BENJAMIN FRANKLIN'S
VISION OF AMERICAN COMMUNITY

VIR

BENJAMIN FRANKLIN'S
VISION OF AMERICAN COMMUNITY

A Study in Rhetorical Iconology

LESTER C. OLSON

University of South Carolina Press

Studies in Rhetoric/Communication
Thomas W. Benson, Series Editor

© 2004 University of South Carolina

Published in Columbia, South Carolina, by the
University of South Carolina Press

Manufactured in the United States of America

08 07 06 05 04 5 4 3 2 1

Library of Congress Cataloging-in-Publication Data

Olson, Lester C.
  Benjamin Franklin's vision of American community : a study in rhetorical
iconology / Lester C. Olson.
    p. cm. — (Studies in rhetoric/communication)
  Includes bibliographical references (p.) and index.
  ISBN 1-57003-525-3 (cloth : alk. paper)
  1. Franklin, Benjamin, 1706–1790—Symbolism. 2. Franklin, Benjamin,
1706–1790—Contributions in art. 3. Art—Political aspects—United States—
History—18th century. 4. Rhetoric—Political aspects—United States—History—
18th century. 5. Art, American—18th century. I. Title. II. Series.
  E302.6.F8O47 2004
  973.3'092—dc22   2003021485

Frontispiece *Benjamin Franklin*, Joseph-Siffrède Duplessis, Paris, 1778. Medium: oil portrait on canvas with a gilded and carved wooden frame featuring a rattle-snake; size, 28 ½" × 23". Photograph courtesy of the Metropolitan Museum of New York, Michael Friedsam Collection.

To my parents,
Donald Clarence Olson and Helen Jean Sisley

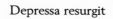
Depressa resurgit

CONTENTS

ILLUSTRATIONS

PREFACE

Benjamin Franklin's Vision of American Community concentrates on an inventive and powerful American's efforts to shape the rhetorical dynamics of images designating British America. Similarly, my previous research in *Emblems of American Community in the Revolutionary Era: A Study in Rhetorical Iconology* focused upon the broad cultural patterns underlying such images. In the earlier book, I defined rhetorical iconology, argued for the value of such research, and situated it beside related approaches to scholarship. Rhetoric, as conceived in the earlier book and here, refers to an aspect of symbolic action in general, not verbal language in particular. Consequently, this book's sense of rhetoric differs noticeably from Franklin's. In the few comments he made on rhetoric, primarily in *Proposals Relating to the Education of Youth in Pensilvania* [*Pennsylvania*] (1749) and "Idea of the English School" (1751), he treated it as a synonym for public speeches, oratory, or persuasion through language.[1]

As before, I have followed fairly standard conventions in transcribing the eighteenth-century texts, retaining the original spelling, capitalization, punctuation, and italics. I have not employed "[*sic*]" in this book; whenever a word, phrase, or sentence appears within quotation marks, the reader may assume that the spelling, punctuation, and grammar have been double-checked for accuracy and reflect the form of expression in the original text. Although secondary eighteenth-century sources often use capital letters for entire words in titles, I have capitalized only the first letter to make the prose easier to read. I have standardized spellings of personal names in the main text but have left the original spellings of them in both quotations and endnotes for accuracy. For example, I have referred to Joseph-Siffrède Duplessis in the main text, even though contemporaries also spelled his name as Joseph Siffred Duplessis, Joseph-Siffred Duplessis, and Joseph-Siffrein Duplessis, which appear in titles of some articles and books in the notes. As this example also illustrates, I supply hyphens in some cases for French names in the main text, which are missing in some primary sources, since the hyphenation of names was not a consistent practice. I have supplied bracketed names in the notes for materials published anonymously at the time. As a simple matter of convenience for readers, I have used brackets to supply missing letters, words, or names within quotations, rather than placing the omitted information in the notes. For the materials written by or to Franklin from the beginning of his life through 1782, I quote from the published volumes in the Yale edition of *The Papers of Benjamin Franklin*. For later materials by Franklin, I cite various collections of his papers when possible, such as Jared Sparks's *The Works of Benjamin Franklin* (ten volumes, initially published during 1836–40), John Bigelow's optimistically titled *The Complete Works of Benjamin Franklin* (ten volumes, 1887–89), and Albert Henry Smyth's *The Writings of Benjamin Franklin* (ten volumes, 1905–7). For the materials after 1782 that are now available on the Packard Humanities Institute's experimental CD-ROM, but which are otherwise unpublished, I provide sufficient information in the notes so that accessing them will be relatively easy when the CD is available commercially.

ACKNOWLEDGMENTS

This project grew out of the research for my earlier book, *Emblems of American Community in the Revolutionary Era: A Study in Rhetorical Iconology*. The grants from the University of Pittsburgh, the National Communication Association (formerly the Speech Communication Association), the National Endowment for the Humanities (NEH), and the American Council of Learned Societies that supported the research for *Emblems* also enabled me to secure primary and secondary materials for this project. Subsequently, in 1989, the NEH provided the Summer Stipend to undertake research for this book in the Papers of Benjamin Franklin held at Yale University, the American Philosophical Society, the Library of Congress, and the National Archives. In 1990, the NEH provided the Travel Award to complete further research in the Public Record Office (Kew and London), the British Library, the British Museum, the House of Lords Record Office, the University of Sheffield Library, and the Sheffield Record Office. The University of Pittsburgh supported this research undertaken in Britain and later, in 1995, in Paris at the Bibliothèque nationale de France, the Archives nationales, the Académie française, the Musée Carnavalet, and the Archives du Ministère des affaires étrangères. In addition, the university granted sabbatical leaves for this project in 1992 and 1998. In 1994 the Packard Humanities Institute, at the suggestion of Barbara B. Oberg, provided me with an experimental CD-ROM containing everything written by and to Franklin. The Richard D. and Mary Jane Edwards Endowed Publication Fund covered certain expenses for permissions, user fees, and production costs for illustrations. I want to thank these institutions and organizations for their confidence in the merit of the project.

Several organizations provided forums for ongoing scholarly conversations in which participants articulated helpful questions and suggestions. I presented preliminary research for this project to the International Society for the History of Rhetoric at Oxford, England, in 1985; the Speech Communication Association at New Orleans in 1988, at San Francisco in 1989, and at New York in 1998; the American Studies Association/Canadian American

Studies Association International Conference at Toronto in 1989; the Eastern Communication Association in 1993; the International Emblems Conference at Pittsburgh in 1993; and the Visual Communication Conference in Rochester, New York, in 2003. The *Quarterly Journal of Speech* granted permission to publish substantially revised and expanded portions of two essays. I now provide a stronger series of arguments that "JOIN, or DIE" posed rhetorical problems for Franklin in 1766. In addition, I present a more complete account of the production, distribution and symbolic reception of Franklin's medal, *Libertas Americana*, in Paris from 1783 to 1784.

For access to materials in their collections and permission to reproduce them, I am grateful to the Académie française, the American Antiquarian Society (Worcester), the American Philosophical Society (Philadelphia), the Archives du Ministère des affaires étrangères, the Archives nationales, the Bedford Estate Offices (Woburn Abbey in Bedfordshire), the Bibliothèque historique de la ville de Paris, the Bibliothèque nationale de France, the Boston Public Library, the British Library (London), the British Museum (London), the Carnegie Mellon University Libraries (Pittsburgh), the Colonial Williamsburg Foundation, the Historical Society of Pennsylvania (Philadelphia), the House of Lords Record Office (London), the Library Company of Philadelphia, the Library of Congress (Washington, D. C.), the Metropolitan Museum of New York, the Massachusetts Historical Society (Boston), the Monnaie de Paris, the Musée Carnavalet, the Musée des arts décoratifs, the Musée nationale de la Coopération Franco-Américaine (Blérancourt), the National Archives (Washington, D. C.), the New-York Historical Society, the New York Public Library, the Public Record Office (Kew and London), the Sheffield City Council, the Sheffield Record Office, the University of Pittsburgh's Darlington and Hillman Libraries, the University of Sheffield Library, the Henry Francis du Pont Winterthur Museum (Delaware), and Yale University.

While I conducted research in the Papers of Benjamin Franklin at Yale University, the staff extended many courtesies. I am grateful to Barbara B. Oberg, who granted me access to the material, and to Ellen R. Cohn, Jonathan R. Dull, Karen Kauffman, Claude-Anne Lopez, Marilyn A. Morris, Catherine M. Prelinger, and Joanne R. Walroth. At the American Philosophical Society, Beth Carroll-Horrocks and Roy Goodman were helpful to me during my visits to the collections. For the French period, Colette Nativel offered several suggestions about accessing materials in French *bibliothèques* and archives for this book, as she did during my research for *Emblems*. Keith Rosemore and Diane Dowdey provided critical readings of two chapters, while Rebecca Carroll and Yves Citton commented in helpful ways on one chapter. David McDougal and Elantu Viovoide improved my prose in the penultimate draft of the entire book. Van Beck Hall, Thomas Kane, Michael Leff, Stephen Lucas, and Trevor Melia wrote on behalf of various grant proposals to fund the research. Marcia Grodsky at the Darlington Library assisted me with locating some important but elusive primary materials. Several friends helped to make possible the necessary travel for research: Frank Feysa, Carol and Dave Hines, Joseph Kielian, Mary Lou Roll, Keith A. Rosemore, Frank and Taylor Slaughter, and Barbara Tisherman. To others who have helped through their scholarship, correspondence, or conversations, thank you.

I would like to thank Barry Blose, my acquisitions editor at the University of South Carolina Press, for seeing the manuscript through the review process in a congenial and supportive manner while maintaining exacting standards for scholarship. Brandi Lariscy-Avant designed the dust jacket with a fine eye for composition to create an exceptional cover. Linda Haines Fogle prepared the marketing materials carefully with timely attention to detail. Bill Adams worked with the anonymous copy editor and me to improve the manuscript throughout the production process, answering my queries promptly and thoroughly. The copy editor's attention to detail was invaluable in making the manuscript clear, consistent, and concise. I alone am responsible for any errors of fact or interpretation.

I had completed a preliminary draft of the entire manuscript for this book in 1993 and 1994, when life intervened with a certain force that, despite my Minnesotan heritage with its tendency for understatement, I can only describe as an ordeal. Some years later, when I returned to the project, the manuscript seemed as if it were the work of an acquaintance who, though still likable, based his interpretations upon some fundamentals with which I could no longer agree. I found it necessary to revise the manuscript with greater attention to the roles of institutions and organizations as they enabled and circumscribed human agency, excluded large numbers of other people altogether, and harmed themselves most deeply in some cases by injuring those who had served them well, as exemplified by Franklin's public humiliation in 1774. A British administration of modest competency focused on him as a scapegoat to deflect attention from its evident ignorance and arrogance in its history of incompetent legislative blunders concerning colonial America. Despite the public shredding of Franklin's reputation in the Cockpit—aptly named for the earlier building there that Henry VIII and his friends had used for bloody games in which birds ripped each other apart for the spectators' pleasure — Franklin possessed the strength of character to continue to pursue conciliation for a time. Finally, in the course of revision, I traced the transformations of symbolic meanings of texts as they moved from one institutional locale into others, noticing—more often than I had in the preliminary manuscript—misunderstandings, willful distortions, and outright appropriations that aided the the partisans' domination and control over relatively vulnerable others.

PART ONE

ONE

Franklin's Emblems and Devices

An Orientation and Conceptual Approach

Benjamin Franklin's Vision of American Community: A Study in Rhetorical Iconology focuses on the pictorial images that Franklin designed to represent those British colonies in America that became the United States. He invented at least one such image during each decade from the 1750s to the 1780s. In 1754 "JOIN, or DIE" represented the colonies as a segmented snake in a wood-cut designed to promote unity among the British colonies during the French and Indian War. A decade later, "MAGNA *Britannia: her Colonies* REDUC'D" portrayed the colonies as the severed arms and legs of Britannia in a political cartoon designed to advocate imperial unity during the Stamp Act controversy of 1765 and 1766. In 1776 "WE ARE ONE" designated the United States as thirteen interlinked rings on the Continental currency to suggest unity among the States during the initial war years. Finally, in 1783, *Libertas Americana* depicted the United States as the infant Hercules strangling two serpents on a commemorative medal issued near the Revolution's conclusion. No other American colonist's pictorial representations designating the emerging nation were more original or influential in their time than those by Benjamin Franklin.

These four pictorial representations of the British colonies in America —"JOIN, or DIE," "MAGNA *Britannia*," "WE ARE ONE," and *Libertas Americana*—were connected by more than their subject of the British American colonial community. All can be classified as belonging to the same general kind of visual rhetoric, based upon three particular features they shared: (1) a pictorial representation, (2) a motto in the vernacular or Latin, and (3) a resulting moral or lesson. As visual rhetoric, they were derived from an aesthetic tradition of emblems and devices. In this brief introduction to the book's subject matter and conceptual approach, I will first explore Franklin's extensive experience with emblems and devices, then comment on my general approach to historical scholarship concerning his visual compositions considered as rhetoric, and, last, preview the structure of the entire book.

Although many varied and sometimes subtle distinctions were drawn between emblems and devices before the eighteenth century, during the era of the American Revolution some individuals used the terms "emblem" and "device" interchangeably or in the combination "emblematical device."[1] An pseudonymous author, "Clericus," outlined essential features that emblems and devices had in common: "An emblematical device, when rightly formed, is said to consist of two parts, a *body* and a *mind*, neither of which is compleat or intelligible, without the aid of the other. The figure is called the *body*, the motto the *mind*." These comments, published initially in the *Pennsylvania Gazette* of September 20, 1775, and reprinted with minor typographical changes in the *Pennsylvania Magazine* of December 1775, neither specified whether a human, animal, plant, or architectural form could be used for "the figure" or pictorial element of the design, nor did they mention whether the motto should be in Latin, a foreign language, or the vernacular.[2] This article by "Clericus" has sometimes been attributed to Franklin.[3] But the attribution is uncertain, however, simply because Franklin never used the expression "emblematical device" in any of his other known prose.

Franklin's comments about and use of emblems and devices reveal that he did not distinguish between them on the basis of either the subject matter depicted in the image or the language of the motto, as did some earlier authorities during the sixteenth and seventeenth centuries in France.[4] Historically, one commonplace distinction was that devices conveyed particular ideas in Latin, while emblems were for general ideas, expressed in the vernacular and applicable to everyone. Nor did he adhere to the common practice of distinguishing as "emblems" those pictorial messages that employed representations of the human form, versus "devices," which did not.[5] In these respects, he was typical of most American colonists in using both terms interchangeably.

Whether the mottos of Franklin's pictorial representations were in Latin or the vernacular was rhetorically consequential because of the messages' accessibility to various audiences. But his choices of language did not necessarily reveal his political commitments, such as a "democratic" impulse, because his use of Latin mottos recurred regularly throughout his entire career.[6] He used them in his emblems and devices for the Associator flags in 1747, for the Continental currency in 1775, again for the various medals commissioned to honor military victories during the American Revolution, and yet again for *Libertas Americana* in 1783. This lifelong pattern of using Latin mottos makes it unlikely that he sought fundamentally to make emblems and devices "democratic," especially since he never explicitly identified himself as having such political commitments. His use of Latin or the vernacular depended, above all, upon rhetorical considerations of the audience and their generic expectations for the particular type of message. Such considerations may have taken priority over adhering to familiar conventions distinguishing emblems from devices.

Franklin's language choice may have depended upon a combination of factors, including not only the conventions for a specific medium, such as the honorary medals, but also the principal audience's level of education. "JOIN, or DIE" and "WE ARE ONE" were both widely distributed among Americans of all backgrounds, the former in newspapers such as the *Pennsylvania Gazette* in 1754, the latter on the Continental currency's fractional notes in 1776; both had vernacular mottos. In contrast, toward the end of his career, *Libertas Americana* was the title of the commemorative medal that he presented in 1783 to prominent political figures in France and the United States: King Louis XVI, Queen Marie Antoinette, the ministers in the French court, and the president and representatives in the American Congress. Franklin used Latin in this instance, because most of these leaders would have had the classical education necessary to comprehend the message. One notable problem with this hypothesis about adjusting to audiences, however, is that Latin mottos accompanied the designs on the Continental currency that circulated widely among the American people in 1775. The same is the case for the paper money issued the following year, with the exception of Franklin's fractional note design ("WE ARE ONE") and the forty-dollar bill printed in English. Perhaps the use of Latin on the rest of the currency reflected the committee's deliberations, not Franklin's judgments.

The choice of Latin for a motto also had rhetorical ramifications for an author's persona. Franklin was aware of this, to judge from humorous commentary in *The New England Courant* on February 11, 1723, when it was published under Benjamin Franklin's editorship instead of under that of his older brother James. The *Courant* commented, "Gentle Readers, we design never to let a Paper pass without a Latin Motto if we can possibly pick one up, which carries a Charm in it to the Vulgar, and the learned admire the pleasure of Construing. We should have obliged the World with a Greek scrap or two, but the Printer has no Types, and therefore we intreat the candid Reader not to impute the defect to our Ignorance, for our Doctor can say all the Greek Letters by heart."[7] Franklin's contemporaries certainly regarded the use of Latin for the mottos as a means of making an author appear well educated. "A. B.," a pseudonymous respondent to "Clericus" in the *Pennsylvania Magazine*, offered amusing commentary "*On the Use and Abuse of MOTTOS.*" In the *Supplement to the Pennsylvania Magazine for the Year 1775*, "A. B." generalized that "Writers of essays, pamphlets, & c. are very fond of mottos. . . . It must be confessed there is sometimes a good reason for this; for, perhaps, the motto is the only thing that shews the author's learning; the work itself being insufficient for this purpose."[8]

In addition to those occasions when Franklin designed images to represent the British colonies that became the United States, he referred to emblems and devices numerous other times. He produced additional pictorial messages in a wide range of contexts and media—frontispieces, Associator flags, paper currency, medals and an honorary sword, a proposal for the Great Seal and for a military monument, metal money, portraits, and even on soap the family produced.[9] Franklin's experiences in suggesting such designs demonstrated that he drew upon the European tradition of emblems and devices regularly throughout his lifetime, not only while he was designing each of the pictorial representations of colonial union in British America.

Along with his productions of other emblems and devices, Franklin's writings about these types of pictorial symbols articulated his familiarity with them. He had certain emblem books in his possession for periods of time, marketing them for sale through the *Pennsylvania Gazette*, a newspaper that he had acquired in 1729 and printed as the sole proprietor until 1748, when he formed a partnership with David Hall. Franklin kept emblem books in his library that he probably consulted as resources when preparing the emblems and devices in his own pictorial messages.

Between February 7, 1740, and December 5, 1751, at least twenty-two advertisements appeared in the *Pennsylvania Gazette* for "Quarles's," "Quarle's," or "Quarrle's" books of "Emblems"—the spelling for the author's name varying in Franklin's *Gazette*. Almost half of these advertisements were for book sales by Franklin between 1740 and 1744.[10] These announcements, which occasionally gave his business location as "near the Market" or "at the Post office, in Philadelphia," spelled the author's name as "Quarles's" and sometimes as "Quarle's," but did not specify the size of the volume. The rest of the advertisements in the *Gazette* were for sales by Franklin's partner, David Hall, who consistently listed the book as "Quarrle's Emblems" and denoted its size as "TWELVES." Between April 1748 and December 1751, Hall advertised at least thirteen such miscellany lists that included this particular volume, often in the same notice with another important emblem book, a folio of "Moral virtue delineated, French and English, with cuts."[11]

The lead-in for the advertisements often mentioned the ship and captain responsible for conveying the books, indicating that perhaps more than one shipment occurred. That yet an additional reference to "Quarles's Emblems," which had been first published at London in 1635,[12] recurred among the "octavos" in *A Catalogue of Choice and Valuable Books*,[13] a 1744 sales list of volumes available through Franklin at the Post Office, suggests strongly that this was among the earliest and most accessible emblem books in his experience. He may, however, have used other collections of emblems as a consequence of his access to the "pretty Collection of Books" in Matthew Adams's library, when Franklin grew up in Boston,[14] or, later, in the "immense Collection of second-hand Books" in John Wilcox's bookshop from 1724 to 1726, when Franklin lived for about a year and a half in London.[15] He also had regular access to James Logan's impressive library in Philadelphia.

As for emblem books in Franklin's own library, a well-known "key" identifies them with a distinctive shelf mark in the following form: "a C followed by one number and an N followed by another" number.[16] The "C" evidently referred to the case in which Franklin stored a book, and the "N" designated the number of the specific book in the case's sequential order. Thus, we know that he owned and used the four volume edition of Joachimi Camerarius, *Symbolorum ac emblematum ethico-politicorum centuriae quatuor* (Mainz: Ludwig Bourgeat, 1702), as evidenced by the presence of shelf marks (C 22 N 23–26) and by the similarity of the designs in this book with the designs that were printed on the Continental currency in 1775.[17] These volumes included designs resembling several denominations of the Continental currency in 1775, but none of them resembled any of the four most important of his emblems portraying a British American community as one body politic. Another emblem book, which bore a distinctive shelf mark (C 112 N 18), was Christoph Weigel's *Ethica Naturalis seu Documenta Moralia e Variis rerum Naturalium proprietatii Virtutum Vitiorumq symbolicis imaginibus collecta* (Nuremberg: [circa 1700]). In this emblem book, each entry had a title, a motto, and a scene with human forms inscribed within a rectangle, plus a Latin verse of ten lines. However, Franklin never referred to the author or the book title in his known prose, including the *Pennsylvania Gazette*.[18]

In a letter to Peter P. Burdett on November 3, 1773, Franklin mentioned having examined a book titled "*Moral Virtue delineated*." Evidently, he was aware of an edition of Marin le Roy de Gomberville, *The Doctrine of Morality: Or, A View of Human Life . . . Exemplified in One Hundred and Three Copper-Plates, done by the Celebrated Monsieur Dart: Written Originally by Monsieur de Gomberville* (London: 1721), because the 1726 edition of it was titled *Moral Virtue Delineated* (London: 1726).[19] In fact, David Hall regularly advertised at least one "folio" edition of *Moral Virtue Delineated* in the *Pennsylvania Gazette*. The advertisements for this emblem book appeared at least eight times between April 5, 1748, and February 6, 1750, with an ever-lengthening description, all of them mentioning that the book was available "at the Post Office." The advertisements on April 5, April 16, and May 12, 1748, simply listed "Moral Virtue delineated." Nearly a year later, the miscellany of books for sale on March 14 and June 22, 1749, specified the languages, "Moral Virtue Delineated, French and English," while subsequent announcements on October 12, 1749, December 19, 1749, and February 6, 1750, added that the volume was illustrated "with cuts."[20]

In his role as a printer, Franklin published at least one book illustrated with several emblems and devices: Johann Arndt's *Sämtliche sechs geistreiche Bücher vom wahren Christenthum* (Philadelphia: 1751), whose audience was the substantial German population that accounted for roughly one-third of Pennsylvania's inhabitants. An early-seventeenth-century German theologian and devotional writer, Arndt was popular among German Protestants.[21] According to C. William Miller, this massive book, consisting as it did of 1,356 pages, was "one of the great publishing feats of the colonial American German press." Some designs in this book resembled those that were later used on the Continental currency in 1775.[22]

Although Franklin's experience with the production of emblems and devices was extensive, it is the four pictorial representations depicting British America that are the most important of his designs for understanding his emerging nationalism, because, in varied ways, they envisioned the British colonies as one body politic. These four images, therefore, constitute the central focus of the present book, which investigates these pictorial images as elements in Franklin's communication about the nature of colonial union, not only because they are a vehicle to explore his evolving vision of a British American community, but also because they reflected and promoted changes in American culture throughout the Revolutionary era. These images, designed with American audiences in mind, can be treated as indices of transformations in American culture. In addition, they reveal changes in his vision of a British American community, because in every instance Franklin modified the depictions of unity among those disparate colonies that became the United States.

Even though Franklin directed all of the pictorial images to Americans, the study is international in scope, because he also directed most of them to audiences in Britain and at least one to a French audience. Franklin was a representative in the Pennsylvania Assembly in 1754, a colonial agent in London in 1765–66, a representative in the Continental Congress at Philadelphia in 1776, and the United States' *ministre plénipotentiaire* to France in 1783, when he lived in Paris. At these moments, each roughly a decade apart, his political and social roles as an American colonist differed significantly. In 1754 and again in

1776, for example, he was well situated as a representative in Pennsylvania to participate directly in the formation of colonial policies. But in 1765–66 and again in 1783, he was located on the periphery of the forums for exercising political power and social privilege—first in the British Parliament and then the French ministry.

Researchers have devoted essays to discussing the iconographic history of each image designed by Franklin to represent British America, but we have yet to study the images collectively as indices of cultural and personal change. Albert Matthews has investigated the iconography of "JOIN, or DIE" by describing the dissemination of the segmented snake in newspapers throughout Pennsylvania, New York, and Massachusetts between 1754 and 1776. Referring to "JOIN, or DIE," Philip Davidson has underscored that Franklin "was a propagandist" who "was the first to see the real possibilities in the use of cartoons." Frederic R. Kirkland and Edwin Wolf II have researched "MAGNA *Britannia*" to document the numerous variants of this image, which were reproduced subsequently in Britain, Holland, France, and America throughout the American Revolution. David P. McBride and Eric P. Newman have investigated the image of the interlinked rings on the Continental currency to conclude that it, too, was of widespread significance, because the design was used on currency, military flags, and housewares produced in the United States, Britain, and China. Finally, Carl Zigrosser and Winfried Schleiner have focused upon *Libertas Americana* to specify the iconographic and textual traditions that informed the design of the commemorative medal.[23] This image was distributed in the United States, France, Malta, Germany, and Italy in the form of medals, engraved broadsides, book illustrations, a textile design, a terra cotta plaque, and poetry.

The existing studies are helpful because they identified several germane artifacts, described the iconographic history of each motif, and provided ample evidence that Franklin's images of America merited a systematic study. However, they failed to account for fundamental differences between the images; ignored the relationship of the images to Franklin's career, objectives, and evolving outlook as his sensibility changed over the decades; and neglected altogether the relationship of the images to the prevailing ideologies and partisan interests of the contemporaneous audiences in America, Britain, and, on occasion, France. A more intellectually satisfying account may be articulated by broadening our focus from the discrete motifs to include the designer and the culture, by foregrounding Franklin's rhetorical practices in the visual communication with which he engaged others. Such an approach is appropriate for this book, because it comports with what R. T. H. Halsey has described as

Franklin's pragmatic view of the arts.[24] Franklin regarded the arts as means to influence public beliefs and actions. In this respect, his use of pictorial images was thoroughly rhetorical. Despite extensive research on Franklin, including Charles Coleman Sellers's study on eighteenth-century portraits of him, no previous book has focused upon Franklin's proposals in the visual arts.[25]

Benjamin Franklin's Vision of American Community describes the transformations in his vision of America as expressed in his rationales for each pictorial image representing America, and it articulates underlying transformations in American culture as suggested by his contemporaries' changing reactions to these images. The value of a book examining Franklin's pictorial representations of the British colonies in America lies, primarily, in the historical understanding to be gained by seeing how he changed his images and ideas about America with the dramatically transformed political, social, and economic circumstances during the Revolutionary era between 1754 and 1784, one of the most dynamic periods in America's past. In addition to being valuable for exploring his use of pictorial rhetoric to influence public policies, his images of America provide a vehicle to explore salient changes within American culture during the French and Indian War, the decade of dissent, and the American Revolution.

For example, rather than initially symbolizing protest or rebellion within the British Empire, the snake device on "JOIN, or DIE" dramatically symbolized the need for well-orchestrated action against the outside threat posed by the French and Indians in 1754. Franklin's idea of union at the time was not radical in its implications for the British Empire; instead, it was a practical, military necessity consistent with the expressed wishes of the British government. Even so, a decade later, during the Stamp Act controversy of 1765 and 1766, American protestors appropriated this image in the *Constitutional Courant* to urge colonial opposition to the British law. Franklin sought to counter this radical use of the image by distributing "MAGNA *Britannia: her Colonies* REDUC'D" in 1766 among Americans to underscore the vital nature of imperial unity and among parliamentarians to advocate moderate political policy. Despite his efforts, the snake device took on a life of its own in American politics: Loyalists sought to connect the image with the biblical traditions wherein the serpent represented guile, deceit, and treachery, while Patriots countered those efforts by associating the image with eternity, vigilance, and prudence.[26] Toward the conclusion of the Revolution, Franklin was once again associated with the snake's image: Joseph-Siffrède Duplessis's portrait of him featured a rattlesnake carved on the gilt wooden frame (see frontispiece).

Each of the pictorial images representing the British colonies in America were details in much broader campaigns. Because the meanings of these images were shaped not only by the palpable form of the messages but also by the audiences' points of view and by the political circumstances surrounding their distribution, it is necessary for me to interpret these images in light of the ephemeral, rhetorical understandings and public address of the period. In this respect, I agree with Douglas Anderson, who commented in *The Radical Enlightenments of Benjamin Franklin* that a study of the meanings of Franklin's prose must take into account that "the social conditions of writing are inevitably an ingredient in meaning."[27] The same insight applies to his pictorial messages. Every one of them had an enduring but changing significance throughout the Revolutionary era, as contemporary partisans appropriated them for a range of reasons and uses in Britain, France, Holland, Germany, Spain, Italy, America, and elsewhere as far away as China.

Although each image portraying a British American community took on a life of its own internationally at the time, each was admittedly a small part of Franklin's extraordinary life. In fact, the pictorial images were of such slight importance as details in his life that even Franklin's best biographers ordinarily mention only one of two of them—typically the most famous of the images, "JOIN, or DIE," but seldom many others.[28] Even Carl Van Doren, who set the standard for subsequent biographies with his Pulitzer Prize winning *Benjamin Franklin* (1938), mentioned only three of them, omitting as he did the designs for the Continental paper currency in 1776.[29] But small details though these visual images certainly were in Franklin's life, I want to argue that careful attention to them will throw into high relief fundamental changes in Franklin's sensibility concerning British America, especially his political commitments as he changed from being an American Whig to a republican.

It is important to remember that Franklin was a colonist; as Anderson has put it, "Franklin is in no sense our contemporary."[30] His role as a colonial agent and, later, as an ambassador usually meant that he actively sought to influence public policy from a position on the margins of the major public forums for exercising political power and social privilege. Seldom did he speak directly to assembled representatives in Parliament. Such was the case of his "Examination before the committee of the whole of the House of Commons" during February 1766. Even then, his role was not as a voting representative, but as a colonial agent, who lobbied for specific colonies' political and economic interests. In general, colonists who wanted to be persuasive in public forums beyond British America had to overcome deeply entrenched and demeaning stereotypes of them in Britain and elsewhere. On December 28, 1765, for example, writing pseudonymously in London in the *Gazetteer and New Daily Advertiser*, Franklin objected, "The gentle terms of *republican race, mixed rabble of Scotch, Irish, and foreign vagabonds, descendants of convicts, ungrateful rebels* & c. are some of the sweet flowers of English rhetorick, with which our colonists have of late been regaled."[31]

In writing this book, I have taken seriously Franklin's comments in a speech that he delivered at the Constitutional Convention on September 17, 1787, toward the end of his life. He affirmed, "For having lived long, I have experienced many Instances of being oblige'd by better Information or fuller Consideration, to change Opinions even on important subjects, which I once thought right, but found to be otherwise."[32] In 1754 Franklin was an American Whig who supported Britain's constitutional monarchy and actively endeavored during the late 1750s and early 1760s to increase the power of the British crown over Pennsylvania by changing the proprietary government into a royal one; ultimately, however, he rejected his commitment to constitutional monarchy and became an advocate of republican politics. These shifts in Franklin's most fundamental beliefs concerning his own political commitments and the relative merits of entire political systems are among the most enthralling aspects of his life. In this book, I dramatize the changes in his commitment to entire political systems by juxtaposing his varied pictorial representations of British America over the decades.

In part, these shifts resulted from a habit of mind that Franklin characterized as his "moderation" and his constant endeavor to locate compromises in the imperial controversies. He understood that such moderation and capacity for compromise left him vulnerable to criticism that he was engaging in partisan tactics and abandoning his principles. During the Stamp Act controversy of 1765 and 1766, for example, Franklin regularly commented on being perceived by the British as "*too much of an American,*" as he put it in a letter to William Strahan on April 8, 1767.[33] Later, along similar lines, Franklin wrote another letter dated November 28, 1768, and published many years later in 1779 in the *Gentleman's Magazine;* concerning his experiences as an American colonist who had lived in Britain, he commented: "Being born and bred in one of the countries, and having lived long, and made many agreeable connections of friendship in the other, I wish all prosperity to both." He added that, having "talked and written so much and so long on" imperial relations, he had rarely carried his point, but had instead rendered himself "suspected by my impartiality; in England of being too much an American, and in America of being too much an Englishman."[34]

The evolutions in Franklin's politics were not merely the result of moderation and compromise, but also, above all, deep and fundamental shifts in his outlook on forms of government, intercolonial commitments, and international relations in the interest of British Americans' survival and growth. Franklin, who in 1754 ardently opposed the French presence in North America as being a threat to the British colonies, later became an ambassador to that country, where his respect and affection for the people left him vulnerable to being considered "too French" by his American contemporaries, as Claude-Anne Lopez has emphasized.[35] These and other extraordinary changes in fundamental aspects of Franklin's outlook tend to make me appreciate the careful and detailed scholarship on his evolving views of empire, as exemplified in Verner W. Crane's examination of Franklin's marginalia on his contemporaries' pamphlets.[36] For these same reasons, I have high regard for scholarship such as Jack P. Greene's essay on factors contributing to Franklin's deepening alienation from Britain's constitutional monarchy during the mid-1760s to mid-1770s.[37] Less satisfying is research affirming that he possessed a democratic sensibility at a time in his life when he was—by both his own words and deeds—an American Whig who supported the constitutional monarchy. Likewise, unconvincing to me is research that accurately identified elements of a democratic sensibility without placing these elements in the context of either his emphatic support of the British monarchy in his early years as an imperialist and land speculator or his equally explicit republican politics toward the end of his life.[38]

The development and flux of ideas in Franklin's outlook are a captivating aspect of his writings, an aspect that deserves even more attention than it has received here. Ultimately, I agree, however, with Douglas Anderson's observation, "Monarchical and republican sympathies coexisted in the culture as a whole, and within particular individuals conservative and radical ideas mingled with an exhilarating disregard for consistency or purity."[39] As Franklin himself put it on February 9, 1789, when he was recollecting the failures of both the British Crown and the American colonies to adopt the Albany Plan of Union in 1754, "The Crown disapprov'd it, as having plac'd too much Weight in the democratic Part of the Constitution; and every Assembly as having allow'd too much to Prerogative. So it was totally rejected."[40] By commenting upon fundamental changes in Franklin's developing political outlook as evidenced in his views on intercolonial union, *Benjamin Franklin's Vision of American Community* complements the research in Gordon S. Wood's brilliant book, *The Radicalism of the American Revolution*, because Wood's work discussed in necessarily broad terms the eighteenth-century shift from monarchy to republicanism and then toward democracy in British American culture.[41] Here those shifts and evolutions acquire a human face as they were instantiated in Franklin's occasionally enraged assertions amid political struggles and his sometimes anguished and agonizing reconsiderations of fundamental elements of his beliefs.

Like many who have commented on Franklin's career before me, I respect and admire his many achievements—as a writer, a printer, a scientist, a politician, and an international diplomat. At the same time, I have taken to heart a few bemused comments by him in the *Autobiography* about his own faults and shortcomings. In connection with his plan to improve his own habits, for example, he affirmed, "I enter'd upon the Execution of this Plan for Self Examination, and continu'd it with occasional Intermissions for some time." He added, "I was surpriz'd to find myself so much fuller of Faults than I had imagined, but I had the Satisfaction of seeing them diminish."[42] Later, in the *Autobiography*, he observed with wry humor, "that such extream Nicety as I exacted of my self might be a kind of Foppery in Morals, which if it were known would make me ridiculous; that a perfect Character might be attended with the Inconvenience of being envied and hated; and that a benevolent Man should allow a few Faults in himself, to keep his Friends in Countenance." Franklin consoled himself with the insight that "tho' I never arrived at the Perfection I had been so ambitious of obtaining, but fell far short of it, yet I was by the Endeavour a better and a happier Man than I otherwise should have been, if I had not attempted it."[43] Perhaps it is in this light of Franklin's humanity where his anti-German, anti-Catholic, and anti-Indian remarks of the 1750s may be situated. Although a dark aspect of his character at the time, his attitude of bigotry underwent significant changes during his lifetime and may have informed his incipient nationalism in the sense that a British American community was formed, in part, by opposition to outsiders not only beyond the borders but also within them.

The following brief, introductory chapter, which examines Franklin's earliest commentary on forming a colonial union in British America, provides a general orientation to his initial views on the subject. Subsequently, four chronological chapters discuss individually each of Franklin's four most important pictorial representations of the colonies that became the United States; the discussions concentrate upon the messages' rhetorical dynamics and explore their production, dissemination, and reception. Each exploration begins with an analysis of the circumstances surrounding the production of a particular pictorial message by identifying the factors that Franklin considered when he developed it. Examples of such factors include the design's specific audiences, his expressed objectives whenever he was explicit about them, and the techniques entailed in production insofar as all these factors illuminate the visual appeals as instruments for persuasion. Of course, drawing any inferences about motivation from expressed objectives is a fallible undertaking such that it cannot be adequate grounds for rhetorical interpretation, but attention to them gives us some sense of his mode of operation and his depiction of his own rhetorical sensibility. Each chapter gauges the ramifications of his social and political roles, as well as his position vis-à-vis political institutions, such as Parliament in London and the French ministry in Paris, since institutions enable and circumscribe some varieties of human agency, while excluding most people altogether.

Each chapter explores patterns of dissemination for the designs by identifying the media through which each motif was distributed among the audiences, not only as used by Franklin but also as redistributed by others, who often had different political agendas. The discussions detail acts of appropriation, subversion, and redefinition of the images by partisans, as the motifs from Franklin's visual works were reproduced on currency, medals, paintings, statues, flags, textiles, housewares, and illustrations in magazines, pamphlets, almanacs, newspapers, and broadsides. As evidence of patterns in the reception of the designs by the principal audiences, I consider other designs featuring the motif on various media and comments concerning the designs in Franklin's contemporaries' diaries, letters, poetic verses, newspapers, magazines, and pamphlets. The extant evidence of active interaction with Franklin's messages is inevitably fragmentary, and it may, in some instances, say more about the viewpoints of the commentators than about Franklin or his messages. So each discussion of reception provides a brief background concerning the commentators's social roles and partisan concerns. My claims about the reception are meant to be suggestive, not conclusive of how contemporaries interacted with Franklin's pictorial compositions to make them meaningful in a range of different circumstances or blunt their political import on occasion.

Examples of the factors and issues considered throughout this process include the value of diverse media for reaching various segments of the audiences; the role of conventional motifs and genres in the formation of the pictorial compositions and in interpretations of the images' meanings; and the underlying political factors impinging upon the diverse audiences' reception of the message and upon its occasional appropriation by rival groups. The best available evidence consists of the pictorial and verbal messages that commented directly on each pictorial representation of the united British colonies. But, in some instances, I found it necessary to draw upon Franklin's and his peers' contemporaneous ideas concerning union to suggest possible interpretations and understandings of the images, simply because they provided the best available evidence.

In attempting to synthesize the rhetorical usage of each of the pictorial images, I have employed a classical vocabulary for organizing both the analysis of the message's role in its time and the analysis of the major appeals to the principal audiences during the Revolutionary era. The classical terms for types of persuasive messages in civic forums—"deliberative," "judicial," and "ceremonial rhetoric"—were salient genres during the eighteenth century, especially among political leaders who ordinarily had the benefit of a classical education. As such, these genres are useful for organizing an interpretation of the visual rhetoric in these specific forums during that time. Well-educated, economically privileged, and politically powerful men in eighteenth-century British and American colonial cultures would have been familiar with these types of persuasive discourse in public life, corresponding as they did to highly visible, public activities in the legislatures, the courts, and ceremonial occasions. Dating back historically to classical Greece, the types of persuasive speeches in these forums were identified and detailed in treatises on rhetoric, especially Aristotle's *Rhetoric*. Each type of public speech had corresponding commonplace lines of public argument that recurred in appeals to specific audiences for consensus on the decisions concerning the expediency or inexpediency of future policies, the justice or injustice of past deeds, or the current praiseworthiness or blameworthiness of individuals or institutions. Early writers on emblems and devices drew upon classical treatises on rhetoric to develop their commentaries about the visual arts.[44]

At the same time, I have employed these classical terms for kinds of discourse under certain strictures, such as a recognition that they were not adequate for understanding broad, popular forms of participation in the rhetorical life of the community. Those without political power and economic privilege often resorted to types of rhetorical appeals in various mundane objects, such as textiles and housewares, as well as popular forums, such as public demonstrations. Also, they frequently relied upon metaphor and allegory, as I have argued in *Emblems of American Community in the Revolutionary Era*, because these were relatively indirect but robust means to assert their views. The utility of the classical terms is ultimately circumscribed in the present study, not only through emphatic strictures upon their use in relationship to specific types of decision making in certain public forums, but also through a conscious broadening of the forms of rhetorical appeal through an examination of common objects used for persuasion in public life: paper money, military flags, textile designs, medals, terra cotta plaques, and the like.

The conclusion consists of two chapters, the first of which situates the major pictorial images in the context of noteworthy transformations in Franklin's outlook by concentrating upon evolutions from 1754 to 1784 in his verbal images representing British America. The following, and final, chapter touches on his criticism of the "Great Seal of the United States," because his remarks condemning the design featuring the bald eagle succinctly summarized some abiding features of his outlook on union. Throughout the book, I argue the thesis that the differences among his pictorial representations of British America as one body politic reflected his complex process of rejecting Britain's constitutional monarchy and ultimately endorsing republicanism as a form of government in the United States. This transformation resulted from his active engagement with diverse, intercultural influences and from his dramatically changing political circumstances. The portrait of Franklin emerging from this study is that of a man whose capacity to reconsider his own most fundamental beliefs resulted in his dramatically changed political commitments over the decades. His visual rhetoric indexes those basic changes.

TWO

Franklin's Earliest Commentary Envisioning Colony Union

At the outset of his remarkable series of changes in political commitments, Franklin's views concerning colony union were expressed in a short but tantalizing letter that he wrote from Philadelphia to James Parker during March 1750 or 1751, after having read an unpublished manuscript for a treatise concerning the "friendship" of Indians. Franklin's expressed views in that moment provide us with a remarkably clear point of reference for noticing elements of his political sensibility that abide and change, sometimes dramatically, over the ensuing decades. In the suggestive letter he affirmed his earliest comments on uniting those British colonies in America that eventually became the United States.[1] He identified numerous factors leading him to conclude that such a union was highly desirable, but improbable. In passing, his letter compared the British colonies in America to the Six Nations of the Iroquois confederacy: the tribes of the Mohawk, Oneida, Onondaga, Cayuga, Seneca, and the recently admitted Tuscarora. He wrote, "It would be a very strange Thing, if six Nations of ignorant Savages should be capable of forming a Scheme for such an Union, and be able to execute it in such a Manner, as that it has subsisted Ages, and appears indissoluble; and yet that a like Union should be impracticable for ten or a Dozen English Colonies, to whom it is more necessary, and must be more advantageous; and who cannot be supposed to want an equal Understanding of their Interests."[2] To Franklin during the 1750s, the Six Nations were both a worrisome military presence along Pennsylvania's borders and a vital source of commerce, even though he would contend in later years that the commerce was a specifically British interest, because most colonists were farmers. Franklin's letter expressed disdain for the "ignorant Savages," but high regard for their "Scheme for such an Union."

Franklin framed his letter as a response to a manuscript by Archibald Kennedy that Parker would later anonymously publish as the pamphlet *The Importance of Gaining and Preserving the Friendship of the Indians to the British Interest, Considered.* Kennedy's argumentation had recognized the value of unifying the colonies, as had periodically been the case among American writers. Franklin remarked, "I have, as you desire, read the Manuscript you sent me; and am of Opinion, with the publick-spirited Author, that securing the Friendship of the Indians is of the greatest Consequence to these Colonies; and that the surest Means of doing it, are, to regulate the Indian Trade, so as to convince them, by Experience, that they may have the best and cheapest Goods, and the fairest Dealing from the English; and to unite the several Governments, so as to form a Strength that the Indians may depend on for Protection, in Case of a Rupture with the French; or apprehend great Danger from, if they should break with us."[3] Franklin was endorsing Kennedy's observation that "Whenever the Colonies think fit to join, *Indian* Affairs will wear quite another Aspect. The very Name of such a Confederacy will greatly encourage our *Indians*, and strike Terror into the *French*, and be a Means to prevent their unsupportable Incroachments, which they daily make with Impunity and Insult."[4] Subsequently, when Parker printed this pamphlet anonymously at New York in May 1751, he published Franklin's letter as a part of it, though without attributing the letter to Franklin by name. During 1752, the pamphlet was reprinted at London, reaching a broader audience in Britain.[5] Consequently, Franklin's ideas on a colonial union circulated throughout the British Empire.

Having focused on the danger posed by the French and possibly by the Indians beyond the British colonies' borders, Franklin turned in his letter to another source of danger within the colony. He added, "The Observation concerning the Importation of Germans in too great Numbers into Pennsylvania, is, I believe, a very just one." He worried, "This will in a few Years become a German Colony: Instead of their Learning our Language, we must learn their's, or live as in a foreign Country."[6] Franklin's remarks exemplified his ethnocentric bigotry, which recurred in another 1751 pamphlet, his *Observations concerning the Increase of Mankind.*[7] In this pamphlet, which he circulated anonymously during the early 1750s, he targeted the influx of German immigrants into Pennsylvania as a danger to the British colonists there. He asked, "Why should the Palatine Boors be suffered to swarm into our Settlements, and by herding together establish their Language and Manners to the Exclusion of ours? Why should Pennsylvania, founded by the English, become a Colony of *Aliens*, who will shortly be so numerous as to Germanize us instead of our Anglifying them." Franklin worried that these Germans "will never adopt our Language or Customs, any more than they can acquire our Complexion."[8]

These were sweeping distinctions between insiders, who belong within an imagined community, and outsiders who threatened it—outsiders located both beyond the borders and within them. As in the letter to Parker, Franklin again juxtaposed his disdain for the Indians beyond the borders with his anxieties about too many Germans within them in yet another letter, written on May 9, 1753, to Peter Collinson, a Quaker mercer residing in London.[9] Such affirmations were commonplace among the British colonists in America throughout the eighteenth century. Like so many features of Franklin's evolving beliefs, however, his condescension toward the "ignorant Savages" underwent dramatic change in later life. In 1784, for example, he opened his pamphlet *Remarks concerning the Savages of North America*, by affirming, "Savages we call them, because their Manners differ from ours, which we think the Perfection of Civility. They think the same of theirs." He added, "Perhaps if we could examine the Manners of different Nations with Impartiality, we should find no People so rude as to be without Rules of Politeness, nor any so polite as not to have some Remains of Rudeness."[10] However concerned he may have been about the German presence in Pennsylvania, he sought to interest them as a market for his publications and, eighteen years after his 1753 letter to Collinson, drew upon their presence in Pennsylvania to argue, "Now that England can no longer monopolize our Commerce, the ancient Connections of those People with their Mother Country will be a Means of opening a considerable American Trade with Germany by the North Seas, & the Mediterranean."[11]

More important than his overt contempt in the 1750s for "Savages" in a study of his emerging but inchoate nationalism, Franklin's remark in the letter to Parker suggested that the Six Nations of the Iroquois confederacy may have contributed to his views on a colonial union of the British colonies in America. Here it may be sufficient to remember that, at the time of his letter to Parker, Franklin was a Whig and a supporter of constitutional monarchy, like most British colonists in America, not a republican. This, too, would change dramatically for Franklin long before the successful conclusion of the American Revolution in 1783. Ultimately, he rejected constitutional monarchy altogether through an agonizing examination and reconsideration of imperial politics during the late 1760s and early 1770s, in the wake of the Stamp Act controversy of 1765–66, the Townshend Duties of 1767, and the Intolerable Acts of 1774. Franklin's dissatisfaction with the British government could only have been magnified by his experience of being publicly denounced by Alexander Wedderburn in 1774 before a British administration of modest competency, an administration that had failed to recognize the value of his services both to America and Britain. But he veered in the early 1760s toward increasing the power of the British crown in Pennsylvania by changing the colony's government from proprietary to royal government. To Franklin, this change was a means to transform, if not resolve, deep conflicts within the colony—conflicts that had recurred with heightened intensity whenever it was necessary to raise funds for the colony's military defense.[12]

But in the early 1750s, Franklin was concerned, above all, about the possible role of the Iroquois confederacy in the ongoing conflict between the British colonies and the French presence in North America. He saw the value of a colonial union among the British colonies in economic and military terms, because it was important to him that the Iroquois be dependable traders and allies of the British in their ongoing struggle for domination over the French in the North American continent. Depending upon how the Iroquois aligned themselves, the Six Nations of the Iroquois confederacy could be powerful allies or a worrisome threat along the western borders of the largest colonies, especially New York and Pennsylvania, but also, in some measure, Massachusetts Bay. Years later, after the British colonies in America had declared their independence from Britain, the Iroquois would again have a comparable role in the conflict between Britain and France, as a relatively vulnerable but crucial weight in the balance of power between the countries. After initially trying to remain neutral during the Revolution, the Six Nations splintered when most tribes aligned themselves with the British and others with the Americans.

In his brief letter in the 1750s, Franklin added that, however desirable such military and economic benefits could be for the British colonists in America, a colonial union was unlikely because of the practical politics within each colony's individual government. He wrote,

> This Union of the Colonies, however necessary, I apprehend is not to be brought about by the Means that have hitherto been used for that Purpose. A Governor of one Colony, who happens from some Circumstances in his own Government, to see the Necessity of such an Union, writes his Sentiments of the Matter to the other Governors, and desires them to recommend it to their respective Assemblies. They accordingly lay the Letters before those Assemblies, and perhaps recommend the Proposal in general Words. But Governors are often on ill Terms with their Assemblies, and seldom are the Men that have the most Influence among them. And perhaps some Governors, tho' they openly recommend the Scheme, may privately throw cold Water on it, as thinking additional publick Charges will make their People less able, or less willing to give to them. Or perhaps they do not clearly see the Necessity of it, and therefore do not very earnestly press the Consideration of it: And no one being present that has the Affair at Heart, to back it, to answer and remove Objections, &c. 'tis easily dropt, and nothing is done.[13]

Despite these conflicts among the varied interests and political factions within and among the British colonies, he contended, "Such an Union is certainly necessary to us all, but more immediately so to your Government," alluding to the situation in New York.[14] His ability to project a political union that he recognized as untenable at the moment, and yet outline a few means of movement toward it, suggested that he was not simply a pragmatist; ultimately, however, his course of action tended to be tempered by a practical sense of the possible.[15]

After outlining how "a Dozen Men of good Understanding and Address" could travel "in the Nature of Ambassadors to the other Colonies," Franklin's letter mentioned that a carefully orchestrated persuasive campaign might possibly bring about a union among the British colonies. He affirmed that "I imagine such an Union might thereby be made and established." Franklin emphasized, "A voluntary Union entered into by the Colonies themselves, I think, would be preferable to one impos'd by Parliament; for it would be perhaps not much more difficult to procure, and more easy to alter and improve, as Circumstances should require, and Experience direct."[16] Then he outlined a possible structure of the Union, placing it unequivocally within the British Empire through the role of a presiding officer appointed by the constitutional monarchy. He suggested, "Were there a general Council form'd by all the Colonies, and a general Governor appointed by the Crown to preside in that Council, or in some Manner to concur with and confirm their Acts, and take Care of the Execution; every Thing relating to Indian Affairs and the Defence of the Colonies, might be properly put under their Management."[17] The detail of supervision by "the Crown" is consistent with the fact that Franklin, like nearly all British colonists in America at the time, believed in constitutional monarchy as the finest system of government known to humankind.

Franklin held that the relative role of the colonies in this "Council" should be determined, not by the population or geographic size, but by each colony's economic contributions to the organization. He was frank about the economic basis of political power within the projected forum for concerted action, despite some passing references to equity: "Each Colony should be represented by as many Members as it pays   Sums of Hundred Pounds into the common Treasury for the common Expence; which Treasury would perhaps be best and most equitably supply'd, by an equal Excise on strong Liquors in all the Colonies, the Produce never to be apply'd to the private Use of any Colony, but to the general Service." (The long blank before "Hundred Pounds" presumably was intended to leave ambiguous the specific sum of money.) Recognizing the importance of familiarity and affiliations in strengthening a community, he added, "Perhaps if the Council were to meet successively at the Capitals of the several Colonies, they might thereby become better acquainted with the Circumstances, Interests, Strength or Weakness, &c. of all, and thence be able to judge better of Measures propos'd from time to time: At least it might be more satisfactory to the Colonies, if this were propos'd as a Part of the Scheme; for a Preference might create Jealousy and Dislike."[18] His ideas outlining a representative council, its duties, and the varied meeting place resembled elements of the New England Confederation of 1643.[19]

Franklin's concern over the role of a union in economic and military dealings with the Indians also stemmed from anxiety about the presence of outsiders within the British colonies. He commented candidly on divisions between the British and German colonists in Pennsylvania, writing, "Already the English begin to quit particular Neighbourhoods surrounded by Dutch, being made uneasy by the Disagreeableness of disonant Manners; and in Time, Numbers will probably quit the Province for the same Reason." He added, "Besides, the Dutch under-live, and are thereby enabled to under-work and under-sell the English; who are thereby extreamly incommoded, and consequently disgusted, so that there can be no cordial Affection or Unity between the two Nations." His allusion to "two Nations" within the colony of Pennsylvania amplified the extent to which he considered the differences between the Germans and British colonists a threat. He intimated, "How good Subjects they may make, and how faithful to the British Interest, is a Question worth considering." Franklin wanted to preserve Pennsylvania exclusively for the British, because, as he put it, "The Number of Englishmen in England, cannot by their present common Increase be doubled in a Thousand Years; but if half of them were taken away and planted in America, where there is Room for them to encrease, and sufficient Employment and Subsistance; the Number of Englishmen would be doubled in 100 Years: For those left at home, would multiply in that Time so as to fill up the Vacancy, and those here would at least keep Pace with them."[20] Population size, as Franklin knew, was the foundation of military and economic strength during the eighteenth century.[21] To him, population growth depended on the availability of land, which, as an imperialist and a land speculator, he sought to secure for British America.

Franklin's letter to Parker sketched in miniature the salient factors that led him to desire a union of the British colonies in America: a military defense from others, economic trade with others, and a common language and set of manners distinguishing the British colonies from others—all undergirded by a fear of outsiders. The transcendent political structure that he envisioned, compared in passing to the "Scheme for such an Union" long in practice among "six Nations of ignorant Savages," blended elements from Western and indigenous American political systems by situating familiar Western practices of constitutional monarchy within a two-tiered structure—each colony preserving its own government, yet each of them participating in "a general Council form'd by all the Colonies."[22] At the time, this Council was to be under "the Crown," an unmistakably British and European element of this scheme. Yet that fundamental element would be eliminated later as he came to reject the constitutional monarchy in favor of a republican government. Most of these elements recurred throughout his imagery designating the emerging nation, albeit with different emphasis and, at times, significant changes.

Franklin drew upon and blended together a concatenation of sources in his conception of colonial union from the outset, as evidenced by his earliest writings on the subject. As Franklin remarked in a speech during the Constitutional Convention on June 28, 1787, "We have gone back to ancient History for Models of Government, and examin'd the different Forms of those Republicks, which, having been originally form'd with the Seeds of their own Dissolution, now no longer exist. And we have view'd modern States all round Europe, but find none of their Constitutions suitable to our Circumstances."[23] His mode of operation, even in his earliest extant commentary on colonial union, was to combine useful ideas that he drew from disparate sources to synthesize a useful scheme appropriate for the circumstances before him.

In 1754, only a few years after the letter to Parker, Franklin revisited his views concerning union in response to French incursions in a frontier area near present-day Pittsburgh. George Washington, who more than two decades later would lead the colonial military during the American Revolution and eventually become the first president of the United States, had sustained a major military defeat at the hands of the French. At the time, he was a soldier in the Virginia military, which was defending that colony's interest in securing land in the area. Concerned by news of the defeat, the British government's Board of Trade called upon leaders throughout British America to coordinate a defense of the empire's interest in the region. During the ensuing controversies throughout British America over how best to engage the French presence, Franklin designed "JOIN, or DIE," the best known of his pictorial messages representing British America as one body politic, for publication in the *Pennsylvania Gazette*, thereby enacting his support of the British government's explicit request. It is that famous image to which we will turn our attention in the next chapter.

PART TWO

THREE

"JOIN, or DIE," 1754

The riots at N York have given fresh spirits to the rioters here. An uniformity of measures it is said will be effectual and join or die is the motto. When you and I were at Albany ten years ago we did not Propose an union for such Purposes as these.

Thomas Hutchinson to Franklin, November 18, 1765

3.1. "JOIN, or DIE," *Pennsylvania Gazette*, [Benjamin Franklin], Philadelphia, May 9, 1754, p. 2, col. 2. Publisher: Benjamin Franklin and David Hall; medium: newspaper woodcut; size: 2" × 2 ⅞". Photograph courtesy of the Prints and Photographs Division of the Library of Congress.

Franklin first published the design of the segmented snake, "JOIN, or DIE," on May 9, 1754, in the *Pennsylvania Gazette* (fig. 3.1), which, over the decades, had become one of the major newspapers in the colony. This was the earliest known pictorial representation of colonial union produced by a British colonist in America. The image of the segmented snake in the *Gazette* consisted of eight sections or parts: the head represented New England, and each of the seven remaining parts corresponded to a single colony, which was identified by its initial letter or letters. The arrangement of the seven remaining parts corresponded from head to tail to the sequence of colonies from north to south: New York, New Jersey, Pennsylvania, Maryland, Virginia, North Carolina, and South Carolina. The image omitted Delaware and Georgia, probably because Delaware shared the same governor as Pennsylvania and because Georgia, a recently developed colony, "could contribute nothing to common security."[1] Further, the British government's use of Georgia for a penal colony may have influenced Franklin, who had denounced the British government's practice of transporting criminals from Britain to colonial America.

Franklin's *Gazette* initially circulated "JOIN, or DIE" to represent the united British colonies in America shortly before the Albany Congress, which was scheduled to convene that summer in response to the beginning of the French and Indian War, known in Britain as the Seven Years War. Before the month of May ended, variations of "JOIN, or DIE" were printed in the *New-York Gazette*, the *New-York Mercury*, the *Boston Gazette*, and the *Boston Weekly News-Letter*. By August the image had been alluded to in the *Virginia Gazette* and the *South Carolina Gazette*.[2] The fairly wide distribution indicates that the pictorial image embodied a message of intercolonial significance from the outset, though the image accrued additional meanings and political import during the subsequent decades of the Revolutionary era.[3] Initially, there was nothing overtly radical or revolutionary about the pictorial composition's meanings as it circulated throughout the British colonies in America. That would develop a decade later after radical protestors appropriated the image to object to a British law known as the Stamp Act.

In 1754 "JOIN, or DIE" promoted a political policy of unity among the American colonies to be formalized at the upcoming Albany Congress. As such, in classical terms of persuasion, it was a deliberative message that employed commonplaces concerning the consequences of enacting or rejecting policies as expedient or inexpedient. Specifically, the image of the segmented snake suggested to the colonists that their political situation was weakened by the divisions among the British colonies. Only through unification could the parts of the snake survive. In addition, the image promoted alliances among the colonies based upon opposition to a shared enemy, the French and their Indian allies. The snake's image represented both unity and opposition, dramatically symbolizing the need for well-orchestrated action against an outside threat.

The British Empire in America could only be protected by well-coordinated military action by several of the colonies. So there was nothing deliberately invidious about what the snake's image implied for the colonies' relationship to Britain in 1754. Indeed, the image complied with the general wishes of the British government's Board of Trade, the national ministry in England responsible for colonial affairs, commerce, and industry, as its expectations were conveyed by Robert D'Arcy, earl of Holderness, in a circular letter to the colonial governors. The Board of Trade handled appointments to offices in colonial America, reviewed legislation pertaining to the colonies, and processed the British government's instructions to governors on a colony-by-colony basis.[4] Franklin's emblem simply affirmed that these colonies should act as a united political community for vital matters of common defense against French encroachment in the region.[5]

In Britain, however, "JOIN, or DIE" was a pictorial appeal that was unlikely to secure support for the policies in Parliament necessary to establish a colonial union, even though the snake's image urging unity was consistent with the Board of Trade's objectives of unifying British America for military defense. By depicting the colonies apart from the rest of the British Empire, the image tacitly suggested that colonial interests were sometimes distinct from British interests. As one consequence, the image of the segmented snake implicitly embodied the concerns of a political faction within the empire. The snake's image seemed to urge the formation of a united body politic in America apart from the rest of the empire. In this light, the image may have contributed in 1754 to raising explicit concerns among the most powerful politicians in Britain that America might seek independence. Such politicians certainly worried that colony union could diminish British control over its American colonies.

Ambiguity in the significance of "JOIN, or DIE" made it possible a decade later, during the Stamp Act controversy of 1765–66, for the image to embody the concerns of a radical political faction within the British Empire. Recognizing the snake emblem's potential use in dramatizing colonial opposition to the British government's act, William Goddard appropriated the image for the masthead on two of three versions of the *Constitutional Courant*, published on September 21, 1765, at Woodbridge, New Jersey, and circulated throughout the northern colonies (fig. 3.2). On the masthead of his publication, "JOIN, or DIE" remained a deliberative message in urging a policy of colonial union, yet it embodied a policy of very different import in that it urged united opposition to the Parliament's recent legislation. Before the Stamp Act controversy was over, the *Courant* was characterized in England as one of the most radical publications opposing the new tax law. Powerful members of Parliament in a committee of the entire legislative body studied the ramifications of the snake's image for imperial relations, because it was featured prominently among the American Papers (figs. 3.3 and 3.4), which documented the

3.2. "JOIN OR DIE," *Constitutional Courant*, [Woodbridge, New Jersey and possibly Boston], September 21, 1765. Publisher: [William Goddard]; medium: newspaper masthead. Photograph courtesy of the Massachusetts Historical Society. This image appeared on two of the three versions of the *Courant* that were published in 1765.

Americans' disobedience and riots. As a consequence, by 1765–66, "JOIN, or DIE" symbolized colonial opposition to Parliamentary sovereignty in America, despite the radical publication's focus only on a specific law.

"JOIN, or DIE" had an enduring but changing significance throughout the decades before the American Revolution. The image constantly promoted colonial union. But it did so in opposition to different adversaries over the decades. Initially, in 1754, Franklin designed it to mobilize a unified military defense against France. But later, in 1765 and again periodically throughout the ensuing decade of dissent, other American protestors appropriated the snake's image to urge colonial unity against British law. For instance, during subsequent American reactions to the British government's Boston Port Act of 1774, perhaps the best known of the Intolerable Acts or the Coercive Acts, the snake emblem was printed repeatedly week after week on the mastheads of three colonial newspapers: the *New-York Journal*, from June 23, 1774, until December 8, 1775 (fig. 3.5); the *Massachusetts Spy*, from July 7, 1774, until April 6, 1775 (fig. 3.6); and the *Pennsylvania Journal*, from July 27, 1774, until October 18, 1775 (fig. 3.7). In the New York and Pennsylvania newspapers, the motto of "JOIN, or DIE" was replaced with "UNITE OR DIE" as the emblem was appropriated to promote colonial unity against the British government's policies.

The meanings of "JOIN, or DIE" were shaped by the design as it was interpreted from the different audiences' points of view in America and Britain. In those locations, the contemporary audiences' interpretations of the image were presumably influenced by the ideas in the political circumstances surrounding its distribution and by the ephemeral rhetorical understandings in the public address of 1754 and 1765–66.[6] Accordingly, the first part of this chapter examines the rhetorical dynamics of "JOIN, or DIE" during 1754,

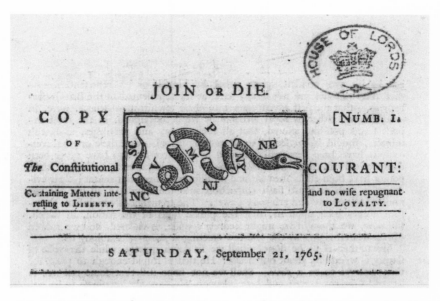

3.3. "JOIN OR DIE," from "Copies & Extracts of Several Newspapers, printed in New England, Sept.-Nov. 1765, and referred to in Gov. [Francis] Bernard's letters," London, February 1766, masthead on the first interior page of text (p. 3). Photograph courtesy of the House of Lords Record Office, London.

3.4. "JOIN or DIE," from the copy of the *Constitutional Courant* held in the official records of the House of Lords, London, as recorded in the *Journals of the House of Commons*, 30:448–50. Photograph courtesy of the House of Lords Record Office, London.

THURSDAY, August 25, 1774.   THE   [NUMBER 1651.]

NEW-YORK
O R,
GENERAL

UNITE OR DIE.

JOURNAL;
THE
ADVERTISER.

Containing the freshest ADVICES,   *both* FOREIGN *and* DOMESTIC.

& PRINTED AND PUBLISHED BY JOHN HOLT, NEAR THE COFFEE-HOUSE.

3.5. "UNITE OR DIE," from the *New-York Journal; Or, the General Advertiser*, from June 23 until December 8, 1774. Publisher: John Holt; medium: newspaper masthead. Photograph courtesy of the Rare Book Division of the New York Public Library, Astor, Lenox and Tilden Foundation.

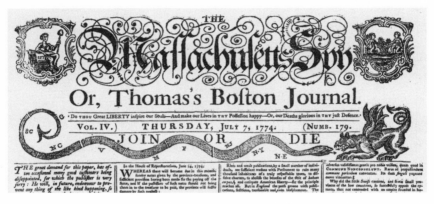

3.6. "JOIN OR DIE," from the *Massachusetts Spy, Or, Thomas's Boston Journal*, woodcut by Paul Revere, Boston, from July 7, 1774, until April 6, 1775. Publisher: Isaiah Thomas; medium: newspaper masthead. Photograph courtesy of the Prints and Photographs Division of the Library of Congress.

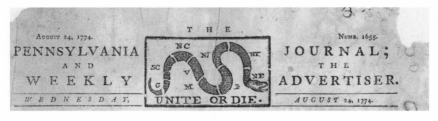

3.7. "UNITE OR DIE," from the *Pennsylvania Journal; and the Weekly Advertiser*, Philadelphia, from July 12, 1774, until October 18, 1775. Publisher: William Bradford; medium: newspaper masthead. Photograph courtesy of the Massachusetts Historical Society.

initially by tracking its circulation with attention to its various meanings in colonial America and then subsequently investigating its ramifications in Britain. Then, the second part of the chapter concentrates on the appropriations of the snake's image in 1765–66, again by beginning with its circulation in colonial America and later its reproductions in Britain. The central argument of this chapter is that the radical appropriation of "JOIN, or DIE" in 1765 so significantly modified its meanings that Franklin had for it a decade earlier in 1754 that, as one consequence, he faced serious rhetorical problems in his roles as a crown officer and as a colony agent in Britain. For a time, he repudiated the snake's image altogether.

Franklin demonstrated his loyalty to the Crown through his political actions during the late 1750s and early 1760s, when he actively campaigned to increase the British government's power over the colony of Pennsylvania by changing its proprietary form of government into a royal government.[7] In fact, in 1754, when he designed "JOIN, or DIE" to promote unified colonial action against the French and Indians, he was complying with the expressed wishes of the British government's Board of Trade and the governor of Pennsylvania's subsequent endorsement of those wishes. In that context, the design "JOIN, or DIE" was benign, even though some evidence suggests that the snake's image may have contributed to concerns in Britain about American independence even then. Yet, the ambiguity resulting from a pictorial image lacking an explicitly depicted adversary made it possible later for radicals in British America to appropriate the snake's image on "JOIN, or DIE" to urge unified colonial opposition to British law in 1765. In short, the meanings of the image had changed during the decade intervening between 1754 and 1765, not Franklin's abiding political commitment to Britain.

"JOIN, or DIE" during the French and Indian War, 1754

In 1754, Franklin actively sought to distribute the image of the segmented snake both in America and Britain. On May 8, 1754, the evening before the emblem was to be published in the *Gazette*, he mailed an advance copy of "JOIN, or DIE" with the accompanying article to Richard Partridge, a Quaker merchant who had been Pennsylvania's agent in London since 1740, with a request that he have it published in the "most publick Papers."[8] Colonial agents like Partridge lobbied on behalf of the various colonies' interests in dealing with the British government's Board of Trade and with the ministry in Parliament, ordinarily trying to coordinate their representations of Americans' interests with those of the British merchants and politicians in London, but sometimes, especially during the decade of American dissent after the

Stamp Act crisis of 1765, bypassing the English merchants and lobbyists altogether by dealing directly with representatives in the British government and, on rare occasion, by submitting petitions to the king.[9] Colonial agents "appeared before the Privy Council, met with members of the cabinet, consulted with the Board of Trade, the attorney general, lords of the Treasury, the Admiralty, and other administrative branches of government," explained Michael G. Kammen. "They were also granted hearings before parliamentary committees, and when the occasion demanded, lobbied among the members of both houses."[10] A few years later, in 1757, Franklin would himself become a colony agent in London for Pennsylvania for a brief time and, eventually, return to such a role in 1764 for over a decade until the eve of the Revolution.

To judge from his letter to Partridge and from the distribution of the image in American newspapers, Franklin's principal audiences consisted of the American colonists and the British. The rhetorical judgment that he asked these people to render was deliberative in the classical sense of persuasive messages concerning expedient and inexpedient courses of action: the image was designed to promote a policy of unity among the colonies to establish a secure military defense against incursions by the French and Indians and to solidify British Americans' alliance with the Iroquois confederacy. He regarded the upcoming Albany Congress to be held at Albany, New York as the principal forum in which a policy of union could be enacted, a forum that had been legitimated by instructions from the British government's Board of Trade. The direct participants in this forum would have been the delegates from each of the American colonies.

By urging a policy of colonial union, Franklin supported the recommendations of the Board of Trade, as expressed in a circular letter from the earl of Holderness to the governors of the North American colonies. Writing from Whitehall on August 28, 1753, he advised each of the governors of Virginia, Maryland, Pennsylvania, New Jersey, New York, Massachusetts Bay, and New Hampshire: "And whereas it may be greatly conducive to His Majesty's service, that all his Provinces in America should be aiding and assisting each other, in case of any invasion, I have it particularly in charge from his Majesty, to acquaint you, that it is his Royal will and pleasure, that you should keep up an exact correspondence with all His Majesty's Governors on the Continent; and in case you shall be informed by any of them, of any hostile attempts, you are immediately to assemble the general assembly within your Government, and lay before them, the necessity of a mutual assistance, and engage them to grant such supplies as the exigency of affairs may require."[11] On February 14, 1754, Gov. James Hamilton provided a copy of this letter to the

Pennsylvania Assembly and asked the representatives to grant supplies to be used for military defense in cooperation with Virginia. He added, "Several Letters have passed between me and the Governor of *Virginia, New-York* and the *Massachusetts*, in which they . . . express an hearty Desire of acting in Concert with us against his Majesty's Enemies [and]; concur in Sentiment with his Majesty's ministers of the Necessity of a general Union of all the Provinces, both in Councils and Forces."[12]

Because Franklin was an active member of the Pennsylvania Assembly, he was aware of these instructions, which the governors of the British colonies in America used to justify plans for the Albany Congress in June 1754.[13] In fact, he was one of seven men appointed to a committee charged on March 6, 1754, with formulating a response to issues raised during the ensuing controversy.[14] As a member of the Pennsylvania Assembly, he may have heard Hamilton's remarks to the Assembly on May 7, 1754, "The Proposals made by the Governor of *Boston* and *New-York*, for an Union of the several Colonies in *Indian* Affairs, is so agreeable to my Sentiments, that I earnestly recommend it to your Consideration."[15] On May 9, 1754, Franklin's *Pennsylvania Gazette* printed a speech by Jonathan Belcher, who was the governor of New Jersey, alluding to the Board of Trade's correspondence and advocating "a strict Union among all His Majesty's Colonies." The same issue carried a speech that Gov. William Shirley of Massachusetts had delivered on March 23, 1754, calling for "Vigorous Measures against the *French*."[16] By creating "JOIN, or DIE" to promote colonial union in the same issue, Franklin not only created a persona of himself as a newspaper editor and member of the Pennsylvania Assembly who was concerned about the colony's security, he also aligned himself with the political policy of the Board of Trade and Pennsylvania's governor. Subsequently, in the *Gazette* for May 16, 1754, Franklin published Governor Shirley's speech of April 2, 1754, advocating colonial union.[17] Reprinting such speeches, articles, and notices from other colonies' newspapers was a conventional feature of eighteenth-century newspapers. Yet, by doing so, Franklin actively constructed an image of a colonial movement toward union exemplified by Boucher's and Shirley's speeches. Among his general objectives in promoting colonial union was securing the existing British alliance with the Iroquois confederacy.

Albany had long been the customary site for the confederacy's treaties with European settlers. That the upcoming congress in June 1754 was scheduled to take place at Albany indicated that colony union was a factor that could enhance the British alliance with the confederacy. Because one of the two major objectives of the Albany Congress was to secure the Iroquois confederacy's goodwill, the first several days of the congress were devoted to meetings with the Iroquois to strengthen the relationship with British America, an activity that Native Americans described metaphorically as "brightening the chain."[18] After the meetings at Albany, Franklin wrote from Philadelphia to Peter Collinson on July 29, 1754: "I am just return'd from Albany, where were Commissioners from seven Provinces to treat with the Indians of the Six nations." He added, "We brighten'd the Chain with them & c. and parted good Friends; but in my Opinion no Assistance is to be expected from them in any Dispute with the French, 'till by a compleat Union among our selves we are enabled to support them in case they should be attacked."[19]

The presence of the Six Nations of the Iroquois confederacy along Pennsylvania's border contributed to Franklin's motivation for a colonial union in certain specific respects. To him, the union among the colonies was a vital interest in strengthening the colonies' alliance with the Iroquois confederacy as both a military and a commercial matter. Thematic in his writings was the vital interest in keeping the Iroquois confederacy as allies of the British colonies in the ongoing conflict with the French.[20] As Franklin was aware, the Iroquois had urged a colony union upon the American colonists as a means of minimizing rivalry among the British colonies over land and goods. In 1744, for example, Canasatego, an Onondaga chief and a spokesman for the Iroquois confederacy, gave a speech during the concluding moments of a treaty conference held in Lancaster, Pennsylvania, where he urged the colonists who were present to develop a union among the British colonies.[21] Addressing commissioners from Pennsylvania, Virginia, and Maryland, Canasatego affirmed,

> We have one Thing further to say, and that is, We heartily recommend Union and a good Agreement between you our Brethren. Never disagree, but preserve a strict Friendship for one another, and thereby you, as well as we, will become the stronger.
>
> Our wise Forefathers established Union and Amity between the *Five Nations*; this has made us formidable; this has given us great Weight and Authority with our neighbouring Nations.
>
> We are a powerful Confederacy; and, by your observing the same Methods our wise Forefathers have taken, you will acquire fresh Strength and Power; therefore whatever befals you, never fall out one with another.[22]

Later that year at Philadelphia, these remarks were published in the treaty proceedings that Franklin "Printed & Sold" under the title *A Treaty, Held at the Town of Lancaster, in Pennsylvania, By the Honourable the Lieutenant-Governor*

of the Province, And the Honourable the Commissioners for the Provinces of
Virginia and Maryland, with the Indians of the Six Nations, in June, 1744.[23]
Because he published the conference proceedings, including these remarks by
Canasatego, he was aware of the Iroquois leader's advice. By 1754, Franklin's
recognition of a colonial union's political worth was influenced, politically, by
such a union's potential value in securing an alliance with the Iroquois in the
British Americans' struggle with the French in North America.[24]

The defense of British America in the interest of survival characterized
the text that accompanied "JOIN, or DIE" during May 1754, as well as his
later comments in "Reasons and Motives on which the Plan of Union was
formed," probably written during July 1754:

> Considering moreover, that one principal encouragement to the French,
> in invading and insulting the British American dominions, was their
> knowledge of our disunited state, and of our weakness arising from such
> want of union; and that from hence different colonies were, at different
> times, extremely harassed, and put to great expence both of blood and
> treasure, who would have remained in peace, if the enemy had had cause
> to fear the drawing on themselves the resentment and power of the
> whole; the said Commissioners, considering also the present incroach-
> ments of the French, and the mischievous consequences that may be ex-
> pected from them, if not opposed with our force, came to an unanimous
> resolution, *That an union of the colonies is absolutely necessary for their*
> *preservation.*"[25]

Certainly defense for survival was an abiding consideration to him throughout the period.[26] Yet, this factor—along with commerce consisting of trade
with the confederacy—was not the only motive that led him to promote
colonial union during the early stages of the Seven Years War.

In addition, he mentioned the value a colonial union would have for
imperial expansion in America in his *Plan for Settling Two Western Colonies*,
written during the fall of 1754 and published much later at London in 1779.
He suggested, "But if the colonies were united under one governor general
and grand council, agreeable to the Albany Plan, they might easily, by their
joint force, establish one or more new colonies, whenever they should judge
it necessary or advantageous to the interest of the whole." He explained, "For
it would be the interest and advantage of all the present colonies to support
these new ones; as they would cover their frontiers, and prevent the growth
of the French power behind or near their present settlements."[27] Whether he
had this objective of imperial expansion in view at the time of "JOIN, or

3.8. "Se rejoindre ou mourir," *Recueil d'emblêms*[,] *devices, médailles, et figures hieroglyphiques* (Paris, 1696 and 1724), plate 61, figure 7 in both editions. Publisher: Nicholas Verrien or Verien; medium: book illustration; size: 1" diameter. Photograph from the 1724 edition courtesy of Special Collections, Carnegie Mellon University Libraries, Pittsburgh. The illustration also appeared in an earlier edition of Verrien's book, *Livre Curieux* (Paris, [1685?]), plate 62, figure 7.

DIE" several months earlier in May 1754, or whether it was an afterthought, is conjecture.

The snake's image dramatized the need for colonial union by featuring a specific, secular belief. As Carl Van Doren observed, the segmented snake's image referred to "the contemporary notion that a 'joint snake' might be broken in pieces and yet live if the parts came together again."[28] As a rhetorical technique, the illustration was a figurative analogy or proportional metaphor: the colonies were to their fate what a segmented snake was to its fate. The caption stated the conclusion: the colonies could join, or die. The image evoked a rhetorical topos of a persuasive appeal based upon the consequences. The image had no direct associations with religious beliefs within the Judeo-Christian tradition, because there are no references to segmented snakes in the Bible. The specific folk belief conveyed an element of urgency, too, because a snake cut into segments could live only by reuniting its parts before sunset.

It was possible that this design was derived from a French emblem book by Nicholas Verrien. In particular, "JOIN, or DIE" resembled the design for "Se rejoindre ou mourir" in N. Verrien, *Recueil d'emblêmes*[,] *devices, médailles, et figures hieroglyphique* (Paris, 1696), plate 61.[29] This design was reprinted in two other editions by Verrien, including his earlier book, *Livre Curieux et utile pour les sçavans, et artistes. . . . Accompangé d'un très grand nombre de devices, emblêmes, médailles et autre figures hieroglyfiques,* published at Paris in 1685 (plate 62), and his subsequent edition of *Recueil d'emblêmes,* published at Paris in 1724 (plate 61). (The latter edition spells the author's name as "Verien" on the frontispiece and "Verrien" on the title page.) The images of the segmented snake in the *Pennsylvania Gazette* and in these French collections were similar (figs. 3.1 and 3.8), except that the motto was translated from French into English, the body of the snake was cut into eight pieces rather than two, and the abbreviations of the colonies were added beside the segments of the snake.[30] But Franklin never mentioned either the author or these book titles in his known prose or in the *Pennsylvania Gazette,* unless he did so with a variant spelling.[31] In the 1724 edition, the design was printed in a general section, the title of which suggested that the snake device had an ancient origin in Latin, Spanish, or Italian texts.[32] Assuming that one of these volumes was the origin of Franklin's device, he had appropriated the message from a French source to urge American colonists to mobilize against the French and their Indian allies, such as the Chippawas and Ottawas.

An article that accompanied the image in the *Pennsylvania Gazette* mentioned the recent military defeat on April 17, the danger of losing the trade of the region, and the importance of avoiding "an eternal Separation made between the Indians and their Brethren the English," referring to the Iroquois confederacy. Then the text reinforced the need for colonial unity in opposition to the French and their Indian allies: "The Confidence of the French in this Undertaking seems well-grounded on the present disunited State of the British Colonies, and the extreme Difficulty of bringing so many different Governments and Assemblies to agree in any speedy and effectual Measures for our common Defence and Security." The article concluded that if the French were permitted to "take an easy Possession of such Parts of the British Territory," then the ineluctable outcome would be "Destruction of the British Interest, Trade and Plantations in America."[33] Newspaper editors reprinted these comments with four other versions of the woodcuts of "JOIN, or DIE." The remarks also appeared in the *Boston Evening-Post* of May 20, 1754, and in the *South Carolina Gazette* of May 28–June 4, 1754, but without the woodcut.[34]

The *South Carolina Gazette* of June 11–20, 1754, stated similar sentiments with an emphasis on "wisdom" and "prudence," ideals often associated with the emblem of the snake. These sentiments were excerpted in the *Boston Gazette* of August 13, 1754, and in the *Boston Evening-Post* of August 12, 1754: "As the Motions of the *French* on the *Ohio* River, and the Measures they are at present pursuing there, threaten to disturb the Tranquillity of the *British*

Provinces; it is greatly to be wish'd that the *British* Provinces would unite in some System or Scheme for the Public Peace and Safety. Such an Union would render us Respected by the *French*, for they are no Strangers to our Power, tho' they may perhaps suspect our Prudence; let us give them this Proof of our Wisdom, and they will hardly make any Experiment of our Strength."[35] The article, which accompanied the segmented snake's image, encouraged viewers to see the serpent as an embodiment of the colonies' need for a united defense against a foreign threat. As Isaiah Thomas observed, the article was published with the emblem to "rouse the British colonies, and cause them to unite in effectual measures for their defence and security, against the common enemy."[36]

The segmented snake was an appropriate metaphor for the colonies, because the image corresponded to the colonies' geography. They were a long, narrow strip of land separated into individual political units running from north to south in the same sequence as on the snake from head to tail. Because a snake lacked many specialized parts, it was also a useful emblem for representing a kind of egalitarianism—not a system wherein all individuals were portrayed as equal, but rather one wherein whole colonial governments were depicted as equal. Had the image depicted only one colony as the head, it may have been seen as making decisions for the other colonies. But because the northernmost colonies were represented collectively as the head, the image distributed the power that was implied by the head, and so mitigated some of the difficulties posed by the difference between the head and tail. It was possible that the reference to New England reminded some viewers of an earlier confederacy among the British colonies in America, the New England Confederation of 1643, consisting as it did of the four colonies of Massachusetts Bay, Plymouth, Connecticut, and New Haven.[37]

The Board of Trade's circular letter had instructed the governors of Virginia, Maryland, Pennsylvania, New Jersey, New York, Massachusetts, and New Hampshire expressly by name to attend the Albany Congress. But, as Thomas Hutchinson later remarked in his *The History of the Colony and Province of Massachusetts-Bay*, "Virginia, and New Jersey, though expressly named [in the circular letter], did not send commissioners. Connecticut and Rhode Island were the only colonies which sent [representatives to the Albany Congress], of those who were not expressly named."[38] The inability of the British colonies to convene in one forum reflected the colonies' disparate concerns and interests in prioritizing their own defense, such as the relative importance of the various indigenous tribes. The colonial leadership's conflicts over participation in the Albany Congress suggest the beliefs and attitudes of the American

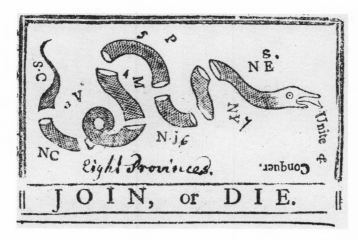

3.9. "JOIN, or DIE," *Boston Weekly News-Letter*, Boston, May 23, 1754, p. 1, col. 1. Publisher: John Draper; medium: newspaper woodcut; size: 1 ⅞" × 3". Photograph courtesy of the Massachusetts Historical Society.

audiences for Franklin's 1754 snake device, "JOIN, or DIE." It is the contemporaneous evidence of those beliefs and attitudes to which we turn our attention now in the next section concerning the American audiences' views of colony union and the snake device.

American Audiences for "JOIN, or DIE," 1754

If "JOIN, or DIE" was designed, above all, to promote unity in British America, then the visual image struck a chord throughout the colonies, to judge from the distribution of its various reproductions. The image was reproduced in woodcut prints in newspapers that circulated throughout New York and Massachusetts, the two largest colonies of the North, which were especially affected by the Six Nations. The images of the segmented snake appeared during May in the *New-York Gazette* and the *New-York Mercury* with only slight variation from the original. Somewhat more substantial revisions were made in the versions of the motif in the *Boston Weekly News-Letter* and the *Boston Gazette*, which also reproduced the snake device before the month of May had ended. The image of the snake in the *Boston Weekly News-Letter* had the words "Unite & Conquer" coming from the snake's mouth (fig. 3.9). The version in the *Boston Gazette*, depicting the snake with an open, threatening mouth, urged "Unite and Conquer" (fig. 3.10).[39]

The *Virginia Gazette* and the *South Carolina Gazette*—newspapers in colonies forming the snake's tail—did not print the image of the snake. Yet

3.10. "JOIN or DIE," *Boston Gazette*, Boston, May 21, 1754, p. 3, col. 1. Publisher: Samuel Kneeland; medium: newspaper woodcut; size: 2" × 3". Photograph courtesy of the Massachusetts Historical Society.

both newspapers indirectly referred to it, and the *South Carolina Gazette* printed an ambiguous representation of it. The *Virginia Gazette* of July 19, 1754, alluded to the image at the conclusion of an article describing another major defeat on July 3 of the British forces under Col. George Washington's leadership: "Thus have a few brave Men been exposed, to be butchered, by the Negligence of those who, in Obedience to their Sovereign's Command, ought to have been with them many Months before; and it is evidently certain, that had the Companies from New York been as expeditious as Capt. Maccay's [James McKay's] from South-Carolina, our Camp would have been secure from the Insults of the French, and our brave Men still alive to serve their King and Country." Having denounced New York, the article concluded, "Surely, this will remove the Infatuation that seems to have prevailed too much among our Neighbours, and inforce a late ingenious Emblem well worthy of their Attention and Consideration." Because the article was not accompanied by the pictorial image of "JOIN, or DIE" and because it did not describe the "ingenious Emblem," the allusion was cryptic. The *Boston Gazette* reprinted the article without explaining the emblem on August 13, 1754.[40]

The *South Carolina Gazette* of August 22, 1754, also reprinted the article from the Virginia newspaper, and added an explanatory note: "The Emblem here mentioned, was a Figure of a Snake, (exhibited in the Pennsylvania Gazette and other Northern News Papers,) divided into 8 Pieces, as represented by the Lines underneath." The *South Carolina Gazette* depicted a line of eight dashes to represent the eight parts of the segmented snake, placing colonial initials alternatively above and below each dash. Underneath the image, the *Gazette* added, "With these Words under the Pieces, 'JOIN, or DIE.'" Since the paper never indicated whether South Carolina or New England was the snake's head, this version of the device was equivocal: readers could have inferred that South Carolina was the head of the snake instead of the tail. Although matters of cost or convenience could have been factors, perhaps the editor omitted the snake's image because being a tail was not a flattering image of South Carolina. On August 1, 1754, Franklin's *Pennsylvania Gazette* also reprinted the news from the *Virginia Gazette*, but without explaining the allusion to an "ingenious Emblem."[41]

Franklin's design for "JOIN, or DIE" was well calculated to promote a policy of colonial union in British America, especially throughout the northern colonies, but also to a degree in the South. The proposal comported well with the views of leaders in other colonies—for example, Gov. William Shirley of Massachusetts Bay, who also recognized the value of colonial union for improving relations with the Iroquois confederacy. In his remarks in his speech on April 2, 1754, to the Council and House of Representatives of Massachusetts, Shirley affirmed, "Such a Coalition of the Colonies for their Defence would be a convincing Proof to them [the Iroquois confederacy], that they might safely depend upon His Maty [Majesty] for Protection, & confirm them in their antient Alliance with the English." Shirley regarded the upcoming Albany Congress as an opportunity to unify the colonies on a basis more permanent than that required by the expected duration of the French and Indian War. In his speech, Shirley remarked: "Such a Union of Councils besides the happy Effect it will probably have upon the Indians of the Six Nations may lay a Foundation for a general one among all His Maty's [Majesty's] Colonies, for the mutual Support & Defence against the present dangerous Enterprizes of the French on every Side of them."[42] These remarks advocating a colonial union were published in the *Boston Weekly News-Letter* on April 25, the *Boston Evening-Post* on April 29, the *New-York Gazette* on May 13, 1754, and Franklin's *Pennsylvania Gazette* on May 16, 1754; in Britain, on July 16–18, 1754, the *Whitehall Evening-Post* published the text of Shirley's speech.[43] Shirley himself sent a manuscript copy of the speech to the Board of Trade, and he later wrote to Sir Thomas Robinson on December 24, 1754, affirming that a plan for colonial union would be useful for defense "as well in time of peace as of war."[44]

Southern leaders appear to have felt ambivalent about plans for colonial union, as illustrated by the rather complicated example of Gov. Robert Dinwiddie of Virginia, who had an official responsibility to protect the colony's frontier and who, as a land speculator, had a personal economic stake in the Ohio Company settling in that region. Although he wrote often to the Board of Trade to underscore the importance of assistance from other American colonies, especially Pennsylvania and New York, in defending a frontier that he claimed for Virginia, he also declined to attend the Albany Congress. He offered the Board of Trade the excuse that "we are at great Expense" from defending the frontiers and from meeting with "the different Nations of Indians at Winchester in May next." He added, "I think the Southern Indians are more to be courted than the Five Nations, being ten Times their Number, yet it's very necessary to keep a strict Friendship with them all, which I shall constantly endeavor to support."[45] Dinwiddie considered colonial union useful, above all, if it would result in protecting Virginia from the "Southern Indians." He persistently and sharply criticized other colonies for failing to concur with his defense priorities.

In New York, the leadership saw the situation differently in that the legislature was most concerned about the Iroquois confederacy along that colony's borders. The General Assembly's message to Governor DeLancey on August 22, 1754, voiced commitment to the general principle articulated by the Board of Trade and endorsed by DeLancey. The Assembly affirmed, "We are of Opinion with your Honour, that Nothing is more natural and Salutary than a Union of the Colonies for their own Defence, and that it is a reciprocal Duty, to be aiding and assisting each other, in Case of any Invasion." Adding that "these Principles your Honour will not extend to an unlimited Sense," the message then made a pointed insinuation about Virginia's repeated demands for assistance: "There may be Instances, where particular Colonies invaded, ought to exert their Strength, and not too loudly call on others, more exposed and more burthened than themselves."[46] The Six Nations were more of a concern to New York than the "Southern Indians" occupying Virginia's attention.

Because "JOIN, or DIE" was a detail in a campaign with much larger social, political, and economic dimensions, and because Franklin realized that such imagery was most useful for promoting broad sentiments, not the specific, mechanical features of a formal proposal, it is inappropriate to judge his rhetorical appeal from the standpoint of securing a formal policy of colonial union. Yet it should be noted that the image and the myriad other appeals on behalf of formal union were not effective when considered collectively, as reflected by the colonial governments' lack of support for the plan developed at Albany. Indeed, Franklin regarded the outcome of the Albany Congress policy deliberations with frustration, because none of the individual colonies subsequently supported the plan for union prepared and endorsed at the congress.[47] Even before that experience, he changed his views on the procedure for implementing a colonial union, a change that deepened as a consequence of the colonies' lack of support for the plan. Initially, in his early 1750s letter to James Parker, Franklin wrote that "A voluntary Union entered into by the Colonies themselves . . . would be preferable to one impos'd by Parliament."[48] Later, but even before the congress at Albany, Franklin's experiences in the Pennsylvania Assembly led him to modify this view. In his "Short Hints towards a Scheme for Uniting the Northern Colonies," written on June 8, 1754, to James Alexander and Cadwallader Colden, Franklin commented under the heading, "Manner of forming this Union": "The scheme being first well considered[,] corrected and improved by the Commissioners at Albany, to be sent home, and an Act of Parliament obtain'd for establishing it." His omission of a stage during which each colony would approve the proposal was suggestive.[49]

After the frustrating experiences following the Albany Congress, Franklin commented in his "Reasons and Motives" for the Albany Plan of Union, probably written during July 1754, that the commissioners while at Albany had resolved *"That it was necessary the union should be established by act of parliament."* He wrote similarly to Peter Collinson on December 29, 1754, enclosing a copy of the proceedings of the Albany Congress and remarking, "All the Assemblies in the Colonies have, I suppose, had the Union Plan laid before them; but it is not likely, in my Opinion, that any of them will act upon it so as to agree to it, or to propose any Amendments to it." He added, "Every Body cries, a Union is absolutely necessary; but when they come to the Manner and Form of the Union, their weak Noddles are presently distracted. So if ever there be an Union, it must be form'd at home by the Ministry and Parliament." Franklin was persistent, as usual, writing again to Peter Collinson on June 26, 1755, "I hope the Plan of Union, which you express your Approbation of, or something like it, will take Place and be established by the King and Parliament," and yet again on August 27, 1755. Likewise, Franklin followed up with another letter to Partridge on October 25, 1755, in which he wrote, "I hope the ensuing Parliament will establish an Union of the Colonies for their common Defence, which will extinguish all these uncomfortable Disputes."[50]

The conviction that Parliament needed to establish the colonial union appears to have been pervasive among American leaders. James DeLancey of New York wrote to the Board of Trade on December 15, 1754, "A general

Union of the Colonies becomes every day more necessary." He amplified, "I have sent your Lordships the general Plan of Union concerted at the Congress at Albany. It was then the general Opinion, that the Colonies would differ in their Measures, and disagree about their Quotas, so that it appeared necessary to have the interposition of the British Parliament to oblige the Colonies; and I think it will not be done otherwise." William Shirley wrote similarly to Sir Thomas Robinson on December 24, 1754, "That an effectual scheme for such an Union can't be carry'd into execution but by authority of the Parliament of Great Britain." James Alexander of New York corresponded likewise in a letter to Cadwallader Colden, also of New York, on September 23, 1755, "Tho' the Colonies to the Northward have now shown a Glorious Spirit in so great & so Speedy reenforcements, yet, little solid, can be Expected, till we are united by act of parliament."[51] But Parliament was unlikely to enact the formal mechanism because of the beliefs and attitudes toward colony union in evidence among British leaders, who were particularly wary of ramifications for British domination and control in America.

British Audiences for "JOIN, or DIE," 1754

The image of "JOIN, or DIE" was not well designed in noteworthy respects to secure British support for a colonial union in 1754, primarily because it envisioned the American colonies as a body politic separate from the rest of the British Empire. By doing so, it may have suggested inadvertently that the colonies could seek independence from Britain, especially if the union was founded on a more permanent basis than necessary to resolve the immediate need for military defense. The life of the segmented snake could only continue through an enduring unity of all its parts. More important, were the British colonies in America united into one body politic, they could as a consequence focus their collective concerns more effectively against the British Parliament than were they disunited. Consequently, the serpent's design did little to assuage British apprehensions of American independence and may have exacerbated them.

Two copies of Franklin's letter of May 8, 1754, to Richard Partridge, written to him in his capacity as Pennsylvania's agent in London, found their way into the "General Correspondence" of the British government's Colonial Office.[52] Only one of the two documents included a hand-drawn copy of the pictorial message "JOIN, or DIE." Exactly when these copies entered the papers of the Colonial Office or who was responsible for examining them are matters of conjecture. Although the penmanship of both copies of these letters was contemporaneous, both copies lack the usual notations specifying a date of receipt and the recipient's endorsement. The documents are located in the "General Series," not associated specifically with the secretary of state or the Board of Trade. It was possible that Partridge conveyed them to the Board of Trade, since he wrote to Secretary John Pownall on December 12, 1754, "I judged it not amiss to give thee some Extracts, if they be of any service make use of them as thou shalt see meet."[53]

During autumn 1754, allusions to and reproductions of "JOIN, or DIE" were sent to the secretary of state, Sir Thomas Robinson. He regarded the accompanying article's account of the French victories in America as important enough to convey it to powerful leaders in the British government: the earl of Hardwicke, the duke of Newcastle, and Lord Albemarle, who was a British diplomat stationed in France. Hardwicke also forwarded the information to First Lord of the Treasury Newcastle, who would, as a consequence, have received it from at least two prominent sources. The earliest allusion to "JOIN, or DIE" in this correspondence was the most cryptic, the version in the *Virginia Gazette* of July 19, 1754. Yet this was also the most important of the two versions sent to British leaders, because of its timing, its association with a major American defeat in Virginia, and its use in the newspapers of London two short months later. The *South Carolina Gazette*'s allusion, which contained the pictorial representation, arrived in Britain considerably later during October 1754, when it, too, came to Robinson's attention.

The Virginia newspaper found its way to Robinson through at least two different routes. An anonymous writer sent the earliest of these copies of the *Gazette* in a letter to John and Capel Hanbury, who subsequently conveyed it and an "Extract of a letter dated Virginia July 23, 1754" to Robinson. The Hanburys were Englishmen and members of the Ohio Company, which sought to settle land and secure fur trade in the region.[54] The anonymous author of the letter to them remarked, "I wrote you two Days ago by Capt. Baker, giving you as full an Account as the time would allow, of our Misfortune at the Ohio. I now enclose you an Abstract of it in the [Virginia] Gazette, wrote by Col. [Philip] Ludwell, & put in with the Approbation of the Govr. [Robert Dinwiddie]."[55] A note on this letter to the Hanburys stated, "In a Private letter from Sir Tho. Robinson to Ld. Alb of 5 Sept. 1754."[56] Evidently, Robinson forwarded the information to William Anne Keppell, earl of Albemarle, in a letter that included an excerpt from the *Gazette*.[57] Lord Albemarle, who had been the British ambassador to France since 1748, would have had an interest in the diplomatic ramifications of the military conflict.[58]

On September 5, 1754, Robinson forwarded another copy of the letter and the article from the *Virginia Gazette* to Philip C. Yorke, earl of Hardwicke, who was Lord Chancellor from 1737 until 1756. Robinson's letter placed the news in the broader context of diplomatic relations between Britain and France:

> I have the honour to send your Lordship by this Messenger the most material papers which have passed in my office since your Lordship left London.
>
> Your Lordship will observe with what warmth the French press for an accommodation of all our disputes in America, and they may well desire to negotiate now that they are in possession of all they pretend to in Nova Scotia, and on the Back of our Settlements.
>
> The inclosed article from the Virginia Gazette came in but yesterday, and that by the way of Scotland. The account however is too true, as it appears by the other inclosed paper to have been inserted with the approbation of Mr. Dinwiddie.[59]

By relating the military developments in the southern colony to those in a northern one, Robinson depicted a broad pattern of French aggression in British America.

On September 7, 1754, the earl of Hardwicke appears to have forwarded a copy of the *Virginia Gazette* to Thomas Pelham-Holles, duke of Newcastle, since his letter alluded to the paragraph in the *Gazette* that Newcastle could "see." Hardwicke commented, "I am very sorry for the check we have receiv'd upon the River Ohio. 'tis monstrous that People will not help themselves, & you see by the Paragraph in the Virginia Gazette that Dinwiddie & his Council lay the Blame on the other Colonies." He added, "I fear we shall find as much, if not more, difficulty to fix them to any thing reasonable in a *general Concert*."[60] Before then, though, Robinson appears to have already conferred with Newcastle about the defeat, since Newcastle had written to Hardwicke earlier on September 4, 1754, "I conclude Sir Thos. Robinson will send your Lordship an Account of our Defeat on the River Ohio where we have been oblig'd to retire, tho' not with so much Loss as the Papers mention." Newcastle did not specify the basis for his skepticism about the extent of the losses. He added, "Our Friend, My Lord Granville, is always talking of our Strength in North America; And I don't see, that we are able to do any Thing. The Situation of our Northern Colonies, & the Encroachments & Insults of the French, require our most serious consideration."[61] Newcastle wrote the following day, September 5, to John Carteret, earl of Granville, commenting similarly on the "Situation of our Northern Colonies" and adding, "The Evil is great & visible. I am sorry to say the Remedy does not seem to me so Easy."[62]

Yet another copy of the July 19 *Virginia Gazette* found its way into the Newcastle manuscripts in the form of a letter from Dinwiddie to Robinson dated July 24, 1754. Dinwiddie commented, "P.S. The News Paper enclosed will give you the Officer's Narrative of the late Action." His political objectives became explicit when he added, "This small Engagem't conducted with Judgm't by the Officers, & great Bravery by our few Forces, gives them Hon'r, & at [the] same Time sh'd Open the Eyes of our neighbouring Colonies, rouse them from their Infatuation, w'n [when] they see their Properties so much Expos'd to a merciless Enemy, but I fear nothing but an Act of Parliam't will oblige them to their Duty." A note on this letter indicated that Robinson received it on September 16, 1754.[63]

During July and August, Dinwiddie sent the article in the *Virginia Gazette* to several other leaders both in Britain and America. He mentioned the newspaper that he enclosed with each of his letters on July 24, 1754, to George Montague Dunk, earl of Halifax; to the earl of Albemarle, the British diplomat in France; to Secretary at War Henry Fox, Lord Holland; to James Abercromby, who was the colony's agent; and to John and Capel Hanbury.[64] That day, Dinwiddie also wrote without explicitly mentioning the newspaper to the Lords of Trade, Sir Thomas Robinson, and the earl of Granville.[65] Yet it seems probable that he included the newspaper in his letters to these figures too, since Robinson's official correspondence included the newspaper with the letter. Later, on July 31, Dinwiddie sent copies to Gov. James DeLancey of New York and to Gov. Horatio Sharpe of Maryland. On August 5, Dinwiddie mailed copies to Pres. Matthew Rowan of North Carolina and to Gov. James Glen of South Carolina.[66]

Dinwiddie's letter to Governor Hamilton on July 31, 1754, was typically evasive on colonial union and sharp in its criticism of Pennsylvania. Dinwiddie detailed the military concerns and mentioned receiving "a Plan for an Union among all the Colonies on this Cont't [Continent]." He added, "As it's an extraordinary Piece, and some new Positions in it not before ventur'd on, I do not care to give any Opinion on it till I hear how it is rec'd at Home [Britain]." Yet, he mentioned, "It is most certain if the neighbouring Colonies had given due Assistance, the last unlucky Affair w'd not have happened; to the Contrary, it's more than probable by this Time we s'd [should] have forc'd the Enemy from the Ohio and had Possess'n of these Lands Ourselves." He then requested financial support from Pennsylvania, "if Y'r Assembly can be bro't to reason, to their Duty to the King and for their own Preservat'n."[67] One significant obstacle for Pennsylvania's governor in responding to Dinwiddie's request, however, was that land speculators in Pennsylvania were interested, as were those from Virginia, in claiming and settling land westward of the two colonies.

The account of the defeat in the *Virginia Gazette* was reprinted in British newspapers, including the *London Evening-Post* and the *Whitehall Evening-Post*,

both for September 5–7, 1754. These articles ended before the cryptic allusion to the "ingenious Emblem." Both commented generally in the conclusion
that "the Account seems to have been drawn up in haste; and tho' it is not
very intelligible in some Places, it may nevertheless be authentick; at least we
may presume it has been published at Williamsburgh by *Authority*" A few
days later, on September 10, the *Public Advertiser* observed, "These Accounts
agree with the Virginia Gazette that the Number of the Killed on our Side
amounted to 30, and that of the Wounded to 70: And that the French had 300
killed or wounded." *Gentleman's Magazine* for September 1754 also described
the defeat in "the account said to be published in the *Virginia Gazette*."[68]

In addition to the allusions to "JOIN, or DIE" in the newspaper account
from the *Virginia Gazette*, Robinson received a pictorial representation of it
in a letter from Gov. James Glen, who enclosed a copy of the *South Carolina
Gazette* for August 22, 1754. Writing to Robinson on August 26, 1754, Glen
alluded to receiving a letter from Dinwiddie, who "refers me for a full account
of the Action to a Virginia Gazette Inclosed which being reprinted in the
[South] Carolina Gazette, I take the Liberty to transmit to you." Robinson received Glen's letter on October 30, 1754, several weeks after his communi-
cations with Newcastle, Hardwicke, and Albemarle based on the same news.[69]
If Robinson had been puzzled by the allusion to the "ingenious Emblem," then
the article in the *South Carolina Gazette* explained it.

In Britain, an underlying contradiction in policy centered on colonial union
in America. On the one hand, a union was vital for military defense against
the French and Indians. On the other hand, a union would have diminished
the Parliament's ability to dominate the colonies, which could be more easily managed were they disunited. In 1754, British apprehensions of American
independence were sufficiently widespread to warrant caution in developing
a plan to unify British America. On September 9, 1754, after having asked the
Board of Trade to develop its own plan for colonial union, Newcastle had asked
the Speaker of the House of Commons about the prospects of a bill for colonial union in the Parliament. The Speaker, Arthur Onslow, indicated that any
such bill would provoke considerable debate, as he put it, on the "ill Consequence to be apprehended from uniting too closely the Northern Colonies
with Each other; an Independency upon this Country to be apprehended from
such an Union."[70] Concerns about the possibility of American independence
were not new among Britain's most powerful political leaders. Horace Walpole, for example, had criticized New York as a "free[,] rich British settlement,
and in such opulence and of such haughtiness, that suspicions had long been
conceived of their meditating to throw off their dependence on their mother
country."[71]

Newcastle received such advice on colonial union from other quarters as well. In Charles Townshend's "Remarks upon the Plan for a General Concert, & c.," probably written during September 1754, Townshend cautioned, "It is well known to those who have attended to the Affairs of America, that the provinces have been for many years engaged in a settled design of drawing to themselves the ancient and established prerogatives wisely preserved in the Crown as the only means of supporting and continuing the Superintendency of the Mother Country." After listing the means by which the colonial governments had sought this end, he warned, "It is as certain that whenever the Bill of supply to follow this scheme of a general Concert is passed, the same Provinces will insert into it the same scheme of Encroachment; and then the Crown will be reduced either to purchase this security to the Colonies by sacrificing our only security for their dependance upon us, or to have a partial supply in Consequence of a general Fund to be settled, or to drop the whole design of an Union upon this Plan."[72]

A similar concern characterized comments by the anonymous author of "Thoughts on the Expediency, & Manner of Supporting a regular military force in the Continent of North America," which had been enclosed "in Mr. Ald*n* [Alden?] Baker's Letter of Octr. 1, 1754," and which had found its way into Newcastle's manuscripts. The anonymous author affirmed, "I cannot see the Scheme of an Union or Confederacy of the Severall governments in any practicable light." This author, too, warned Newcastle that "an act of Parliament here would with difficulty be framed to adjust the Quotas & past with more difficulty against the outcry of those who almost claim an independency on this country."[73] The snake's image on "JOIN, or DIE" would almost certainly have heightened such concerns about British control over its dominions.

Meanwhile, the military defeat in America heightened the British government's urgent need for action and justified setting aside the plans for uniting the colonies. As early as August 15, 1754, Halifax had written to Newcastle, indicating that "the Delay which must necessarily attend the Execution of this or any other Plan for an Union of the Colonies would not admit of its answering the Purpose of present Exigency." After receiving this letter and after Newcastle's September 9 conference with Onslow, in which the Speaker mentioned concerns about independence, Newcastle wrote to William Murray on September 28, 1754, "You will have all that has passed, about the General Concert for establishing some provision for the Joint deffence of our Northern Colonies, but as no Scheme of that kind can be of service in the present Exigency, *that* may be a matter of future consideration."[74]

As a consequence both of British leaders' misgivings concerning American independence and of the urgent need for action following the defeat on the Ohio River, the plans for colonial union—both the one developed by the Board of Trade and the one developed at the Albany Congress—were set aside, though not without having been shown to King George II and having undergone some continued discussions through December.[75] No meaningful action was taken on either of the plans of union, not because of its democracy, as Franklin later claimed, but rather because of the danger posed by "the anticipated permanence of its institutions, the regularity of its intercolonial meetings, and the federal nature of its authority."[76] Instead of finalizing a formal union, the British sent a military commander to take charge of the military in America and Robinson sent a circular letter on October 26 to the governors requisitioning contributions to a "Common Fund, to be employed, provisionally, for the general Service of North America, . . . until such Time, as a Plan of general Union of His Majty's [Majesty's] Northern Colonies, for their Common Defence, can be perfected."[77] The British ministry negotiated the tensions posed by a colonial union by providing British control over colonial military forces, while requisitioning the colonies' funds to finance them.

Although the outcome of bureaucratic controversy over the plans of union had been resolved by late October, Americans fed lingering concerns about the possibility of independence, sometimes inadvertently, sometimes in the process of seeking advantage over political rivals within a particular colony, and other times by intimation. The last can be illustrated by Governor Shirley's letter on December 24, 1754, to Robinson about the Albany Plan. Shirley had been an enthusiastic advocate of a colonial union and, as recently as October 21, 1754, had urged the new governor of Pennsylvania, Robert Hunter Morris, "to lose no time for promoting the Plan of an Union of the Colonies for their mutual Defence to be concerted at home, and establish'd by Act of Parliamt as soon as is possible." But Shirley remarked in his letter to Robinson that the Albany Plan "doth not appear well calculated to strengthen the dependency of the Colonies upon the Crown, wch seems a very important Article in the consideration of this affair."[78] The prominent colonial leader overtly undercut prospects for a colonial union. In his other correspondence from that time, Shirley sparred with Franklin over alternative plans of colony union, with the former endeavoring to blunt the implications such a union would have for British control over America.[79]

Similarly, during early October 1754, the "Report of a Committee, Chosen by the General Assembly of Connecticut," listed several objections to the Albany Plan, among them that "His Majesty's subjects, now inhabiting this country, are a very great body; and in every twenty-five years the increase of inhabitants is so great, they are supposed to become double." Because growth in population size was a conventional means of gauging military strength, the committee cautioned, "This power and strength being brought into one point, all to move under the direction of said president-general and council, we fear, may in time be of dangerous consequence to his Majesty's interest, and the good of his loyal subjects here." The Connecticut Assembly's October 2, 1754, expression of concern about the plan of union was worded similarly.[80] Ambivalence in the American colonies' leadership reflected deep tensions in British politics as well, tensions likely to have been evoked, in part, by Franklin's "JOIN, or DIE."

Exploiting anxieties in Britain about independence, other Americans, such as William Smith of Pennsylvania, sought to undermine his political opposition in the Assembly, especially his adversaries among the Quakers. In Smith's anonymous pamphlet, *A Brief State of the Province of Pennsylvania*, which was published at London in 1755, he sought to explain Pennsylvania's failure to contribute funds for defense by blaming the Quakers. Smith, who was an Anglican clergyman and provost of Philadelphia College, referred to the Quakers as people who "are factious, contentious, and disregard the Proprietors and their Governors. Nay, they seem even to claim a kind of Independency of their Mother-Country, despising the Orders of the Crown, and refusing to contribute their Quota, either to the general Defence of *America*, or that of their own particular Province."[81] Because the paragraph switched between plural assemblies and the singular assembly of Pennsylvania, it was not altogether clear whether Smith meant to describe a broad pattern in several colonies or a specific one in Pennsylvania, though the general tenor of his commentary strongly suggested the former. In any event, in the context of concerns about the prospect of the colonies' independence, "JOIN, or DIE" almost certainly elicited a conflicted response in Britain: the support for union in the interest of military defense was circumscribed by fears that such a union would endanger British dominance in America. The latter response was magnified a decade later in British responses to "JOIN, or DIE" during the Stamp Act controversy of 1765–66.

"JOIN, or DIE" during the Stamp Act Controversy, 1765–66

The snake device on "JOIN, or DIE" acquired modified meanings in 1765, when the image was reproduced on the masthead of a radical publication in British America urging united colonial opposition to recent British legislation, the Stamp Act, which was to go into effect on November 1, 1765. The provisions of the legislation affected most colonists, especially newspaper publishers throughout the colonies. "Stamped paper would have to be used for newspapers, many classes of legal documents, ships' clearance papers, appointments to public offices, liquor licences, surveys, grants and conveyances of land, assurances, mortgages, cards, dice, pamphlets, advertisements, calendars, and apprentice contracts," explained Peter D. G. Thomas. "The tax would be paid regularly by merchants, lawyers or their clients, and newspapers printers; often by publicans and sinners—or at least gamblers; and at infrequent intervals by virtually every colonist." The Stamp Act was calculated both to raise a revenue and to assert the sovereignty of the British Parliament over British America.[82] Although such Stamp Acts were familiar to British citizens as a commonplace means to raise a revenue in Britain, the British government's use of such taxation in British America was an innovation that, to the American colonists, set a dangerous precedent in that it could provide a legal means for the British to shift their economic burdens onto the colonists without any harmful ramifications for the British constituents of the representatives in Parliament. In fact, these constituents could find their own tax burdens eased as a consequence of raising the necessary taxes in British America.

In adamant opposition to the new taxation, William Goddard appropriated "JOIN, or DIE" for the masthead on two of three versions of the *Constitutional Courant* that were published on September 21, 1765, and circulated throughout the northern colonies (fig. 3.2 on p. 30). Goddard printed the *Courant* at Woodbridge, New Jersey, on James Parker's press, having secured permission to use it occasionally.[83] On October 7, 1765, the *Boston Evening-Post* reproduced "JOIN, or DIE" with a description of the *Courant* (fig. 3.11). On October 7, the *Courant* was also described in the *Newport Mercury* of Providence, Rhode Island, but without reference to the snake's image.[84] The images of the segmented snake in the *Courant* and the *Boston Evening-Post* had the usual eight parts, but they differed from the earlier versions of the device in that the motto, "JOIN, or DIE," was printed above the snake instead of below it. Isaiah Thomas commented in *The History of Printing* that "A large edition was printed, secretly forwarded to New York, and there sold by hawkers selected for the purpose. It had a rapid sale, and was, I believe, reprinted there, and at Boston."[85]

Only a month before the Stamp Act Congress of the American colonies was to be held at New York in October 1765, the publisher of the *Courant* appropriated the segmented snake's image to urge unity in colonial opposition to the tax law.[86] This radical appropriation of the segmented snake came to the attention of the most powerful politicians in Britain by various means. The two most important of these were correspondence from Cadwallader Colden of New York to Henry Seymour Conway and from Sir Francis Bernard

3.11. "JOIN OR DIE," *Boston Evening-Post*, Boston, October 7, 1765, p. 3, col. 1.
Publisher: Thomas Fleet; medium: newspaper woodcut; size: 1 ¾" × 3 ⅛".
Photograph courtesy of the Massachusetts Historical Society.

of Massachusetts to the Board of Trade in London: both letters were later
exhibited before the entire Parliament among the American Papers with a reproduction of the snake's image prominently placed at the beginning as the masthead of the "Extracts" (fig. 3.3 on p. 31). As one consequence, the significantly
altered meanings of the snake's image posed serious rhetorical problems for
Franklin in his roles as a crown officer and a colonial agent in London.

On October 12, 1765, Lieut. Gov. Cadwallader Colden wrote to Henry
Seymour Conway, secretary of state for the Southern Department, enclosing
a copy of the *Constitutional Courant* with the snake device on the masthead:
"Since the last which I had the honour to write to you of the 23rd of September, this Town has remain'd quiet, tho' inflammatory Papers continue to
be publish'd exciting the People to oppose a Stamp Duty in the Colonies.
The most remarkable of these Papers is inclosed. This was distributed along
the Post Roads by the Post Riders. I examined the Post Master in this Place to
know how this came to be done. He assured me that it was without his knowledge; that he had examined the Post Riders and found, that one or more bundles of them were deliver'd at Woodbridge New Jersey, to the Post Rider by
James Parker Secrettary to the General Post Office in N. America." Having
alerted Conway to the distribution of the *Constitutional Courant*, Colden indicated that the government of New York had taken notice of the publication.

He commented that "The Gentlemen of the Council think it prudent at this time to delay making more particular inquiry least it should be the occasion of raising the Mob, which it is thought proper by all means to avoid."[87] To judge from the date written on the envelope upon its arrival at Conway's office and from Conway's later report to the House of Commons, he received these materials from Colden on November 15, 1765. A subsequent letter on December 15 from Conway to Thomas Gage, who was stationed in New York, indicated that Conway had learned "with the utmost Concern the disordered State of the Province where you reside, & the very riotous & outrageous Behavior of too many of the Inhabitants." He added, "I did not fail to lay Your Dispatches, together with those of Lieut. Governor Colden before His Majesty."[88]

Yet another American figure, Gov. Francis Bernard of Massachusetts, also took notice of the *Constitutional Courant* with the snake device in his correspondence with the Board of Trade and with John Pownall. Both of these letters, too, ultimately came to Conway's attention. Governor Bernard had opposed the British government's passage of the Stamp Act, but, after it was formally enacted by the British Parliament, found himself in the tenuous position of having to enforce it.[89] On October 12, 1765, he wrote to the Board of Trade, "The inclosed paper has been handed about here under pretence that it was printed at a private press at New York, but is supposed to have its birth nearer to this Town than New York. It is of so seditious a Nature & so flagitious a tendency, that I have thought it my duty to transmit to your Lordships immediately." Subsequently, on October 17, 1765, Bernard wrote to the "Board" that "On Monday last, Oct. 14th, a Town meeting was held at Cambridge, 4 Miles from this Town, to consider of giving instructions to their Members: and the honble [honorable] William Brattle Esqr. one of his Majesty's Council & Colonel of a Regiment was chose Moderator, that is, Chairman." Bernard continued, "A Motion was made that the Governor's Speech to the Assembly should be read; which was done. Upon which the Mover said he had a paper in his hand, which he thought was a full Answer to the Governor's Speech, & he moved that it might be read. The Chairman received it with a seeming surprize as if he knew Not what it was, & having first put the Question he read it out. This Paper which I enclose, is an Infamous libell against the Government of Great Britain so outrageous & indecent, that it has been printed at a private Press, either at this Town or at Rhode Island, it matters not which, & handed about Gratis."[90] This letter, too, was read by the Board of Trade and the Privy Council and placed before the entire Parliament among the American Papers.

Although Bernard's letters to the Board of Trade did not specify the *Constitutional Courant*, it was certainly a copy of the *Courant* with the snake device that he enclosed, as evidenced by his reference to the "one in a Cover to their Lordships" and the similar wording in his letter a few days later on October 19, 1766, to John Pownall:

> Among the Papers I send you now you will see one in a Cover to their Lordships with an Emblem of a Snake cut in pieces. This is pretended to be printed at New York and to favour that Pretence It was first communicated here this Day fortnight (or Eleven Days I am not sure which) on the day the New-York post came in. But it is generally understood it was printed here or at least in the Neighbourhood from a Copy sent from hence. However it has been reprinted here; the Copy I send to you having been purchased here for that Purpose. It has also been printed, a great Part of it in the Newport Gazette, which I send you, to show how much bolder the Rhode Island Printers are than ours. I send one of the original Impressions to their Lordships. I have no Doubt but it comes from the same Mint wch [which] produces the Boston Gazette, wherever it is printed or reprinted. It has been called a Answer to my Speech.[91]

Bernard's claim that the *Courant* had been republished at Boston was probably accurate, though yet another copy had also been produced earlier near New York.[92] His letter intimated that he was placing great confidence in Pownall's discretion, presumably because, as the governor of Massachusetts, Bernard would be vulnerable were his letters made public. Bernard prefaced his remarks, "I continue to send you the seditious Papers published here, leaving you to communicate such Part of them as you shall see Occasion to your Board, or elsewhere as you shall see fit. I send them to no one else."[93] Contemporaneous notations on these letters indicated that the Board of Trade received them on December 13, 1765.

When Pownall received these materials from Bernard featuring "JOIN, or DIE" on the *Constitutional Courant*, coming as they did in a steady stream of information to British officials about riots and unrest in America, Conway also took notice of the situation in New York as a result of his own correspondence with Colden and Thomas Gage. Conway wrote to Charles Lennox, duke of Richmond, who was in France. After assuring Richmond that the "violence" was "confined to the Northern Provinces," and that "in the South there has been no Uneasiness," Conway observed, "These affairs certainly call for the serious Attention not only of His Majesty and His Servants, but of the whole legislative Authority, and will accordingly obtain it, and will be the first Business which the Parliament will go upon in the ensuing Session. I do not however at all despair, that the Wisdom and Prudence of that Body will find a Remedy for these Disorders; and possibly the Constitution may hereafter find itself strengthened by the Remedy that is now become necessary." Intimating the potential of the riots for causing complications in Britain's diplomatic relationship with France and other European nations, Conway added, "It is not unnatural to believe our Neighbours may affect at least to suppose this Affair to be of a more alarming Nature than it really is; for tho' it is serious, it is not alarming; and I may presume to say, that nothing but Prejudice and Passion can make it so; for there is no Disaffection at the Bottom, nor any misplaced Attachment, to which a present Discontent could have Recourse, and expect Support from."[94] Conway's final line suggested the possibility that the French would meddle by supporting the protestors in British America. Conway affirmed his recognition during the early stages of the controversy that the American protestors' opposition was not to the Parliament, but rather to specific legislation by that governing body.

According to the *Journal of the Commissioners for Trade and Plantations*, two letters from Francis Bernard to the Board of Trade on October 12 and 17 were read along with "extracts" from his letters to Pownall. The *Journal* also indicated that Bernard enclosed "certain seditious papers printed and published in that province." These "seditious papers" certainly included the *Constitutional Courant* with the snake device on the masthead, even though numerous other protests were in circulation, because the *Courant* was included later among the American Papers, when they were studied by the entire Parliament in 1766. On December 17, 1765, the *Journal* also recorded an order that these documents "be copied to be laid before his Majesty, and a representation thereupon to his Majesty was prepared, transcribed and signed."[95] The letter from William Legge, earl of Dartmouth, Jeremiah Dyson, and William Fitzherbert to George III on December 17, explicitly included "the publick Papers & Prints" as well as copies of the letters from Bernard, suggesting that the king himself had seen the *Constitutional Courant* with the snake device.[96] An anonymous note in the records of the House of Lords indicated that "The original Newspapers, which were referred to in Governor Bernard's Letters to Mr. Pownall, were transmitted to the Council Office; and no Copies of them taken in the Office of Trade and Plantations," another way of referring to the Board of Trade.[97] Subsequently, the *Acts of the Privy Council* recorded on December 17, 1765, that the Privy Council read Francis Bernard's letters as represented to them by the Board of Trade, including his letters of October 12, October 17, and an extract of his letters of October 19 and 26, 1765.[98]

Meanwhile, during December, Thomas Pelham-Holles, duke of Newcastle, and Charles Watson-Wentworth, marquis of Rockingham, contemplated the king's upcoming speeches to the Parliament, one to open the session on December 17 and, after the holidays, another on January 14, 1766.[99] As planned in an exchange between the powerful politicians, King George III's speech to the Parliament on December 17 affirmed, "as matters of importance have lately occurred in some of my colonies in America, which will demand the most serious attention of parliament; and as further informations are daily expected from different parts of that country, of which I shall order the fullest accounts to be prepared for your consideration; I have thought fit to call you now together in order that opportunity may thereby be given to issue the necessary writs on the many vacancies that have happened in the House of Commons since the last session." In the Lord's traditional reply, an "Address of Thanks" delivered in response to the king's speech opening the session, the earl of Hardwicke remarked, "The state of affairs in America, which is the subject pointed out to us in the Speech is indeed of the highest magnitude." Hardwicke added, "When we enter into this arduous matter, my lords, it should be discussed deliberately, wisely, . . . and thoroughly with all the materials necessary to inform and direct our judgments; with joint deliberation and concurrence of both Houses of parliament, and with the fullest attendance of their members."[100]

The following day, on December 18, 1765, the Privy Council considered a "Letter from the Duke of Grafton for copies of all letters, papers, and orders to be laid before the House of Lords; also letters from H. S. Conway for copies for the House of Commons 19 Dec." Augustus Henry Fitzroy, duke of Grafton, had written to the Board of Trade, the Privy Council, and the Treasury Department, remarking, "I am commanded to signify to your Lordships His Majesty's Pleasure, that you do give orders for preparing without loss of Time, & transmit to me, copies of all such Letters & Papers as relate to the Riots, which have lately happened in America, in opposition to the putting in Execution the Stamp Act in His Majesty's Colonies in that Country, as well as every Information of every kind that may have been received, together with all orders & such issued by your Lordships, since the passing of that Act to this present Time, in order that I may lay the same before the House of Lords."[101] Conway's letters to the board, the council, and the Treasury were similar on behalf of the House of Commons.[102] During December, the Treasury Department also received abstracts of the American Papers, including the letters by Colden and Bernard.[103] An entry in the *Acts of the Privy Council* indicated that the "Copies & Extracts of Several Newspapers, printed in New England,

Sept.–Nov. 1765, and referred to in Gov. Bernard's letters," consisting of 108 pages, were printed "for the Parliament," along with a "list of letters, papers and Orders, 27 Aug to 6 Nov."[104]

On December 19 the administration was confronted by a motion in Parliament from John Russell, duke of Bedford, requesting the American Papers relating to the Stamp Act.[105] Horace Walpole's *Memoirs* recorded Bedford's maneuver to secure the papers: "The Duke of Bedford moved for all papers that had been sent to America relating to the Stamp Act, and since the passing of it. The Duke of Grafton quashed that proposal, by promising *all* the papers should be produced." Walpole added, "[Richard] Rigby moved the same question in the Commons, and was severely treated by [William] Beckford, and the motion was rejected, the Duke of Grafton forgetting to acquaint the Ministers in that House that he had granted the demand to the Lords. This obliged the King to send the papers to the House of Commons likewise."[106] Grafton did not, in fact, have the king's authorization to make this commitment, because he explained his actions to the king later by remarking that he had sought "to save that days Discussion, & thinking it would have a better appearance, presumed to answer that he had already received your Majesty's Commands on the Subject."[107] The king assured Grafton that his answer had been "perfectly right."[108]

On December 19, Conway reported the Parliamentary proceedings to the king, noting that "A Motion was most insidiously & I may say indecently made to call for the American Papers which Your Majesty promis'd the Parliament." Although the motions by Bedford and Rigby failed, the king wrote later that day to Rockingham: "The Duke of Bedford's motion seems to be most extraordinary, for one would think it were necessary to weigh every paper carefully before they either themselves or by any committee, direct any of them to be printed."[109]

During December, before the American Papers were officially presented to Parliament, they were circulated among the most powerful political figures in Britain. On December 14, 1765, Newcastle sent a note to Conway remarking, "I am much obliged to you, for the American Letters; which, I find, are The Originals; I should have wished rather, That they had been Copies, as I might have kept them longer; for such important Letters as these, should not be read in a Hurry." Evidently, Conway later supplied copies, because Newcastle wrote to him again on December 25, "P.S. I have, this Moment, received from you, The American Correspondence, & thank you for it. I will send it back to you, the Moment I have done with it." He added, "It is very Voluminous; & Every Paper very material, for the Knowledge of those, who may take any Part in the Debate, in Either House. And so, I find, the Duke of Grafton thought, by sending them to My Lord Holdernesse, & My Lord Hardwicke; which I was very glad to hear."[110]

On December 25, Newcastle recorded a question in his list of "Items for My Lord Rockingham only": "Stamp Act—Q: What is intended to be done in it.—What mention of it in The Speech."[111] In early January, Charles Yorke and William Dowdeswell both provided Rockingham with drafts for the king's speech, and Dowdeswell's was used.[112] On January 14, 1766, the king commented in his speech to both houses of Parliament, "When I met you last, I acquainted you that Matters of Importance had happened in America, which would demand the most serious attention of Parliament." He added, "That no information, which could serve to direct your Deliberations in so interesting a Concern, might be wanting, I have ordered all the Papers, that give any Light into the Origin, the Progress, or the Tendency of the Disturbances which have late prevailed in some of the Northern Colonies, to be immediately laid before you."[113] Subsequently, the speech was published in the *London Chronicle* for January 14–16, 1766 and in Franklin's *Pennsylvania Gazette* for March 27, 1766, among other outlets.[114]

Horace Walpole's *Memoirs* recorded that "Mr. Conway, then, by order of his Majesty, presented at the bar the letters and different intelligence to and from America, and moved to have them taken into consideration on the Thursday sevennight following." Walpole then commented on British politicians' efforts to print the American Papers in a published form: "Mr. [Richard] Rigby proposed to have them printed. Mr. Conway observed, that those papers mentioned particular names of men and their transactions, and therefore objected to the printing. Mr. [Edmund] Nugent said, Too much had been done now to leave any room for secrecy; and Mr. Conway gave it up." *The Journals of the House of Commons* recorded that on the same day, January 14, Conway placed the letter from Colden along with a "Printed Copy of the *Constitutional Courant*" among the papers before the committee of the entire House of Commons.[115] In addition, the American Papers included Francis Bernard's letters alluding to and enclosing a copy of the *Courant*.

The records of the House of Lords indicated that on January 16, 1766, a motion was put forward in Parliament "That the several papers relating to the informations and advices received from North America of the riots & tummelts there be printed under proper restrictions."[116] Yet Parliament found the question of publishing the intelligence from America provocative, because, as Edmund Burke put it in a letter on January 18, to Charles O'Hara, "the Lives of some in America would be endangerd by such a publication."[117] Parliament also had more selfish motives than this to be concerned about publishing the names. John Huske, according to Walpole's *Memoirs*, remarked that "if they printed the names, they would never have any more intelligence."[118] In a marginal note, George Villiers observed in his journal similarly, "Motion for printing the papers unguardedly consented to in the H. [House] of Commons: It had the same day been made & withdrawn in the H. of Lords."[119] Subsequently, the Parliament resolved, as Burke put it, "to refer the dangerous Papers to the Speaker, that he might cut out the parts which might expose those who communicated intelligence to Government, to the resentment of the populace in America." Burke added, "Yesterday the Speaker was of opinion that no precaution of that kind would be sufficient for the purpose. And Mr[.] Dowdeswell moved, on the Speaker[']s report, to discharge the order for printing."[120] Recognizing this aspect of the situation, Lord William Wildman Barrington wrote to Governor Bernard a letter on February 6, 1766, that intimated the possibilities: "Your Correspondence with the Ministry laid before both Houses of Parliament is universally admired; I wish the Publication of it may not produce any inconveniences in America."[121]

Eventually, several copies of the lengthy "Copies and Extracts of Several News Papers Printed in New England in the Months of September, October and November, 1765, and Referred to in the Letters Transmitted from Francis Bernard, Esq; Governor of the Massachusetts Bay to the Lords Commissioners for Trade and Plantations" were printed especially for the members of Parliament to study with care.[122] In the published version, the snake device from the *Constitutional Courant* was reproduced prominently as the masthead on page three, which was the first page of text (fig. 3.3 on p. 31). The text of the *Courant* was reprinted on the pages from three to ten, the first document in the series to be placed before the Parliament. Yet additional extracts from the *Courant* as reported in the *Newport Mercury* of October 7, 1765, were reprinted on pages seventeen through twenty. Thus the image of "JOIN, or DIE" became readily available in pictorial reproductions and verbal descriptions to all parliamentarians.

To judge from correspondence of colonial agents and parliamentarians, the reading of the American Papers, either in their original form or in the publication itself, occupied the Parliament throughout January. In Villiers's entry in his journal for January 28, 1766, he remarked, "Both Houses began reading the American Papers. Many days are spent in reading these Papers & examining the most considerable Merchants to give lights into the State of the Trade." The same day, Philip York, earl of Hardwicke, wrote to Charles Yorke, "Reading the papers will take up a day more, and I suppose we shall not sit on the 30th of January." On January 31, Hugh Hamersley, the colonial agent for Maryland, reported to Governor Sharpe, "Both Houses of Parliament have been employed this week in reading the Papers Laid before them by the Crown, which has been done in the most secret manner by Excluding every other Individual from their Walls, for, as the Private Correspondence of the Governors and other Servants of the Crown in the different Colonys makes a considerable part of the Collection, they are justly apprehensive of the consequences to particular Persons, shd [should] the contents, by being made Publick, find their way back to their proper Colonys. The Discussion of the Papers is appointed for the beginning of next week."[123]

Another colonial agent, Charles Garth, reported on progress reading the American Papers in his letter to the South Carolina Committee of Correspondence on February 9, 1766: "Upon the 28 of Jany the Committee of the whole House in the affairs of America & c. commenc'd; reading the Papers mention'd in the Votes." He added, "Very sorry I am to observe, that the Contents of many of the Papers, particularly from ye Northern Colonies, touching the Legislative Authority of Parliament, for Language and Expression, together with the Accounts of the tumultuous proceedings, the nature and extent thereof, were received by the Committee with an impression far from favourable to the great object in view." He noted, "It is very unfortunate that the steps to prevent the Act taking place were in some places carried to that Length and extremity they have been."[124]

While examining the papers prior to their publication, either during preparations for the sessions in December or during the formal meetings in January, several members of the concerned departments in government and other members of Parliament took extracts of the letters, as evidenced by manuscript collections of such political leaders as George Grenville, Hardwicke, Newcastle, Rockingham, and Dartmouth. "JOIN, or DIE" was mentioned specifically in a document among George Grenville's papers labeled "Lord Temple's notes on reading of American papers," dated January 1766. An entry for Bernard's October 19 letter to Pownall, received December 13, 1765, elicited this comment: "*Madness of the people* far from abating, sends seditious papers"; a reaction to Cadwallader Colden's letter was more specific: "Enclosing printed Copy of Constitutional Courant[,] a snake cut in pieces[,] Join or Die."[125]

Hardwicke's manuscripts contained a complete copy of the *Constitutional Courant* in the form reproduced with the snake device in the "Copies and Extracts of Several News Papers Printed in New England." A handwritten note on the title page indicated that it had been "Annexed to the Representation of the Board of Trade, dated 17 December 1765." Among Hardwicke's papers, a summary of the letter from "Lieut. Govr. Colden Octr 12th Ry [Received] Nov. 15th" stated, "The Town remained quiet, but inflammatory papers dispers'd about to keep up the resentment of the People to the Stamp Act. Mentions & incloses a remarkable one distributed along the Post roads by the Post Riders, supposed to be printed by one Parker, but the enquiry into it deferr'd to a more proper time."[126] It was unlikely that this was the copy that Conway had prepared for Hardwicke, since the other copies prepared from the records of the Board of Trade were exact duplicates, not paraphrases.

Another paraphrased version of Colden's letter was in Newcastle's manuscripts in a document labeled "America Correspondence relative to the Disturbances Abstracted," with the notation "Oct. 12: 1765 Rec'd Novr. 9 [sic:15] Vide Printed Paper." The abstract noted, "No public Disturbances had yet happened but licentious Papers Swarm'd; of which he incloses the most inflammatory, which he supposes to have been printed by James Parker Secretary to the General Post Office in North America, who was formerly a Printer in New York, prints now occasionally and was known to have distributed Bundles of these Papers."[127] William Legge, earl of Dartmouth, who had been appointed president of the Board of Trade on July 20, 1765, also apparently made abstracts of the letters from Bernard and Colden. In addition, Dartmouth's manuscript collections contained two original copies of the *Constitutional Courant*.[128] Most important, because of the leadership of Charles Watson-Wentworth, marquis of Rockingham, in the Parliament, the Rockingham papers contained a "Précis of Letters from the America Governors," including references to Colden's letter of October 12, 1765. In fact, at least four "copies" and "duplicates" of these abstracts were among Rockingham's papers.[129]

Clearly, when George Onslow wrote on January 30, 1766, to William Pitt about "having read all the American Papers," commenting that "The House is so fatigued with these long sittings, and attention to useless uninforming papers," he was only partly correct, insofar as the meetings were both long and tiring. But the most powerful figures in Parliament devoted careful attention to details in the "useless uninforming" American Papers. Moreover, the minority in the House of Lords specifically mentioned letters from Bernard and Colden by name in justifying their votes against the repeal.[130] Some parliamentarians' notes on the American Papers attributed the publication of the *Courant* to James Parker, because of the inaccurate speculation in Colden's letter. On January 31, the Parliament finished reading the American Papers and turned its attention to examining various witnesses, Franklin among them during mid-February.[131]

On February 1, Conway reported to the king, "What relates to the American business was that the Papers & Examinations were all finish'd & that it was agreed to go on the Resolutions & c. on Monday." During Parliament's ensuing debates about whether to receive or reject a petition from the Stamp Act Congress that had convened in New York, a potential colonial union became the subject of controversy.[132] According to the Parliamentary diaries of Nathaniel Ryder, on February 3, 1766, for example, Hans Stanley expressed concerns about resolves in Massachusetts, commenting in general, "They have begun a Federal Union: we do not meet without the Crown's authority." Later in his speech to Parliament, he remarked, "From the letter from Governor Bernard, it is apparent that there is an intention of improving the present ill humour into an actual breach with Great Britain."[133] Grey Cooper, a new member of the Parliament who had only months earlier become a secretary of the Treasury, recorded that, at some moment during the debates, Stanley also denounced the actions of the legislature of Massachusetts Bay: "They have exceeded what this House has ever done Meeting in a federal Union not to be dissolved by the Crown." Stanley worried, "They will soon become more useful Allies to France than to you as appears from the papers."[134]

The *Memoirs of Rockingham* suggested that Stanley was not alone in expressing such concerns: "Messrs. [Charles] Jenkinson and [Jeremiah] Dyson, both holding office under Lord Rockingham, as did [Edmund] Nugent and [Wilbore] Ellis, belonged to the Court Party, who called the [Stamp Act] Congress a 'dangerous federal union.'"[135] Likewise, Walpole commented in his *Memoirs* that Edmund Nugent and Wilbore Ellis "called it [the congress] a dangerous federal union."[136] An undated, contemporaneous "Notes on Lord Halifax's comments to Parliament" stated: "But the Fact is as it appears from the Papers on ye Lds Table that it is not the Stamp Act that is opposed but the Authority of this Legislature."[137] According to Hardwicke's notes, Henry Howard, earl of Suffolk worried, "May it not be that the Americans will make further Demands till they by Degrees gett to Independency and at last give Law to these from whom they have received it?"[138]

In a similar vein, Lord Buckinghamshire wrote to the mayor of Norwich during January 1766. Alluding to "the transactions in North America," Buckinghamshire cautioned, "Whatever false pretences they may alledge those who are acquainted with the whole tenor of their conduct cannot doubt that their intention is to shake off all connection with their Mother Country." He added ominously, "If their Plan succeeds the Glory of England is no more."[139] Among the Bedford manuscripts was a sheet listing arguments to be used during the Parliamentary debate about repealing the Stamp Act. Under the heading, "If it was right to tax America, the Stamp Act should not be repealed for these reasons," the fifth of the eight lines of argument was that "the Spirit of indepency should be checked & not encouraged by ye repeal of the Act."[140] As interpreted by powerful politicians in Parliament, the meanings of the Americans' protests, such as "JOIN, or DIE" on the *Courant*, broadened from the specific issue of taxation to encompass, in general, the Parliament's right to govern altogether in British America.

On January 27, during the Parliamentary debate over the Stamp Act Congress petition, William Pitt endeavored to assuage members' widespread concerns that the congress was an illegal assembly. Referring to Britain, Pitt contended, "It was the evil genius of this country that had riveted amongst them this union, now called *dangerous and federal.*"[141] Pitt minimized the concerns by comparing the congress in New York with various political gatherings in Britain. Subsequently, on February 3, 1766, late in the evening, Col. Isaac Barré sought to assuage misgivings by remarking to Parliament, "As to the idea of a Federal Union, did their committees at New York settle the quota of men and arms?" Because the congress had not raised a militia, Barré's rhetorical question was calculated to diffuse British anxieties about an American movement toward independence. Yet Barré added the conventional wisdom that "All colonies have their date of independence. The wisdom or folly of our conduct may make it the sooner or later."[142] His observations were not compelling to some parliamentarians. On February 24, for example, Hans Stanley reaffirmed his anxieties about the consequences of a colonial union: "If this Act is repealed, the provinces of America will either quarrel with one another about the levying the money left by this country, or they will unite in such a manner as to be superior to any power we can send against them."[143]

Months before the American Papers had been placed before Parliament, where the ramifications provoked intense discussion and where the *Courant*'s snake device amplified anxieties over a new body politic in British America, several British publications described the *Courant* to the British public. During the controversy over repealing the Stamp Act, at least four such publications interpreted "JOIN, or DIE" as being radical in its implications. The *Annual Register* for 1765 described the emblem and the *Courant*, observing that subsequent to the passage of the Stamp Act,

> Essays soon followed, not only against the expediency, but even the equity of it, in several news-papers, one of which bore the significative title of "The Constitutional Courant, containing matters interesting to liberty, and no-wise repugnant to loyalty, printed by Andrew Marvel, at

the sign of the Bribe refused, on Constitution-Hill, North-America;" and wore a still more significative headpiece; a snake cut in pieces, with the initial letters of the names of the several colonies from New-England to South-Carolina, inclusively, affixed to each piece, and above them the words JOIN or DIE. To these were added caricatures, pasquinades, puns, bonmots [bon mots], and such vulgar sayings fitted to the occasion, as by being short could be more easily circulated and retained, at the same time that, by being extremely expressive, they carried with them the weight of a great many arguments.[144]

In early November 1765 the *London Evening-Post* reported that "By yesterday's North American Packet is received a News Paper, under the Title of 'the CONSTITUTIONAL COURANT, containing matters interesting to *Liberty* and no wise repugnant to *Loyalty*'; printed by *Andrew Marvel*, at the sign of the *Bribe refused*, on *Constitution-Hill*, North America." The newspaper added, "It has an emblematical head piece of a snake or serpent cut into several pieces, on each of which are the initial letters of the names of the several colonies, as N.Y.— N.E.—P. for New York, New England, Philadelphia, & c. and over it are the words "JOIN, or DIE," in large letters." The *Gazetteer and New Daily Advertiser* for November 6 and *Lloyd's Evening Post* for the same date relayed similar information, with both newspapers making the same error of substituting "Philadelphia" for Pennsylvania.[145] Such elementary errors in the names for the colonies would have amplified the concerns in America that the British were ignorant about what they often referred to as their "dominions."

On November 16, 1765, the *Public Ledger* of London reported "Rationalis's" comments on the *Courant*'s publication, and the *Pennsylvania Journal* reprinted excerpts on February 20, 1766: "A printed paper is just now fallen into my hands, from North America; the Title of which is, The CONSTITUTIONAL COURANT: *containing matters interesting to Liberty, and no wise repugnant to Loyalty*. It is dated, Saturday, September 21, 1765, and marked No. 1, printed by *Andrew Marvel*, at the sign of the Bribe-refused on Constitution-Hill, North America: and is a half sheet, containing an introduction and two political pieces, with an ill-executed stamped emblematical device in the middle of the front, representing a writhing serpent divided into eight parts, marked with the following initials, NE, NY, NI [NJ], P, M, V, NC, SC, and over all these words, JOIN OR DIE." Judging from contemporaneous newspaper accounts, "Rationalis" was a pseudonym of New York native Nicholas Ray, who was a merchant residing in London and the author of *The*

Importance of the Colonies of North America, and the Interest of Great Britain with regard to them, Considered.[146] The reprinted article suggested how a contemporary public in Britain had interpreted the *Courant:* "From the extraordinary publication which I have mentioned [the *Courant*], . . . and indeed from all intelligence we receive from that quarter of the world, we must have reason to believe, that union is forming, which, according to the wisest opinions, it must ever be for our greatest interest and security [to] give no cause for being effected, and therefore the policy must have been erroneous which has contributed thereto."[147] "Rationalis's" article criticized the Stamp Act for inadvertently promoting a colonial union that could threaten the British Empire's political stability. The colonial union advocated in "JOIN, or DIE" was interpreted as endangering the British government's legitimacy in colonial America.

"Rationalis" did not go unopposed in articulating such views, even though his strategy in the article was to discredit the British government's policy of taxing America by underscoring the developing union as one undesirable consequence of the policy. "Pacificus," a pseudonym that although used at least once by Franklin during the Stamp Act controversy was more often used by another writer, responded in the *Gazetteer and New Daily Advertiser* on November 15, 1765, to the whole tenor of "Rationalis's" series of letters criticizing the American colonies for conspiring to unite against Britain. "Pacificus" commented, "The public are strongly impressed, with the fears of a rebellion on the continent of America; and the labours of your correspondent Mr. Rationalis seem calculated to encrease these apprehensions, altho' nothing can be plainer to a geographer than this proposition, *That the continent of America cannot be so much strengthened by population as ever to be able to dispute any point with that European power which is master of the seas.*"[148] Even so, during the controversy, "JOIN, or DIE" amplified the image of America in a state of open rebellion against the British government.

Conclusion

Specific allusions to the *Constitutional Courant* with the snake device on the masthead recurred throughout the Revolutionary era, not only in the newspaper literature in America and Britain, but also in a political pamphlet, *The Charters of the Following Provinces of North America . . . To Which is Prefixed, a Faithful Narrative of the Proceedings of the North American Colonies, In Consequence of the Late Stamp-Act*, published in London in 1766, a copy of which found its way into Hardwicke's papers. In addition, further references to "JOIN, or DIE" as published on the masthead of the *Constitutional Courant* recurred in a contemporaneous history, Edward Barnard's *The New, Comprehensive and*

3.12. "DON'T TREAD ON ME," a coiled rattlesnake on the device for "North Carolina Currency" for "TWENTY DOLLARS," probably North Carolina, April 2, 1776. Engraved by "G. L.," medium: state paper currency; size: 2 ¼" × 3 ½". Photograph courtesy of the American Antiquarian Society.

Complete History of England, published at London in 1782. The snake's symbolism had changed such that it had revolutionary implications concerning the status of British law in colonial America.[149]

The snake as an embodiment of anticipated American union and independence persisted in numerous verbal and pictorial forms, especially after the image was transformed into an American rattlesnake on the colonists' military flags. The imagery was reproduced widely on newspaper mastheads (figs. 3.5, 3.6., 3.7 on p. 32), almanac illustrations, paper currency (fig. 3.12), military flags, portrait frames (fig. 3.13), political prints (figs. 3.14 and 3.15), and even housewares.[150] Partisans in America and Britain vied with each other to shape the meanings of the snake's image. Depending upon the partisans' political commitments, the snake represented guile, deceit, and treachery on the one extreme, or prudence, wisdom, and virility on the other. The unified rattlesnake became internationally recognized in Britain, France, and the United States as a symbol of the new nation.

As soon as other Americans employed the snake's image politically to oppose the British government, Franklin quickly and tacitly repudiated both its use in such a manner and its radical implications for the British Empire. He

DONT TREAD ON ME

GEORGE WASHINGTON,
Commander in Chief of ye Armies of ye
UNITED STATES of AMERICA.

Engrav'd by W. Sharp, from an Original Picture

London, Published according to Act of Parliament Feb!: 22!: 1783.
by J. Stockdale Piccadilly.

did so, in part, by creating a political card, "MAGNA *Britannia: her Colonies* REDUC'D," to depict the entire British Empire as one body politic with the American colonies serving only as the extremities. Although this political card had forward-looking political uses during Parliament's deliberations over repealing the Stamp Act, the pictorial image also signaled Franklin's distancing himself from the radicalism of the snake's image on the *Constitutional Courant:* the body politic could not survive dismembered. The February 20,

Left: **3.13.** "DON'T TREAD ON ME," as an element in a portrait frame of "George Washington Commander in Chief of ye Armies of ye United States of America," engraved by W. Sharp from an original picture by John Trumbull, London, February 22, 1783. Medium: engraved print as the frontispiece of a book, *The Constitutions of the Several Independent States of America* (London, 1783); size: 6 ⅛" × 4 ¼". An almost identical engraving appeared earlier in Charles Henry Wharton's *A Poetical Epistle To His Excellency George Washington* (London, 1780), frontispiece, which Richard Brunton copied in an American edition of the same book published at Providence, Rhode Island, in 1781. Other later variations of this portrait were reproduced in Britain, France, and the United States. Photograph courtesy of the Prints and Photographs Division of the Library of Congress.

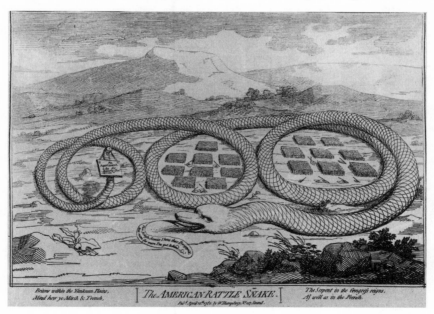

3.14. "The AMERICAN RATTLE SNAKE," [James Gillray], London, April 12, 1782. Publisher: W. [William] Humphrey; medium: engraved print; size: 9 ⅞" × 14". Photograph courtesy of the Colonial Williamsburg Foundation, Williamsburg, Virginia.

3.15. "MAGNIFICAT," or "Tu la voulu," also known by "Omni animal post coïtum triste" and other names, [France], 1779–80. Medium: line engraving; size: 9 ¾" × 6 ¾". Photograph courtesy of the Colonial Williamsburg Foundation, Williamsburg, Virginia.

1766, date of the *Pennsylvania Journal* article proves that news of "Ratio-nales's" comments concerning the snake device as reported in the *Ledger* already had re-crossed the Atlantic before Franklin's earliest extant reference to "MAGNA *Britannia*" on February 24, 1766. Despite misgivings about specific acts and policies, Franklin remained constant in his politics as an American Whig, an imperialist, and a supporter of Britain's constitutional monarchy. Although the meanings of his famous image from the *Pennsylvania Gazette* had changed in its political uses, he had not in the fundamentals of his political commitments.

Even so, Franklin's views on imperial unity did undergo significant refinement and development during the Stamp Act controversy of 1765–66. Specifically, Franklin understood British America to be within the *dominions* of the king, but outside the *realm* comprehended in the Parliament. Especially important in his marginalia during the decade of dissent from 1765 to 1775 were his recurring comments distinguishing between the Crown and the Parliament, the former corresponding to the father of the American colonies and the latter representing their "mother country." Even though Franklin's account of the differences in power between the Crown and the Parliament was accurate historically in that the king had founded the colonies and the Parliament had not contributed economically to that process, his account would have been perplexing to the English, because he depicted the Crown as the sole legitimate source of authority over British America.

During the previous century, the relative power of the Crown and of Parliament had significantly shifted. This shift was at times gradual and incremental, but at others, such as the 1688–89 revolution, dramatic, such that the Parliament had increased its authority to govern in Britain in ways that most of the English would have considered as strengthening the English citizens' rights. In Franklin's rhetoric, however, the Parliament's rise in power vis-à-vis the Crown posed dangers to the colonies, because Parliament was now claiming the king's rightful authority over the colonies and, in the process, making the British Americans subordinate to English subjects in Britain—"the Subjects of Subjects," as Franklin put it toward the end of 1767 in *Gentleman's Magazine.*[151]

During the process of repealing the Stamp Act, several members of the House of Lords who opposed rescinding the act prepared two protests in March 1766, one following the second reading of the repeal legislation in the House of Lords, the other following the third reading. These protests were published shortly later, possibly during the same month, but certainly before mid-April 1766, in two pamphlets: *Protest against the Bill To repeal the American Stamp Act, of the Last Session* and *Second Protest, with a List of Voters against the Bill to Repeal the American Stamp Act, of Last Session.* A summary of these pamphlets was printed in the March 1766 *Gentleman's Magazine,* which was published in early April. On April 12, 1776, Franklin sent copies of the pamphlets to the Pennsylvania Committee of Correspondence. His marginalia in both of these pamphlets was suggestive, distinguishing between the power of the Crown and the Parliament, and between the dominions of the British Empire and the realm of the British Parliament. During the subsequent decade of dissent, Franklin overtly transformed his vision of American community as he further developed the implications of these distinctions.[152]

The lords' *Protest* had depicted the colonists' protests during the Stamp Act controversy as an affront, not just to the power of the Parliament, but as *"derogatory to the honour of his Majesty's Government."* To this assertion, Franklin replied bluntly, "Neg. All acknowledge their Subjection to his Majesty." The *Protest* continued to denounce the colonists' protests as "destructive of the *legal and constitutional* dependency of the said Colonies, on the imperial Crown and *Parliament* of Great Britain." Franklin interjected simply: "Neg." Continuing the sentence, the *Protest* amplified, "Which resolutions were founded on a full examination of the papers on our table, manifesting a denial of the *legislative authority* of the Crown and *Parliament* of Great Britain." Franklin's response was unequivocal: "Thrust yourselves in with the Crown in the Governmt. of the Colonies." He wrote, but then struck out, "Do your Lordships mean to call the Parliamt. *imperial."* When the *Protest* went on to allude to "OUR *North American Colonies,"* Franklin corrected the possessive: "Not *our,* the King's."[153]

Such language on the lords' part obfuscated crucial distinctions in Franklin's understanding of imperial relations. Yet these were distinctions that may not have appeared important to the English, because it was a commonplace in England that the Crown and Parliament united the inseparable parts of government, combining as it did the monarch, the aristocracy, and the Commons. When the lords alluded to the power of the British government as *"inseparable from the Three Estates* of the *Realm* assembled in Parliament," Franklin commented, "Agreed, *within* the Realm," underscoring *"within"* to emphasize that such inseparable power of the Crown in Parliament did not extend beyond the borders of Britain to the American colonies.

Other passages in the lords' *Protest* also elicited handwritten responses from Franklin, revealing his assumptions about the distinct powers of the Crown and the Parliament beyond the borders of Britain. As for the power of the Parliament to legislate for the colonies, which the lords' *Protest* depicted as "their *antient, unalienable rights of supreme jurisdiction,"* Franklin's position was unequivocal. He wrote categorically, "They have no such Rights." In his judgment, such rights resided in the colonial assemblies alone. But this was a power in the colonial legislatures that the lords' *Protest* denied. As for the crown's authority to delegate the power to initiate legislation "exclusively to the subordinate Provincial Legislatures *established by prerogative*, the *Protest* objected that this was never intended or thought of, and is *not in the power of prerogative to bestow.*" In his response Franklin remarked, "Dispute this with the King my Lords, he has done it." Later in the *Protest*, when the lords alluded to "*the whole legislative authority of Great Britain, without any reserve or distinction whatsoever,*" Franklin observed, "This is encroaching on the Royal Power." Thus, in Franklin's rhetoric, the Parliament's recent legislation not only violated the colonies' rights as granted by the Crown as a matter of historical record, but also eroded the Crown's power in relationship to the Parliament. While such an erosion of power would not have been threatening to the English, it was insidious to the British Americans in that the Parliament could use such power to shift the economic burdens of the English onto the colonists without accountability.[154]

Franklin's marginalia in the lords' *Protest* examined these relationships of power under the key term "sovereignty," which designated the nature and location of ultimate power in the government. "In the last analysis," as Bernard Bailyn has written, "it was over" the issue of sovereignty "that the Revolution was fought."[155] Alluding to "independency of the Provinces" and the conviction of the Americans that they "are not subject to the legislative power of Great Britain," the *Protest* observed, "This opinion of their strikes directly at the Act of Navigation, and other subsequent laws, which from time to time have been made in the *wise policy* of that Act." Franklin commented, "The Policy *wise* with regard to foreigners. Selfish with Regd. to Colonies." The *Protest* continued to worry, "Should they ever be encouraged to procure for themselves that absolute freedom of trade, which they appear to desire, our plantations would become, not only of *no benefit*, but in the highest degree prejudicial *to the commerce and welfare* of their Mother-country." To this, Franklin replied, "Other Advantages of Colonies besides Commerce. Selfishness of Commercial Views." Then the lords referred to the American colonists' protest as "so much contempt of the *Sovereignty* of the *British Legislature.*" In response, Franklin wrote, "The Sovereignty of the Crown I understand. The Sov[ereignt]y of the British Legislature out of Britain, I do not understand."[156]

The lords' *Protest* deplored the behavior of the American colonists who "have dared to insult with impunity and success" and worried that the Stamp Act's repeal would "*sacrifice* the Sovereignty of the Realm." This outrageous misbehavior on the part of Americans and sacrifice on the part of Britain's government would come now "at a time when the strength of our Colonies, as well as their *desire of a total independence on the Legislature and Government of their Mother country,* may be greatly augmented, and when the circumstances and dispositions of the other powers of Europe, may render the contest far more dangerous and formidable to this Kingdom." To these claims about independence, Franklin commented simply that the authors had made "a Mistake."[157] While Franklin's experiences had led him to sharpen the distinctions between the Crown and Parliament, these remarks reveal that he also drew an equally sharp distinction between "the Realm" and the "dominions."[158]

As for the unity of the entire British Empire, a few decades later, on February 9, 1789, Franklin assessed the long-term implications of the mutual failures of the colonies' assemblies and the Parliament to adopt the Albany Plan of Union in 1754, which he had advocated earlier with "JOIN, or DIE." Referring to the Albany Plan, he observed:

> On Reflection it now seems probable, that if the foregoing Plan or some thing like it, had been adopted and carried into Execution, the subsequent Separation of the Colonies from the Mother Country might not so soon have happened, nor the Mischiefs suffered on both sides have occurred, perhaps during another Century. For the Colonies, if so united, would have really been, as they then thought themselves, sufficient to their own Defence, and being trusted with it, as by the Plan, an Army from Britain, for that purpose would have been unnecessary: The Pretences for framing the Stamp-Act would then not have existed, nor the other Projects for drawing a Revenue from America to Britain by Acts of Parliament, which were the Cause of the Breach, and attended with such terrible Expence of Blood and Treasure: so that the different Parts of the Empire might still have remained in Peace and Union. But the Fate of this Plan was singular. For tho' after many Days thorough Discussion of all its Parts in Congress it was unanimously agreed to, and Copies ordered to be sent to the Assembly of each Province for Concurrence, and one to the Ministry in England for the Approbation of the Crown. The Crown disapprov'd it, as having plac'd too much Weight in the democratic Part of the Constitution; and every Assembly as having allow'd too much to Prerogative. So it was totally rejected.[159]

FOUR

"MAGNA *Britannia: her Colonies* REDUC'D," 1765–66

When the Feet are wounded, shall the Head say, It is not me; I will not trouble myself to contrive Relief! *Or if the Head is in Danger, shall the Hands say,* We are not affected, and therefore will lend no Assistance! *No. For so would the Body be easily destroyed: But when all Parts join their Endeavours for its Security, it is often preserved.*

Benjamin Franklin, Plain Truth, *1747*

4.1. "MAGNA *Britannia: her Colonies* REDUC'D," [Benjamin Franklin, London, 1765–66]. Medium: engraved print on a card; size: 4 ⅛" × 5 ⅞". Photograph courtesy of the Library Company of Philadelphia.

Franklin's engraving "MAGNA *Britannia: her Colonies* REDUC'D" had an enduring significance throughout the American Revolution and proved immensely popular among those critical of the British government's American policies (fig. 4.1).[1] Originally printed at the end of 1765 or the beginning of 1766, "MAGNA *Britannia*" was distributed by him in England and America on note cards. During the subsequent decade of dissent, various illustrators reproduced the engraving in modified forms in America, France, England and Holland. Between 1766 and 1769, an enlarged broadside version with an accompanying explanation and moral was printed anonymously at Philadelphia and distributed in the colonies (fig. 4.2). In December 1768, the frontispiece of a liberal English magazine, *The Political Register,* incorporated the illustration above another pictorial work, "Its Companion" (fig. 4.3). Then on November 29, 1774, M. Darly—either Matthew or Mary—published yet another British version of the engraving, retitled "BRITTANNIA MUTILATED. or the Horrid (but true) Picture of Great Brittain. When Depriv'd of her Limbs. BY HER ENEMIES" (fig. 4.4). Sometime around 1775 in France an additional version of Franklin's illustration was printed, modified by the absence of brooms on the ships in the background and by the repositioning of Britannia's spear (fig. 4.5). An inscription in French on the back referred to it as a "prophetic card." Finally, probably in 1780, the Dutch adapted yet another version of the print, deriving it from Darly's version but placing French and German legends beneath (fig. 4.6). The idea of the American colonies as the limbs of a self-destructive empire had recurring relevance throughout the imperial dispute.

These illustrations succinctly dramatized a way of viewing the colonies and their relationship to Britain. The colonies were parts, or limbs, of Britannia. The separateness of the colonies, not only from England but also from each other, was emphasized by labeling Britannia's four severed limbs "Virg," "Pennsyl-," "New York," and "New Eng." These colonial parts were subordinate to Britain, since the colonies constituted the extremities while Britain was the head and torso. Yet, because together they formed one body, the print underscored the interdependence of the colonies and England: the cause of one was identified with the cause of the other. Finally, internal divisiveness within the empire, especially the use of force to subjugate the colonies, became the equivalent of suicide for the empire. Although this last association was emphasized in an accompanying text from the 1766–69 broadside version, each of these ideas depended upon the others. The pictorial metaphor resonated with commonplace ideas and attitudes condensed and consolidated in the single image.

In addition to visualizing some of Franklin's most vital appeals to the Parliament, "MAGNA *Britannia*" also constituted a significant shift among his pictorial representations of the united American colonies, because the emblem

4.2. "MAGNA *Britania her Colonies* REDUC'D," [Philadelphia], 1766–69. Medium: engraved print on a broadside; size: 15" × 10". Photograph courtesy of the Library Company of Philadelphia.

4.3. "The Colonies Reduced" and "Its Companion," *Political Register* 3 (December 1768): frontispiece. Medium: engraved print in a magazine; size: 2 ⅜" × 3 ⅞" and 3 ½" × 3 ⅞" respectively. Photograph courtesy of the Prints and Photographs Division of the Library of Congress.

4.4. "BRITTANNIA MUTILATED. or the Horrid (but true) Picture of Great Brittain. When Depriv'd of her Limbs. BY HER ENEMIES," London, November 29, 1774. Publisher: M. [Mary or Matthew] Darly; medium: print; size: 11 ¾" × 15 ½". Photograph courtesy of the Library Company of Philadelphia.

4.5. "MAGNA *Britannia her Colonies* REDUC'D," [France], [circa 1775]. Medium: print on woven paper; size: 3 ⅝" × 5". Photograph courtesy of the Historical Society of Pennsylvania.

4.6. "La Grande Bretagne mutilé. Das verstümmelte Britanien," Amsterdam, [1780–1783]. Medium: engraved print with colored and uncolored versions; size: 8 ¼" × 13 ¼". Photograph courtesy of the Prints and Photographs Division of the Library of Congress.

was a marked departure from his earlier image of America, "JOIN, or DIE." Both "MAGNA *Britannia*" and "JOIN, or DIE" depicted each colony as a part of a larger unity. The colonies were separated even among themselves. But while the implied need to unify the segmented snake was restricted only to the colonies, the implied need to unify Britannia entailed the union of the colonies with the entire British Empire. While the segmented snake obscured any relationship of the colonies to England, Britannia's severed body emphasized colonial interdependence with Britain. Most important, while the segmented snake implied that autonomous colonial action was possible if the colonies would unite, Britannia's severed body implied that autonomous colonial action was impossible. Although both "JOIN, or DIE" and "MAGNA *Britannia: or her Colonies* REDUC'D" were reproduced widely in the colonies and England throughout the American Revolution, each of these compositions presented a markedly different vision of the American colonies, the former image suggesting in 1754 that the colonies could form a united community apart from Britain (fig. 3.1 on p. 27), the latter image suggesting in 1766 that neither the colonies nor Britain could survive apart from each other (fig. 4.1).[2] What were Franklin's underlying reasons for this fundamental shift in his portrayals of the British colonies in America?

In classical terms of persuasive discourse, Franklin's political card, "MAGNA *Britannia*," was both a deliberative message directed to the Parliament concerning a public policy and an apologetic message directed to a moderate segment of the colonial public concerning Franklin's performance as a colony agent. He used the engraving both to advocate the repeal of the Stamp Act in Parliament as an inexpedient policy and to defend his own reputation in America; there, some had accused him of complicity in the Stamp Act, while others had noted the radical implications of his emblem "JOIN, or DIE," as it had been used anonymously on the masthead of the seditious *Constitutional Courant*. The central argument in this chapter proceeds in three stages—first an examination of the historical evidence that "MAGNA *Britannia*" was a deliberative message designed to promote a forward-looking political policy, then an examination of the historical evidence that it was also an apologetic message in countering criticism of Franklin's political commitments and public performance, and, finally, an interpretation and assessment of the engraving in light of those two kinds of rhetorical discourse. This sequence underscores how the meanings of "MAGNA *Britannia*" were shaped by the points of view of the British and American audiences who viewed it and by the political circumstances at the time of its distribution: an image that had several associated meanings to parliamentarians was likely to have had alternative and supplementary meanings to Americans.

Franklin's public role had changed significantly during the decade between "JOIN, or DIE" in 1754 and his later production of "MAGNA *Britannia*" during the Stamp Act controversy of 1765 and 1766. In 1754 he had been an elected representative to the Pennsylvania Assembly, an office to which he was reelected annually in Philadelphia until 1764, when, for the first and only time in his political career, he lost an election to public office. His allies in the Assembly, who still held a majority of seats, then voted to make him the colony's agent in London with the expectation that he would lobby to change the colony's form of government from proprietary to royal. That fall Franklin left for Britain, where he would served in London as an agent for roughly a decade before returning to America in 1775. Other consequential changes in his public role between 1754 and 1765 were his election to Fellow of the Royal Society in 1756 and his appointment as the postmaster general of the colonies. The former enhanced his public image as a man of intellectual accomplishment, while the latter complicated his political life by creating some possible conflicts between his roles as a colony agent and a Crown officer, conflicts that partisans of the proprietor exploited to his detriment in Pennsylvania politics during the 1765–66 Stamp Act controversy.

The Deliberative Use of "MAGNA *Britannia*"

In several letters from Franklin to Americans, he suggested that "MAGNA *Britannia*" was designed to convince the Parliament that imposing the Stamp Act with military force was an inexpedient policy. Writing from Craven Street in London, he sent the earliest of these letters on February 24, 1766, to David Hall, a printer, former apprentice and partner, and friend in Philadelphia, the publisher of the *Pennsylvania Gazette*. Franklin's letter described how he used the pictorial composition as colony agent, articulating in the letter the engraving's central contention: "I enclose you some of the Cards on which I have lately wrote all my Messages; they are to show the Mischiefs of reducing the Colonies by Force of Arms."[3] He repeated this information and more in a letter dated March 1, 1766, when he wrote to his sister, Jane Mecom: "I congratulate you and my Countrymen on the Repeal of the Stamp Act. I send you a few of the Cards on which I wrote my Messages during the Time, it was debated here whether it might not be proper to reduce the Colonies to Obedience by Force of Arms: The Moral is, that the Colonies might be ruined, but that Britain would thereby be maimed."[4]

In these letters, Franklin portrayed himself as having written political messages on the engraving; he professed to have used the engraving as note cards for his political correspondence. He affirmed that the policy issue was whether force should be used to impose the Stamp Act on America and that his appeal was to a "moral" based on an argument from consequence: such a policy was inexpedient because in the process the whole empire would be maimed. By implication, the primary audience consisted of parliamentarians, because they were debating the issue, and because he was actively lobbying them as Pennsylvania's agent. Precisely when he used "MAGNA *Britannia*" is open to some speculation, though it was most likely during mid-January or February 1766, when he intensified his lobbying activities against the Stamp Act.[5]

Additional letters were sent to Deborah Franklin, his wife, as well as to Joseph Galloway, Franklin's political ally, who was a prominent member of the Pennsylvania Assembly.[6] In a letter to William Franklin dated April 29, Galloway alluded to his own letter from Benjamin Franklin and forwarded a copy of the engraving: "I suspect the Print inclosed by Mr. Fn. [Franklin] to me and several others is his own. Quere. It is certainly a good one. Explains the Subject deeply. The Launce [lance] from the Thigh of New Eng. pointed at the Breast of Brittannica, is striking, as is indeed every other Emblem. If you have not one inclosed to you keep it, if you have please return it by the Bearer."[7] This letter classified the engraving as an "Emblem," so identifying it with a tradition of aesthetic images designed to influence belief. Galloway intimated that the positioning of the lance was important in his interpretation, a comment insinuating that he had pondered the placement's significance. As a group, these letters—especially those sent to Hall and Galloway—suggest that Franklin also directed "MAGNA *Britannia*" to a sympathetic and influential segment of the colonial public.

An American reprint of the composition, probably published at Philadelphia between 1766 and 1769, was inscribed in a contemporary hand: "The above piece was invented by Benja. Franklin & a Number of them struck off on Card paper on which it is said, he used to write all his Messages to Men in power in Great Britain; he also emplyd a Waiter to put one of them in each Parliament Mans hand as he entred the house the day preceding the great debate of the Stamp Act—The meaning of the spear from N[ew] England your own Sagacity will point out."[8] The inscription elaborated on the distribution of the emblem and the nature of the audience, by claiming that a waiter gave one to each minister in Parliament as he entered the house. Like Galloway, the anonymous commentator attached significance of some sort to the positioning of the "spear from N England." But because the author of this inscription was anonymous and because the description was made in America at a remove from the events, the description of the distribution ought to be accepted provisionally.[9]

To date, not a single note card with Franklin's handwriting on it has been found.[10] Although there was a half-sheet version dated 1765–66, it was located among the papers of an American colonist, Pierre Eugène Du Simitière (fig. 4.1). This provenance of the half-sheet version was consistent with its distribution in British America. Furthermore, to date, no quotations from the memoirs, correspondence, journals, or speeches of *any* minister of Parliament have corroborated that Franklin actually used the engraving to urge the repeal of the Stamp Act. Yet it was likely that he employed the print to influence policy in Parliament, since nothing the engraving expressed was more bold or more provocative than what he was willing to state publicly in his examination on February 13, 1766, before the entire House of Commons.[11] One Briton definitely knew about the print: Mrs. Margaret Stevenson, his landlady in London, who sent Franklin a letter dated November 22, 1766, several months after the repeal. She wrote, "Pray Dear Sir send a Carid [Card] that Ingravaed about the Colnies."[12]

But other, more politically noteworthy evidence confirmed that Franklin distributed "MAGNA *Britannia*" in England toward the conclusion of the Stamp Act controversy. Thomas Hollis wrote to Jonathan Mayhew on June

19, 1766: "He [Franklin] is certainly a Man of Knowledge, Ability; wishes well to what is right; loves his Country, N. A. [North America] even to partiality; & yet, according to old observings, to me, he is a *Trimmer*. His *Card* too, which came forth in such numbers, appeared *not*, if I am well informed, till after the Death of the D. of C. [duke of Cumberland], and till the Spring, that the Leaders in the Ministry had taken party and *resolved* to repeal the Stamp Act. All this *in Confidence*." Hollis observed, "No Measure certainly was *wiser*, than that of securing an Influence over the Public Prints, which influence evidently has been of highest Utility on both sides the Water & may & will & must be again."[13] Hollis's letter affirmed that "MAGNA *Britannia*" was used in England to advocate political policy. Accordingly, the meanings of "MAGNA *Britannia*" were ascertained in light of both that rhetorical use and that British audience. Hollis's reference to Prince William, duke of Cumberland, who had suddenly collapsed and died on October 31, 1765, suggested that Franklin distributed the political card in the final months of 1765 or early in 1766.

Yet, if Hollis was correct, Franklin distributed "MAGNA *Britannia*" only after the change from the Grenville ministry to the Rockingham ministry had made the Stamp Act's repeal probable.[14] Indeed, Richard Jackson, Franklin's fellow agent, believed in 1766 that, had the duke of Cumberland not died, the government would have sent soldiers to America to enforce the tax.[15] So Hollis's comment raised additional questions about how, if at all, Franklin was a "Trimmer"—one who trims between opposing parties in politics or who inclines to each of two opposing sides as interest dictates—when he distributed "MAGNA *Britannia*." Years later, when Hollis's *Memoirs* were published at London in 1780, the letter criticizing Franklin as a "Trimmer" became public and the subject of a gracious exchange between Hollis's son and Franklin.[16]

The Apologetic Use of "MAGNA *Britannia*"

Although commentators on "MAGNA *Britannia*" uniformly have treated it as a deliberative work concerned with the Parliamentary debate over a policy to use military force to impose the Stamp Act, the rhetorical uses of the engraving were more complex than that.[17] An audience for Franklin's engraving also existed in the colonies: he sent several copies of it to Americans. Indeed, most of the extant evidence about the political use of "MAGNA *Britannia*" was written in the form of letters from Franklin to Americans. Therefore, the engraving was interpreted from that colonial audiences' particular viewpoints, for surely these colonists were not debating whether Parliament should use military force to impose the Stamp Act.

The appropriation of "JOIN, or DIE" for use on the masthead of a radical publication, *The Constitutional Courant,* was one salient reason for Franklin's use of new imagery to represent America: he sought to protect his own reputation from the taint of radicalism that had become associated with the snake's image from "JOIN, or DIE." A second and independent development that may have motivated him was his need to counter the Proprietary party's allegations in Pennsylvania that he had not adequately represented the colony throughout the Stamp Act proceedings. In light of these two political developments in British America, "MAGNA *Britannia*" was an apologia in the sense that it was used both to circumvent potential criticism of Franklin for the incipient radicalism of "JOIN, or DIE" and to counter partisans' actual contentions about his complicity in the passage of the Stamp Act.

Did William Goddard's radical use of "JOIN, or DIE" on the *Constitutional Courant* motivate Franklin to publish "MAGNA *Britannia*" as a means to demonstrate his own loyalty to the British government? During the Stamp Act controversy, he knew that the *Courant* had been published with "JOIN, or DIE" on the masthead months before he published "MAGNA *Britannia,*" if the latter's mid-January or February 1766 publication date is accurate. Long before then at least two colonial officials had written to him about the *Courant.* Enclosing a copy of it with "JOIN, or DIE" on the masthead, the acting governor of New York, Cadwallader Colden, wrote to him on October 1, 1765, about the publication's radicalism:

> My regard to you makes me give you the trouble of the inclosd Printed Paper [*Constitutional Courant*], one or more bundles of which, I am well informd, were deliver'd to the Post Rider at Woodbridge [New Jersey] by James Parker, were distributed by the Post Riders in several parts of this Colony, and I beleive [believe] likewise in the Neighbouring Colonies: the doing of which was kept Secret from the Post Master in this Place. It is beleived that this Paper was Printed by Parker after the Printers in this Place had refused to do it, perhaps you may be able to Judge from the Types. As he [James Parker] is Secrettary to the General Post Office in America, I am under a necessity of takeing notice of it to the Secrettary of State by the return of the Packet which is daily expected, and I am unwilling to do this without giving you previous notice by a Merchant Ship which Sails Tomorrow.[18]

Although Colden's letter erroneously attributed the *Courant* to James Parker, rather than to William Goddard, Franklin almost certainly knew about the radical use of "JOIN, or DIE," because Colden enclosed a copy of it with his letter.[19] The consequences of Colden's mistaken attribution appear to have been consequential for Parker, whose alleged role was discussed among powerful parliamentarians. Parker subsequently wrote an abject letter to Franklin on January 4, 1766: "Last Post, I had a Letter from New York, telling me a Rumour prevail'd there, that I was turn'd out or superseded in that Place in the Custom-House: tho' I do not know what Grounds there are for such Report, yet as tis possible, I can't contradict it: Those who gave it, can doubtless take it away, and if it is so, I submit." He added, "If it is not so, I shall proceed to New-York assoon [as soon] as I can, and know the Truth: I shall endeavour to execute it faithfully and honestly to the best of my Skill, that I may not disgrace your kind Recommendations."[20]

Colden's letter to Franklin depicted the publication of the *Courant* as a secretive and seditious act. The letter also suggested to him some potential for political embarrassment: he was deputy postmaster under the Crown and his personnel had been implicated in the printing and distributing of the *Courant*, and he had designed the emblem that appeared prominently on the masthead of the seditious publication. Although Colden expressed his personal regard for Franklin, he also intimated that Franklin could vindicate himself by identifying the printer's types. Had Franklin examined the types with care, he would not have been in a position to correct Colden's inaccurate attribution of publication to Parker, because Goddard had printed the *Courant* at Parker's printing house, having secured permission previously to use it on occasion.[21] Using the typeface as the basis for identifying the printer was reasonable, but also fallible. The mistaken attribution deflected attention from Colden's son, Alexander, whom Colden protected when he wrote that the *Courant's* delivery "was kept Secret from the Post Master in this Place."[22]

Colden had corresponded with Franklin a decade earlier concerning the Albany Plan of Union and had been active in New York politics in 1754 when reproductions of "JOIN, or DIE" had circulated in both of New York's major newspapers to urge unified colonial action against the French and Indians. Although Colden's 1765 letter to Franklin left unanswered the question of whether the acting governor of New York definitely connected the *Courant's* "JOIN, or DIE" with the design Franklin had executed prior to the Albany Congress of 1754, a letter from the lieutenant governor of Massachusetts-Bay, Thomas Hutchinson, did not. Hutchinson's home had been ransacked and destroyed by a mob in Boston on August 26, 1765 (Gov. Francis Bernard detailed the damage in a letter to the Board of Trade on August 31).[23] Hutchinson wrote to Franklin on November 18, 1765: "The riots at N York have given fresh spirits to the rioters here. An uniformity of measures it is said will be effectual and join or die is the motto." He added, "When you and I were at Albany ten years ago we did not Propose an union for such Purposes as these."[24]

Like Franklin, Hutchinson had prepared a plan of union to be considered during the Albany Congress in 1754. During the congress, in fact, he had worked on the committee that Franklin had chaired to prepare the plan of union.[25] More important for understanding the changes in Franklin's pictorial representations of British America, not one, but two high ranking colonial officials had informed him that "JOIN, or DIE" had been appropriated for radical purposes during the Stamp Act protests and riots in New York and Boston. Further, Hutchinson's letter connected the motto to Franklin's design prior to the Albany Congress, where both men had contributed ideas for colony union. Hutchinson affirmed his own confidence in Franklin's benign intent when he distributed "JOIN, or DIE" in 1754, by emphasizing a disparity between the initial use of "JOIN, or DIE" in 1754 and the subsequent use of it only a decade later in 1765, during the Stamp Act riots.[26] Moreover, when Hutchinson wrote to notify British officials about the publication of the *Courant*, he provided an excerpted version of it as printed in the *Newport Mercury* on October 7, 1765, without the masthead's snake device.[27]

Even so, recognizing that the radical appropriation of "JOIN, or DIE" had transformed its meanings by emphasizing opposition to the Parliament's legislation, Franklin may have designed "MAGNA *Britannia*" to repudiate such seditious use by demonstrating his own continuing loyalty to the government. More important, the design was consistent with most of the American rhetoric during the Stamp Act controversy: both denied any colonial attempt to gain independence from the Crown. So "MAGNA *Britannia*" was not simply a personal apologia; it also represented the ethos of responsible opposition to the Stamp Act. "MAGNA *Britannia*" did not resist interpretation as an adept pictorial response to the problems created by the radical use of "JOIN, or DIE," since the image of Britannia surrounded by her severed limbs emphatically visualized the interdependence of the American colonies and the British Empire.

There is, then, reason to believe that "MAGNA *Britannia*" was in part a response to the radical appropriation of "JOIN, or DIE." In addition to the personal letters that Colden and Hutchinson sent to Franklin, no fewer than seven publications could have informed him that his emblem, "JOIN, or DIE," had been used on the masthead of the *Constitutional Courant*. These publications included the *Courant* itself, the *Boston Evening-Post*, the *London Evening-Post*, the *Lloyd's Evening Post*, the *Gazetteer and New Daily Advertiser*, the *Public Ledger,* and the *Annual Register.*[28] The two American publications, printed at least three full months before "MAGNA *Britannia*" likely first appeared, would have reached him in London by the probable publication date of mid-January or early February 1766. Any of the five British publications might have informed him of the radical use of "JOIN, or DIE," because the articles in at least four newspapers were available two months before his earliest extant reference to "MAGNA *Britannia*" and because the *Annual Register* may have been available by then, though whether Franklin was aware of these specific developments is conjecture. He probably was aware of the article in the *Ledger,* since he himself occasionally had articles printed in the paper under pseudonyms during this period.[29] Any one of these publications may have suggested to Franklin the necessity of protecting his own reputation from radicalism's taint and of reshaping British and colonial perceptions about the appropriate way to represent colonial opinion. Most important, the reproduction of the image and references to it in the American Papers placed before Parliament made it highly likely that Franklin recognized the potential for political and rhetorical problems: both of the American leaders who had written to alert him had also corresponded in their official roles with the British government, and Colden's letter had expressly mentioned taking notice of the *Constitutional Courant* in his correspondence with British officials.

While the radical appropriation of "JOIN, or DIE" posed a threat to Franklin's political reputation in the northern colonies and in England, powerful members of the Proprietary party assaulted his political reputation in Pennsylvania, giving rise to yet another rationale for Franklin to employ "MAGNA *Britannia*" as an apologia. Earlier, during the fall and winter of 1764, the party had initiated a campaign of vilification that initially sought to oust him from the Pennsylvania legislature; subsequently, the party endeavored to prevent his appointment as Pennsylvania's colonial agent to the British Parliament in London. By using anonymous pamphlets, newspaper articles, and broadsides to discredit Franklin,[30] the Proprietary party was successful in preventing him from retaining the Pennsylvania Assembly seat he had held since 1751, but unsuccessful in obtaining enough seats to prevent the Assembly party from still dominating the legislature. When the citizens of Philadelphia finished casting their votes in October 1764, the outcome was Franklin's only loss during his lifetime in an election for public office, a loss that he attributed to "the wretched Rabble brought to swear themselves intitled to a Vote."[31]

An array of lively issues divided the political parties in Pennsylvania in 1764, but, above all, the central concern of most colonial leaders was Benjamin Franklin and Joseph Galloway's endeavor to change Pennsylvania's political system from a proprietary government to a royal government. Franklin and Galloway's proposal for reform was simple and straightforward, even though their opponents represented it in many different ways to the voters in Pennsylvania. Instead of allowing the Penn family to appoint the colony's governor, as it had been doing for over a century, the king would appoint the colony's governor, as was the practice in colonies with a royal government. The proposal was a relatively simple change in the process for appointing and instructing the governor of the colony, but the stakes in the political struggle were extensive. For example, because the proprietor, Thomas Penn, had the authority to appoint and instruct the colony's governor, the governor routinely vetoed any legislation from the Assembly that threatened the Penn family's powers and privileges. Further, the proprietor could effectively force the governor to act in keeping with the family's instructions by requiring a bond in exchange for the appointment to office; a governor who dared to disregard or disobey the proprietor's instructions could suffer substantial financial losses.[32] This power to appoint and instruct the governor was the linchpin of the Penn family's political power in Pennsylvania, and, as a consequence, had become the central focus of Franklin and Galloway's endeavor to change the form of government.

In addition, Pennsylvania's charter granted the proprietor the authority to appoint and commission "all necessary executive officials for the province's internal administration: judges, sheriffs, coroners, quit rent collectors, tax assessors, tax collectors, excise collectors, provincial customs collectors, commodity inspectors, justices of the peace, Indian agents, military officers, and court recorders, as well as the clerks, registrars, and surveyors of the Penn's personal land office. After 1701 the electors in each county were permitted to choose nominees for the posts of sheriff and coroner; but, between 1754 and 1764, Thomas Penn still controlled patronage and judicial appointments." Of course, the proprietor could transform these elements of his authority into derivative power of great consequence. For example, the proprietor had substantial means of controlling the judicial system, because he appointed all of Pennsylvania's judges, who continued to serve at his pleasure. Through the appointment and control of such judges as the Supreme Court's chief justice William Allen, the proprietor could determine the careers of would-be lawyers in the colony, because "Allen and his associates on the Supreme Court were the sole examiners of young lawyers seeking admission to the bar in Pennsylvania."[33]

In addition to these forms of direct and indirect political power, the proprietor enjoyed extensive economic resources and privileges in Pennsylvania. He controlled "approximately 40,000 square miles of unsettled land; of the remaining 5,000 square miles of land alienated to private buyers in Pennsylvania and Delaware, Penn maintained indirect control through the imposition of quitrents payable in silver, the yearly revenues of which amounted (on paper, at least) to £10,000."[34] In addition, the proprietor benefitted economically from the privilege of paying no taxes on the Penn family's vast land holdings, a privilege that Franklin and Galloway had openly opposed in the Pennsylvania legislature because of the high cost of defending the western frontier during the French and Indian War. Their efforts to tax the proprietor's land had been an ongoing source of open conflict. Further, the Penn family appeared to have rewarded members of the Proprietary party for satisfactory service by granting them land warrants and waiving the cash down payments. The principal recipients of such rewards were Col. John Armstrong, Rev. William Smith, and Rev. Richard Peters.[35]

The Penn family regarded the attempt to reform the government as a villainous threat to their power and privileges. Their judgment of Franklin was unequivocal. On May 5, 1764, the governor of Pennsylvania, John Penn, commented at length on Franklin's character and conduct in a letter to Proprietor Thomas Penn: "Mr: Franklin may be consider'd as the chief Cause of this faction being carried to it's present height, for it is observ'd by every body that while he was in England there was at least an appearance of Peace and Quietness, but Since his return, the old Sparks are again blown up and at present the flame rages with more violence than ever." He added, "I really believe there never will be any prospect of ease or happiness here, while that Villain has the liberty of Spreading about the poison of that inveterate Malice and ill Nature, which is so deeply implanted in his own black heart. He certainly looks upon Mischief, in the light other people do upon Virtue, as carrying with it its own reward."[36]

Of course, if Thomas Penn lost his political power within the colony, so would the men who continued to serve at his pleasure, such as Chief Justice William Allen. With their own political careers at stake, members of the Proprietary party were highly motivated to protect and preserve the existing form of government. That motivation animated the Proprietary party's scurrilous assault on Franklin's reputation, although numerous other issues within the colony—such as the defense of the western frontier, the need for reapportionment within the colony's assembly, and the extent of religious tolerance —also figured prominently in the political turmoil. Above all, to prevent Franklin and Galloway from altering the form of the government, the Proprietary party assaulted their public image to oust them from the Pennsylvania Assembly, thereby minimizing their ability to lead the legislature toward a royal government. In the pamphlet *A Looking-Glass for Presbyterians, Number II*, Isaac Hunt anonymously explained that if the Assembly leaders were not reelected in the October election, "the rest wou'd be like a Body without a Head."[37]

Franklin probably lost the election for a combination of reasons. His influential and monied opponents in the Proprietary party criticized his humble origins and his plan to change the colony's form of government, and they entwined religious and political considerations when suggesting, as they sometimes did, that the change might bring with it the Church of England.[38] Pamphleteers and political cartoonists reminded Germans, who voted in substantial numbers in Philadelphia, that Franklin had referred to them as Palatine "BOORS *herding* together" who "swarm into our Settlements."[39] The Proprietary party widely reprinted this remark in pamphlets, broadsides, and political prints alike, using it to drive a wedge between Franklin and his German constituency. Franklin reported in a letter to Richard Jackson on September 1, 1764, a month before the election, "I bore the personal Abuse of five scurrilous Pamphlets, and three Copperplate Prints, from the Proprietary Party, before I made the smallest Return; and they began to think they might continue to affront me with Impunity."[40]

The campaign caricature "The Counter-Medly" showed a German standing in a long line of voters and saying, "None call us Boors but Sons of Whores," an emphatic depiction of German antipathy for Franklin as a consequence of his widely publicized comment. Beneath the print, among numerous verses, the slur was amplified:

> Drink a Health to the Boors
> Who turn'd BEN out of Doors
> And like Heroes erected their Banners
> For he said they were Swine
> Who did *Herd* and combine
> To spread both their Language and Manners.[41]

In addition to driving a wedge between Franklin and the German constituency, the Proprietary party included "two Germans on the Philadelphia slate for their appeal to that large element in the county's population." As Samuel Purviance Jr. explained in a letter to Col. James Burd on September 10, 1764, "The design is, by putting in two Germans, to draw such a party of them as will turn the scale in our favor."[42]

Over a decade after Franklin's printed remarks in his *Observations concerning the Increase of Mankind*, Franklin's allies attempted to explain away his offensive views concerning the German presence in Pennsylvania. For example, *The Plot. By way of burlesk, to turn F[rankli]n out of the Assembly* responded in the form of verse:

> Not one [German] with F_____n [Franklin] seems offended,
> At length *Hans* who knew *English* better,
> Clear'd the Point with his Visage pleasant,
> Your *Wisdoms* have mistook a Letter[.]
> *Boars* may be Hoggs, but *Boor* is Peasant.[43]

Another of Franklin's defenders endeavored in 1765 to explain, "'Tis well known that *Boor* means no more than a Country Farmer; and that *herding* signifies flocking or gathering together, and is applied by the best English Writers to harmless Doves, or Ladies in Distress."[44]

The anonymous assaults on Franklin's reputation were successful for the Proprietary party in that Franklin lost the election for public office by a narrow margin. Franklin observed in a letter to Richard Jackson on October 11, 1764, "I am no longer in the Assembly. The Proprietary party by great Industry against great Security carried the Election of this County and City by about 26 Votes against me and Mr. Galloway; the Voters near 4000. They carried (would you think it!) above 1000 Dutch from me, by printing part of my Paper sent to you 12 Years since on peopling new Countries where I speak of the Palatine *Boors herding* together, which they explain'd that I call'd them a *Herd of Hogs*." Franklin added, "This is quite a laughing Matter. But the Majority of the last Assembly remain, and will I believe still be for the Measure of changing the Proprietary for a Royal Governor." In contrast, William Allen of the Proprietary party wrote a victorious letter to Thomas Penn on October 21, 1764. Allen's analysis of the underlying political factors agreed with Franklin's, "No doubt you will hear that we have been able to turn out the two grand incendiaries, in effecting which, we had great help from the Lutherans and Calvinists among the Dutch, from their other sects we had great opposition: We had about half of the Church of England, and the Presbyterians to a man."[45]

After the defeat in the campaign to serve in the Pennsylvania Assembly, Franklin's political allies in the Assembly then nominated him to serve as Pennsylvania's agent in London. Subsequently, during the fall of 1764, the Proprietary party initiated a campaign to prevent Franklin from assuming the position. Contending that he could not adequately represent the colony because of a conflict of interests, they observed on October 26, 1764, that Franklin and his son were officeholders under the Crown and therefore, "the

Remonstrants cannot expect that a Gentleman of his moderate Fortune will sacrifice his Interest for the Sake of the Province, which he must necessarily do, if he but seems to oppose the Measures of the Ministry."[46]

On October 26, 1764, twelve members of the Proprietary party, among them John Dickinson, signed a *Protest Against the Appointment of Benjamin Franklin as Agent*, which was published on November 1 in the *Pennsylvania Journal*. They offered seven reasons for their opposition to his appointment. To discredit him, they objected that he was the chief author of measures to change the proprietary government under the Penn family into a royal government under the king. They claimed that "enmity" between Franklin and the proprietors would "preclude all Accommodation of our Disputes with them." They added that Franklin, "as we are informed, is very unfavorably thought of by several of his Majesty's Ministers." Further, his appointment was "so very disagreeable to a very great Number of the most serious and reputable Inhabitants of this Province." The authors affirmed that his appointment was questionable because it was made in "unnecessary haste," and they alleged that he had misused public funds "whereby this Province suffered a loss of £6000." In general, they claimed that they wished "to avert the mischiefs" arising from Franklin's appointment.[47]

To these charges, Franklin responded less than a week later on November 7, 1764, with the brief pamphlet *Remarks on a Late Protest*, which the *Pennsylvania Journal* reprinted on November 22. Claiming that his principle motivation in writing the pamphlet was concern for the reputation of the Assembly, he systematically responded to the seven charges, choosing not to dispute the first two charges about his intention to change the proprietary form of government and instead endeavoring to refute the remaining five charges.[48] He never disputed the contention that he faced a conflict of interests in his roles as a colonial agent and deputy postmaster under the Crown. Instead, he emphasized that the Crown appointment was proof that he was regarded favorably by the king and his ministry. As Verner Crane observed, the Crown appointment in the Post Office "did not make him [Franklin] anti-American," as the proprietor's partisans later insinuated; however, it "confirmed him in his instinctive prudence" and impelled him "to draw the veil of anonymity over much of his writing" during the Stamp Act controversy. While his use of several pseudonyms in newspaper articles had the advantage in England of making the pro-American arguments seem to originate from several sources and "to come from a less interested source than a colonial agent," his rhetorical strategy of anonymity had the serious disadvantage in America of leaving him vulnerable to criticisms both of inactivity and of complicity with the government, criticisms that developed during the continuing controversy over his appointment as agent.[49]

Even as he departed for London to assume his new duties, critics continued to relentlessly assault his reputation. On December 7, 1764, over a month after Franklin's response to the *Protest*, William Smith extended the attack upon Franklin's political reputation in Pennsylvania by anonymously publishing *An Answer to Mr. Franklin's Remarks*. On December 20, 1764, and again on January 10, 1765, Franklin's political ally John Hughes wrote in response to the "false, malicious, and scandalous" *Answer*. He deplored the anonymous nature of the pamphlet and offered to pay ten pounds toward building a public hospital for every charge proven true, if the author of *An Answer* would agree to pay only five pounds for every charge proven false.[50] Later, when it was alleged in Pennsylvania that Franklin had helped to plan and to promote the Stamp Act, his son, William, responded vehemently in the *Pennsylvania Journal* of October 3, 1765, that "it is grossly false, and consequently a shameful imposition on the people." He added, "Not a gentleman of the proprietary party, even among those, who scruple not to aver the truth of it in conversation, can, I am convinced, be found so hardned [that is, calloused] as to avow in print, with his name subscribed, that he believes it to be true, or to undertake to produce any proofs in its support."[51] His father was kept informed of such developments. In a letter on November 27, 1765, for example, Hugh Roberts urged Benjamin Franklin to "keep up thy Spirrits for thou hast yet a numerous set of Advocates who dare to speake their Sentiments with freedom and vindicate thy Conduct."[52]

Franklin had not, in fact, colluded with George Grenville's ministry in Parliament on the Stamp Act legislation.[53] However, he had suggested an alternative means to raise a revenue in British America through the creation of a "General Loan Office in America," as he explained to Galloway later in a letter on October 11, 1766, months after the repeal of the Stamp Act: "This I then thought would be a lighter and more bearable Tax than the Stamps, because those that pay it have an Equivalent in the Use of the Money; and that it would at the same time furnish us with a Currency which we much wanted."[54] Like the Post Office, which charged a fee to those Americans who used that specific service, the "General Loan Office" would have provided interest to Britain paid by those Americans who benefitted directly from the loans provided to them. His plan would have raised a revenue for the British, provided a much needed currency for the Americans, and strengthened the British merchants' confidence in the Americans' currency, because it would have been backed by the Bank of England.[55] He complained that Grenville "paid little Attention" to the ideas for the loan office, "being besotted with his Stamp Scheme."[56] Galloway suppressed news concerning Franklin's plan, to judge from his letter to William Franklin, affirming, "This part of his Letter I shall keep private, as I have heard from many very warm objections against such a Plan, and in the present Temper of Americans, I think it wd occasion great Clamours."[57] However, Franklin's ideas were published contemporaneously— albeit without attribution to him by name—in the fourth edition of Thomas Pownall's ever expanding *The Administration of the Colonies*, published in London in 1768.[58] Franklin had sent his "Scheme for Supplying the Colonies with a Paper Currency" sometime during mid-February 1765 to Pownall, an Englishman who had been present at the Albany Congress in 1754 in an unofficial capacity and who had been the governor of Massachusetts for about three years beginning in 1757. Franklin had known him for over a decade by the time of the Stamp Act controversy in 1765.[59]

Although Franklin had neither proposed nor supported the Stamp Act, he had concluded that the legislation was inevitable. He wrote to Charles Thompson on July 11, 1765: "Depend upon it my good Neighbour, I took every Step in my Power, to prevent the Passing of the Stamp Act; no body could be more concern'd in Interest than my self to oppose it, sincerely and Heartily." But, he added, "We might as well have hinder'd the Suns setting. That we could not do. But since 'tis down, my Friend, and it may be long before it rises again, Let us make as good a Night of it as we can. We may still Light Candles."[60] Having recognized the inevitable, he proposed to George Grenville that John Hughes be appointed Stamp distributor, perhaps making the best of the situation by using it for patronage.[61] In a March 1766 Parliamentary speech made during the subsequent debates over the Stamp Tax's repeal, Grenville rationalized the reasonable nature of the failed policy by seizing upon Franklin's willingness to suggest "his friend Hughes to that employment."[62]

In Pennsylvania, the appointment of Hughes as a stamp distributor left Franklin vulnerable to his adversaries' charges of complicity with the British administration, because, in an act of political patronage, he was willing to recommend a friend for the role.[63] Even after the Stamp Act's repeal, allegations persisted that he had promoted the legislation to gain personal favor in the eyes of the ministry and to secure places for his political allies. The *Pennsylvania Journal, Supplement* on September 18 and September 25, 1766, published lengthy essays purporting to prove that Franklin had been responsible for promoting the law. Since the Stamp Act had been repealed much earlier that year, the writer doubtlessly intended to influence voters in the upcoming fall election by discrediting members of the Assembly party. Although the author wrote in the persona of an anonymous observer of political life in England, the writer's own concern about Pennsylvania's form of government was evident in his conclusion: "As Dr. F[rankli]n has evidently nothing else in view than to obtain a Change of the Government of Pennsylvania, and get himself placed at the head of it; . . . As he is so regardless of your real liberties, as to engage warmly with the weight of all his friends, in protecting and encouraging the most ignominious law, the Stamp-Act; . . . And as he is for every other reason, under such strong suspicions of betraying his constituents, and is certainly known to have deserted them, and not to have served them with any zeal; Whether he can safely be continued as the Agent, and Patron of the Liberties of your province, is a question that I apprehend the people of your side [of] the water will easily solve."[64] As the anonymous author's conclusion suggested, the central thrust of Franklin's political adversaries was to create such distrust for him that he would be removed from office. The issues of Pennsylvania's form of government and Parliament's Stamp Act became entwined in Pennsylvania politics: the Stamp Act provided a basis for amplifying Pennsylvanians' concerns about replacing the proprietary government with a royal government, which would make the colony even more vulnerable to British domination.[65]

Because the continuing controversy over Franklin's political conduct during the Stamp Act proceedings stood to influence the fall elections in Pennsylvania, David Hall, although no longer a partner in publishing the *Pennsylvania Gazette*, printed and distributed copies of *The Examination of Doctor Benjamin Franklin, before an August Assembly, relating to the Repeal of the Stamp Act, & c.*, in Pennsylvania in an effort to vindicate him. William Strahan had secured a copy of the proceedings from an unnamed "clerk" in the Parliament, whom Strahan expressly asked Hall not to mention in the publication.[66] In the *Gazette* of September 18, 1766, Franklin's defenders announced the publication of the *Examination*, using it as incontrovertible proof that he had acted decisively on the colonies' behalf. A German edition was published to secure support from that constituency.[67] The campaign to restore Franklin's reputation in Pennsylvania extended beyond the distribution of his *Examination*, but that performance was the cornerstone of the endeavors during the fall of 1766.[68]

Indeed, Franklin himself had written more than a dozen letters in British publications, using perhaps as many as eight different pseudonyms, including "W. S.," "F. B.," "N. N.," "Homespun," "A Friend to Both Countries," "Pacificus," "Pacificus Secondus," and "A Lover of Britain."[69] The *Pennsylvania Chronicle*, edited by William Goddard, reprinted several of these articles to rehabilitate Franklin's reputation.[70] Franklin's friend and ally John Fothergill, a Quaker doctor reputed to have the largest practice in London, wrote a letter to James Pemberton on February 27, 1766, concerning Franklin's efforts as colony agent: "From my own Knowledge, I can safely aver; that Benja[min] Franklin did all in his power to prevent the Stamp-act from passing; that he waited upon the Ministry that then was, to inform them fully of it's mischievous Tendency, and that he has uniformly opposed it to the utmost of his Abilities; that in a long Examination before the house of Commons within these few Weeks, he asserted the Rights and Privileges of America, with the utmost Firmness, Resolution and Capacity." Fothergill emphasized that "he has been, an able, usefull, Advocate for America in General, the Province of Pennsylvania in particular, during his Stay here." On May 8, 1766, portions of this letter and others pertaining to Franklin's performance during the Stamp Act controversy were published in the *Pennsylvania Gazette*, which had also printed some extracts of similar letter the previous week.[71] "MAGNA *Britannia*," sent by Franklin to several Americans and subsequently distributed in Philadelphia on a broadside, was probably used as additional evidence of his efforts during the controversy.

In summary, by the 1765–66 winter, Franklin recognized that his public image was under attack in Pennsylvania, where some believed that he failed to defend the colonies' best economic interests and others thought him an accomplice to the Stamp Act. Elsewhere, in the northern colonies and in England, the previously quiescent implications of his emblem "JOIN, or DIE" were being described as seditious, so making manifest the ideas of faction and sedition. By mid-November of 1765, both of these political developments in America had been related in personal letters from prominent colony officers to Franklin. In light of these developments, "MAGNA *Britannia*" was, in part, an apologia directed to a moderate and sympathetic segment of the colonial public. For Franklin certainly realized that the Proprietary party's advocates would never respond favorably to any rhetorical appeal from him or his supporters.

Interpreting "MAGNA *Britannia*" in Britain and America

Franklin probably designed "MAGNA *Britannia*" to fulfill both deliberative and apologetic functions. Recognized as an attempt to influence public opinion in Britain and in America, features in the composition evoked a range of likely meanings and appealed to specific Parliamentary and colonial interests. Attention to the engraving's rhetorical functions suggests that different audiences may have interpreted identical features of the composition in dissimilar ways. For example, parliamentarians were likely to see the subordination of the colonial limbs as a tacit recognition of Parliament's sovereignty, so satisfying one of their expectations during the policy debates.[72] In contrast, moderate colonial protestors, who knew about the radical appropriation of "JOIN, or DIE," could see the same subordination of Britannia's limbs as both a reminder that all parts of the empire were interdependent and as a denial that the colonies could survive as an autonomous community, so satisfying the colonial expectation that Franklin demonstrated his own moderate tactics to obtain repeal while eliminating the taint of radicalism.

When Franklin represented the whole British Empire as one body politic, he almost certainly realized that he was relying upon a metaphor to influence his British and colonial audiences, because he had specified some differences between the human body and a political government in his earlier writings.[73] Therefore, he used the pictorial metaphor of a human body politic for a strategic reason: the metaphor rendered the interdependence of the parts vital to an extent that a mechanistic metaphor could not have conveyed. Since force would have irrevocably harmed the well being of the whole body politic, the pictorial metaphor developed his appeal for moderate conduct both in Britain and in America.

Franklin chose the specific image of Britannia because she represented a shared British heritage; by convention, Britannia represented varying geographical scopes within the empire, usually denoting England, Great Britain, or, rarely, the entire empire. Britannia's image obscured the diverse descent of some colonial populations: Franklin estimated that Pennsylvania, for example, was roughly one-third German.[74] Even so, his use of Britannia emphasized a heritage shared by many Americans and the English in an attempt to reduce the psychological distance between them. During his examination before the House of Commons, and probably for similar reasons, he observed that the British colonies in America "consider themselves as a part of the British Empire, and as having one common interest with it; they may be looked on here as foreigners, but they do not consider themselves as such."[75] His endeavors to promote identifications between Americans and the English was thematic in his writings.

Britannia's image located the imperial dispute precisely in Parliament: another of Britannia's conventional referents was the Parliament, and her head presumably corresponded to the governing part of the body politic.[76] As such, Britannia's image granted Parliament's demand that the colonies recognize its sovereignty. As the head of the body politic, Britannia was placed in a role of both political authority and moral culpability. In that sense, Britannia's image was well adapted to parliamentarians, who were almost unanimously perturbed by the colonies' protests and riots as an affront to their power. The pictorial representation of Britannia was designed to remind these parliamentarians that they, not the colonies, were morally responsible should the government decide to implement the Stamp Act with military force, even as her butchered body depicted the dire consequences of that policy.

Britannia's image implicitly dissociated the dispute from the king, thus maintaining for the colonists an important distinction between royal and Parliamentary authority. While the colonists had by convention acceded to the authority of Parliament, Franklin and others privately noted that the colonial charters specifically acknowledged only the king's sovereignty. To Franklin, the colonies' past compliance with Parliament proved that those laws were prudent and acceptable to Americans, not necessarily that Parliament had a right to pass such laws.[77] Therefore, for a limited group of confidants, as well as for some colonial pamphleteers during the controversy, the dissociation of the dispute from the king may have reduced somewhat the legitimacy of Parliament's American policies.

Finally, Britannia's image obfuscated any colonial responsibility for various legislative acts or social unrest. Arms and legs could not have been held morally accountable, because the mind dictated the activities of the extremities. In addition, such limb imagery obscured aspects of colonial unity: different limbs served different bodily functions and, more important, colonial unity was possible only through Britannia's torso. Franklin was adapting to the ministers' apprehensions of a united colonial rebellion by noting aspects of colonial disunity, much as he had in 1760 in his political pamphlet *The Interest of Great Britain Considered, With Regard to her Colonies*.[78] At the same time, he attempted to assuage moderate colonists' concerns about the radical implications of "JOIN, or DIE," since the arms and legs of the empire could neither form an autonomous community nor survive severed from Britain.

Franklin depicted his home colony of Pennsylvania as an arm and hand near an olive branch; in contrast, New England was represented as a leg and foot with a nearby lance directed at Britannia's heart. Both Joseph Galloway and an anonymous contemporary writer attached significance to this positioning of the weapon. Both chose to intimate rather than specify its meanings. Both described it as "from N England," rather than near or beside that limb. New England had been the site of two violent Stamp Act riots in which persons had been assaulted and homes destroyed. Franklin was well aware of the riots in Boston, because of correspondence such as Hutchinson's letter during November, which had mentioned violence in New York as well.[79] Pennsylvanians, in contrast, had protested in comparatively peaceful ways; the vigilance of a group of men known as the White Oaks enabled the colony's government to prevent acts of violence. This difference between the olive branch and the spear may have ingratiated Pennsylvania to Parliament by reminding its members of that colony's comparatively peaceful protest, while amplifying another difference within the colonial community.[80] If so, then, "MAGNA *Britannia*" was better adapted to parliamentarians, who would have found some reassurance in evidence of colonial disunity, than to American colonists, who probably would have found evidence of divisiveness counterproductive to continued concerted action against the act. Alternatively, the olive branch falling from Pennsylvania's hand may have implied that the normally peaceful Quakers were prepared to separate themselves from the body politic. Seen from this point of view, both the olive branch and the spear emphasized intense colonial dissatisfaction with the tax law, though each colony's means of expressing those sentiments still differed.

"MAGNA *Britannia*" amplified the vital interdependence of the colonies and the empire by emphasizing rhetorical commonplaces concerning the harmful consequences of employing military force. By adopting such a policy, Britain would destroy her own means of obtaining nourishment, her resources for military defense, her international stature, perhaps even her life. Franklin amplified each consequence by incorporating background and foreground imagery. A similar emphasis on harmful consequences recurred in his private correspondence and his examination before the House of Commons.

Franklin visualized the potential economic consequences of enforcing the Stamp Act, by placing ships with brooms attached to their masts in the background. As a text accompanying the 1766–69 broadside version of the print explained, "The British Ships, the Instruments of her Trade, with Brooms on their Topmasts, denoting that they are Advertised for Sale, being no longer either necessary or Useful to her People."[81] Such imagery of brooms on the masts of ships was commonplace in political prints during the Stamp Act controversy.[82] This background imagery drew upon the economic consequences of the colonies' non-importation agreement, which was contributing further financial pressure to an existing recession in Britain, to prove that policies harmful to America were disastrous for Britain's own economy.[83]

The placement of Britannia's shield and spear on the ground behind her developed a second harmful consequence: a policy of force to impose the Stamp Act would render the whole empire less able to defend itself should a French or Spanish adversary seize the opportunity to attack her. Although the

London version of the print did not textually amplify this appeal, the version printed at Philadelphia did: "Her Shield which she is incapable of Weilding, laying useless by her. The Lawrel Branch droping from the hand of Pennsylvania, which She is renderd unable to retain. And in Fine, Britania herself Sliding of[f] the World, no longer Courted by the Powers of Europe; no longer Able to Sustain its Ballance; No longer respected or Known among Nations."[84] Such appeals to military factors dovetailed with argumentation in Parliament during January and early February that enforcing the Stamp Act with military force was impractical. Such military considerations were perhaps more fundamental to parliamentarians than the public emphasis on economic considerations may have suggested to constituents.[85]

Such language on the broadside as "No longer respected or Known among Nations" amplified a third harmful consequence: "MAGNA *Britannia*" visualized the lost international stature of the whole empire. This consequence was developed both by Britannia's placement in the composition and by a comparison to Belisarius. Britannia's torso was propped up beside a globe, a placement that depicted her inability to dominate world politics should she dismember herself. Draped across the globe and Britannia's lap was a banner reading *Date Obolum Belisario*, "Give Belisarius a Penny." Although this classical allusion was not explained in the original London version of the print, presumably because well-educated parliamentarians could grasp the comparison, the Philadelphia version of the print commented at length upon the comparison of Britannia with Belisarius:

Belisarius was one of the Greatest Heroes of the Antients. He lived under Justinian the Emperor. He Gain'd a Victory over and concluded an Honourable Peace with Cabades King of Persia, Took Carthage and Subdued Gilimes the Usurper of the Crown of the Vandals, Overthrew Vitiges and refused the Throne of the Goths when offer'd to him; Rebuilt the Walls of Rome after they were distroy'd by Tolita, and performed many other Military Atchievements too tedious to enumerate. In this Part of his Character is represented the late Successful and Flourishing State of Great Britain, which Aided the King of Prussia against the Powerful Armies of Hungary and Russia; Supported Portugal against the Spaniards, and reduc'd France and Spain to the most Advantageous Terms of Accommodation.

By the latter Part of Belisarius's Life is represented the Unhappy and Miserable State of Great Britain, should the late Measures against America take Place. This General at length being Accused of a Conspiracy against Justinian, That Emperor barbarously Ordered his Eyes to be pulled out, which reduced him to the Greatest Poverty, and Obliged him to Subsist on the Alms of others. The Motto is also Stricking, and elegantly Expressive of this Truth DATE OBOLUM BELISARIO—Give Poor Belisarius a Penny.

View the Countenance of Great Britain under this Character, and you Percieve nothing but Abject Despondency: Her Eyes, and the Stumps of her mangled Arms raised towards Heaven in Vain. Behold her Colonies, the Source of Her Commerce, Wealth and Glory, Separated from her Body, and no longer Useful to her.[86]

The comparison to Belisarius synthesized several appeals: it underscored the colonies' assistance in past international conflicts; it suggested the military harm Britain would do to herself by weakening the colonies; and it visualized the loss of international stature resulting from the conflict within the empire.

Perhaps because the comparison concisely summarized so many harmful consequences, the comparison of the mangled British Empire's decline to the life of Belisarius recurred in an undated song that was titled "A New Ballad: *Date Obolum Belisario.*" The lyrics invoked the image of Britannia's disabled body, much like the print in "MAGNA *Britannia.*" Referring to Britannia, the verse affirmed, "A Wretch forlorn, kind Sir, you see / That begs from Door to Door: / Oh Stop & give for Charity / *A Penny to the Poor*!" The penultimate verse of the song lamented, "A Shield & Lance once grac'd My Hands / Perhaps you've heard my Fame / For I was known in distant Lands / *Britannia* is my Name." This lament over lost British strength and glory, written in a contemporaneous hand and located among Franklin's papers, drew upon the comparison to underscore the destruction of the British Empire as a consequence of misguided British partisans' envy and fear of the American colonies' accomplishments and augmenting strength.[87]

Franklin's final appeal from consequence stressed that the dispute within the empire could destroy the life of the body politic. This was his most emphatic appeal, and it was amplified in the foreground by the addition of a mutilated oak, the healthy English oak being a conventional symbol of England. A text on the Philadelphia version of the print noted: "The Famous English Oak Diprived of the Wide Extended Top and late flourishing Branches, save a few, and those with its Body witherd and Decay'd. The Ground Beneath it producing nothing but Bryars and Thorns."[88] This image, like that of Britannia's mangled body, portended decay and death. All of these appeals were designed to dissuade Parliament from a policy of military force and to demonstrate for Americans how Franklin sought to protect colonial interests in the moderate manner of a loyal opposition.

Conclusion

In several senses, Franklin skillfully designed the London version of "MAGNA *Britannia*" to influence parliamentarians. The image conciliated, because it recognized, rather than challenged, Parliament's authority as Britannia's head. The emblem sought to discredit the policy of military force, which the Grenville faction had advocated in Parliament, by depicting that policy's dire consequences: lost trade, lost defense, lost international stature, lost life of the body politic. The emblem sought to dissuade the country faction from military force by diminishing their financial motivations: although the new tax in America might provide a means for those ministers to reduce the land taxes in Britain, this financial benefit for the landed gentry would be less than the costly consequences of military enforcement for the empire. In the background, ships for sale in "MAGNA *Britannia*" reminded the mercantile faction in Parliament that their own economic prosperity depended on the act's repeal.

The arrangement of the pictorial composition reflected a prudent weighing of these appeals. Franklin did not need to make lost economic benefits the central appeal of "MAGNA *Britannia*," because the mercantile interests were already convinced of the merits of repeal. As the *Annual Register* of 1766 asserted, during the debate that resumed in mid-January of 1766 over the Stamp Act: "Petitions were received from the merchants of London, Bristol, Lancaster, Liverpoole, Hull, Glasgow, & c. and indeed from most of the trading and manufacturing towns and boroughs in the kingdom. In these petitions they set forth the great decay of their trade, owing to the new laws and regulations made for America."[89] So as a reminder, Franklin made a peripheral appeal in "MAGNA *Britannia*" to commercial matters, but emphasized matters of authority and imperial unity through the central placement of Britannia's dismembered body.

Yet these appeals to parliamentarians were also counterproductive, given some of Franklin's other concerns. One of these was what he saw as Parliament's gradual usurpation of the Crown's authority over the colonies. As detailed at length in the previous chapter, Franklin believed that the colonies, which had complied with past Parliamentary policies, were legally subject only to the king's dictates. "The Sovereignty of the Crown I understand," he wrote in the margin of the lords' first *Protest against the Bill To repeal the American Stamp Act* in 1766. "The Sov[ereignt]y of the British Legislature out of Britain, I do not understand."[90] Because Franklin was apprehensive of Parliament's encroachment on the king's rightful authority, his own choice of

Britannia was counterproductive to the extent that it reinforced Parliament's sense of rightful authority over America.[91]

Intimately related to what Franklin perceived as encroachment was Franklin's perception that British subjects in general had come to believe that they, like the king, properly had authority over the colonial dominions. As Franklin wrote to Henry Home, Lord Kames, in 1767, "Every Man in England seems to consider himself as a Piece of a Sovereign over America; seems to jostle himself into the [royal] Throne with the King, and talks of OUR Subjects in the Colonies."[92] Although Franklin recognized that this pervasive attitude of smug superiority posed serious problems for the maintenance of imperial unity, his depiction of Britannia seemed to reinforce such sentiments of rightful domination, for by implication the extremities were less vital and therefore less significant than the head and torso. One abiding consequence of the controversy was his keen awareness of the low status that the colonists held in the eyes of the English, a prejudice that he commented upon thematically in his writings.[93]

A final counterproductive consequence of Franklin's appeal with "MAGNA Britannia" was that it may have undermined his own efforts to develop what he called a "consolidating Union." He also wrote to Lord Kames during 1767, "I am fully persuaded with you, that a consolidating Union, by a fair and equal Representation of all the Parts of this Empire in Parliament, is the only firm Basis on which its political Grandeur and Stability can be founded."[94] Earlier, during the Stamp Act controversy, he had written in an unpublished pamphlet: "Representation [is] necessary to consolidate the Empire—to inform Government of the State of the remote Parts— & them of the Motives & Measures of Government. People in Colonies will never be convinced that they are virtually represented, &c." In the notes for this pamphlet, he also alluded to the dangers resulting from imposing the Stamp Act with force, such as "Mortification in the Foot."[95] Yet, while he saw representation as vital to consolidate the empire, "MAGNA Britannia" seemed to grant Parliament's authority to legislate without the actual representation of America.

Moreover, the image may have lent itself to a form of rhetorical reversal in which recognizing the colonial assemblies' separate power of taxation constituted a form of imperial dismemberment, especially if Parliament could not tax British Americans, since such a practice would decentralize authority. In a later context, Franklin engaged precisely such concerns. Sometime after 1770, Franklin wrote marginalia on An Inquiry into the Nature and Causes of the Present Disputes between the British Colonies in America and Their Mother-Country, an anonymous pamphlet published in London in 1769. At one juncture, the anonymous author quoted another source to the effect that "If there are many assemblies, one is supreme and the powers of the rest abridged; otherwise there would be 'many different governments *perfectly independent of one another.*'" Alongside the quoted passage, Franklin wrote, "This is the only clear Idea of their real present Condition." He added, "Their only Bond of Union is [the] King." The anonymous writer continued, claiming, "The American assemblies cannot have an authority equal to that of Parliament '*without actually dismembering the British empire*'; for government implies subordination as well as union. All its constituent parts, however, have a right to participate in regulating the affairs of the whole." In reply on the margins, Franklin commented, "It would not be dismembring of it, if it never was united, as in truth it never yet has been." He added, "Breaking the present Union between England and Scotland would be dismembring the Empire; But no such Union has yet been formed between Britain and the Colonies."[96]

During 1774 Matthew or Mary Darly endeavored to counter the notion that could be rhetorically implied in "MAGNA *Britannia*" that the separate power of taxation was responsible for the empire's dismemberment. Darly depicted her in "BRITTANNIA MUTILATED. or the Horrid (but true) Picture of Great Brittain. When Depriv'd of her Limbs. BY HER ENEMIES" (fig. 4.4), which blamed the reduced state of the empire upon unidentified "ENEMIES," thus eliminating implications of self-destruction. The image omitted Britannia's spear and showed her chained to the trunk of the English oak; the text specified that she had been deprived of her limbs "BY HER ENEMIES."

"MAGNA *Britannia*" seemed well designed as an apologia to a moderate segment of the American public. "MAGNA *Britannia*" succeeded as proof that Franklin acted to protect colonial interests to the extent that it demonstrated his own moderate way of obtaining repeal. The work was moderate in its emphasis on colonial subordination and interdependence in the empire, even as it placed responsibility for just policy upon the Parliament. In these ways, the print was also well designed to counter the radical implications of "JOIN, or DIE" as used in the *Constitutional Courant*, because "MAGNA *Britannia*" suggested that the colonies could not survive severed from the British Empire. In addition, by placing ships for sale in the background, "MAGNA *Britannia*" pointed to the efficacy of the united colonies' non-importation agreement.

Franklin's political allies in Pennsylvania actively sought to restore his reputation there by publishing accounts of his activities in London. Referring to David Hall's recent publication at Philadelphia of *The Examination of Doctor*

Benjamin Franklin, before an August Assembly, relating to the Repeal of the Stamp Act, & c., Baynton, Wharton, and Morgan wrote from Philadelphia to Franklin on August 28, 1766, "Your Enemys acknowledge—That if it is genuine—You have been the great Defender of their Liberties—But They affect to doubt its Authenticity, As it is not signed, by the Clerk of the *House.*" The authors added with reference to Franklin's enemies, "They are, as Mr. Pope says 'Willing to wound, But yet afraid to strike'—It has had a very happy Effect, In confirming the wavering, awakening the Neutrals and dividing Our Opposites."[97] As such remarks conveyed, Franklin's enemies of long-standing affected to disbelieve any evidence of his merits, and continued the assault on his performance as colony agent. Despite the false criticism, Franklin actively constructed an image of himself as secure in the merits of his performance. He wrote to Joseph Galloway on November 8, 1766, for example, that "Dirt thrown on a Mud-Wall may stick and incorporate; but it will not long adhere to polish'd Marble."[98] Even so, he was rhetorically savvy enough that he also supplied his allies with the evidence to vindicate him. Yet, "MAGNA *Britannia*" possibly failed to satisfy adequately certain demands of a colonial audience. The emblem did not, for example, maintain a basis to distinguish between internal and external taxes, since all taxes within a single body politic must be internal. Because that distinction provided one of the colonists' chief bases for protesting the Stamp Act, a basis that Franklin himself had relied upon repeatedly during his examination, this implication of the emblem could not have been very satisfying to some colonial protestors.[99] More important, even though "MAGNA *Britannia*" indicated to a colonial audience that their unity in the non-importation agreement contributed to the repeal of the Stamp Act, the pictorial message may have exacerbated a sense of divisiveness among the colonies, by contrasting Pennsylvania's olive branch with New England's lance. The image suggested, counterproductively, that various colonies objected in a disunited manner to the act.

Obviously, Franklin could not satisfy in this pictorial work all the diverse demands of the English and the Americans. Certain of these seeming failings could be explained by his pragmatic sensibility. While he viewed the Parliament as encroaching on the king's authority, deplored the pervasive attitude among the English that they had a degree of authority over America, and awaited the development of a consolidating union, he was also pragmatic enough to recognize that the situation would not be changed by his lone appeal, no matter what its form, no matter how persistent his efforts.[100] Even though Franklin wanted to see the various dominions represented in a consolidated union, he commented several times in his correspondence that such a development was unlikely, and, in a letter to Lord Kames, after articulating his doubts about Parliament's sovereignty over America, Franklin added, "On the other hand[,] it seems necessary for the common Good of the Empire, that a Power be lodg'd somewhere to regulate its general Commerce; this . . . can be plac'd no where so properly as in the Parliament of Great Britain."[101] Political pragmatism and the habitual complicity of subordinated peoples accounts, in part, for Franklin's strategic choices in "MAGNA *Britannia.*"

Franklin's caution and political moderation also went far to explain the seeming shortcomings of "MAGNA *Britannia*" for an American audience. Recognizing on the one extreme that his political career was threatened within Pennsylvania by allegations that he did not protect colonial interests and on the other extreme that the radical appropriation of "JOIN, or DIE" developed implications that could taint his own career with hints of inappropriate conduct for a Crown officer, Franklin with "MAGNA *Britannia*" demonstrated his loyalty to American interests while circumventing criticism for the incipient radicalism of "JOIN, or DIE."

At the time of "MAGNA *Britannia,*" Franklin was a Whig supporter of constitutional monarchy, though in later years he became a republican. During the Stamp Act controversy of 1765 and 1766, for example, his marginalia on *Protest against the Bill To repeal the American Stamp Act* commented "I am a Subject of the Crown of Great Britain have ever been a loyal one, have partaken of its Favours." He added, "I came over here to solicit in Behalf of my Colony a closer Connection with the Crown."[102] Subsequently, Franklin commented on "republicanism" by listing it among other "Evils" in his marginalia on Josiah Tucker's anonymous pamphlet, *A Letter from a Merchant in London to His Nephew in North America,* published in London in 1766. Tucker had written about the consequences of the colonists' behavior for the American colonies: "Soldiers will be needed for defense against Indians and against neighbors, and fleets as well. All these burdens will soon disillusion the people and open their eyes until, surfeited with republicanism, they will petition for reunion with the mother country." In response, Franklin commented on the margin, "These Evils are all imaginations of the Author. The same were predicted to the Netherlands, but have never yet happened." He added, "But suppose all of them together, and many more, it would be better to bear them than submit to Parliamentary Taxation: We might still have something we could call our own: But under the Power claim'd by Parliament we have not a single Sixpence." His argument conceded a premise that republicanism was among the "Evils" and "imaginations of the Author," but he considered them preferable to the consequences of taxation by the British Parliament without representation.[103]

Earlier in November 1765 during the Stamp Act controversy, Joseph Galloway, Franklin's closest political ally in Pennsylvania, wrote to him in terms that suggested serious liabilities in some colonies' democratic form of government. Galloway observed, "That the first Settlers of America came over possessed of the highest Ideas of Liberty. That their Posterity have been educated in the same Notions. Several of their Governments are meerly Democratical, and Consequently very liable to discontent and Insurrections." He added, "Their Distance from their mother Country will Lessen her Awe, and the Idea of her Power, and when in a more Opulent State, and increased in Numbers, will probably prompt them to throw off their Subordination. I do not think this can possibly Happen in our Day, God Grant it never may." Galloway continued, "But certainly these Considerations indicate the Prudence, if not the Necessity of Uniting the Colonies to their Mother Country by every Prudential Measure that can be devised."[104] Shortly later, he wrote again to Franklin on January 13, 1766, confiding that "A certain Sort of People if I may Judge from all their late Conduct Seem to look on this as a favorable opportunity of establ[ish]ing their Republican Principles, and of throwing of[f] all Connection with their Mother Country." He added, "Besides I have other Reasons to think, that they are not only forming a Private union Among themselves from one End of the Continent to the other, but endeavouring also to bring into their union, the Quakers and all other Dissenters if possible." Galloway emphasized, "But I hope this will be impossible. In Pennsylvania, I am Confident it will."[105]

Although significant differences were developing between Franklin and Galloway during this period, and although Galloway eventually over the next decade became a Loyalist, as did Franklin's son, William, it was unlikely that anyone so familiar with Franklin's outlook would have sent such letters to him had he been either an avowed democrat or republican during the mid-1760s. While Galloway would move more deeply into an orthodox Whig political commitment in British America,[106] Franklin moved in the opposite direction: in the ensuing decade he would reject Britain's constitutional monarchy in the process of becoming a republican. Despite Franklin's earlier political commitment to constitutional monarchy, he could write decades later, in a June 3, 1779, letter to his daughter, Sarah Bache, "as I intend him [Franklin's grandson Benjamin Bache] for a Presbyterian as well as a Republican, I have sent him to finish his education at Geneva."[107]

Roughly a decade after the production of "MAGNA *Britannia*," when Franklin was being denounced publicly in England during 1774 and 1775 because he had sent copies of Thomas Hutchinson's private correspondence with British government officials to Americans, Franklin sought to justify his conduct by reviewing the political principles that had guided his handling of imperial issues throughout the preceding decade of dissent. In that narrative apologia, written but left unpublished, his explanation and assessment of his public works during the Stamp Act controversy aptly explained and evaluated his performance with "MAGNA *Britannia*," a detail within the campaign:

It has long appeared to me that the only true British Politicks were those which aim'd at the Good of *the Whole British Empire*, not those which sought the Advantage of *one part* in the Disadvantage of the others. Therefore All Measures of procuring Gain to the Mother Country arising from Loss to her Colonies, and all of Gain to the Colonies arising from or occasioning Loss to Britain, especially where the Gain was small and the Loss great; every Abridgment of the Power of the Mother Country where that Power was not prejudicial to the Liberties of the Colonists, and every Diminution of the Priviledges of the Colonists, where they were not prejudicial to the Welfare of the Mother Country, I in my own Mind condemned as improper, partial, unjust, and mischievous, tending to create Dissensions, and weaken that Union, on which the Strength, Solidity, and Duration of the Empire greatly depended. And I opposed, as far as my little Powers went, all Proceedings either here or in America, that in my Opinion had such a Tendency. Hence it has often happened to me, that while I have been thought here too much of an American, I have in America been deem'd too much of an Englishman.[108]

FIVE

"WE ARE ONE," 1776

Knowing how naturally men allow themselves, to be guided by words and images, they cause the bills to be decorated with great care.

Benjamin Franklin (apocryphal attribution), concerning Massachusetts's "Sword in hand" paper money

---

5.1. "One Sixth of a DOLLAR," [Benjamin Franklin], Philadelphia, 1776. Printer: [David] Hall and [William] Sellers; medium: colonial paper currency; size: 3 ¼" × 2 ½". Similar designs were printed on "One Third," "Half," and "Two Thirds of a DOLLAR." Photograph courtesy of the Rare Books Division of the Library of Congress, the Thatcher Collection.

In 1776 the design for "WE ARE ONE" on the fractional notes of the Continental paper currency circulated in large quantities throughout British America.[1] The image consisted of thirteen interlinked rings arranged in the form of a circle around a radiant center (fig. 5.1).[2] The rings, each of which was inscribed with either the full name or the abbreviation of a colony, were arranged, clockwise, in geographical order from north to south. Inserted at the center of this large circular pattern were two small concentric circles, with "WE ARE ONE" inscribed within the center circle and "AMERICAN CONGRESS" imprinted within the outer circle. This language affirmed an oxymoron—a plural was a singular—and it identified the Congress as the authority sanctioning the paper currency. The concentric circles were framed by thirteen rays interspersed by thirteen thin lines, each of which connected the radiant center to one of the linked rings. Printed beneath this geometric design for "WE ARE ONE" were the surnames and location of the printers, David Hall and William Sellers at Philadelphia. The rhetorical figure of an oxymoron, so central to the rhetorical appeal of this message, endeavored to call into being a condition of colonial union that had not previously existed: a unified American community in the British colonies that subsequently became the United States.[3]

The organization of "WE ARE ONE" amplified equality among the distinct colonial governments in Congress, because each colony had equal size and stature as a link within the circle. Despite this image implying equalitarian status among colony governments, Franklin believed that some colonial governments should have more power in the Congress than others, based upon two factors: the number of individuals within each colonial government and the amount of economic support that each government was prepared to contribute to the mutual cause.[4] During debates on the Articles of Confederation, as John Adams recollected, Franklin had commented bluntly, "Let the smaller Colonies give equal Money and Men, and then have an equal Vote. But if they have an equal Vote, without bearing equal Burthens, a Confederation upon such iniquitous Principles, will never last long."[5] Even so, he depicted as equal the distinct colonial governments in Congress, by portraying them as thirteen rings of equal size and by using geographical considerations as the principle underlying the sequence: the abbreviations within the rings began with New Hampshire at twelve o'clock and proceeded clockwise from north to south. The participation of every colonial government in Congress gave life to the continuity of the circle, just as the diverse American citizens' active acceptance of the Congress affected its authority, legitimacy, and power.

Franklin underscored the underlying legislative basis for American unity and the sanctioning authority, whose political and military power gave credit to the paper money, by inserting the words "American Congress" in the center of the design. Americans placed confidence in the paper money as a medium of exchange to the extent that they had confidence in the Congress's power to support it. Circulating with the currency among Americans were tightly intertwined factors concerning the Congress's legitimacy and authority; an additional factor was Congress's need for evidence that Americans supported it despite innumerable protests by Loyalists, ongoing military battles with Britain, and international diplomacy. Depending not only on trade but also on victories and defeats during the Revolutionary War, the fluctuating economic value of the Continental currency impinged on the Congress's ability to finance the conflict. As the British approached Philadelphia, for example, the paper currency's value plummeted throughout the city and surrounding region.

Like Franklin's other images representing British America, "WE ARE ONE" was widely distributed throughout the colonies and as far abroad as China. The image on the fractional notes was reproduced on an immense variety of mundane objects, ranging from military flags, metal coins, state paper currency, newspaper mastheads, portrait frames, buttons, and carpeting to various housewares employed in daily use, such as pitchers, bowls, and plates. Yet, unlike the other pictorial images designed by Franklin, few contemporaneous poems and commentaries were written concerning the design's meanings, presumably because the design was an even smaller detail during war preparations than had been the two earlier images in their relatively circumspect conflicts. That the Congress's American supporters were less expressive about the persuasive potential of the various currency's designs, worrying as many of them did instead about its depreciating worth, may have indicated the effectiveness of the designs as propaganda: the currency was almost unnoticed as such by those in rebellion. Regardless of whether the American supporters of the Congress recognized the currency designs as pictorial rhetoric, clearly the Loyalists and the British did. The most powerful indicators of the pictorial rhetoric's significance came from the Congress's adversaries, the most emphatic of whom were American Loyalists such as Joseph Stansbury, who ridiculed and redefined several elements of the design in an attempt to appropriate it to the Congress's detriment. British newspaper accounts detailed the American citizens' rejection of the Continental paper currency a evidence of the Americans' disunited state.

Above all, Franklin's "WE ARE ONE" exhorted the Americans to unify— to constitute a new government in the ongoing war with the British military forces. Colonists could demonstrate their commitment to this unity simply by using the paper money to finance the war. At the same moment that the

Americans did so, they tacitly recognized, affirmed, or acquiesced to the Congress's legitimacy as the authority sanctioning the paper money. Yet this legitimacy was much in doubt among Americans, especially because of substantial opposition to Congress from Loyalists, who made up one-third of the colonists; perhaps another third were neutral on the proposition of independence from Britain. Throughout America since 1774, the Loyalists in all of the largest colonies had published a deluge of pamphlets condemning the creation of the American Congress.[6] Among their extensive writings in newspapers and pamphlets were numerous poetic verses condemning the Congress's paper money as a worthless sham by criminals.[7]

At the time of the production of "WE ARE ONE" during February 1776, Franklin was back in Philadelphia, having returned there from London in 1775. Since the repeal of the Stamp Act in 1766, which had been accompanied by legislation affirming Parliament's right to legislate for British America, Franklin had lived in London, where he served for about a decade as a colony agent, lobbying and waging a newspaper campaign against the Townshend Duties of 1767, all of which were ultimately repealed except for the duty on tea. As his reputation spread throughout British America, he became the colony agent for New Jersey, Georgia, and, most important, the Massachusetts House of Representatives. Subsequently, in 1774, Franklin was publicly condemned in the Privy Council by Alexander Wedderburn, the king's solicitor general, because two years earlier, in 1772, Franklin had sent to Boston leaders copies of Thomas Hutchinson's and Andrew Oliver's correspondence with Thomas Whately concerning politics in Massachusetts. (Hutchinson served as governor there, with Oliver as his lieutenant governor.) Franklin had imagined that, by revealing how certain key American leaders had misled the British government, it would be possible to ease tensions between America and Britain. Franklin's stipulation that the letters not be published was ignored by the radical leaders of Boston, thus ending Hutchinson's political career in Massachusetts. Franklin's role in transmitting the letters became public knowledge when he admitted it in a newspaper notice to prevent another party from being blamed for the deed. In the ensuing political spectacle, he was denounced in the Cockpit by the British government's Privy Council on February 29, 1774. The next day, he was dismissed from being postmaster general, his reputation in Britain in shreds. Despite this humiliating treatment by the British government, he continued his final efforts in negotiations to preserve the British Empire in the wake of the Boston Port Act of 1774, which severely punished Boston for dumping huge quantities of tea into Boston Harbor, known popularly as the Boston Tea Party. In 1775 he returned to America.

Subsequently elected to the Continental Congress, Franklin participated in the deliberations over issuing paper currency and served on a committee that designed the emblems on the currency in 1775 and again in 1776.[8]

The Production of "WE ARE ONE"

During the early stages of the Revolution, in June 1775, the Congress voted unanimously to print and circulate paper currency, not only to facilitate commerce among the colonies and abroad, but also to finance the American military forces that were engaged in armed combat with the British army in New England. Because issuing the paper currency violated British law, the Congress's act of authorizing it enacted their rejection of British authority. Within a few months, the mounting expenses of the war required additional paper currency, even though the delegates to the Congress worried about making it credible to the American public. As one delegate put it during October 1775, "We must keep up a Notion that this Paper is good for Something. It has not yet a general Circulation."[9] The problem was exacerbated when each of the colonies also began to circulate paper currency to support the individual state governments. As the currency began to depreciate, slowly at first and then with increasing rapidity, sometimes plunging in value, the Congress found it necessary to institute laws on January 11, 1776, to impose the paper currency upon American citizens who had begun to refuse to use it.

Despite the environment of apprehension about the Congress's ability to support the currency, the Congress unanimously resolved on February 17, 1776, to print another 4 million dollars in paper money because of the continuing expense of the war. A few days later, on February 21, Richard Smith recorded in his diary that Congress had approved a report from the Treasury committee "establishing the Denominations of the 4 Millions. One Million of them is to be in 2/3ds, 1/2, 1/3d & 1/6th of a Dollar & the other 3 in Bills of One Dollar, 2, 3, 4, 5, 6, 7 & 8 Dollars, but more of the 1 & 2 than of the others." The new design for this paper currency was also ordered on February 21.[10] This paper money was to be imprinted with various designs and mottos, with "WE ARE ONE" on all of the fractional dollar notes. To judge from Smith's account, Franklin's design circulated on about 1 million dollars worth of paper currency on the fractional notes, not to mention on innumerable counterfeits.

The design was sufficiently elaborate to discourage counterfeiting, though some did occur despite this obstacle. In general, the printers of the paper currency used several methods to authenticate the currency and to discourage counterfeiting of the paper money: elaborate designs, numerous type fonts on the same design, use of two different colors for imprinting a single bill, designs featuring complex natural symbols such as leaves, paper embedded with colored threads, and lists of authorized signers on the currency. The last of these also helped control the issuing of more paper money than Congress had authorized, since more than one signature was ordinarily necessary on each and every bill. In addition, the paper money bore distinct numbers in consecutive sequence that could be used to verify the legitimate money. However, even the death penalty in some colonies and punishments ranging from "branding, ear cropping, whipping, or the pillory" in other colonies did not eliminate the problem of counterfeit currency. For various reasons, "counterfeits of early issues survive in far greater quantity than genuine bills."[11]

Franklin's design for the fractional notes was original and inventive in representing British American unity. The design for "WE ARE ONE" was attributed to him, primarily because various preliminary sketches for it were extant on two sheets among his papers (figs. 5.2 and 5.3),[12] and because he served in 1775 on the first congressional committee that prepared paper currency for America and served again in 1776 on the committee responsible for the new designs, including "WE ARE ONE."[13] Franklin had previous experience printing paper currency, having occasionally produced notes during the 1740s and 1750s in Pennsylvania.[14] On April 3, 1729, while he was still young, Franklin had written about the utility of paper currency in an essay titled "The Nature and Necessity of a Paper-Currency."[15]

In addition to his sketches for "WE ARE ONE," he prepared yet another sketch for the Continental currency that featured the wind moving waves across a body of water (fig. 5.4).[16] He had mentioned his idea for the imagery, which was used on twenty- and thirty-dollar bills, on two earlier occasions, both of which focused on the conflict between British America and Britain. In 1760, in *The Interest of Great Britain Considered, With Regard to her Colonies*, he remarked anonymously with reference to a union of the American colonies against Britain, "When I say such an union is impossible, I mean without the most grievous tyranny and oppression. People who have property in a country which they may lose, and privileges which they may endanger; are generally dispos'd to be quiet; and even to bear much, rather than hazard all. While the government is mild and just, while important civil and religious rights are secure, such subjects will be dutiful and obedient. The waves do not rise, but when the winds blow."[17] Subsequently, Franklin evoked this emblematic imagery again in a letter over the pseudonym "F + S.," published in the *London Chronicle* on January 5–7, 1768. He used the maxim *"The Waves never rise but when the Winds blow"* as a proverb to begin this letter, perhaps best known under

5.2. [Preliminary ink sketch of thirteen interlocked rings], Benjamin Franklin, Philadelphia, 1776. Medium: ink sketch; size: 4 ½" × 4 ½" (single completed design only). Photograph courtesy of the American Philosophical Society.

Right at top: **5.3.** [Two preliminary ink sketches of thirteen interlocked rings], Benjamin Franklin, Philadelphia, 1776. Medium: ink sketch; size: 4 ¼" × 4 ¼" for the upper left design and another sketch measuring 4 ½" × 4 ¼" for the lower right design. Photograph courtesy of the American Philosophical Society.

Right at bottom: **5.4.** [Preliminary ink sketch of wind blowing waves, design for Continental currency], Benjamin Franklin, Philadelphia, 1776. Medium: ink sketch; size: 4" × 3 ½" (design with the handwritten Latin motto only). Photograph courtesy of the American Philosophical Society.

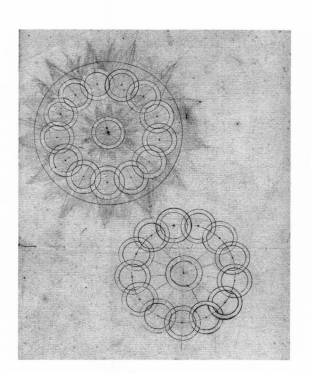

VI VENTORUM CONCITAT

Another Motto

Cessante Vento, conquiescimus

the title "Causes of the American Discontents before 1768." Among Franklin's most famous contributions during the decade of dissent, "Causes" summarized several concerns in the imperial dispute.[18]

The design on the obverse of the fractional notes, also attributed to Franklin, consisted of a sun and sundial accompanied by two mottos. One of these mottos was a Latin expression, "FUGIO," meaning "I fly." The other motto, "MIND YOUR BUSINESS," was printed in English. Taken together, the images and terms suggested that time flies, so concentrate on business.[19] An unpublished entry by Samuel Breck also underscored Franklin's general role, along with Charles Thompson's, in proposing currency designs. Breck commented, "On each bill is stamped a rudely printed Emblem with a latin motto, amounting in number to twenty. They are marked by pith and point, and are supposed to have been composed by Benjamin Franklin and Charles Thompson, aided by the latinists of the Continental Congress."[20] Breck's "list of these devices" included the fractional notes and reference to the motto "Fugio. Mind your business." Similar expressions in Franklin's *Poor Richard's Almanack* in 1748 and again in 1758 suggest that the design was his.[21] After 1776, this design emphasizing time and industrious labor circulated with the design of the interlinked rings on the notes for fractions of a dollar: "One Sixth of a DOLLAR," "One Third of a DOLLAR," "Half a DOLLAR," and "Two Thirds of a DOLLAR" (fig. 5.1).[22] Except for the forty-dollar note, these were the only bills with English mottos in that issuance of paper money.[23]

The Congress sanctioned the initial and subsequent printing of paper currency in a way that fostered unity among the thirteen colonial governments. As Samuel Ward wrote from Philadelphia in a letter to Henry Ward on June 15, 1775, "The Congress continues vastly unanimous on going on with proper Measures for supporting the Troops already raised & putting all the Colonies into a Posture of Defence, a continental Currency is agreed upon & will soon be emitted." Again and again, the delegates to Congress wrote about the unanimous decision to create the paper currency primarily as a vehicle to support the American army.[24] On June 18, 1775, John Adams wrote from Philadelphia to Elbridge Gerry, "The Congress have voted, or rather a committee of the whole house have unanimously agreed, that the sum of two million dollars be issued in bills of credit, for the redemption of which, in a certain number of years, twelve colonies have unanimously pledged themselves."[25] At the time twelve colonies were unanimous since Georgia did not formally vote to join the Congress until early July 1775.

Yet, despite such moments of unity implied by the unanimous decisions, Congress was deeply divided over fundamental issues, such as whether to resist the British military while seeking reconciliation or to declare their national independence. This divide was much in evidence during debates over "Proposed Articles of Confederation," on or before July 21, 1775. The contingencies specified in the resulting resolutions underscored the delegates' ambivalence. They affirmed, for example, "The *Union* thereby establish'd is to continue firm till the Terms of Reconciliation proposed in the Petition of the last Congress to the King are agreed to; till the Acts since made restraining the American Commerce [*interlined:* and Fisheries] are repeal'd; till Reparation is made for the Injury done to Boston by shutting up its Port; for the Burning of Charlestown; and for the Expence of this unjust War; and till all the British Troops are withdrawn from America. On the Arrival of these Events the C[olonies are to] return to their former Connection and Friendship with Britain: But on Failure thereof this Confederation is to be perpetual."[26] Lack of consensus on the war's objectives undercut the currency's legitimacy, because issuing money was a national government's activity, not merely that of a political faction within the empire, since British law forbid it.

In addition to Franklin's central concern of promoting colonial union, the depreciation of the currency was another major factor in the rhetorical context, which would have been evident to anyone in Congress, given the lengthy debates over the money. As the paper currency began to depreciate during the early winter of 1775, Americans requested payment in hard currency— silver or gold. Some colonists refused to accept the paper money altogether. As early as November 23, 1775, this problem had become serious enough to warrant the creation of a special committee in the Congress.[27] Subsequently, on December 26, 1775, Richard Smith's diary alluded to a report from the committee: "inter alia that all Persons who refuse the Continental Bills shall be declared Enemies to their Country was postponed." Only a month later, on January 11, 1776, Smith's diary contained an entry observing that "a proposition of [James] Duane's took Place implying that all who refuse to take the Continental Curr[enc]ey shall be treated as Enemies to their Country."[28] Within a few days, the new law was published widely in the newspapers throughout America. In retrospect, on September 11, 1783, after the war's conclusion, Franklin criticized the Congress's handling of the depreciating currency: "It is some Consolation to me, that I wash'd my hands of that Evil by predicting it in Congress, and proposing Means that would have been effectual to prevent it, if they had been adopted."[29]

The Design of "WE ARE ONE"

The design for the thirteen interlinked rings relied upon two figurative strategies: the metaphor of eternity as a circle and the oxymoron "WE ARE ONE." Because Franklin depicted each state as a circle, he recognized the authority of each individual government as an institution to be valued and perpetuated throughout all time. At the same time, by arranging the thirteen distinct circles to constitute a larger circle, he suggested that the authority of the transcendent government, the Congress, should also be valued and perpetuated throughout eternity. By combining thirteen individual circles in the pattern of an encompassing circle, he sought to negotiate an underlying tension between recognizing the distinct power of the individual states and portraying the transcendent power of the Congress as an enduring political body authorizing and supporting the military force. Other designs produced at the time likewise employed various patterns of thirteen identical stars, stripes, pillars, arrows, candles, or bees at the same hive to acknowledge the distinct governments of the members participating in the American Congress.[30] Paradoxically, the governments were, at once, distinct and united. This apparent contradiction rested at the center of the constitutive rhetoric, even as the act of striking the currency enacted the Congress's unified resistance to British authority by violating its laws concerning issuing paper money.

The design was an original device to designate a union of distinct governments. Although there were some similarities with the interlinked rings in the symbolism of the ancient Greek Olympics, in which the various city states convened for athletic competitions, the interlinked rings for the Olympic games never designated a transcendent government unifying the distinct city states.[31] A more likely source for Franklin's idea of using interlinked rings to designate distinct governments within an overarching government may have been the imagery evoked by the Iroquois confederacy. He knew that the Six Nations had a unified form of government, embodied in the image of the long house. He also knew that among the Iroquois "brightening the chain" was a pervasive image for unity among the distinct governments.[32]

The evidence that the Iroquois confederacy influenced Franklin's design for "WE ARE ONE" is suggestive, but inconclusive.[33] Between 1736 and 1762, Franklin printed at least thirteen treaties made with the Indians, usually between Pennsylvania and the Iroquois confederacy, a factor that indicated his deepening familiarity with the Iroquois confederacy long before his earliest comments on colonial union.[34] Most of these Indian treaties used such phrases as "brighten the chain," "chain of friendship," "covenant chain," "chain of peace," and even, on occasion, "chain of union," all of which symbolized the relationship between the parties to the specific treaty. Typical of these references was the language in a treaty at Lancaster in 1744: "We will brighten the Chain, and strengthen the Union between us; so that we shall never be divided, but remain Friends and Brethren as long as the Sun gives Light; in Confirmation whereof, we give you this Belt of Wampum."[35] Chain metaphors, such as "chain of peace" and, above all, "covenant chain," also appeared in other treaty proceedings and in contemporaneous comments in Franklin's *Pennsylvania Gazette*.[36]

In 1753 Franklin had represented Pennsylvania at the Carlisle treaty, preparation for which would have required his careful attention to the Six Nation's practices.[37] Visualizing the union between the Six Nations and the various British colonies as a chain was so common that the image was evoked in instructions to some commissioners at the subsequent Albany Congress in 1754.[38] The "Journal of the Proceedings of the Congress Held at Albany, in 1754," where Franklin was an active participant, contained numerous references to "renewing" the "covenant chain," "brightening" the "covenant chain," and the "chain of friendship."[39] Often, these metaphors were ascribed to the practices of the Iroquois confederacy, even though the English terms themselves combined Western language and indigenous social practices.[40] In British America, references to a covenant chain may have resonated with ideas embedded in covenant theology.[41]

It was noteworthy, too, that Franklin's contemporaries in the Congress also alluded to the conventional images of the treaties with the Iroquois confederacy, sometimes in their correspondence with Franklin, as did Francis Hopkinson on November 30, 1781. In reference to the use of pen, ink, and paper to write a letter to Franklin, Hopkinson commented, "I set down to brighten the Chain between us." John Adams, the ambassador to Holland, also referred to brightening the chain in his correspondence with Charles Dumas on September 10, 1783. Adams wrote, "It has ever been my Intention to come in Person to the Hague, and take Leave of their High Mightinesses with all the Respect in my Power, before my departure for America." He added, "If it is the usage of their High Mightinesses, as you say it is, to make a Present of a Chain upon the occasion, it will be very agreeable to me to accept it, and in the Language of my Countrymen I hope it will prove the Chain of perpetual Peace and invariable Friendship, and brighten more and more with Time."[42]

On the currency in 1776, Franklin used the vernacular language of most colonists when he expressed the motto, "WE ARE ONE," in English to describe the pictorial design. This use of the vernacular was of strategic importance in that it enabled the message to reach a broader segment of the American population than would have been possible with a Latin motto, though there was a large population of Pennsylvanians who spoke German and for whom English may have been unfamiliar. The motto may have had some relationship to another motto, "*E Pluribus Unum*," which may be translated, "Out of Many,

One." This Latin expression—proposed as early as 1776 by Pierre Eugène Du Simitière for the Great Seal and formally adopted in 1783—had a disadvantage in that it excluded Americans who had not had the benefit of a classical education.[43] Even so, the process of forming one government out of several distinct governments made more temporal and logical sense than the oxymoronic "WE ARE ONE," in which a plural was at the same time a singular, as Loyalist Joseph Stansbury noticed in a series of verses ridiculing Franklin's design for the Continental currency.

Franklin may have considered several audiences in 1776, when he prepared the design for "WE ARE ONE," though his principal objectives at the time are a matter of conjecture, because his papers contain no written commentary concerning his rationale for the design. The Americans were most likely to have been central to Franklin, because (1) the currency's design would circulate most widely among them; (2) the Congress's legitimacy was much doubted by colonists; and (3) the Congress's ability to supply and pay the military forces depended upon the colonists' acceptance of the paper money. The reflexive, constitutive qualities of the motto, "WE ARE ONE," provides additional evidence that Americans were the principal audience. Beyond suggesting that they could demonstrate their commitment to the aims of the Congress by using the paper currency, Franklin sought to strengthen American unity in general for diplomacy abroad. An image of American unity would suggest to the British that America was a formidable power and suggest to various European powers that the new country was sufficiently unified to be a plausible political force in the war with Britain. For example, on October 3, 1775, he wrote from Philadelphia to Joseph Priestley at London: "America is determined and unanimous; a very few tories and placemen excepted, who will probably soon export themselves."[44]

Even though he projected an image of confidence in American unity to the British and French correspondents, Franklin's correspondence with American leaders indicated that he recognized disunity in the Congress. For instance, he remarked in a letter to Charles Lee on February 11, 1776, only a few days before the Congressional approval of the currency, "There is a kind of Suspense in Men's Minds here at present, waiting to see what Terms will be offer'd from England. I expect none that we can accept; and when that is generally seen, we shall be more unanimous and more decisive." It would not have been possible to be "more unanimous," if the colonies were already unified, as Franklin suggested in letters abroad during this time.[45] In a sense, the oxymoron "WE ARE ONE" was self-directed to the Congress to call into being a condition among its members that had not and did not, in fact, exist.

During this period, delegates in Congress sought to strengthen the unity among them through carefully considered political actions such as the appointment of George Washington, a Virginian, as the head of the American military forces in New England. On June 16, 1775, Eliphalet Dyer explained in a letter to Jonathan Trumbell Sr. that Gen. George Washington's "appointment will tend to keep up the Union & more strongly Cement the Southern with the Northern Colonies, & serve to the removing all jealousies Army composed principally of New Englanders (if happily they prove Successfull) of being formidable to the Southern Colonies."[46] From Philadelphia, George Washington wrote to his brother, John A. Washington, on June 20, 1775: "I have been called upon by the unanimous Voice of the Colonies to take the Command of the Continental Army—An honour I neither sought after, nor desired, as I am thoroughly convinced that it requires greater Abilities, and much more experience, than I am Master of, to conduct a business so extensive in its nature, and arduous in the execution."[47] The delegates to Congress often wrote to their constituencies to assure them of the unanimity of the Congress.[48] While delegates' comments affirmed a commitment to maintaining unity, they also revealed that the delegates were aware of the distinct interests and divisive fractures among the states. These were so varied and deep that, reminiscing on the American Revolution years later in 1818, John Adams remarked that "Thirteen clocks were made to strike together—a perfection of mechanism, which no artist had ever before effected."[49] At the time, however, American Loyalists and British partisans disparaged the Continental currency in order to challenge any images of Congressional unity and to undermine economic support for the American forces. Their efforts to undermine the currency focused, in part, on the meanings of its designs.

Partisans Discrediting "WE ARE ONE" and the Continental Paper Currency

Loyalist poems often referred to the Continental currency to discredit the Congress and the Revolutionaries' cause. For example, one Loyalist verse alluded to: "That conj'rer, which conveys away your gold, / And gives you paper in its stead to hold." Another Loyalist verse described "Knave after knave as easy we could join, / As new emissions of the paper coin." Still another verse commented,

> Here Anarchy before the gaping crowd
> Proclaims the people's majesty aloud;
> There Folly runs with eagerness about,
> And prompts the cheated populace to shout;

> Here paper-dollars meager Famine holds,
> There votes of Congress Tyranny unfold.[50]

Still other poems alluded to the motto on the fractional notes, as did "Mud Island," a verse among the *Loyalist Rhapsodes* in December 1777: "Amid all the Plenty of Goods, this Vexation / Arises, where shall we get the Money to buy / For all our Old Paper's of no Valuation / With these great Importers of Wet Goods and Dry. / They mistake it, my honey! For the Congress Money, / Whose Motto, you know, it is 'Fugio,' I fly!"[51]

American Loyalist Joseph Stansbury, who wrote at Philadelphia over the signature "R.R.," responded at length to Franklin's design on the currency for February 17, 1776, regarding it as a resource for ridiculing the Congress.[52] After devoting several stanzas of "The History of Peru & c." to clever puns and reversals that focused upon the Continental currency issued in 1775, Stansbury penned several to the design for "WE ARE ONE" in 1776. "Peru" was slang for gold and silver money. So the title of the poem focused on the history of money. Having little confidence in his readers' abilities to understand his allusions to the various designs on the currency, Stansbury provided explanations within notes. Not all of Stansbury's notes were accurate, however. Beside stanzas 10 and 11, for example, he wrote, "The lesser Continental Bills of fractions of a Dollar intended for Change, the Device by Francis Hopkinson."[53]

In stanza 10, Stansbury redefined the image of thirteen interlinked rings and challenged the Congress's legitimacy:

> But the last fashion'd Money
> we all must commend,
> Where a Circle of Rings
> join in Rings without end,
> Each Ring is a State,
> and (the Motto explains)
> They all are a Congress—
> a Congress in Chains!

This reversal of the meanings for the image on "WE ARE ONE" suggested that the design foreshadowed the delegates' imprisonment, presumably for violating British laws forbidding the production of paper money, among other offenses.

The next stanza amplified the idea of the confinement, through yet another rhetorical reversal. He portrayed the lines around the sun, typically a symbol of the glory of the rising sun, as a confining picket fence.

> In the midst a small Circle
> resplendent is seen
> Surrounded with Glory
> and *Picketed* in,
> To make Jest of our Creed
> this was certainly done,
> For who can believe
> that *Thirteen* are but *One?*

This stanza undermined the motto by portraying it as a contradiction. Because being one and many at the same time was logically impossible, the verse ridiculed the phrase "WE ARE ONE" as nonsense, an imposition on credulity.[54] The verse challenged the credibility of the constitutive rhetoric that had affirmed British American's unity, because it enacted disunity among British Americans and displayed attitudes underscoring the impossibility of amity among them.

Turning next to the opposite side of the paper money, playfully referred to as the "reverse," Stansbury suggested that the sun was not rising, but setting. As such, the sun was an emblem of the American colonies' ineluctable decline, presumably because they had chosen military conflict with Britain rather than legal compliance.

> On the Face of the Bill
> the *reverse* doth appear,
> Almost Shorn of his beams,
> the Sun's quitting the Sphere,
> "I am going," he cries,
> "who was late your delight,
> Mind your Business—Repent—
> I must bid you good night."

The motto on the reverse side of the paper money, "Mind your Business," which had urged the colonists to be industrious because time flies, became transformed into an appeal to "repent" one's political blunders, introducing an element of religiosity. Moreover, Stansbury exploited the pictorial ambiguity of the rising sun in a rhetorical reversal by suggesting that it was, on inspection, a setting sun.

Years later, Franklin likewise would exploit such pictorial ambiguities in the rising and setting suns by commenting on the carved design on the back of a chair. Toward the end of his life, Franklin participated in the Constitutional Convention, where he delivered perhaps his best-known speech.

Subsequently, toward the conclusion of the ratification of the United States's Constitution, as each of the delegations in geographical order from New Hampshire to Georgia signed the Constitution, Franklin noted an image of a sun on the chair of the president. "Whilst the last members were signing it," James Madison mentioned in his account of the event, "Doctr. Franklin[,] looking towards the Presidents Chair, at the back of which a rising sun happened to be painted, observed to a few members near him, that Painters had found it difficult to distinguish in their art a rising from a setting sun. I have, said he, often and often in the course of the Session, and the vicissitudes of my hopes and fears as to its issue, looked at that behind the President without being able to tell whether it was rising or setting: But now at length I have the happiness to know that it is a rising and not a setting Sun."[55] Such remarks were well-known allusions to symbolism of the rising or setting sun in various books of emblems and devices, in which a rising sun corresponded to increasing glory and a setting sun represented decline.

But, during the mid-1770s, the outcome of the conflict was not yet known. In Stanbury's poem concerning the paper currency, the subsequent series of stanzas mocked the delegates to the Continental Congress and the officers leading the military forces, using as his starting point the appeal to "Repent." If these men had not become prominent in the current political and military affairs, the poem suggested, they would be recognized as a common gang, who could perhaps be entrusted with distilling rum, making snuff, or, worse, governing children. In brief, the poem suggested that the leaders in the Congress and the military were acting from a desire for personal power, not the best interest of the community. Further, the Loyalist charged that the members of Congress had violated the social codes of conduct by entertaining aspirations beyond the norm for men of their character and social status.

Having castigated the delegates and officers, and having belittled them as pretentious, Stansbury addressed his penultimate stanza to fellow citizens:

> Mind your Business, good folks,
> of this raving give o'er.
> Convinc'd of your Errors
> your Folly deplore,
> Return to your Duty,
> Great Britain is kind,
> And all past Offences,
> She'll give to the Wind.

The poem's moral suggested that the citizens could take responsibility for improving the state of affairs by ignoring the Congress's pretensions and reuniting with the British government. Of course, a Loyalist would have deplored the design for "WE ARE ONE." The principal value of Stansbury's poem was how it exploited pictorial ambiguities rhetorically to reverse the symbolism's meanings, while employing ridicule to denounce the Congress.[56] In addition to illustrating how symbolism depended upon perspective in the politically charged environment, the poem indicated to the Congress's adversaries that the paper currency was a useful target.

British partisans also assailed the paper currency. During 1776, the *London Chronicle* carried a few articles about the Continental currency, but did not describe the design for "WE ARE ONE," or reactions to the pattern. Instead, the *Chronicle* described the problems arising from depreciation and the punishment of those Americans who refused to accept the paper money, targeting the issuance of currency by both the Congress and the states. In the June 4–6, 1776, edition, for example, the *London Chronicle* reported the Congress's punitive actions to impose the paper money upon the citizens: "The Congress have seized the books and shut up the stores of several Quakers at Philadelphia, who were capital traders, but who were unwilling to accept the Congress paper in payment for their goods." In the November 5–7, 1776, newspaper, the *Chronicle* reported that "no one takes the paper currency that can help it, though the Congress have punished several for refusing it." Again, the December 28–31, 1776, issue of the *London Chronicle* portrayed the depreciation of the paper currency by comparing the value of the paper with that of hard money: "The current rate that Congress dollars passed at New York, ever since General Howe landed at Staten Island, was twelve for one, that is, twelve Congress or paper dollars, issued by the American Congress, for one hard dollar, or silver dollar; and no person took them at this rate but those who could dispatch them to the New England provinces, where they were in rather better credit, though it was every day falling off."[57]

Similarly, reports in the *London Chronicle* depicted the Americans' resistance to accepting paper bills at the state level. In early March 1776, for example, the *London Chronicle* reported the North Carolina government's resolution "that if any person shall refuse to receive the public bills of credit by this congress enacted to be emitted, in payment of any debt or demand, or shall refuse to give them credit, or speak disrespectfully of the said bills, or shall offer a greater sum of the said bills in exchange than at the rate of eight shillings for a dollar, such [a] person shall be treated as an enemy to his country." The report in the *Chronicle* added, "They have made a large sum of money out of a few sheets of paper; which I can easily see is to pass, by a magic trick, out of the hands of the leaders into the pockets of the poor people of the provinces." The same issue of the *Chronicle* reported a similar resolution by

the Continental Congress.[58] These news reports concerning Americans rejecting the paper currency doubtless undercut whatever images of American
unity the colonists, including Franklin, endeavored to enhance in the British
citizens' imaginations.

To judge from the letters by delegates to the Congress, the Loyalists were
largely successful in undermining Americans' acceptance of the paper money,
though their success was presumably aided by the currency's rapid depreciation and its backing by a new government, whose future was uncertain. In a
letter on October 2, 1776, Edward Rutledge informed Robert R. Livingston,
"We have great Reason to think that the Quakers have determined to refuse
our Continental Currency. If they make a point of it, we must make a point
of hanging them, which will bring on a storm that will take the Wisdom of
all our wise Men to direct." William Hooper wrote likewise to Joseph Hewes
on November 5, 1776 that "The Tories have taken the hint & with Israel Pemberton at their head openly and avowedly decry the Currency and refuse to
take it in payment of their debts. The prejudice is becoming general & timid
whigs are catching the infection." He added, "This is striking radically at our
struggle and unless vigorous & immediate steps are taken to cure the evil we
are a ruined Country." Referring to the paper currency, Robert Morris commented to Silas Deane in a letter on December 20, 1776: "Our internal Enemies, who alas are numerous & rich have always been undermining its value
by various artifices and now that our distresses are wrought to a Pitch by the
Success and near approach of the Enemy they speak plainer & many perem-
torily refuse to take it at any rate. Those that do receive it, do it with fear &
trembling." Benjamin Rush wrote to Richard Henry Lee on December 21,
1776, "I need not inform you of the general disposition of the people in &
near Philada to refuse continental money upon the late prospect of Genl
Howe's getting possession of the city." He added, "I tremble every time I think
of the danger of the further progress of the refusal of our money."[59]

Partisan's Reproducing "WE ARE ONE"

Franklin sought primarily to promote unity among the American colonies, and,
although he was aware of the difficulties arising from depreciation, he probably recognized that solving those difficulties rested upon other factors such
as laws, commerce, and military victories. Of course, the design did little if
anything to change the pattern of a depreciating and increasingly unpopular
currency. Changing that would have required Congressional attention to the
material resources supporting the currency. Americans continued to reject the
paper currency because acceptance of a failing currency had a profound impact

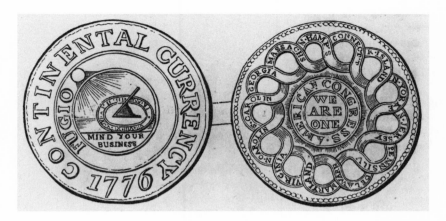

5.5. Continental currency, "E.G." [Elisha Gallaudet], [possibly Philadelphia], 1776. Medium: United States currency in silver, brass, and pewter; size: 1" diameter. There were at least four variants of this coin. Photograph of a facsimile courtesy of the Prints and Photographs Division of the Library of Congress.

on their economic circumstances.[60] Indeed, the situation seemed so desperate by December 1776 that Benjamin Rush advocated concealing from the public any further issuances of currency by the Congress, especially if the Congress was now prepared to offer interest on the amounts.[61]

Yet revolutionaries and nationalists enthusiastically reproduced the design for "WE ARE ONE." After it circulated initially on the paper money, the design was reproduced widely on metal money, state currency, newspaper mastheads, flags, carpeting, housewares, portraits, buttons, and the like. The motif recurred on almost every imaginable object from the mundane to the highly refined in public spaces as well as in the home. During the Revolutionary War, a similar design recurred on the metal Continental Dollar in 1776 (fig. 5.5), a coin struck from silver, brass, and pewter. Instead of thirteen rings, two strands were interwoven thirteen times. On each of the thirteen outer loops was inscribed the name of a colony.[62] An inscription on some pieces of "E. G. FECT" meant "made by Elisha Gallaudet," who was a New York engraver of paper currency.[63] The December 21–24, 1776, *London Chronicle* announced, "The Congress have established a Mint at Philadelphia, where they coin copper and silver pieces about the size of half a crown: In silver go for twelve shillings, in copper for fourteen pence."[64] Silver coins were probably used as currency, brass ones as dies used to form the coins, and pewter ones as symbols distributed to members of Congress to gain their support for the coins.[65]

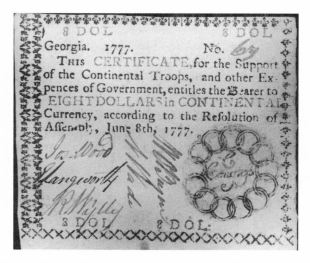

5.6. "C Congress" as an element on a "CERTIFICATE" for "EIGHT DOLLARS in CONTINENTAL Currency," [Georgia], June 8, 1777. Medium: paper money for the state of Georgia. Size: 3 ¼" × 3 ½". Photograph courtesy of American Antiquarian Society.

Beyond this, the motif also circulated on two states' paper currency: Georgia's for June 8 and September 10, 1777, and Vermont's for February 1781.[66] On Georgia's currency (fig. 5.6), the interlocked rings appeared on the eight-dollar denominations, which featured "a simple linked rings device in the lower right corner. Printed in blue, the rings around 'C Congress' in script."[67] A few years later, during February 1781, the Vermont currency also circulated with the interlocked rings in at least two different designs. Printed by Judah Spooner and Timothy Green at Westminster, Vermont, one of these designs showed a separate circle located at the top of the coin and between the un-joined ends of the otherwise interconnected circle of thirteen rings, presumably to represent Vermont's possible addition to the existing union.[68] This pattern recurred on Vermont's notes for "*One Shilling,*" "*Six Shillings and Eight Pence per Ounce,*" and the "*Two Shillings and Six-Pence.*"[69] Another type of paper currency in Vermont for "One Shilling and Three Pence" placed the thirteen linked rings in a continuous curve rather than a completed circle. A fourteenth ring representing Vermont was inserted above the curve, as though awaiting there to be added to the existing states.[70] Ironically, each state's efforts to secure loans abroad to finance its own currency may have undermined Franklin's efforts to secure loans for the United States, because the states competed with him on interest rates, and because, as Franklin put it, "The Agents from our different States running all over Europe begging to borrow Money at high Interest, has given such an Idea of our Poverty and Distress, as has excedingly hurt the general Credit, and made the Loan for the United States almost unpracticable."[71]

In addition to recurring on the currency of the Congress and certain states during the war, the interlinked rings appeared with "WE ARE ONE" printed in black lettering against a gold-painted background on the 1777 buff-colored silk flag of the New Hampshire Second Regiment, though without the words, "AMERICAN CONGRESS."[72] In some additional instances, designs from the paper currency were featured on the military flags of various regiments, associating the economic medium with the war that the paper currency enabled the Congress to finance.[73] The Americans who accepted the currency in transactions would have needed to fight for their material well-being, as one consequence of having placed their resources behind the military.

A revised version of the motif was distributed widely in a newspaper, the *Massachusetts Spy: Or, American Oracle of Liberty*, in which the image appeared on the masthead week after week during 1781, long after the alliance had been formed between the United States and France. Isaiah Thomas, the editor of the *Spy*, described how the device "on the right was, a chain of thirteen links, with a star in each link, representing the union of the thirteen states; this chain was placed in a circular form, leaving an opening for the arms of France, to which the ends of the chain were attached, and which perfected the circle. Above the arms were two hands clasped, and directly over them a sword, with its hilt resting on the clasped hands; the motto—'UNION.'"[74] Thomas modified the image to acknowledge the alliance between the United States and France, though he continued to use the motif to emphasize the central idea of unity among the American governments. Then, sometime after September 3, 1783, a version of the two strands interwoven thirteen times, much like the pattern on the metal Continental Dollar of 1776, was used on a Revolutionary War peace medal, *FELICITAS: BRITANNIA ET AMERICA* ("Happiness: Britain and America"), commemorating the treaty of Paris on September 3, 1783 (fig. 5.7).[75]

After the war's conclusion, the image of the interlinked rings recurred on various metal coins produced for the United States, circulating as the motif did among citizens throughout the new nation: John Chalmers's "Rings" shilling, produced at Annapolis, Maryland in 1783;[76] the "Washington the Great" copper, otherwise known as the "Ugly Head," in 1784;[77] and both versions of the Fugio cent (also identified as the Franklin cent) of 1787,[78] perhaps the best-known of the metal coins, having been approved by a Congressional

5.7. "Peace of Versailles" or "FELICITAS: BRITANNIA ET AMERICA" ("Happiness: Britain and America"), probably America, 1783. Medium: a peace medal made of tin commemorating the treaty of Paris, September 3, 1783; size: 1 ⅝" diameter. Photograph courtesy of the British Museum, Department of Coins and Medals.

resolution on July 6, 1787.[79] The design for the fractional bills was noteworthy in numismatics because the first coin issued by the United States, the Fugio cent of 1787, was patterned after it.[80] In 1793, the interlocked rings were used on the United States large cent, a usage of particular interest because of a debate that centered around the meanings of the design.

The rings on the United States large cent were modified to more closely resemble a chain and, as a consequence, caused a public controversy, because the chain was thought to connote slavery and bondage rather than liberty. A letter, which was published in *The Mail or Claypoole's Daily Advertiser* at Philadelphia on March 18, 1793, and again in *The Argus* published at Boston on March 26, 1793, objected, "THE American *Cents* . . . do not answer our expectation. The chain on the reverse is but a bad omen for liberty, and liberty herself appears to be in a fright -- May she not justly cry out in the words of the apostle, '*Alexander the copper-smith, has done me much harm; the Lord reward him according to his works*'?"[81] "Alexander" was a mocking reference to Secretary of the Treasury Alexander Hamilton, and the biblical allusion was to 2 Timothy 4:14. More important, the debate echoed Joseph Stansbury's criticism in ridiculing verses of the earlier design for "WE ARE ONE" on the paper currency.

By 1785 the interlocked rings began to appear frequently as a commonplace motif on a wide variety of housewares—dinner plates, bowls, pitchers, and the like—produced by the use of transfer designs on creamware manufactured at Liverpool and on porcelain exported from China. Of these, perhaps the best-known example was the Martha Washington "States" China, a design on cake and dinner plates produced circa 1792–96 (figs. 5.8 and 5.9).[82] At the rim, a blue rattlesnake biting its tail encircles a chain composed of fifteen links separately named for each state. The *ouroboros*, or image of a circular snake biting its own tail, also served as a reference to Franklin's earlier "JOIN, or DIE." But another noteworthy example of "WE ARE ONE" recurred on the Gen. Richard Humpton bowl, likewise produced circa 1798–1805 as Chinese Export porcelain.[83] A type of Liverpool Creamware transfer design placed an image of the Arms of Virginia at the center of the interlinked rings, presumably for market in that state sometime after 1785.[84] Yet another design for Liverpool Creamware, produced sometime after 1790, placed an eagle from the "Arms of the United States" on plates at the center of the image (fig. 5.10), a design that recurred over the years on various housewares, such as pitchers (fig. 5.11).[85] Still another Liverpool production of housewares, circa 1795, featured fifteen interlinked rings, including Vermont and Kentucky, in a circle around representations of the Great Seal, the female figure of Liberty, and a portrait of George Washington.[86] Such images on ordinary housewares prove that the home was not separated from political life, but rather that the nationalistic and state commitments of a household were displayed on a daily basis.

The motif even recurred on buttons for clothing. In 1789 the interlocked rings appeared on the metal commemorative buttons known as the "Linked States Border Pattern," celebrating the inauguration of George Washington as the president of the United States.[87] In addition, the motif recurred on portraits, peace medals, and carpeting. The interlocked rings formed a framing device for the "Display of the United States of America," a 1788–89 engraving by Amos Doolittle, reprinted in 1789, 1791, 1794, and 1796—a sign of the popularity of the pictorial composition in which the design of linked circles encircled a portrait of the president.[88] Sometime before 1790, the motif was used on the "United States Indian Peace Medal," designed by either Thomas Goadsby or Albion Cox.[89] In 1791, the interlocked rings were a prominent motif on the United States Senate Chamber carpet in Congress Hall.[90] Between 1820 and 1825, a cotton textile print, featuring the text of the Declaration of Independence, was circled by sixteen rings: thirteen designated the original states and three at the top featured portraits of Presidents George Washington, John Adams, and Thomas Jefferson.[91] Franklin's image of American unity, "WE ARE ONE," struck a chord throughout the United States, sounding the distinct governments abiding within the transcendent American Congress. The image simply resounded throughout the culture on almost every conceivable medium.[92] It was a powerful image within eighteenth-century

5.8. Cake plate with rim design featuring interlinked rings and snake ouroboros known as "State" service, or "Martha Washington" service, produced in China, circa 1792–96. This was part of a set presented to Martha Washington by Andraeas Everardus van Braam Houckgeest. Medium: painted hard-paste porcelain housewares; size: 2" high × 13 ⅞" diameter. Photograph courtesy of the Henry Francis du Pont Winterthur Museum.

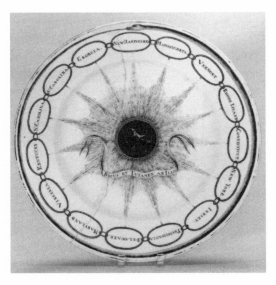

5.9. Dinner plate with rim design featuring interlinked rings and a snake ouroboros owned by Martha Washington, produced at Jingdezhen, China, circa 1785. Medium: painted hard-paste porcelain housewares; size: 1" high × 9 ¼" diameter. Photograph courtesy of the Massachusetts Historical Society.

5.10. "Thirteen States" plate, Herculaneum factory, probably at Liverpool, Britain, 1790–1820. Media: Liverpool transfer design on earthenware creamware for housewares; size: 1 ⅛" high × 9 ¹³⁄₁₆" diameter. Photograph courtesy of the Henry Francis du Pont Winterthur Museum, Gift of Mr. and Mrs. John Mayer.

5.11. Pitcher, Britain, circa 1800–15. Medium: Liverpool transfer design on earthenware housewares; size: 7" high × 6 ¾" wide. Photograph courtesy of the Henry Francis du Pont Winterthur Museum.

American culture, even though the medium on which it was initially distributed was not worth a Continental.

Conclusion

Franklin's design for the Continental currency, "WE ARE ONE," depended
for its popular appeal on the rhetorical figure of an oxymoron, a paradox that
the Congress was both many and one. Further, the pictorial design suggested
that the colony governments, despite their widely varying population densi-
ties and geographic sizes, had equal stature within the American Congress as
necessary links in the circular chain. Above all, Franklin's "WE ARE ONE"
exhorted the Americans to unify—to constitute a new government in the ongoing war with the British military forces. Colonists could demonstrate their
commitment to this new government simply by using the paper money to
finance the war. At the same moment that the Americans did so, they tacitly
recognized, affirmed, or acquiesced to the American Congress's legitimacy as
the authority sanctioning the paper money. Yet the Congress's legitimacy was
much in doubt among Americans, especially because of the Loyalists' criticisms of it. Widely distributed throughout the United States and abroad, the
design became one of the most popular images employed on a wide range of
mundane objects throughout the Revolutionary era. The image appeared on
military flags, metal coins, state paper currency, newspaper mastheads, frames
on portraits, bottons for clothing, and carpeting. After the war, the motif
recurred on numerous types of housewares displayed in daily life, such as
decorative pitchers, bowls, and plates.

Franklin had employed a somewhat similar rhetorical strategy of pictorial
communication roughly two decades earlier, when he designed the image of
the segmented snake, "JOIN, or DIE," during 1754, because it suggested that
unity conferred strength. The snake's image had likewise suggested egalitarianism, not among all individuals but rather among whole colonial governments, because each had been depicted as a segment of a larger creature. As
with the image of the interlinked rings, he arranged the segments from North
to South, using geography as the underlying principle of arrangement. Where
the organic form of the snake inadvertently suggested that New England, as
the snake's head, was more important than the other colonies, as evidenced
by a 1774–1775 newspaper debate about the image,[93] the mechanical form of
the thirteen interlinked rings resolved the difficulties implied by the varied
status of differentiated parts. In response to the snake's image on various newspaper mastheads in Pennsylvania, New York, and Massachusetts (figs. 3.5,
3.6, and 3.7 on p. 32), for example, the *New-York Gazetteer* on Aug. 25, 1774,

and, subsequently, the *Boston Weekly News-Letter* on September 8, 1774, had quipped, "NEW-ENGLAND's the Head too;—NEW ENGLAND's abused; / for the *Head of the Serpent* we know *should be* bruised.[94] The interlinked rings, in contrast, never suggested differences of any consequence among the relative importance of the thirteen links.

"WE ARE ONE" and "JOIN, or DIE" may be compared in additional respects. Where the snake device had to be severed each time that another colony joined the union, as had been the case when Georgia joined the colonial cause in 1775, the interlinked ring device could be expanded through the simple addition of links within the circle. This was an improvement over the image of the snake, because severing the snake into additional parts had suggested a weakening of the creature's condition, even though the addition of states in the union strengthened it. In contrast, the addition of new links could suggest increasing strength in the Congress as a whole. Further, "WE ARE ONE" suggested respect for the political unity of the individual states, each of which was a complete ring, while "JOIN, or DIE" suggested that the individual colonies could only constitute a complete body politic through a transcendent unity with other colonies. The shift from organic metaphors depicting the body politic in both "JOIN, or DIE" and "MAGNA *Britannia*" to the mechanical imagery of "WE ARE ONE" indicated a shift from vital, living connections among the colonies to artificial mechanisms depicting a unity that, at best, was contrived to conceal deep divisions in Congress over fundamental issues, such as whether the war was for national independence. In this respect, the currency design was a myth and a deflection from actual political conditions, such as the deep divisiveness not only in Congress but also in British America between the American Loyalists and the Patriots.

Most important, Franklin had distributed the image of the segmented snake on "JOIN, or DIE" to urge colonial unity during the military struggle with the French and Indians, but the interlinked rings on "WE ARE ONE" represented American unity in the military struggle against Britain. While the snake's image had urged unity among the colonies within the British Empire as a practical military necessity, "WE ARE ONE" urged unity among the colonies in Congress as a governing authority in opposition to the rest of the British Empire. Gone altogether were images of an interdependent empire, as in "MAGNA *Britannia: her Colonies* REDUC'D." As for interdependent colonies, the rhetorical oxymoron's recognition of the deep divisions among the distinct governments perhaps served as a strategic ambiguity and paradox that contributed to the image's rhetorical power and resonance at the time. The chain links were also bonds subject to reversal by adversaries, precisely

because of the political dangers that confederation posed to the state governments, and because of the illegal proceedings of the Congress in light of British
laws, as Stanbury's poem admonished on behalf of American Loyalists.

Sometime before July 21, 1775, Franklin had written an "Intended Vindi-
cation and Offer from Congress to Parliament, in 1775," which the *Public
Advertiser* subsequently printed on July 18, 1777. Alluding to the French and
Indian War, Franklin commented again upon the British failure to endorse the
Albany Plan of Union in 1754. He said, "In the last War it is true Britain sent
a Fleet and Army, who acted with an equal Army of our's in the Reduction
of Canada, and perhaps thereby did more for us than we in the preceding
Wars had done for her. Let it be remembered, however, that she rejected the
Plan we formed in the Congress at Albany, in 1754, for our own Defence, by
an Union of the Colonies; an Union she was jealous of, and therefore chose
to send her own Forces; otherwise her Aid, to protect us, was not wanted."[95]
Two decades after the Albany Congress of 1754, Franklin's "WE ARE ONE"
in 1776 corresponded to his political commitment to the Continental Congress, the Articles of Confederation, and the unified American opposition to
the constitutional monarchy of Britain.

SIX

Libertas Americana, 1782–83

The gratitude of most men is merely a secret desire to receive greater benefits.

François, duc de La Rochefoucauld

6.1. *Libertas Americana*, obverse and reverse, proposed and commissioned by Benjamin Franklin, executed by Augustin Dupré, environs of Paris, 1783. Medium: gold, silver, copper, and bronze medals; size: 1 $^{15}/_{16}$" diameter. Photograph courtesy of the British Museum, Department of Coins and Medals.

In March of 1782, as the war for American independence was nearing its denouement, Franklin proposed that a medal be designed to commemorate the military victories over Britain at Yorktown and Saratoga. The medal that resulted from his proposal, *Libertas Americana*, became recognized internationally as an expression of the United States's gratitude to France for economic, diplomatic, and military assistance during the American Revolution (fig. 6.1). The gratitude that Franklin expressed with *Libertas Americana* was neither simply a gesture of appreciation for the past support from France nor merely a means to display the civic virtue of the United States. Above all, his expression of gratitude was a pragmatic, diplomatic move designed to help strengthen the United States's relationship with France in the interest of future national security. At the same time, his distribution of the medal suggested to other European nations that initiating diplomatic relations with the United States was acceptable to France, the most powerful nation on the western European continent. Franklin intimated that establishing a timely alliance now with the United States could create a debt of gratitude that would be of economic and political value in the future.[1]

Franklin designed *Libertas Americana* primarily to influence the beliefs and actions of those in the centers of political power in France and the United States. In his role as *ministre plénipotentiaire*, the United States's plenipotentiary ambassador to France, he presented originals of *Libertas Americana* to the most powerful figures in France: King Louis XVI and Queen Marie Antoinette received gold medals, and "each of the Ministers" in the French court—such men as Charles Gravier, comte de Vergennes, the minister of foreign affairs, and Philippe-Henri, marquis de Ségur, the minister of war—received one made of silver.[2] In addition, Franklin sent several medals in letters to the secretary of foreign affairs for the United States, Robert R. Livingston, with requests that he distribute them to every member of the U.S. Congress: the president of the Congress, Elias Boudinot, was presented with a silver one, and each state representative was given a copper medal, as was the secretary himself. Later, Franklin sent enough medals so that President Boudinot was able to distribute a copper version to each governor in the United States.

The act of striking the commemorative medal, a common practice at the time among more established nations, was in itself symbolically significant.[3] By the act of striking the medal, Franklin depicted the United States conducting itself as a member of the community of nations. He had been charged by the Congress with preparing several other medals to commemorate military victories, including those for Gen. George Washington, Maj. Gen. Horatio Gates, Brig. Gen. Anthony Wayne, Lieut. Col. Louis de Fleury, Lieut. Col. John Stewart, and Lieut. Col. Henry Lee.[4] But Franklin proposed, prepared, and presented *Libertas Americana* on his own initiative for diplomatic uses in his role as ambassador. As a consequence of distributing *Libertas Americana* to the most influential figures in the United States and France, gratitude for generosity became the hallmark of his diplomacy throughout this period.[5]

The commemorative medal was designed to praise those qualities of the United States and France that would be esteemed in the community of nations: for the United States, the medal depicted courage, military skill, and youthful potential for greatness; for France, the medal portrayed generosity, loyalty to an ally, and beneficent concern for an emerging nation. Franklin sought to design *Libertas Americana* so that it appealed to the interests of the distinct, principal audiences in the United States and France, whose cultural points of view placed different demands upon the medal's conception and interpretation. Equally important, he employed the design to commemorate past military victories, and, by doing so, he urged future political actions in a diplomatic situation charged with ambiguity and tension. Although he used the medal primarily to praise the national characters of France and the United States in those two countries, he also used it to influence a government policy in Malta and to vindicate himself from a published criticism of his character in England. This chapter investigates these ceremonial, deliberative, and apologetic functions of *Libertas Americana* to illustrate the range of its meanings for various audiences interpreting the commemorative medal under diverse political circumstances.

First, this chapter considers Franklin's rhetorical objectives as he developed a proposal for the medal, by noting how his correspondence with Americans suggested the centrality of the design's commemorative functions. Then, the underlying rhetorical strategies and tactics of the design will be inferred from his choice of visual elements recorded among others in three preliminary sketches and from his comments about the audiences. Finally, the recipients' written and pictorial responses to the design will be discussed in relationship to their diverse circumstances in the United States, France, Malta, Germany, Holland, Spain, and England. Notable national figures in France and the United States were able to interpret the medal differently than Franklin originally had planned, because of the design's allegorical structure and the changing political circumstances during the period between his proposal for the medal and its formal presentation.

At the time of Franklin's production of *Libertas Americana* in 1782 and 1783, he had been in Paris representing the United States for several years, initially serving alongside Silas Deane and Arthur Lee as one of three commissioners, later acting as the sole ambassador for the United States. Before having left America for France on October 26, 1776, he had participated in designing "WE ARE ONE" for the Continental currency and, shortly thereafter, in signing the Declaration of Independence. During December 1777, news reached Paris concerning British general John Burgoyne's surrender at Saratoga to American forces. Subsequently, during 1778, Franklin negotiated and signed a treaty of alliance with France (fig. 6.2), whose entry into the war was crucial, not only because it resulted in financial, military and diplomatic

6.2. "[Louis XVI and Benjamin Franklin]," probably Charles-Gabriel Sauvage, known as Le Mire Pere, produced at Niderville factory, Niderville, France, circa 1782–85. Medium: soft-paste porcelain; size: 12 ⅞" high with base and figures, base 8 ¾" × 4 ¹⁵/₁₆". Photograph courtesy of the Henry Francis du Pont Winterthur Museum.

support for the United States from France, but also because French diplomacy brought Spain into the war, despite Spanish misgivings about the United States's war for independence.[6] As a result, the British were unable to concentrate their military efforts only in British America, having become engaged in battle at Gibraltar and having been forced to gauge the risk of an attack from across the English Channel. Then, during fall 1781, came news of the decisive victory over the British forces under the command of Gen. Charles Cornwallis at Yorktown, which prompted Franklin's proposal for a commemorative medal, *Libertas Americana*.[7]

The Proposal for *Libertas Americana*

In a letter to John Adams on November 26, 1781, Franklin made his earliest allegorical reference to the recent military victory over Britain at Yorktown: "Most heartily do I congratulate you on the glorious News! The Infant Hercules in his Cradle has now strangled his second Serpent, and gives Hopes that his future History will be answerable." He added, "It is a rare Circumstance, and scarce to be met with in History, that in one War two Armies should be taken Prisoners compleatly, not a Man in either escaping. It is another singular Circumstance, that an Expedition so complex, form'd of Armies of different Nations and of Land & Sea-Forces, should with such perfect Concord be assembled from different places by Land & Water." Again, on January 19, 1782, Franklin wrote to John Jay about "the Reduction of Yorktown and Gloucester" as a "great and important Event!" He added, "The Infant Hercules has now strangled his second Serpent that attacked him in his Cradle, and I hope his future History will be conformable."[8]

Evidently, John Adams was impressed with the image, because he responded to Franklin on December 1, 1781, "I am much pleased with your Reflections on the Glorious News." The same day, Adams appropriated the imagery to describe America's future in a letter to Maj. William Jackson, "The Infant Hercules will go through all the twelve Labours, as triumphantly as he has strangled the two serpents Burgoine & Cornwallis." John Jay responded favorably to the imagery and, like Adams, situated the achievements among the tasks of Hercules. Jay replied to Franklin on February 11, 1782, "I am much mistaken if the Young Hercules does not one Day shake the pillars of the old," an allusion to the tenth labor.[9]

With the allusions to the infant Hercules, Franklin rejected the commonplace belief that Britain was the mother country of the British colonies in America, as he had done explicitly in his correspondence as early as 1778. For over two centuries, the English and colonists alike had claimed that the relationship between Britain and America resembled that between a mother and her child. The analogy between the British Empire and a family had been ubiquitous in pamphlets, newspapers, magazines, public speeches, diaries, letters, and satirical prints. However, in the classical myth, Hercules's stepmother, Juno, had sent the two serpents into his bedroom to kill him while he slept one evening. Those familiar with the myth would have noted the implication that Britain, by sending military forces into America, had emulated Juno's role as a stepmother. In this light, the allusion to the classical myth developed an allegory to influence American and European perceptions of Britain's role vis-à-vis the United States.[10]

On March 4, 1782, Franklin articulated his preliminary proposal for a medal in a letter to Robert R. Livingston, the secretary of foreign affairs for the U.S. Congress. After referring to Livingston's request for a sketch of an emblem for a memorial, Franklin's letter specified the central figures in his own design for *Libertas Americana*: "This puts me in mind of a Medal I have had a Mind to Strike since the late great Event you give me an Account of; representing the United States by the Figure of an Infant Hercules in his Cradle, strangling the two Serpents, and France by that of Minerva, sitting by as his Nurse with her Spear and Helmet, and her Robe speck'd with a few Fleurs-de-lis. The extinguishing [of] two entire Armies in one War, is what has rarely if ever happen'd, and it gives a presage of the future Force of our growing Empire."[11] Franklin's letter expressed a commemorative purpose for the medal by specifying its use to perpetuate the memory of the military victories at Yorktown and Saratoga. By doing so, he identified the proposed medal with a tradition in rhetoric of ceremonial messages designed to praise or blame prominent public figures or consequential achievements through representations of the noble and the base. Such messages were employed generally to unify a community through the public celebration of civic virtue.

A month later, on April 2, 1782, Franklin wrote a letter to Gen. George Washington that alluded once again to the infant Hercules and the two serpents, this time with a telling omission that indicated he had adapted his remarks to the American general. He said, "I received duly the Honour of your Letter accompanying the Capitulation of Gen. Cornwallis. All the World agree that no Expedition was ever better plann'd or better executed. It has made a great Addition to the military Reputation you had already acquired, and brightens the Glory that surrounds your Name and that must accompany it to our latest Posterity. No News could possibly make me more happy. The Infant Hercules has now strangled the two Serpents that attack'd him in his Cradle, & I trust his future History will be answerable."[12] His reference to the infant Hercules omitted any reference to the role of French protection embodied in Minerva, a role that he had noted in his earlier letter to Livingston and that he later endeavored to recognize through the distribution of *Libertas Americana*. He probably omitted that portion of his design, which would have suggested the United States's dependence upon France, so that he could underscore the merit of Washington's accomplishment. This objective was suggested by the design of *Libertas Americana*, wherein the infant Hercules used his own strength to strangle the two serpents, while France as Minerva protected him from a separate threat, a crouching leopard. To recognize the merits of the American and French leaders' accomplishments, the medal portrayed their struggle against distinct embodiments of the same British enemy.

Although all of Franklin's letters transfigured a major military victory into the suffocation of a serpent—an emblem of evil—to suggest the triumph of the virtuous over the wicked, the letters shifted in focus from the past victories to the promising future. He noted that Hercules's youthfulness was significant, because the United States's successful exercise of military strength at Yorktown and Saratoga foreshadowed the emerging nation's future accomplishments. The initial letters to Adams and Jay had recognized the interval between the two military victories by referring to the killing of a "second Serpent." The subsequent letters to Washington and Livingston alluded more vaguely to a moment when the infant had killed the "two Serpents." Eventually, however, the four years between the two military victories became condensed into a single fictional moment when the infant simultaneously strangled the two serpents, one in each hand. In subsequent years, this condensation of narrative time upset some Americans, among them Robert R. Livingston, whose initial response was enthusiastic.

To Franklin's proposal for a commemorative medal, Livingston responded in a letter on May 30, 1782, "I am charmed with your idea of a Medal to perpetuate the memory of York and Saratoga. The thought is simple, elegant and strikingly expressive of the subject. I cannot however but flatter myself, that before it can be executed, your Hercules will have tasked your invention for a new Emblem."[13] This pun on tasks, referring as it did to the labors facing Hercules after his infancy, placed the victories in the broad context of the myth, as had Adams and Jay in their earlier correspondence with Franklin. Livingston's support was only a personal endorsement, since the secretary of foreign affairs did not mention any economic support or sanction from the Congress for the medal's execution. That fall, on August 12, 1782, Franklin wrote to thank Livingston for approving of the proposed medal, even though he was not entirely satisfied with this form of support: "Your approbation of my Idea of a Medal to perpetuate the Memory of York & Saratoga Victories gives me great Pleasure, and encourages me to have it Struck." Later, on April 15, 1783, he expressed his hope that Congress would officially "approve of" the medal so that he could "add something on the Die . . . to show that it was done by their Order, which I would not venture to do till I had Authority for it." To Franklin, such a Congressional endorsement would have been invaluable, because it would have transformed his personal and diplomatic expression of gratitude to France into a national expression of gratitude.[14]

The Production of *Libertas Americana*

Sometime between mid-August and mid-September 1782, Franklin discussed his proposal for the medal with Alexandre-Théodore Brongniart, who, on December 14, 1782, became the architect and general controller of the Military School, having been suggested for that role by Ségur.[15] Brongniart's earliest correspondence with Franklin about the medal transpired before his formal appointment, however. A member of the Royal Academy of Architecture since 1781,[16] Brongniart wrote to him in his role as the "Architect of the King" on September 22, 1782: "I have at last obtained two rather large sketches for the medal from the sculptor whom I had the honor to speak with you about." He added, "I also requested one from a painter among my friends who designed a sketch of the same subject and I believe that he has succeeded."[17]

The capacity in which Brongniart wrote to Franklin, writing as he did from the Academy of Royal Architecture, may explain why there was no mention of the design for *Libertas Americana* among either the records of the French institution that ordinarily would have been engaged in such productions, the Royal Academy of Inscriptions and Belles-Lettres, or that institution's history, *Histoire de l'Académie royale des Inscriptions et Belles-Lettres.*[18] This history listed the medals authorized and commissioned by Congress in honor of George Washington, Horatio Gates, Nathaniel Greene, Daniel Morgan, William A. Washington, John Stewart, and John Paul Jones, but made no mention of *Libertas Americana;* thus, the lack of Congressional authorization for Franklin's medal may have been another cause for its omission from the list.[19]

Although Brongniart did not name the sculptor or the painter in this letter, he secured the preliminary sketches he mentioned from two French artists, Augustin Dupré and Esprit-Antoine Gibelin. The former was a goldsmith and medalist, and the latter, a member of the French Academy of Painting and Sculpture, who had completed several frescoes for the School of Medicine and the Royal Military School.[20] Between them, these men developed three extant sketches for *Libertas Americana*. Gibelin prepared one sketch, which is now held by the Musée nationale de la Coopération Franco-Américaine à Blérancourt (fig. 6.3). He later wrote to Franklin on February 7, 1785, "The medal of the United States of America that you had struck last year was modeled on the design that I composed at the request of Mr. Brongniart."[21] Dupré prepared the other two sketches, one in the American Philosophical Society (fig. 6.4), the other in the Musée des arts décoratifs au Louvre (fig. 6.5).[22] The sketches differed from each other in at least three noteworthy respects: the type of weapon held by Minerva, the position of the weapon, and the position of the leopard's tail. The sketch at the Musée des arts was less elaborate than that at the American Philosophical Society, and the design was the reverse of the final medal (with Minerva to the right of the composition and the leopard to the left). But the visual elements in the sketch at the Musée des arts more closely resembled the final medal than either of the other sketches. More important, all the sketches differed from Franklin's original

6.3. "[*Libertas Americana*—preliminary sketch]," Esprit-Antoine Gibelin, environs of Paris, 1782. Medium: pen and ink sketch. Photograph courtesy of the Musée nationale de la Coopération Franco-Américaine à Blérancourt, France and the Réunion des Musées Nationaux Art Resource, New York. Inventory CFAC 209.

6.4. "[*Libertas Americana*–preliminary sketch]," Augustin Dupré, environs of Paris, 1782. Medium: pencil sketch; size: 4 ⅞" × 4 ⅜". Photograph courtesy of the American Philosophical Society.

6.5. "[*Libertas Americana*—preliminary sketch]," Augustin Dupré, environs of Paris, 1782. Medium: pencil sketch; size: 7 1/16" × 9 1/2". Photograph courtesy of the Musée des arts décoratifs, Paris, France. Photograph by Laurent-Sully Jaulmes.

proposal in that they significantly changed the narrative action and introduced an additional pictorial element.

On January 13, 1783, Antoine-Alexis-François Cadet de Vaux, who was a royal censor, a chemist, and a translator, wrote to Franklin about the preparations for the medal.[23] Cadet de Vaux remarked, "Mr. Brongniart of the Academy of Royal Architecture has prepared a preliminary stamp of the medal destined to consecrate the union of the United States with France; he would like the honor of presenting the proof to Mr. Franklin." The rhetorical purpose ascribed by Cadet de Vaux to the medal differed significantly from those Franklin had articulated in his letter to Livingston, because Franklin had affirmed as his objective the commemoration of a rare military achievement. Yet such commemorative rhetoric had the value of unifying communities. Cadet de Vaux, who signed in his role as royal censor, requested time later in the week to arrange for Brongniart to meet with Franklin about the medal.[24]

Shortly later, Brongniart wrote to Franklin on January 23 about sending two more "new proofs of the medal." Commemorative medals traditionally bore specific types of illustration on each of the two sides, the obverse and the

6.6. Augustin Dupré's plaster proof for *Libertas Americana*, environs of Paris, 1782–83. Medium: plaster proofs gilded and framed; size: 1 ⅞" diameter. Photograph courtesy of the Print Department of Boston Public Library.

reverse. The former ordinarily featured the head of the honored figure, while the latter often represented the specific achievements in an allegory. The architect observed that the "head is not yet perfect," presumably a reference to the image of the head of the beautiful woman representing Liberty on the obverse. He also criticized the size of the serpents on the reverse, because they were "too large and too typical." Evidently at least one of the mottos on the medal was integrated into the design by this time, because he mentioned the need to correct the spelling: the engraver had mistakenly printed "intans," not "infans." Yet, Brongniart added, "I have the honor to remind Mr. Franklin that he has promised that he will write the two dates at the base of the medal and that this is the only matter that hinders completion of it."[25] Evidently, more than one such proof was prepared for the medal, judging from the correct spelling of "infans" on the plaster cast held at the Boston Public Library (fig. 6.6).[26] The process of production also entailed preparing wax and plaster casts and actually casting and engraving the medal.

Evidently, the decision about how to handle the dates at the base of the medal's reverse was a source of some difficulty for Franklin, unless he was simply too preoccupied with other matters to respond quickly to the reminder, because Brongniart wrote to him again a week later on January 31, 1783. After alluding to the "two new proofs" that he had presented to Franklin the previous week, along with "others depicting the head of Liberty," Brongniart added, "Apparently Mr Franklin has forgotten to send to me what he wants to place at the base of the medal for each date." That, he pointed out, was all that prevented the engraver from completing the project, and, Brongniart stressed, "he wants to finish this work." The date on the reverse on the medal was a concern, because ordinarily there was only one date at the bottom, but the references to both Saratoga and Yorktown required two. Ultimately, this aspect of the design was resolved by placing the month ("OCT.") at the center of the bottom with both days ("17" and "19") before it, one day printed above the other, and both years ("1777" and "1781") after it, again with one above the other, so as to include the complete dates for the victories.[27]

Because Franklin neither remarked in his papers about the preliminary pencil and ink sketches for *Libertas Americana* nor indicated his selection criteria for visual elements from the sketches, the underlying reasons for his choices can only be inferred on the basis of the differences among the sketches. Before exploring the possible rhetorical bases for these choices, two other pragmatic concerns merit mention because they probably influenced his choices: First, because he considered the arts in pragmatic terms, he probably used several elements from Dupré's designs in order to adapt to the principal audiences in France and the United States.[28] Second, Franklin's friendship for Dupré and certain technical considerations may also have influenced his selection of certain visual elements.[29]

In certain respects, all the sketches complied with Franklin's proposal in his letter to Livingston. America was represented as an infant Hercules, who was portrayed strangling two serpents, one in each fist. In addition, France was represented by the figure of Minerva, whose association with France was established with fleurs-de-lis. One minor departure from Franklin's proposal was the placement of the fleurs-de-lis: a sketch by Gibelin (fig. 6.3) and another by Dupré (fig. 6.4) placed three of the fleurs-de-lis on Minerva's shield, instead of on her "Robe" as proposed by Franklin. To judge the character of each nation by Franklin's choice of pictorial metaphors, the civic virtue of France and the United States were commended through representations of them as a goddess and a mythical hero, while Britain's moral depravity was disparaged by its depiction as two serpents.

All three extant sketches departed from Franklin's preliminary proposal by significantly changing the narrative action and by introducing an additional element. Instead of depicting Minerva "sitting by as his Nurse," as Franklin had planned in his letter to Livingston, the three sketches portrayed Minerva standing beside the infant where she defended him with a weapon. Equally important, although the original proposal's two serpents represented the sole suggestion of a threat from Britain, the sketches included an additional threat:

a leopard prepared to pounce on the child, who was preoccupied with strangling the serpents. Suggesting that only Minerva's forceful intervention could thwart the leopard's attack, the added visual element transformed the image of France from passive nurse into an active protector. By doing so, the sketches visualized the nature of French generosity to the United States, implicitly expressed gratitude for it, and embodied an appeal concerning the respective roles of France and America in the war. The consistent modifications to the design in the sketches were probably not accidental. Perhaps Franklin initiated these changes when he arranged for the artists to prepare sketches, since they were common to all three drawings. Alternatively, one artist could have prepared an initial sketch with the changes and the subsequent sketches could have been influenced by that preliminary drawing.

The changes violated the familiar plot of the classical myth, perhaps reflecting a calculated strategy on Franklin's part. He had described the French to Livingston in the letter in which he had proposed the medal: "This is really a generous Nation, fond of Glory and particularly that of protecting the Oppress'd." The depiction in the medal may have been intended to play to that French attribute. Moreover, the modifications reflected his convictions about the way the United States was most likely to secure foreign assistance. In the same letter, he had written, "In my Opinion the surest Way to obtain liberal Aid from others, is vigourously to help ourselves. People fear assisting the Negligent, the Indolent and the Careless, lest the Aids they afford should be lost."[30] Consistent with this, the infant Hercules defended himself from the serpents to illustrate the United States's efforts on its own behalf. In this light, the depiction flattered the French and asserted the character of the new nation.

The tactics underlying the visual appeals were reflected by the differences among the three sketches, which indicated some options that Franklin considered for *Libertas Americana*. For example, although all three sketches depicted the infant Hercules in a cradle, in keeping both with Franklin's proposal to Livingston and with classical mythology, the sketch by Gibelin depicted the infant Hercules in a conventional crib (fig. 6.3), while both of Dupré's sketches placed the infant in a military shield that served as his cradle (figs. 6.4 and 6.5). A brief pamphlet commissioned by Franklin in 1783 and a subsequent broadside produced by Jean-Baptiste Bradel in 1784 associated the image of the military shield with the classical theme in Theocritus's *Idyll* (24.4). The pamphlet and the broadside both explain that "The United States are represented by the infant Hercules, rising from his military shield which in Theocritus served as his cradle." While either type of cradle would have suggested the youthfulness and vulnerability of the victim, Franklin probably selected the shield to highlight the military nature of the commemorated event and to project the character of the emerging nation.

Gibelin followed Franklin's suggestion that Minerva carry a spear in his sketch (fig. 6.3), as did Dupré in one of his sketches (fig. 6.5). In another, Dupré considered depicting Minerva with a sword (fig. 6.4). Perhaps Franklin ultimately chose the spear, because it was Minerva's conventional weapon. Furthermore, the spear implied that France was able to guard the United States, but not slay the snakes herself, because a spear was less suitable than a sword for killing snakes. More important, the sketches portrayed Minerva holding the spear in different positions, which conveyed distinct visual messages. Gibelin depicted Minerva with the spear upraised over her shoulder and pointed down toward the leopard. In contrast, Dupré depicted the spear at her waist level, although still aimed at the leopard. Franklin probably selected the lower placement to underscore the defensive role of France as protector of Hercules, rather than as an independent attacker of Britain, since such a position for the spear suggested that it could be employed to intercept the leopard's pounce. He may also have selected the lower placement for the technical reason that the whole design could be executed in a somewhat larger size. The upraised spear in Gibelin's sketch would have required foreshortening the spear or reducing the entire design, which was to be executed within a circle that had Minerva near the perimeter.

Finally, the varied position of the leopard's tail in the sketches suggested the attitude of Britain. The leopard's tail was between its legs in sketches by both artists (figs. 6.3 and 6.5), although Dupré considered drawing the tail upward in one of his sketches (fig. 6.4). Franklin probably selected the image of the leopard with its tail between its legs to suggest cowardice. Other features of the composition reinforced implications of cowardice: the leopard prepared to pounce on an unarmed child, who was distracted by a different threat from the serpents. The visual appeal contrasted the dishonor of Britain as cowardly leopard with the honor of France as divine protectress.[31]

To the design for the medal Franklin added a motto that William Jones had suggested to him: *"NON SINE DIIS ANIMOSUS INFANS"* (Not without divine help is the child courageous).[32] Jones was a lawyer, a scholar, and a brilliant linguist who codified and explained the legal system in India.[33] The motto amplified the alterations in the narrative action to highlight French assistance. In a letter on March 17, 1783, Franklin thanked Jones for contributing the motto and reminded him that he had proposed the medal "before the Peace." This comment noted the timeliness of the medal's conception earlier in 1782 and eliminated any impression that he sought to perpetuate wartime values after the peace settlement. He added, "None are yet struck in hard Metal, but will be in a few Days: In the meantime . . . I send you one of the *Epreuves*."[34] Presumably, he secured Jones' suggestion for the motto during 1782, while he was in Passy, a visit that had inspired speculation in British newspapers about peace negotiations.[35]

Franklin's correspondence on March 26, 1783 from Robert de Cotte indicated the number of medals that he ordered for the initial distribution: "2 gold, 20 silver, and 20 bronze." Robert de Cotte was probably a member of the family of Jules-François de Cotte, who for over a decade had been the director and controller of the "Mint for Medals at the Louvre."[36] French laws required that all coins, jettons (tokens used for calculating prices), and medals in the country be produced by this institution, or risk confiscation.[37] But Franklin must have subsequently ordered many more than the original forty-two medals, to judge from the extensive distribution that he later detailed. Robert de Cotte also identified Dupré's role in preparing the medals, by remarking that Dupré had asked de Cotte to write to Franklin about the progress made in preparing "not only the medals that you want to have at this moment, but also the very large number that you need. The 2 of gold, 20 of silver, and 20 of bronze, that you have requested, will tomorrow be in a state ready for the person whom you may charge with securing them from the hands of S. Roger," the principal commissioner of the Mint for Medals.[38]

The description of the distribution alone would indicate that several more medals were eventually struck at the mint, identified in William Temple Franklin's correspondence with Caleb Whitefoord as the "Mint for Medals at the Louvre." Benjamin Franklin's letter to Livingston on April 15, 1783, for example, included a shipment of two medals—one silver and one copper. A month later, George Fox, who routinely shipped materials to the United States, wrote to William Temple Franklin on May 15, 1783, about a shipment of medals. Fox remarked, "Traveling here hath entirely destroyed the paper which contained the Medals addressed to the Secretary for Foreign affairs & made some havock amongst my Linen—but I have repapered them in number fifty & hope that they will reach their address." On September 16, 1783, Boudinot wrote to Livingston about another shipment of "several more" medals that Franklin had "sent by Capt. Barney," yet another shipper. In a letter to Boudinot on September 13, 1783, Franklin mentioned, "Since the two first which you mention as received, I have sent by different Opportunities so many as that every Member of Congress might have One."[39] In 1783, there were ninety-six members of Congress, including the president.

Franklin subsequently commissioned a four-page pamphlet in parallel French and English texts to explain the significance of the medal, a document mentioned in several contemporaneous letters as "The Explanation." Abbé André Morellet's unsigned note to Franklin has established Morellet's authorship "of the text or at least the French translation" for the written explanation.[40] Franklin had known Morellet for just over a decade, having met the writer and political economist during 1772.[41] In the note on March 31, 1783, Abbé Morellet assured Franklin that he had followed his wishes by emphasizing the timeliness of the medal during the war. The explanation did not announce "your liberty, your political existence as entirely and completely established but simply *the events designated in the medal.*"[42] This note and Franklin's remark to William Jones suggested that Franklin was concerned about the timeliness of the medal. To judge from the date of Morellet's note and the reference in it to Franklin's upcoming journey to Versailles, he probably secured the translation in preparation for the formal presentation of the two gold medals to the king and queen in early April.[43]

Franklin's written plans for the medal made no reference to the image of the woman's head representing Liberty; later, however, he alluded with evident pride to the "countenance of my *Liberty*" in a letter referring to the medal on October 5, 1783, to Thomas Brand Hollis.[44] At the time of the medal's production, Morellet's "Explication de la Médaille Frappée par les Américains en 1782" commented on the meanings of the Liberty's head, as Franklin may have envisioned the significance of the image, since the French explanation was prepared at his request. According to this text, "The head represents American Liberty with her hair flowing behind her to show that she is in action; and her ordinary emblem, the bonnet on the tip of a spear. At the base of the image one sees the date of July 4, 1776, the day when the United States declared their independence." Innumerable references had been made to liberty as the central objective of the American Revolution, an objective embodied on the medal by the image of a beautiful woman.

Although the image of the United States as an infant Hercules in his cradle did not originate with Franklin, the application of such imagery to the victories at Yorktown and Saratoga was inventive. He may have been aware that some early colonists had used an image of the infant Hercules to represent British America, as in Cotton Mather's *Magnalia Christi Americana*, a copy of which Franklin had owned and read, having written notes in red crayon inside the back cover of his copy. Alluding to the Native Americans as the serpents, Mather commented, "The Infant Colonies of *New England* finding themselves necessitated unto the *Crushing of Serpents*, while they were but yet in the *Cradle*, Unanimously resolved, that with the Assistance of Heaven they would root this *Nest of Serpents* out of the World."[45] British parliamentarians had also evoked the image of the infant Hercules to describe the colonies, as in Temple Luttrell's comments during a debate over American policy in 1775. Luttrell had inquired, "What has been the fate of your famous Bills passed in the last session of the deceased parliament? I mean, Sir, the Boston Port Bill, and the Bill for altering the charter of Massachusett's Bay. America, as an earnest of her triumph over the future labours for which envy and malice may reserve her, has, like another Hercules in the cradle, already grappled with those two serpents sent for her destruction."[46] Earlier references to the classical myth suggested that it provided a typology within which recent events could be organized and understood by those who recognized the allusion. Such strategic uses of the classical myth in rhetorical appeals were not unusual in the evocation of typologies during the eighteenth century.[47]

The Distribution and Reception of *Libertas Americana*

Libertas Americana became especially well known in the centers of political power in France and the United States. During the spring and summer of 1783, some recipients commented on *Libertas Americana* in ways that disclosed the patterns of distribution and reception of the medal in the United States and France. These comments by Franklin's contemporaries are invaluable in a rhetorical analysis and interpretation of the medal, because they provide evidence of how the diverse recipients' interests and values influenced their interpretations of the design. Their remarks suggested that the timing of the medal led some recipients to interpret the design differently than Franklin had originally planned. For example, instead of regarding the medal primarily as a commemoration of the past military victories at Yorktown and Saratoga, some commentators in France viewed it in connection with the future peace settlement and as a sign of Franklin's confident anticipation of a final victory.

More important, the recipients' comments suggested that the medal functioned in the following ways: it praised the United States and France in those two countries; it influenced a political policy in Malta while serving additional diplomatic uses in Holland, Germany and Spain; and it vindicated Franklin from a published criticism of his character in England. The uses to which he put the medal, the diverse points of view of the recipients, and the salient circumstances of the moment had an impact on the rhetorical functions of the design. *Libertas Americana* functioned as ceremonial, deliberative, and apologetic messages for the recipients from different countries, who interpreted the allegory in light of their own circumstances. The visual allegory between the international struggle and the classical mythology allowed flexibility in how the recipients interpreted the images. The next section of this chapter begins first with the distribution and reproductions of the medal in France, then turns to its distribution in the United States, and, finally, its use internationally in diplomacy with Malta, Holland, Spain, Italy, Germany, and Britain, noticing how recipients and other partisans made the medal meaningful in a variety of ways, to judge from their comments concerning it.

Distribution of Libertas Americana in France

In France, Franklin used *Libertas Americana* as an expression of gratitude to praise the national character of France and, thereby, strengthen the diplomatic relations of the United States. On April 8, 1783, he presented the commemorative medal to King Louis XVI, an event noted by the *Gazette de Leide* (as the *Nouvelles extraordinaires de divers endroits* was commonly known) on April 18, the *Gazette des Deux-Ponts* on April 19, and the *Courrier de l'Europe* on April 22. The first and last of these papers reported under a dateline from "Paris, April 11" and "April 12," that "Last Tuesday, Mr. Franklin, Minister for the United States of America, had the honor of presenting to the king a medal that the Commissioners of the Congress have had struck here, on the occasion of their country's independence. This medal, which will transmit throughout the centuries the events of the most remarkable revolution in the history of humankind, is exactly the one that we had announced in an earlier edition of this newspaper."[48] In addition, Franklin distributed silver medals to "each of the Ministers" in the French court. Each presentation of the medal to a French leader enacted American gratitude to France, even as it expressed pleasure in the achievements of the international alliance.

Franklin sought to make the design of *Libertas Americana* known, not only to the most privileged and powerful figures, but also to the people of France. He did this through the explanation prepared by Morellet, which Franklin later had published, and through published newspaper accounts of the design and its presentation. Perhaps the earliest of the newspaper accounts was a notice in the *Gazette des Deux-Ponts* on March 4, 1783. The newspaper reported, "Doctor Franklin has had struck at Paris a medal representing on one side America with the emblem of Liberty & the inscription: *libertas Americana*; on the other side is an infant who endeavors to crush two seprents in the presence of a furious leopard & under the protection of a beautiful woman whose mantle is replete with lilies." This description was not exact in that it misplaced the lilies on the mantle, not the shield, and asserted that the infant "crushes" rather than "strangles" the serpents. The account also omitted the names for the classical figures, probably because the design was not consistent with the narrative in the classical myth. Subsequently, this newspaper eventually carried at least two more notices about *Libertas Americana*, another on March 11, 1783, describing the designs on the medal more completely and accurately, and yet another article on April 19, 1783, reporting on Franklin's presentation of the medal to King Louis XVI.[49]

A full month before this formal presentation of the medal, even weeks before any had been struck in hard metal, the *Gazette des Deux-Ponts* and the *Gazette de Leide* carried similar descriptions of its design on the same day, March 11, 1783. The *Gazette de Leide* reported:

> If ever an event has merited remembrance with a durable monument, it is doubtless the war in *America* and the recognition of *Independence* that has resulted from it. As a consequence, Mr. *Franklin* has had struck here [in Paris] a Medal about these great events. It represents *Hercules* in a cradle strangling two serpents: A leopard, surprised by his strength, wants to pounce upon the child. The animal is repelled by *France*, who, under the figure of *Minerva*, protects the child with her shield, decorated with three fleurs-de-lis. At the base are the dates 1777. & 1781. denoting the years of the capitulations of the Armies of *Burgoyne* and of *Cornwallis*, represented by the two serpents. On the reverse [obverse] is Liberty, under the emblem of a beautiful woman, and in the exergue: *Libertas Americana*.[50]

The article in the *Gazette des Deux-Ponts* was somewhat longer than this, referring "to the creation of an independent Republic on this [American] Continent," misspelling Cornwallis's name as "Cornouallis," and recalling its earlier account of the medal. On March 14, the *Courrier d'Avignon* reprinted this description of the medal's design under a dateline, "Paris, March 4," suggesting that there was yet another earlier source for the article.[51] On March 15, 1783, *The Journal politique de Bruxelles*, which, despite its title, was published in Paris, did likewise, having only recently been reunited with the *Mercure de France*.[52] This article was somewhat shorter, omitting as it did the line about Liberty being represented as a woman. Subsequently, the article describing the medal was reprinted yet again in the April 1–15, 1783, edition of *Journal politique, ou gazette des gazettes*, perhaps better known as the *Journal de Bouillon*, and in the *Affiches Américaines* on May 21, 1783.[53]

Ultimately these descriptions and the newspaper accounts of the presentation to the king were translated for printed notices throughout Europe, Britain, and the United States. The Swiss *Journal historique et politique de*

Genève reprinted it on March 15, 1783, under the dateline "Paris, March 11," and the *Courrier de l'Europe*, published in London and Bologna, reproduced it on March 18, 1783, under the earlier dateline "Paris, March 4."[54] In Britain, the description of the design was published in the March 13–15 edition of the *London Chronicle*, the March 15 editions of the *Morning Herald* and the *Morning Chronicle*, and the March issue of *Gentleman's Magazine*.[55] In the United States, republished accounts appeared in various American newspapers, including the *Maryland Journal* for May 23, 1783, under a dateline headed "LONDON, March 6," and the *Virginia Gazette* for May 31, 1783, headed "LONDON, March 1," which claimed dubiously that the excerpted letter was dated two days later on the third of March from Paris.[56] Such datelines suggested an even more extensive distribution of the article in British outlets than the few newspaper titles mentioned here.

The articles in the European newspapers made the design of the medal widely known among the French people even before the medals had been struck at the mint, or, for that matter, before Franklin had formally presented it to the king and queen. In fact, during late March and early April, he received requests from diplomats who had read newspaper accounts of the design and who wanted to be remembered with one of the medals. From The Hague, Charles-Guillaume-Frédéric Dumas, for example, wrote to Franklin on March 14, 1783, "I saw with pleasure the description of a medal, which, according to the newspapers, you have had struck in Paris. *The infant Hercules* strangling some *serpents*." Dumas evidently wanted one of the medals so intently that he also wrote to John Adams on March 18, 1783, to request one of them, indicating that he did so in response to request from a die sinker in Amsterdam.[57] Perhaps Dumas was signaling his willingness to help distribute the design's imagery since a "die sinker" was a mechanic who cut dies for producing medals. Franklin received another request for a medal from Mr. Luigi de Pio, the "Chargé des Affaires" from the court of Naples, who was the secretary of the Neapolitan legation in Paris. He wrote to Franklin on March 20, 1783, "Mr. de Pio is so bold as to ask Mr. Franklin if the new medal that he has recently had struck here for the Republic is already finished and if Mr. de Pio will be happy about being able to have one." That Franklin responded to this request is evident from de Pio's letter of April 20, 1783, indicating that he "has received with the greatest possible pleasure the medal, which Mr. Franklin was generous enough to give to him."[58]

After the actual presentation of *Libertas Americana* to King Louis XVI on April 8, 1783, numerous additional newspaper articles throughout Europe, Britain, and the United States mentioned the medal. In France, another series of such articles about *Libertas Americana* was published with only minor variations in the *Gazette de Leide* on April 18, the *Gazette des Deux-Ponts* on April 19, and the *Courrier d'Avignon* on April 22, 1783. In other parts of Europe, articles about this event appeared in such newspapers as the *Suite des nouvelles d'Amsterdam* on April 18 and *Courrier de l'Europe* on April 22, 1783. In Britain, a translated account of the presentation was published in the April 22–24, 1783, edition of the *London Chronicle*. In the United States, more of these accounts were reprinted, appearing in the *Pennsylvania Journal* for June 18, 1783, and the *New-Jersey Gazette* for June 25, 1783, both of which represented the article as an "Extract of a letter from Paris, April 13." As for noteworthy differences among all of these accounts, some mentioned having published earlier an account of the design for *Libertas Americana*, and some represented the article as an extract of a letter, instead of printing it under a dateline from Paris. No account mentioned that Franklin also presented a medal to the queen.[59]

During April 1783, Franklin was inundated with notes of thanks from various French ministers who acknowledged receiving the medal. Minister of War Philippe-Henri, marquis de Ségur, wrote to him on April 11, remarking that he "had receive the medal that Mr. Franklin had given him the honor of sending to him."[60] Franklin also distributed the medal to additional ministers who served prominently in the French court during the American Revolution, including the minister of finance, Jean-François Joly de Fleury, and the minister of the interior, Antoine-Jean Amelot de Chaillou, who was the royal secretary for household affairs. Both of these men wrote notes of thanks to Franklin in mid-April.[61] Joly de Fleury had recently resigned his position in the French ministry, and Amelot did likewise later during 1783. To judge from this pattern of distribution to these secretaries of state who were also members of one or another of the four councils of the king, which included the Council of State, the Council of Finances, the Council of Dispatches, and the Council of Commerce,[62] it is highly probable that Franklin presented a medal to Charles-Eugène-Gabriel de La Croix, marquis de Castries, who was the minister of the Navy, though he does not appear to have acknowledged receiving a medal by sending a note of thanks to Franklin.[63] Nor, apparently did another probable recipient, Vergenne, the powerful minister of foreign affairs who had been named president of the Council of Finances in February 1783.[64]

Franklin gave additional medals to military leaders who had served at Yorktown, such as the French admiral, François-Joseph-Paul, comte de Grasse.[65] He wrote effusively to Franklin on April 13, "I am very pleased that my services

for American liberty have merited the flattering testimony that your republic has had the goodness to honor me with one of the medals that you had
the kindness to send me by an envoy." He added, "I take pride in having formed
and executed the project for the conquest of Yorktown that has decided the
independence of a people so worthy of being governed by their own laws and
who have so publicly expressed their gratitude to the king."[66] Likewise, Franklin would almost certainly have provided a medal to Jean-Baptiste-Donatien
de Vimeur, comte de Rochambeau, and George Washington, whose leadership at Yorktown was vital and who, like comte de Grasse, signed the articles
of capitulation at Yorktown, though de Grassi's signature was by a delegated
representative.[67]

Within the military, Franklin also presented a medal to Yves-Marie Desmaretz, comte de Maillebois, who was a "Lieutenant General of the Armies
of his Majesty and Chevalier of his Orders," an officer in the Order of Saint-
Esprit, and a member of the Royal Academy of Sciences. The comte de
Maillebois, who referred to Franklin as "my dear colleague," thanked him in a
letter on May 15, 1783, for a *Libertas Americana* medal. Maillebois wrote,
"You know that I have always held in my heart the glory of the Congress, and
the success of my respectable colleague and friend."[68] Commissioner of War
Palteau de Veimerange, who served in the military under the marquis de
Ségur, wrote on April 13, 1783, to thank Franklin for having given him one of
the *Libertas Americana* medals.[69] To judge from Franklin's correspondence
with him, Palteau de Veimerange was heavily involved in the shipment of
military supplies to America.[70] Others involved in financing the war asked for
medals from Franklin, as did vicomte de la Houssaye, the principal treasurer
of the war in the province of Brittany, who wrote to Franklin from Rennes
on May 1, 1783, to request one.[71]

Marianne Camasse, who represented herself as the Countess Forbach,
"duchesse douairière du duc de Deux-Ponts" (even though she was not of royal
blood), wrote a letter to Franklin on April 13, thanking him for the medal that
he had sent to her, evidently in recognition of the military contributions of
her sons.[72] Her sons, Christian and William, both fought with the regiment of
Deux-Ponts at Yorktown, a battle in which William was injured. An official
account of the military maneuvering at Yorktown, which was published on
November 20, 1781, as a lengthy "Supplement" to the *Gazette de France*,
reported that William had been "slightly wounded" by a "discharge from a
canon" during the battle.[73] William was honored with the "cross of Saint-Louis"
on December 5, 1781.[74] Additional medals were conveyed to her through
Agathon Guynement, chevalier de Kéralio, who "had been her children's tutor

and now functioned as her 'private secretary,' a title vague enough to cover a multitude of occupations."[75]

Chevalier Agathon de Kéralio was also an inspector of the military school in France, a position that he resigned during May 1783.[76] Writing from the Royal Military School on April 18, the chevalier de Kéralio also thanked Franklin for remembering him with "the ingenious medal that eternalizes your glory and that of your country."[77] Later, during May, Kéralio secured additional medals through William Temple Franklin, one of which was for display in "the Library of the Royal Military School."[78] Yet another medal conveyed by Kéralio was for Jean-Baptiste-César, marquis de Timbrune, who for a decade had served as the governor of the Royal Military School.[79] Kéralio conveyed yet another medal to Louise-Francis, baron de Moyria, who was a Lieutenant-Colonel of the Cavalry and the Captain in Command of the Company of Gentlemen Cadets at the Military School.[80] A member of the baron de Moyria's family, Joseph-Marie-Anne de Moyria, had been "dangerously wounded" during the battles at Yorktown and was honored by the king with the "cross of Saint-Louis" on December 5, 1781. *Histoire de l'ordre royal et militaire de Saint-Louis* indicated that he died from the injuries later that year, but two other accounts detailed the subsequent developments in the injured man's military career.[81] Still later, during July 1783, Kéralio requested yet another medal from Franklin to replace the one that the duchess had given to a man identified as "Mr. de Vauban," probably Jacques-Anne-Joseph Le Prestre, comte de Vauban, who had served at Yorktown.[82]

Yet additional medals of *Libertas Americana* were presented to Claude-Gabriel, marquis de Choisy, and a Pierre-François, chevalier de Béville, who replied together with a note of thanks to Franklin on April 28, 1783.[83] De Choisy had served in the infantry as a brigadier under Rochambeau at Yorktown, performing exemplary military service that was noted when he became camp marshall on December 5, 1781, and commander in 1784.[84] Both of the official accounts of the military victory at Yorktown—one written by comte de Grasse and another by Rochambeau that were published together in a ten-page supplement of the *Gazette de France* for November 20, 1781—had mentioned de Choisy's role at Glochester near Yorktown.[85] Evidently, de Béville's military service was of comparable importance, because he, too, became a camp marshall during December as a consequence of his performance at Yorktown, as mentioned in Rochambeau's *Mémoires*. Rochambeau commented that the king recognized several of the military leaders in the combat at Yorktown, identifying by name the specific ranks of both de Choisy and de Béville among several others, including also "le marquis de Deux-Ponts," who became a brigadier in recognition of his service.[86] These same factors would have explained Franklin's presentation of *Libertas Americana* to Barnabé-Eugène, comte de Messey, because he, too, was recognized as a camp marshall in 1781 as a consequence of his service in the cavalry. He thanked Franklin in a long and effusive undated letter presumably written during 1783.[87]

The *Libertas Americana* medal appears to have been cherished and coveted among military figures in France. Guy-Claude, comte de Sarsfield, a French officer of Irish origins whom Franklin had known since 1767 in London,[88] cautioned him in a letter of May 4, 1783, that "some of the general officers of our navy who were at the Chesapeake Bay when Cornwallis was defeated are proposing to visit you to request a medal." Evidently, distribution of the medal entailed the risk of slighting those who did not receive one, however unintended. He suggested that Franklin avert this scenario by making a gift of the medals to the officers. The comte de Sarsfield not only suggested providing a medal to "M. Le Chev[alier] de Monteil, but also the others who follow him."[89] François-Aymar, chevalier de Monteil, had been one of the commanders of the Naval Service since 1781, had served in America during August and September 1781 under comte de Grasse and was listed among the "Grand Cross, Commanders, and Officers" of the Royal and Military Order of Saint-Louis.[90] Evidently, Franklin heeded the advice, because chevalier de Monteil, who had become a "Lieutenant-General" of the navy only recently on March 11, wrote to him on May 23, 1783, to thank him for his attention.[91]

Another note of thanks combined appreciation for the gift of a *Libertas Americana* medal with a request for further recognition. On January 2, 1784, Jacques-Dominique de Cassini fils, who was an astronomer and a fellow member of the Royal Academy of Sciences, wrote to Franklin to comment that the medal for his brother-in-law, "vicomte de Mory," was to him "the most precious reward for his military service" in America.[92] After alluding to "five campaigns, four sieges, a naval combat and two wounds" experienced by the brother-in-law, the son of Jacques-Dominique de Cassini added a request that the man be considered for membership in the Society of the Cincinnati. André-Jérôme de la Mire, vicomte de Mory, who had been wounded in 1779 at Savannah during his military service in America, eventually did become a member of the society.[93] Other members of this organization who had received a *Libertas Americana* medal from Franklin included Pierre-François, chevalier de Béville, Claude-Gabriel, marquis de Choisy, François-Joseph-Paul, comte de Grasse, François-Aymar, chevalier de Monteil, and, probably, Charles-Eugène-Gabriel, marquis de Castries, Joseph-Marie-Anne de Moyria (whose father had received the medal via Kéralio) and Jacques-Anne-Joseph Le Prestre, comte de Vauban.[94]

Members of various French institutions requested *Libertas Americana* medals from Franklin on behalf of their academies and museums. There appears to have been a socially awkward moment resulting from the expectation that Franklin would present such French institutions with the *Libertas Americana* medals, as suggested in the comte de Sarsfield's correspondence with Franklin on May 4, 1783. Sarsfield apologized to him for "an indiscretion in asking you in front of Mr. De Brecquigny if you have sent a medal to his academy."[95] Sarsfield was probably referring to Louis-George-Oudart Feudrix de Bréquigny, who had been a member of the Academy of Inscriptions and Belles-Lettres since 1759 and a member of the French academy since 1772.[96] That Franklin provided a medal of *Libertas Americana* only as an afterthought to this academy may be inferred from a letter later that summer from the institution's recently chosen perpetual secretary, Bon-Joseph, baron Dacier. On June 6, 1783, he wrote with two other members, Désormeaux and Desaultx, in their role of "deputies" of the Academy to thank Franklin for the medal. Dacier added his regret that it had not been inscribed with the name of the "author" for the "most beautiful revolution in modern times."[97] Evidently, this letter to Franklin was prepared on the same day that the academy received the medal from him, as evidence by the formal, handwritten *Assemblées et délibérations de l'Académie Royale, 1783–84*. An entry for June 6 mentioned, "M. Dacier presented on the behalf of Mr. Franklin a Medal struck by the order of the Congress of the United States on the occasion of the liberty of America," an entry inaccurately attributing the production of the medal to a Congressional order.[98]

Active and honorary members of the Royal Academy of Sciences whom Franklin remembered with a *Libertas Americana* medal included Antoine-Jean Amelot de Chaillou, who had served as president of the Academy in 1779, Louis-Alexandre, duc de La Rochefoucauld, Jean-Baptiste Le Roy, and Yves-Marie Desmarets, comte de Maillebois.[99] The son of Jean-Dominique de Cassini, who had written on behalf of his brother-in-law's membership in the Society of the Cincinnati, was likewise a member of the Academy. Jean-Baptiste Le Roy, who was a famous scientist in his own day, a historian for the Royal Academy of Architecture, and one of Franklin's friends, wrote during April 1783 to thank him for one of the medals.[100] Le Roy alluded to himself as "a member of the club of the beautiful medal that you have given." He added that he was sensible of "so flattering a favor" on Franklin's part. Then Le Roy turned to the idea, evidently conveyed to him by William Temple Franklin, that "M. Priestley" be elected to the prestigious Academy to replace "M. Hunter" following his anticipated death.[101] On February 26, 1784, Joseph Priestly was admitted to the Academy as an "Associated Foreigner," but as a replacement for "de Wargentin," who had died.[102] Le Roy was also a member of the Academy of Inscriptions and Belles-Lettres, yet another basis for his having received *Libertas Americana*.[103] In short, Franklin's distribution of *Libertas Americana* included several members in these two of the five academies that constituted the French Academy.

In some cases, Franklin remembered various French and Italian writers with one of the *Libertas Americana* medals. Louis-Alexandre, duc de La Rochefoucault, who was engaged in translating *Constitutions of the United States* into French for Franklin under the title *Constitutions des Treize Etats-Unis de l'Amérique*, wrote on April 12, 1783, to express his gratitude for the "beautiful medal."[104] On April 11, Joseph Bartoli, an Italian writer who was residing at the time in Paris, wrote likewise to thank Franklin for a *Libertas Americana* medal "before the time of its distribution." Bartoli was an antiquarian and a member of the Royal Academy of Inscriptions and Belles-Lettres. He exclaimed that "the subject, the inventiveness, the execution of the medal, all merit an encomium." Evidently, this was precisely what Bartoli supplied, to judge from an allusion in his letter to a verse that he had written about the "glorious monument," a verse about which more will be said later.[105] Franklin also presented one of the medals to a famous lawyer, author, and friend of Voltaire: Jean-Baptiste-Jacques Elie de Beaumont, who was respected for his familiarity with British and French legal systems. He referred to the gift in his letter to Franklin on April 14, 1783, as "a monument for the greatest event" of the period.[106]

Requests for one of the *Libertas Americana* medals were not limited to diplomats like Luigi de Pio, judging from the numerous pieces of correspondence that people across France sent to Franklin. Even before Franklin had presented the medal to the king and queen of France, Jean-André Mongez, who identified himself as the author of an agricultural dictionary, the *Cours d'Agriculture*, as well as a journal of physics, requested a medal from Franklin in a letter on April 1, 1783. Mongez probably sought this medal for his brother, Antoine, who was a curator at the Cabinet de Médailles and a member of the Academy of Inscriptions and Belles-Lettres. Jean-André Mongez described the medal as "a sign of the union between the states of America and France."[107] The same day, writing from Versailles, Brother Félix Nogaret asked for a medal, and, like Dumas, de Pio, and Mongez, he made his request before Franklin had presented the medal to the king.[108] Nogaret, who appears to have written some literature, had been among the "Secretaries of the King" since 1774.[109]

During May, Jean-Baptiste Artaud, who identified himself as the "author of the *Courrier d'Avignon*," wrote likewise to Franklin to request a medal out of recognition for the role that he claimed for his writings during the American Revolution. On May 10, Artaud remarked that, through his writings, he "had celebrated your country's conquest of liberty," but that the Congress had neglected him.[110] Franklin does not appear to have replied to Artaud's request. Yet another author, Michel-Guillaume Saint John de Crèvecoeur, whose *Letters from an American Farmer* had been published in 1782, wrote to Franklin to mention, "I forgot the other day to Inquire of you where I cou'd [could] procure Two of your Medals which I have Imprudentely promised in Normandy —after Fruitless Inquiries, I find myself obliged to ask you that Question."[111] Crèvecoeur had dined with Franklin and the comtesse Elisabeth-Françoise-Sophie de la Live de Bellegarde d'Houdetôt during March 1782, four months after which Crèvecoeur had sent Franklin a copy of his pamphlet.[112] It was through comtesse d'Houdetôt that Franklin had met Crèvecoeur, whose letters to Franklin regularly mentioned her.[113] A shipper, George Fox, requested a medal, too, in his letter on May 15, 1783, to William Temple Franklin. After mentioning how the shipment of the medals had affected the paper used to wrap them, he added, "If perchance you should have one of them to spare to a Friend I flatter myself that you will favor me with it."[114] Quite a bit of such maneuvering to secure a medal involved William Temple Franklin.[115]

Franklin employed a Parisian printer, Philippe-Denis Pierres, to print a four-page pamphlet that explained the images on *Libertas Americana* in parallel French and English texts. (Vergennes had recently authorized Pierres to prepare and publish the French translation of the *Constitutions of the United States*.)[116] There hundred pamphlets were delivered to Franklin on May 5, 1783.[117] They were probably prepared so that he could use them to influence interpretations of the medal. Even though Morellet had drafted the handwritten explanation or, at least, the French translation of it, earlier during March, Franklin probably had an explanation printed to respond tactfully to a general concern expressed later by the comte de Beaujeu, who had been honored with a medal in recognition of his service on the seas. Like many other recipients, he was named a chevalier de Saint-Louis in 1781.[118] In a letter of April 18, 1783, he thanked Franklin for sending one of the medals "by courier," observed that "this monument interests all of Europe and eternalizes the glory of America," but added, frankly, that it was not possible to respond to the letter accompanying it, "because I do not know English."[119]

On March 19, 1783, the author of *Mémoires secrets pour servir à l'histoire de la république des lettres en France, ou journal d'un observateur* referred to *Libertas Americana*. These comments framed the production of the medal primarily in the context of the future peace settlement in 1783, not the past military victories, even though the description noted the internal references to the dates of the victories at Yorktown and Saratoga: "Now that independence, already secured *de facto* by the United States, is legally confirmed by the peace treaty, Mr. Franklin has had a medal made commemorating this great event."[120] Because of recent changes in the political circumstances—the coalition ministry of Lord Frederick North and Charles James Fox had replaced Lord William Fitzmaurice, earl of Shelburne's ministry in Britain, and the final peace settlement had become imminent, though not with terms as favorable as those Shelburne had been willing to accommodate[121]—*Mémoires secrets* gave the commemorative use of *Libertas Americana* a more generalized meaning than the one Franklin had noted in his original proposal. These comments attributed to Franklin foresight and confidence about the war's outcome: by implication, he had undertaken preparations for the medal in anticipation of the peace agreement; however, Franklin's plans for the medal made no mention of such an agreement.

The April 1783 *Correspondance littéraire, philosophique et critique* of Friedrich Malchior Grimm and Denis Diderot contained an entry referring to *Libertas Americana*, further evidence that the medal was widely known in France. This description suggested that, at least in some French circles, the execution of the design for the infant Hercules was not as highly regarded as Franklin claimed later in correspondence with Elias Boudinot, the president of the U.S. Congress. *Correspondance littéraire, philosophique et critique* observed: "The execution of the opposite side *('revers')* is mediocre; but the sole fault, no doubt, that one could find with the motto is of being too beautiful; it is drawn from the Ode of Horace to Calliope, Book III, Ode 4." Even so, the commentary praised the beauty of the woman symbolizing Liberty on the medal's obverse: "This medal represents the bust of a very beautiful head, of pure features, frank and vigorous in expression, her hair in the wind and the liberty cap surmounted on a lance carried on her right shoulder." Some members of the French audience regarded the aesthetic merits of the medal as a sign of the value to be attached to the expression of gratitude.[122]

During April 1783, the design for *Libertas Americana* became the central image for a poem by an Italian writer, Bartoli, who was in Paris at the time. He, too, associated the medal with the peace settlement, as indicated by the title in French, "Description of the Medal about the Independence of America on the Occasion of the Peace."[123] A relatively immediate response to the design, this poem was further evidence that the timing of the medal shaped interpretations in Europe. Although the poem was in French with attention to rhyme, the ideas may be translated:

Cornwallis, Burgoyne, at the feet of America
Carry with them the fate of Albion [Britain].
Let's celebrate forever the Union of the States,
The heroic valor of an infant Empire.
Depict, O Bronze, animated by the aid of the Arts,
The majestic independence of the wise American.
That with her free embellishment, with her disheveled hair
She announces the ardor, glory, and assurance.
That from the grand Jupiter the new offspring
Strangles two Serpents, the game of your youth.
A shield must serve, Alcides [Hercules], as your cradle,
And as your guardian God, either Athena, or France.
May she display her Lily, arm herself with a spear,
Opposing her shield to the ardent leopard.
Franklin spoke. His voice, which to the heavens soars,
Commands successfully to Nature, to the Arts.

Bartoli's poem amplified the imagery of the infant Hercules representing the new nation, "an empire born in heroic valor," while the allusions to the "fate of Albion" amplified the losses to Britain resulting from the successful revolution of the American colonies.

Several months later, on August 1, 1783, Coquillot, the prior of Epinay, also wrote a verse to Franklin titled "Ode 5" with the introductory note, "To his Excellency Mr. B. Franklin Ambassador for the United States on receiving a medal from him struck by the Americans in 1782."[124] Consisting of fourteen stanzas of seven lines each, these verses were written in rhyming French, which, when combined with allusions to military leaders and events in ancient Greece, created a highly contrived, convoluted expression of regard for the peace and for Franklin's role in achieving it. The ideas in a few stanzas about the medal's design suggested how the medal was interpreted in the months following its distribution. The first stanza focused upon "Liberty":

What do I see? O sacred Liberty!
Divinity cherished by Mortals,
Everywhere worthy of their altars,
Without being everywhere adored,
You reign then on the Thirteen States,
Where the beginning of the Days of Jupiter's daughter
    [Astrée; i.e., celebrity]
Follows the horrors of battles?

After alluding to the image of the woman representing Liberty as a goddess, later stanzas situated the versifier's own sentiments in relationship to the image of the infant Hercules on the other side of *Libertas Americana:*

> Emblem of magnanimous hearts
> I admire this infant Hercules,
> Who represents a People being born
> Of Heroes and of Sublime Spirits:
> Already two tortuous Serpents,
> Seized by him, are the victims
> Of his impetuous courage.
>
> But, who covers him with a Shield
> Embossed with a burst of Lilies?
> Is it Minerva? Ah! It is Louis;
> The friend, the Benefactor of Alcides,
> Who, with a piercing Spear,
> Stops the murderous ardor
> Of the ravenous Leopard.

Beyond commenting on *Libertas Americana*'s imagery, the poem framed the medal's visual narrative in ways that amplified the significance of the creation of the United States. Referring to Franklin, perhaps, the poem continued,

> Thus triumphs the Minister
> Who touched the heart of a great King,
> And managed to get him to take up Arms in his favor
> Against the most sinister Fate.

Later verses compared the birth of the American empire with the birth of Rome, Carthage, and Athens, city-states that subsequently became powerful empires. Still later verses compared the victories over Britain at Yorktown, Saratoga, and Trenton with those by the Athenian general Miltiades over the Persians at Marathon. The penultimate stanza focused upon Franklin,

> . . . whose wisdom
> Never exerted itself in vain,
> Friend of the Gods, you, whose hand
> Guides their Vengeful Blows;
> Light of our days! Oh You,
> Whose Genius, with skill,
> Parried the blows of a People-King.

6.7. "Explication de la Médaille Frappée par les Américains en 1782," Jean-Baptiste Bradel, Paris, circa 1784. Medium: engraved broadside; size, 13 5/16" × 9 3/4". Photograph courtesy of the American Philosophical Society.

The final lines invoked clichés about knowledge and light dispelling darkness and then called upon the readers to "Revel, with us, in the Peace."

One year after the formal presentation, the design for *Libertas Americana* was reproduced at the top of a broadside in French titled "Explanation of the Medal Struck by the Americans in 1782" (fig. 6.7), engraved and distributed by Jean-Baptiste Bradel.[125] Whether Franklin employed Bradel to design this broadside is not known, although an early type of the Franklin coat of arms was inserted at the bottom of the broadside and the French text was identical—except for typographical changes—to the explanation in his commissioned pamphlet.[126] This broadside was advertised for general sale in *Affiches, Annonces, et Avis Divers* as early as April 15, 1784.[127] Focusing on the peace settlement, the broadside framed the engraved reproduction of *Libertas Americana* to generalize the commemorative purposes of the medal.

Beneath the engraved design of both sides of *Libertas Americana* was an explanation that described the medallion as an expression of the United States's gratitude to France, even though Franklin had received neither a formal Congressional endorsement nor financial support for the medal's production. "This medal is destined to be an enduring monument of the designated events, at the same time that it is a recognition from the United States of their grand and generous benefactor." The explanation amplified France's contributions: "Minerva, armed with a shield decorated with the arms of France, comes to his aid, & characterizes the generous protection that the king has given to America." The entire explanation on Bradel's broadside was inscribed within the fur hide of a leopard, the remnant of the aggressive animal that represented Britain. This framing of the medal indicated the conclusion of the narrative depicted in *Libertas Americana:* the hide of the leopard was a trophy to dramatize a victory perfected by the enemy's death. Franklin's use of the allegory, selecting as he did a climactic moment in the classical myth, allowed the recipients to participate in constructing the message by completing the narrative action.

Moreover, the design on the medal was integrated in a textile pattern by Jean-Baptiste Hüet, a member of the Academy of Painting and Sculpture, for mass reproduction on fabric produced at Oberkampf's famous cotton factory in Jouy, where it was probably produced in the mid-1780s (fig. 6.8).[128] Sometimes called "La Liberté Américaine," the fabric bearing the *Libertas Americana* design was produced sometime after June 19, 1783, because that was when the king granted the factory at Jouy its status as the "Royal Manufacturer," a phrase that the factory imprinted in French on the border of this textile.[129] The *toiles de Jouy*, as the imprinted cotton fabrics were known, were at the height of their popularity both in America and Europe, where there were

6.8. "[*Libertas Americana* im-printed textile]," Jean-Baptiste Hüet, Jouy, France, circa 1784. Medium: textile (printed can-vas). Photograph courtesy of the Musée nationale de la Coopéra-tion Franco-Américaine à Blérancourt, France and the Réunion des Musées Nationaux Art Resource, New York. Inven-tory MNB CFA 207.

strong markets for it.[130] These fabrics were highly regulated by French law and, because of their political import and economic ramifications, had been pro-hibited altogether in France between 1686 and 1759.[131] In addition, textile industry representatives sent letters to Franklin early in 1783 that expressed strong interest in accessing the U.S. market, possibly an underlying factor in the production of the pattern at Jouy.[132] Evidently, an interest in producing a textile version of the design extended beyond France to the Austrian Nether-lands, because "de Coch" may have had a role in arranging for another fabric version of the design. On March 17, 1783, he wrote from Brussels to Franklin that "the subject of the ingenious medal which you have had struck will not be less impressive on fabric than in Bronze."[133]

Eventually, the design of the infant Hercules was reproduced on a large terra cotta plaque, sometimes attributed to Claude Michel Clodion, now held by the Musée nationale de la Coopération Franco-Américaine à Blérancourt (fig. 6.9). This plaque was probably completed in the terra cotta factory that was managed by Jean-Baptiste (Giovanni-Battista) Nini, an Italian, and owned by Jacques-Donatien Le Ray de Chaumont, the well-known host of Franklin during his nine-year stay at Passy.[134] In 1777 and again in 1779, Nini had

6.9. "[*Libertas Americana*—allegory of the American Revolution]," Claude Michel Clodion, France, circa 1783. Medium: terra cotta; size: 14 ½" diameter. Photograph courtesy of the Musée nationale de la Coopération Franco-Américaine à Blérancourt, France and the Réunion des Musées nationaux Art Resource, New York. Photograph by Gérard Blot. Inventory MNB 49C2.

produced at least two portraits of Franklin in this medium, one without a cap and another with a fur hat identifying him with Rousseau.[135] Because of distribution to prominent political, military, and diplomatic figures at the French court; reproduction on an almanac, terra cotta, and textiles; and descriptions of its design in numerous newspapers, *Libertas Americana* gained widespread visibility within France and beyond.

Yet, during 1783 in France, complaints about elements in the design on *Libertas America* were employed to highlight criticism of the situation at the war's conclusion. For example, in Linguet's *Annales politiques, civiles, et littéraires,* a publication prohibited by the French government,[136] an article about the situation facing the American Loyalists in the United States alluded to the "cradle" as "bloody" and "drenched in tears."[137] To the author, the terms concluding the war had been severe in the treatment of the American Loyalists. Subsequently, in another article devoted to the American paper currency and the amount of the Congress's public debt, Linguet again alluded to imagery from *Libertas Americana*, complaining that "for an infant state" it would have been "difficult to have a more expensive cradle."[138]

Distribution of Libertas Americana *in the United States*

In addition to distributing *Libertas Americana* in France for the diplomatic purposes of commemorating the military victories and of expressing the United States's gratitude, Franklin also sought to influence an American audience with the medal. His April 15, 1783, letter to Livingston specified the most politically significant recipients of *Libertas Americana* and intimated the symbolic significance of the material—copper, silver, or gold—from which each medal was made: "I have caused to be struck here the Medal which I formerly mentioned to you, the Design of which you seem'd to approve. I inclose one of them in Silver for the President of Congress, and one in Copper for yourself: The Impression in Copper is thought to appear best; and you will soon receive a Number for the Members. I have presented one to the King and another to the Queen[,] both in Gold, and one in silver to each of the Ministers, as a monumental Acknowledgement, which may go down to future Ages, of the Obligations we are under to this Nation. It is mighty well received, and gives general Pleasure."[139] Because gold was reserved by convention for medals presented to kings and queens, silver was appropriate for the president's medal.[140] More important, this letter suggested that Franklin's plans for the medal were more complex than a simple matter of commemorating the military accomplishments at Yorktown and Saratoga. He wanted to remind Americans of their obligations to France for the military, economic, and diplomatic assistance. By doing so, he hoped to make Americans grateful for that assistance. He suggested that the Congress could express that appreciation officially by endorsing the medal so that he could include a reference to the U.S. Congress on subsequent copies. As Gerald Stourzh has observed in his description of Franklin's general strategy of diplomacy at this time, Franklin fostered "'The essential interests of our reputation' . . . as a substitute for material power."[141]

On June 18, 1783, the president of the U.S. Congress, Elias Boudinot, wrote to Franklin about the medal: "Your Letter to Mr. Livingston of the 15th April enclosing the two Medals, came to hand this Morning. . . . I feel myself much indebted for your polite Compliment of the Medal; it is thought very elegant and the device and workmanship much admired. You will be pleased Sir to accept my acknowledgement on this Occasion[.] As I doubt not but the Copper one was designed for Mr. Livingston personnally, I shall send it to him by the first Convenient Opportunity. He is a worthy deserving Character and the

United States will suffer greatly by his Resignation, tho' I think him justified in attending to the calls of his private Affairs."[142] Franklin's letter to Livingston had tactfully remarked that the copper medal seemed to look better than the silver one, perhaps to offer Livingston an aesthetic compensation for the differences in the economic value of the medals. Unfortunately for Franklin, the letter apparently reached Congress after the secretary's formal resignation; thus, it was received and read by Boudinot, the president of the Congress himself, whom Franklin had designated as the recipient of the silver medal. Nonetheless, Boudinot's response was gracious.

Franklin responded on September 13, 1783, to Boudinot's letter: "I am happy that both the Device and Workmanship of the Medal are approv'd with you, as they have the good Fortune to be by the best Judges on this Side the Water. It has been esteem'd a well-timed as well as a well-merited Compliment here, and has had good Effects." He added, "Since the two first which you mention as received, I have sent by different Opportunities so many as that every Member of Congress might have One. I hope they are come safe to hand by this time."[143] Franklin endeavored to reinforce the general aesthetic and pragmatic merits of the medal as a diplomatic act, perhaps to enhance his own image as a skilled diplomat whose timely compliment had strengthened the United States's relationship with France. He sought also to ensure that every member of Congress would receive one of the commemorative medallions, perhaps to help them realize the United States's obligations to France, and to enhance his reputation in the Congress, where he had been criticized sharply in letters from John Adams for inactivity and for excessive deference to France.

Elias Boudinot's correspondence confirmed that he had distributed the medals to major political figures in the United States, among them Robert R. Livingston. On September 16, 1783, while Boudinot was presiding over the Congress in Princeton, New Jersey, he wrote a letter to Livingston. There were two slightly different versions of this letter, each of which provided information about the distribution of the medal. In one version, Boudinot remarked, "I take the opportunity of sending the Medal, I have twice mentioned to you. I recd. with the public Letters 19 or 20 of them which I distributed among the States."[144] The other version of this letter specified that Boudinot enclosed the medal "with the Explanation," mentioned that his two earlier remarks about the medal had been made "in two of my former Letters," and commented that Franklin had sent "several more" by a shipment through "Capt. [Joshua] Barney."[145] Later, on September 27, 1783, Boudinot forwarded an additional medal to Livingston, "I wrote you lately pr Post & enclosed a Medal recd from Dr Franklin. I add another herein."[146] A month later, on November 1, Boudinot described the distribution of the medals in a letter to Franklin: "I have received the additional number of Medals, which, not having any particular directions from you, I distributed among the Members of Congress —presented one to the Governor of each State, and the Ministers round Congress."[147] On December 26, 1783, Franklin acknowledged receiving this letter from Boudinot, but without further comment about the medals. By distributing the medals, Boudinot had complied with Franklin's requests and helped him to reach those Americans whom he sought to influence with the medal.

On September 29, 1783, Livingston wrote to Boudinot to acknowledge receiving the medal. He then articulated several sources of discontent about the design and commented generally that the medal "does not please me as much as the first design," by which he meant Franklin's written description. Livingston complained that "Hercules & the serpents which should have been principal figures are too diminutive" and that "the great contest seems to be between Minerva & her antagonist." To Livingston, Hercules and the serpents were so small in comparison that they "only serve as contrastable auxileries." He noted "an important error in the history of this revolution," namely that the design "keeps out of sight what we should most pride ourselves upon that the first serpent was strangled before France had armed in our defence & when our infant Hercules received nothing more from her than now & then a spoonful of pap." To Livingston, the condensation of historic time in the pictorial narrative was flawed because it implied a debt of gratitude at a time when none was due. At the time of Saratoga, France had seemed to ignore American requests for aid, providing only enough covert financial support to sustain a nuisance to Britain. Livingston worried, "By the bye, I am fearful that the serpent will continue to be our emblem." He concluded, "I pray your Excellency to transmit me so much of Dr. Franklin's Letter to me as relates to the Meddal as it will be necessary I suppose to return some answer, in my private character."[148]

Livingston does not appear to have followed through on his plans, as remarked to Boudinot, even though Boudinot's later letter to Livingston assured him that a copy of Franklin's letter was forthcoming.[149] Nor does Livingston appear to have ever responded to Franklin's explicit request in a letter on July 22, 1783, for an opinion of the medal. Franklin had written, "I send you herewith a few more of the abovementioned Medals which have given great Satisfaction to this Court and Nation. I should be glad to know how they are liked with you."[150] In contrast with Livingston's complaint that the "serpents" were "too diminutive," a Frenchman, Brongniart, had worried during the production that the serpents were "too large and too typical."

None of the governors or members of Congress ever wrote to Franklin to acknowledge receiving the medal, much less thank him for it, to judge from Franklin's extant papers. Whether this specific silence resulted from the press of demands upon the American politicians' time, a feeling that the president had responded on their behalf, or their tacit agreement with criticism that Franklin was "too French" is speculation, though there is ample contemporaneous evidence of a general concern in America about Franklin's attitudes toward France.[151] In an entry in his diary, William Dunlap recorded a Congressman's criticism of the medal's design. On November 30, 1797, almost a decade after Franklin had died, Dunlap wrote that he had dined "with Dr Jedediah Morse." Dunlap noted that Morse "read to me a letter from a Member of Congress in 1782 giving an Acct. of a Medal which Dr Franklin had had struck at Paris & 2 impressions of which he had sent to Congress for their approbation, on which he had represented France as Minerva, shielding America, a helpless infant in the Cradle, from England, a Lion." Evidently, the writer of the letter did not recognize the infant as Hercules, nor mention the serpents—factors that support the probability that this was a different criticism than Livingston's letter to Boudinot; Livingston, whose letter mentioned both the infant as Hercules and the serpents, was no longer active in Congress when he wrote his criticism. The entry continued, "The writer reprobates the design & the designer." Dunlap added, "Morse likewise read to me letters, (I believe from Mr [John] Adams in 1783) from Holland, in which the designs of France at that period are exposed as inimical to us & Franklin represented as the Dupe of that court."[152]

John Adams's well-known conflicts with Franklin had surfaced in numerous earlier contexts, one of which Franklin himself reported on August 9, 1780, to Congress concerning the United States's gratitude to France. After mentioning that Vergenne himself had asked Franklin to forward copies of Adams's correspondence offending the French court, Franklin commented that Adams "thinks as he tells me himself, that America has been too free in Expressions of Gratitude to France; for that she is more obliged to us than we to her; and that we should shew Spirit in our Applications." Franklin observed, "I apprehend that he mistakes his Ground, and that this Court is to be treated with Decency & Delicacy." With regard to the United States's gratitude to France, Franklin amplified, "The King, a young and virtuous Prince, has, I am persuaded, a Pleasure in reflecting on the generous Benevolence of the Action, in assisting an oppress'd People, and proposes it as a Part of the Glory of his

Reign: I think it right to encrease this Pleasure by our thankful Acknowledge-
ments; and that such an Expression of Gratitude is not only our Duty but
our Interest."[153] This earlier conflict between Adams and Franklin over gratitude foreshadowed a deep divide years later, when Franklin's appreciation of
France's assistance left him vulnerable to being considered too French. Yet, in
1780, Franklin was in a position to add, "I cannot but imagine that he mistakes the Sentiments of a few for a general Opinion." Franklin then alluded
to a recent letter in which the Congress had expressed its gratitude for the
king's "unremitted Attention to the Interests of these United States."[154]

The silence of the American politicians in response to *Libertas Americana*
must have seemed deafening to Franklin in France, juxtaposed as it was with
the effusive responses from the ministry there. Years later, on September 16,
1789, Franklin sent in a letter to James Logan a copper copy of *Libertas Americana* and two other medals for "our Public Library," presumably the Logan-
ian Library, which was held in public trust and later annexed to the Library
Company of Philadelphia.[155] Thus, just as he had done for various French institutions, Franklin provided a medal to an American library, which he also happened to serve as a trustee. In this letter, he described the distribution of the
medal and commented that he intended it "partly as a grateful Compliment
to France for the Assistance afforded us; and partly to record the two great
Events of the Taking of Burgoyne & Cornwallis with their Armies." He added,
"I presented one of these in Gold to the King & another to the Queen, which
were extremely well taken. I distributed also a Number of Silver ones among
the Ministry, and the Officers of the French Army that had served in America." Although Franklin reiterated this information about the distribution in
France, he made no mention whatsoever of any American distribution of *Libertas Americana*. He also contrasted it, a medal "struck by me," with another
medal for M. Fleury, "struck by Order of Congress."[156]

Perhaps the candid response of Livingston to Boudinot and the diary entry
of William Dunlap revealed the underlying reasons explaining why Congress
never officially sanctioned *Libertas Americana*, even though Franklin had requested that the Congress do so and had hoped the medal would remind
these powerful Americans of their obligations to France. Evidently, he regarded
the rhetorical functions of the medal as so important to the diplomacy of the
Revolution that he was prepared to finance the production of *Libertas Americana* himself as the plenipotentiary ambassador; Congress never funded or
endorsed the project. Although American politicians may have held private
concerns about the medal, various American newspaper accounts of 1783
—such as those appearing in the *Maryland Journal* for May 23, the *Virginia*

Gazette for May 31, the *Pennsylvania Journal* for June 18, and the *New-Jersey Gazette* for June 25—would have made the medal well known throughout the United States.[157]

Distribution of Libertas Americana *in International Diplomacy*

During the spring of 1783, about the same time that he distributed originals of *Libertas Americana* to powerful leaders in France and the United States, Franklin used the medal to influence government policy in Malta by presenting it to Emmanuel de Rohan, Grand Master of the Order of Saint John of Jerusalem and the ruler of Malta. To promote a diplomatic policy in the island country that would benefit the United States, Franklin enclosed a medal with his written request that the government protect American citizens and their property in the ports of Malta. On April 6, 1783, Franklin wrote to Emmanuel de Rohan, "I have the honor of addressing to your Eminent Highness a medal, which I have recently had stuck. It is, your Highness, a homage of gratitude, which is due to the interest that you have taken in our cause, and we no less owe it to your virtues and to your Eminent Highness's wise administration of government." He then broached his request, "Permit me, your Highness, to ask your protection for those of our citizens that circumstances may lead to your ports. I hope that your Highness will be pleased to grant it to them."[158] Although the medal was a gift to the ruler of Malta in appreciation for his past assistance, the design on the medal depicted the alliance between the United States and France, not Malta. Perhaps in addition to ensuring the safety of American citizens and property in Malta, Franklin sought to remind the ruler that the most powerful nation on the western European continent had established an alliance with the United States and that Malta's best interest might lie in doing the same.

On June 21, 1783, Emmanuel de Rohan responded to the gift and the request by Franklin: "I received with the most lively sensibility the medal which your Excellency sent me, and the value I set upon this acquisition leaves my gratitude unbounded. This monument of American liberty, an event which your Excellence has had the glory of preparing and conducting, has a distinguished place in my cabinet." He responded positively to Franklin's concerns about safety, "Whenever chance or commerce shall lead any of your fellow-citizens or their vessels into the ports of my island, I will receive them with the greatest welcome. They shall experience from me every assistance they may claim, and I shall observe with infinite pleasure any growing connection between that interesting nation and my subjects."[159] Emmanuel de Rohan's allusion to commerce underscored an economic rationale for improving diplomatic relations as well. Because the United States's navy was too weak to protect American merchants in the area, Malta's cooperation was consequential for American commerce. To judge from Grand Master de Rohan's response, the medal enhanced diplomatic relations by generating gratitude for the present from Franklin and by placing an image of American liberty before the ruler's eyes. As a result, Franklin obtained a formal government policy that he had requested from the ruler of Malta.

Franklin also presented the commemorative medal to various ambassadors, envoys, and "chargé des affairs" representing foreign nations at the French court, including, for example, those from the United Provinces, Denmark, and the Court of Naples in Italy. On April 29, 1783, Gerard Van de Brantsen, who was the Extraordinary Ambassador from the United Provinces designated to work on the preliminaries for the peace, wrote to Franklin to thank him for a *Libertas Americana* medal.[160] The following day, on April 30, Baron Otto de Blôme, "Extraordinary Envoy of the King of Denmark," wrote likewise to Franklin to acknowledge a gift of a *Libertas Americana* medal. In his letter, de Blôme mentioned that he was writing on behalf of "M. le Baron de Rosencrone," who was the minister for foreign affairs from Denmark.[161] The medal that Franklin presented to Luigi de Pio in response to his request for one would have been warranted by his role as a representative from the Court of Naples in France.[173] Evidently, Franklin presented the commemorative medal to these various representatives in his role as an international diplomat.

This pattern indicates that Franklin may have distributed the medal even more widely among national leaders from various countries. But the extent of this international distribution is difficult to ascertain, because some recipients may not have replied with notes of thanks, others did so only after a lapse of time, and, on occasion, Franklin distributed the medals through intermediaries. In a letter of January 17, 1786, for example, Peter P. Burdett, "Major of the Guards and Chief Engineer" for the Prince of Baden, mentioned receiving a gift of the medal toward "the latter end of last year," along with a copy of *Constitutions des Treize Etats-Unis de L'Amérique*. After mentioning that these gifts had been conveyed to him by an intermediary, Burdett commented, "If these articles were ment [meant] as presents from Your Excellency to me, I then beg you will be persuaded to believe that I have employed the very first favorable opportunity of returning you Sir my most grateful thanks." About the design of the medal, Burdett commented, "The device on the reverse of this Medal is as strong & flattering to the Arms of France as it is humiliating & disgraceful to those of England." He added a note that looked to the future, writing, "How far the allusion may bear a resemblance to truth, the annals of time are left to unfould, confirm & record."[163]

Other Americans in Europe recognized the value of the *Libertas Americana* medal for diplomacy. William Carmichael wrote to William Temple Franklin from Madrid on November 26, 1783, "I wish to have some copies of the Constitutions of the States translated into French & published at Paris as also some of the Medals struck to commemorate the era of our Independance [Independence], because I have been sollicited for the one & the other by people of high Consideration here." Carmichael added, "There are things which I presume ought to be furnished by the Public to public Servants to be employed for public purposes." Subsequently, in a letter of January 15, 1784, Carmichael wrote directly to Benjamin Franklin to request "the French Translation of our Constitutions" so that he could present it "in your name" in the court of Spain.[164] He framed his request in the context of having been presented with "two Spanish productions" from the head of the "Council of Castile" to be conveyed to Franklin.

At the time of the peace negotiations, Franklin may even have presented the *Libertas Americana* medal to a member of the British delegation in Paris, Caleb Whitefoord, who served as secretary for the delegation. Whitefoord had been chosen for this role because was a close friend of Franklin's, having been a neighbor on Craven Street in London. A wine merchant, he also had supplied Franklin with rum and Madeira.[165] On April 26, 1783, Whitefoord wrote to William Temple Franklin to thank him "for the medal which was inclosed in your Letter," but added that he wished "to have an order for some in *Silver* & Copper, as the man at the Mint tells me, he wont give me any without it." Having left Paris for London on April 27, 1783, Whitefoord subsequently wrote from London to William Temple Franklin on May 9, 1783. Whitefoord affirmed, "On the Eve of my Departure from Paris I had the pleasure to receive your Letter, with the Medal & c for which I thank you." This gift appears to have blended the Franklin family's personal friendship for Whitefoord with a political courtesy in the interest of international diplomacy.[166]

Moreover, Franklin used *Libertas Americana* to enhance his own reputation in the United States as an able diplomat and, more important, to strengthen the reputation of the United States abroad. In his letters to the president of the Congress and to the secretary of foreign affairs, he portrayed himself as having employed the medal to improve the United States's diplomatic relations with Malta and with France. Franklin sent the one of these letters to Secretary Robert R. Livingston on July 22, 1783: "I made the Grand Master of Malta a Present of one of our Medals in Silver writing to him a Letter of which I enclose a Copy; and I believe our People will be kindly receiv'd in his Ports; but that is not sufficient; and perhaps now [that] we have Peace, it will be proper to send Ministers with suitable Presents to establish a Friendship with the Emperor of Morocco, and the other Barbary States, if possible."[167] Franklin not only informed Livingston of the improved relations between the United States and Malta, he also featured his use of *Libertas Americana* in obtaining those improvements and observed that the medal could be employed to initiate diplomatic relations with nations throughout North Africa, where French influence was especially strong.

Two months later, on September 13, 1783, Franklin wrote to Elias Boudinot. After responding to Boudinot's note of thanks, Franklin added, "I sent before a Copy of the Letter I wrote to the Grand Master of Malta, with a present of our Medal; with this you will have a Copy of his Answer." The president of the Congress read these letters with interest, because after assuring Franklin in his letter of November 1, 1783, that the medals had arrived and been distributed among the powerful leaders in the United States, he added, "The compliment to the Grand Master of Malta, I doubt not, will produce good effects and for which the commercial interest of this Country will be much indebted to you." By writing to the president and the secretary of foreign affairs, Franklin fulfilled his diplomatic responsibility to keep them informed about the nation's foreign relations with Malta. At the same time, he enhanced his own image as a skilled and successful diplomat.[168]

Finally, beyond his efforts to convey American gratitude through the distribution of *Libertas Americana* in various public circumstances, Franklin used the medal to further his own diplomatic efforts toward friends and foes. A primary example is his attempt to vindicate himself in England from some of the criticism that *The Memoirs of Thomas Hollis* had leveled at his character and conduct. The *Memoirs* had included Hollis's letter depicting Franklin as "a Trimmer" during the Stamp Act controversy, making the private assessment of Franklin a public document. The publication of this criticism created a circumstance in which the medal functioned as an apologia in the broad sense of an explanation or vindication of his conduct. On October 5, 1783, Franklin commented on Hollis's *Memoirs* in a letter to the son, Thomas Brand Hollis, who had presented a copy of the book to Franklin. "I find besides, in perusing these Memoirs, that I was a doubtful Character with him." Franklin assured Hollis, "I do not respect him less for his Error; and I am obliged to the Editors for the Justice they have done me." Franklin gave the medal to Hollis's son as a sign of his own continuing good will toward the family, a sign that could ease the rather delicate circumstance created by the deceased Hollis's writings. Furthermore, the design on the medal constituted proof of Franklin's commitment to America and, consequently, protected his character from Hollis's accusation. An expression of gratitude became transfigured into a sign of loyalty, patriotism, and good will.[169]

In reply, Thomas Brand Hollis wrote to Franklin on June 21, 1784, "It is some time since I received from you a medal to commemorate the glorious events of the Independency of America & the total subjugation of their enemies[,] events which I rejoice at as I have always detested and abhorred the principle of enslaving mankind and depriving them of the rights of human nature, under any pretence whatsoever." Hollis continued, "The medal I esteem on all accounts a great honor from the donor, it is a most valuable addition to my friends collection of Liberty coins as he used to call his cabinet." Referring to the design on the medal and responding to Franklin's pride in the countenance of Liberty, Hollis amplified, "The head of your Liberty would have pleased him. It is simple & noble the execution is good but I could have wished the names & dates of your victories had been wrote in capitals & also the date of your independence that every part might be intelligible." He pointed out, though, that "There is a mistake in the word *Juil* which might yet be altered." In Hollis's letter, he highlighted the achievements of the United States, by adding, "The three noble Subjects united in your medal claim each a distinct medal and had I the honor to be an American it should be done, for never in the Annals of mankind such events have had such glorious consequences. The divine rights of human nature are declared & established against all the Arts of Priests & Tyrants & there is now an Asylum for the injured & oppressed." Turning later in the letter to the concern posed by publication of the *Memoirs*, Hollis explained that "candor to the publick obliged the compilors of the Memoirs not to conceal any sentiment of my late friends." Attempting to explain his late father's stance toward Franklin, Hollis wrote, "His anxiety for the publick weal made him suspicious of Characters eminently great but which by their strenuous exertions have demonstrated to the world how much they are superior to detraction."[170] The exchange of letters between the two men was a model of grace.

Beyond this use of the medal to counter published criticism, Franklin gave *Libertas Americana* to some friends and family members. Jan Ingenhousz, a friend, physician, and a fellow scientist who was residing in Vienna, had written to Franklin on April 29, 1783. After reporting on an experiment, he mentioned, "I see in the papers that a medal has been struck in Paris by your direction." Perhaps as a hint, he added, "None of them have yet arrived here." Subsequently, on May 16, 1783, Franklin sent a medal to Ingenhousz, who served as the imperial physician to Emperor Joseph II and Empress Maria Theresa. On August 15, Ingenhousz wrote to thank Franklin for "the medal, which was much and justly admired."[171] As in the instance of Whitefoord, the gift may have blended friendship with diplomacy.

Franklin conveyed yet another medal, possibly *Libertas Americana* though probably another medal with his profile on it, such as the Franklin Medal, sometime before May 23, 1785, to George Whatley in London. Whatley was the author of *The Laws and Policies of England Relating to Trade* (1765). Franklin had contributed ideas in lengthy notes to the second edition in 1774, with a much revised title. In a reply on July 22, 1785, Whatley remarked, "Your said Present of your Medallion, I Shall ever prize; & it will ever be present before me. Not that I want it to serve as a Remembrancer: for your Friendship is too deeply impressed in my Mind."[172] After returning to Philadelphia, Franklin sent a medal on June 1, 1788, to the Reverend Doctor Mather Byles, who had been a preacher at the Hollis Street Congregational Church in Boston and who had recommended him many years earlier for what Franklin referred to in the letter as "my first Academical Honours." Byles remained in Boston throughout the American Revolution, a Loyalist who sympathized with the Crown and who prayed for America's defeat. (Somewhat ironically, he was a descendant of Cotton Mather, whose writings may have been a source of the imagery on the medal.) Whether Byles ever saw the medal Franklin sent is uncertain, because he passed away the same year.[173]

While he was still in Paris, Franklin gave *Libertas Americana* to his grandson and namesake, Benjamin Franklin Bache. Writing from Geneva on March 30, 1783, the grandson mentioned, "I heard . . . that you have made medals for the Liberty of my Dear Country." He requested three of them: "One for Mr. Marignac, an other for Johonnot and an other for me." Gabriel-Louis Galissard de Marignac was the young Bache's tutor, and Samuel Cooper Johonnot was his playmate and schoolmate in Geneva. On May 2, Franklin replied with a letter to his grandson by sending one requested medal. On May 30, 1783, the young Bache wrote to thank him for it.[174]

After returning to the United States, Franklin remembered an additional member of his family with *Libertas Americana*. When Franklin wrote from Philadelphia to his sister, Jane Mecom, on September 4, 1786, he enclosed "three Medals," including "One that I struck to commemorate our two important Victories, and in honour of France for the Assistance she afforded us." In addition, Franklin enclosed "The other two struck as Compliments to your Brother, One by the Lodge of the Nine Sisters, of which he was President, the other by a private Friend."[175] Because the Nine Sisters had struck two

6.10. "The Infant Hercules," [Thomas Rowlandson], London, February 3, 1784.
Publisher: W. [William] Humphrey; medium: engraved print with colored and
uncolored versions; size: 7 13/16" × 12 3/4". Photograph courtesy of the British
Museum, Department of Prints and Drawings.

different medals depicting Franklin—one in 1778 and the other in 1783—the
letter may have enclosed either of them. But the latter medal "by a private
Friend" had been struck by Augustin Dupré in 1784.[176] In Jane Mecom's letter on September 13, 1786, she replied to the gift. After first mentioning the
safe arrival of her "grandson" at Boston with the "3. Medals," she commented,
"Your Device in the first is very Striking, the others are very Pritty." She added,
"Multitudes that have a disposition to shew you Respect, has no other means
than an Honest Acknolidgement of yr Vertues and Servises."[177] Subsequently,
in a letter written on May 22, 1787, Mecom alluded to having received "The
Explanation for the Medal" and thanked Franklin for it.[178]

Once the medal became well known in the major centers of power, the
design was even more widely described and reproduced in Britain and Europe.
On February 3, 1784, William Humphrey published a print titled "The Infant
Hercules" (fig. 6.10), attributed to Thomas Rowlandson. Instead of the two
defeated armies, the serpents represented two British ministers, Fox and North,
to depict their political demise as a consequence of the peace treaty of 1783.
During 1784 in Germany, an engraved image of *Libertas Americana* was reproduced by D. Berger in Matthias Christian Sprengel's *Allgemeines historisches
Taschenbuch*, in which the medal illustrated a German history of the American Revolution (fig. 6.11).[179] Published at Berlin by Charles Spener, the book's
inclusion of these designs may have resulted from Hilliard d'Auberteuil's
request to Franklin in a letter on April 12, 1783. Hilliard d'Auberteuil, whose

6.11. "[*Libertas Americana* and the Continental Currency]," by D. Berger in
Matthias Christian Sprengel's *Allgemeines historisches Taschenbuch* (Berlin: Haude
and Spener, 1784). Medium: book illustration, mixed method; size: 4 ¼" × 4 ½".
Photograph courtesy of the Rare Books Division and the Prints and
Photographs Division of the Library of Congress.

own book, *Essais Historiques & Politiques,* had only recently been published,
had included a list of French officers who had served in the American army.[180]
He wrote, "I would like to have the designs for the medals struck by Congressional order and those for the mausoleums erected by your care." He explained, "Mr. Charles Spener, Bookseller of the King of Prussia, wrote to me
to request a copy of the designs" for an almanac "commemorating the glorious revolution."[181] Subsequently, writing from Berlin on May 26, 1783, Spener
himself directed a letter to Franklin outlining the plans for an almanac, listing
the specific designs that Spener was seeking for it, and sketching Mr. Sprengel's credentials as a history professor familiar with the English language.[182]
Eventually, in 1784, the designs for the obverse and reverse of the *Libertas
Americana* medal were engraved beside each other, above the designs for both
sides of the Continental Dollar, the first metal money coined by the United

States with a version of "WE ARE ONE" on it. As a consequence of the distribution of the medal itself and the representations of it in pamphlets,
broadsides, textiles, terra cotta, poetry, and book illustrations, the image of
Libertas Americana became internationally recognized as an expression of the
United States's gratitude to France.

Long after the conclusion of the American Revolution, allusions to the
United States as an infant Hercules recurred in the political discourse of the
period. For example, Fisher Ames, the Federalist statesman and publicist who
resided on the outskirts of Boston and who served in the Congress, commented in a letter from New York to William Tudor on April 25, 1789, "The
federal government is not an Hercules, and if it was, it is yet in the cradle, and
might come off second best in a struggle with the serpent." Ames believed
that the federal government was inherently weak. Almost a decade later in
the introduction of *A View of the Causes and Consequences of the American
Revolution* in 1797, Jonathan Boucher, the American Loyalist who had been
a preacher in Maryland and who had moved to Britain in 1775, compared the
outcome of the American Revolution with the result of the French Revolution of the 1790s. Evoking images of both an infant and an adult Hercules,
he remarked, "Heavy to this nation [Britain] was the loss of Thirteen of the
best of her Continental Colonies: but it becomes intolerable to us now only
when, as one of it's consequences, another republic is about to arise at our very
doors; a republic to which that of America can be compared only as an infant
Hercules may be compared with an Hercules at his full growth."[183] The image
of the infant and the adult Hercules became associated with the spread of
republicanism so threatening to supporters of the constitutional monarchy in
Britain.

Throughout this period, Franklin's own image was also widely reproduced
in an immense variety of French popular media; so extensive were the reproductions that they later were made the subject of an exhibit in France.[184]
Franklin's image was reproduced in portraits exemplified by Joseph-Siffrède
Duplessis's well-known painting of him framed by a rattlesnake carved out
of wood (frontispiece), mass-produced textile designs imprinted by copperplate on cotton and linen fabrics used throughout the home (fig. 6.12), as well
as pictorial allegories, such as Antoine Borel and Jean Charles La Vasseur's
"L'Amérique Indépendante" in 1778 (fig. 6.13), Jean-Honoré Fragonard's "Au
Génie de Franklin" in 1778 (fig. 6.14), and an anonymous engraver's "Benjamin Franklin" in 1780, published by H. T. Bligny (fig. 6.15).[185] Augustin
Dupré immortalized his friend's profile on a medallion, "The Franklin Medal"
(fig. 6.16), the reverse for which had the classic motto from Anne-Robert

6.12. "The Apotheosis of George Washington and Benjamin Franklin," Britain, circa 1785–90. Medium: mass-produced textile designs imprinted by copperplate on cotton and linen fabrics used throughout the home, such as window hangings. Photograph courtesy of the Henry Francis du Pont Winterthur Museum.

Turgot's epigram about Franklin's having snatched lightening from the sky and a scepter from the tyrant (fig. 6.17).[186] One of Dupré's preliminary sketches for this medal's reverse featured an adult Hercules as the central figure, standing with his foot on a prostrate crowned figure (fig. 6.18). This sketch would presumably have pleased Livingston had it been used for the design of *Libertas Americana*. But Dupré chose instead a slender, winged male to represent the Genius of Liberty on the "Franklin Medal." This was the medal that Franklin described as having been made by a "private Friend" when he enclosed it with *Libertas Americana* in the letter to his sister, and it may have been the medal that he sent to Whatley.

Referring to the portrait Jean-Baptiste Nini made of him on a clay medallion at Chaumont's factory, Franklin commented in a letter to his daughter, Sarah Bache, on June 3, 1779:

6.13. "L'Amérique Indépendante," Jean Charles La Vasseur's engraving after a drawing by Antoine Borel, Paris, 1778. Medium: line engraving on a broadside; size: 17" × 13 ¾". Photograph courtesy of the American Philosophical Society.

6.14. "Au Génie de Franklin," also known as "Eripuit Coelo Fulmen, Septrumque Tirannis," etching by Marguerite Gérard after a drawing by Jean-Honoré Fragonard, Paris, 1778. The print features Turgot's epigram, "He snatched the lightning from the heavens and the scepter from the tyrants." Medium: etched print, probably an aquatint; size, 19" × 14 ½". Photograph courtesy of the Bibliothèque nationale de France (Paris).

6.15. "BENJAMIN FRANKLIN," under the pseudonym N.L.G.D.L.C.A.D.I., Paris, July 14, 1780. Publisher: H. T. Bligny; medium: line engraving; size, 10 ½" × 8". Photograph courtesy of the American Philosophical Society.

6.16 and 6.17. Obverse and reverse of "The Franklin Medal," Augustin Dupré, environs of Paris, 1784. Medium: silver, bronze or brass medal; size: 1 ¾" diameter. Photograph courtesy of the American Philosophical Society.

6.18. [Preliminary sketch for "The Franklin Medal]," Augustin Dupré, environs of Paris, 1784. Medium: sketch; size: approx. 4 ¾" diameter. Photograph courtesy of the American Philosophical Society.

The clay medallion of me you say you gave to Mr. Hopkinson was the first of the kind made in France. A variety of others have been made since of different sizes; some to be set in lids of snuff boxes, and some so small as to be worn in rings; and the numbers sold are incredible. These, with the pictures, busts, and prints, (of which copies upon copies are spread every where) have made your father's face as well known as that of the moon, so that he durst not do any thing that would oblige him to run away, as his phiz would discover him wherever he should venture to show it. It is said by learned etymologists that the name *Doll*, for the images children play with, is derived from the word IDOL; from the number of *dolls* now made of him, he may be truly said, *in that sense*, to be *i-doll-ized* in this country.[187]

He was not exaggerating. Beneath the wordplay in this letter was his keen sense of the ramifications that pictorial representations of individuals and nations posed for relationships among symbols, self, and society. Throughout his life, Franklin was mindful of the symbolic significance attached to depictions of him in portraiture. It has been said that, as a consequence of his diplomacy and the symbolic significance of his widely reproduced image during the decade, he became a cult figure among the French.[188] In his person, Franklin embodied a powerful symbol.

Conclusion

Franklin's commemorative medal, *Libertas Americana*, illustrated some of the underlying rhetorical functions of an expression of gratitude during the diplomatic phase of the American Revolution. The range of uses to which Franklin put *Libertas Americana* were as diverse as the major audiences to whom he presented it, but in each instance an expression of gratitude was paramount. Franklin gave *Libertas Americana* to the French rulers and citizens as a means of thanking France and acknowledging publicly the United States's debt for its ally's past military, economic, and diplomatic assistance. By expressing gratitude in his public role as *ministre plénipotentiaire*, Franklin sought above all to strengthen the future relationship between the United States and France as a practical matter of national security, recognizing that Britain could attempt to regain her lost lands. Indeed, Franklin's letters repeatedly advised American leaders that maintaining the friendship of France was a vital national interest. With *Libertas Americana*, he offered France symbolic compensation for economic assistance.

As important, by making such a public acknowledgment of his gratitude to France, Franklin intimated to other potential allies in Europe and Africa that the United States possessed a praiseworthy character, one that publicly recognized the sources of its being and that would, insofar as possible, reward those who provided assistance. *Libertas Americana* focused upon gratitude to develop the reputation of the emerging nation in a way that demonstrated its commitment to its allies. Although the United States had few economic or political benefits to bestow at the end of the war—indeed, the nation was burdened with a heavy national debt and was not inclined to play a further role in the European balance of power—the symbolism of *Libertas Americana* suggested the United States had the type of character that could provide commercial and political benefits to allies in the promising future.

Libertas Americana illustrated the role of perspective and circumstance in the rhetorical functions of a visual message. Franklin's letters and the comments by contemporary recipients suggested that nothing inherent in the tangible design for the medal limited it to ceremonial, deliberative, or apologetic uses, as revealed in the public and private distribution of *Libertas Americana*. The meanings of the medal resulted not only from the design, but also from the manner in which Franklin framed the gift's presentation and from the perspectives of those who received a medal. Accordingly, the French could see the medal as praise for their nation's generosity, loyalty to an ally, and beneficent concern for an emerging nation, while the Americans could see the medal as a depiction of their nation's courage, military skill, and youthful potential for greatness. Beyond this, the ruler of Malta could see *Libertas Americana* as an appeal on behalf of policy because the medal portrayed American liberty and the strength of the international alliance between the United States and France, while Thomas Hollis's son could view it as a vindication of Franklin's character from criticism in his father's *Memoirs*. The visual allegory was so loosely structured that it enabled the recipients to participate in completing the appeals of the message.

The timing of the medal's presentation in France was a rhetorical concern to the extent that it shaped the medal's impact. When Franklin made his preliminary plans for the medal in 1782, he sought to commemorate a rare military accomplishment at Yorktown and Saratoga, namely the defeat of two major armies in one war. The passage of time between his proposal in the spring of 1782 and the completion of the medal in the spring of 1783 saw significant changes in the political circumstances of the United States and France: a change of ministry had occurred in Britain and the peace settlement had become imminent. To prevent possible implications that Franklin sought to perpetuate wartime values when he presented *Libertas Americana* to France, he stressed the timeliness of the medal in connection with the past military victories. Yet the published broadsides in France, the title of Bartoli's poem, and the commentary in *Mémoires secrets* redefined the commemorative purposes of the medal so that it was an expression of Franklin's confident anticipation of the peace settlement, not simply a retrospective celebration of military victories. Then, as now, for works of praise or blame the crucial consideration was timeliness.

PART THREE

SEVEN

Interludes and Transformations

Franklin's Verbal Images Representing British America

And when the wolf is determined on a quarrel with the lamb, up stream or down stream 'tis all one; pretences are easily found or made, reason and justice are out of the question.

Franklin, "Reply to Coffee-House Orators," April 1767

Franklin employed an array of verbal metaphors to represent the British colonies in America, especially during the decade of dissent between the Stamp Act controversy of 1765–66 and the Declaration of Independence in 1776. Like other colonists during the eighteenth century, Franklin extensively employed the parent and child analogy to depict the relationship of Britain to the colonies, an analogy that was ubiquitous in Britain and America: The king was the father; England or, more generally, Britain was the mother country; and the colonies were their children.[1] In Franklin's prose, innumerable references to the "mother country" recurred until the U.S. Congress issued the Declaration of Independence in 1776, after which his references diminished so noticeably that they virtually disappeared, except in an occasional reminiscence, in which the image was replaced by allusions to Britain as a stepmother. Sometimes he used other images to represent the colonies, by alluding to them as parts of a "Polypus" (a freshwater polyp now known as a hydra) or by depicting them as the goose that laid golden eggs, a herd of cows, a cat, the classical figure of Antaeus, or even a shattered porcelain vase.

This chapter focuses upon Franklin's verbal representations of British America as a means of identifying shifts and evolutions in his outlook as the imperial crisis deepened and as the United States achieved independence. In the process, it traces the developments in Franklin's verbal imagery depicting a colonial union during major political changes, such as the peace negotiations at the conclusion of the French and Indian War (known in Britain as the Seven Years War), which resulted in the British Empire's acquisition of French Canada. During the decade of dissent from 1765 until 1776, several controversies disrupted imperial relations between the American colonies and Britain:

the Stamp Act in 1765 and 1766, the Townshend Duties in 1767, the Boston Massacre in 1770, and the Intolerable Acts in 1774, to name a few. Examining Franklin's verbal images of British America during the controversies provides a means for reviewing major developments in his representations of the colonies; such an examination also identifies factors contributing to the transformations in his outlook between the production of each of the four major pictorial representations discussed in the preceding chapters.

Although the vast majority of Franklin's verbal images focused upon the mother country in relationship to the colonies understood as her children, Franklin's prose employed other sustained images to designate British America. In 1751, for example, he compared the empire to a "Polypus" in his *Observations concerning the Increase of Mankind, Peopling of Countries, &c.* to convey his vision of an expanding British Empire: "A Nation well regulated is like a Polypus; take away a Limb, its Place is soon supply'd; cut it in two, and each deficient Part shall speedily grow out of the Part remaining. Thus if you have Room and Subsistence enough, as you may by dividing, make ten Polypes out of one, you may of one make ten Nations, equally populous and powerful; or rather, increase a Nation ten fold in Numbers and Strength."[2] The implications of this imagery for imperial politics varied with the location of Franklin's readers. Where British Americans may have welcomed the prospect of an increased population, the settling of new territories, and the creation of numerous nations, the British could have understood him to be insinuating a potentially ominous development.[3] Ordinarily during the eighteenth century, a nation's population was the most dependable indicator of its military strength. But the British had a conflicted position on the increasing population in America. On the one hand, the increase of this population strengthened the British Empire as a whole in its military strength against other nations. But, on the other hand, this increase could also result in the military strength necessary for the American colonies to become independent of Britain. Accordingly, the diverse political interests of American and British audiences influenced understandings of Franklin's images depicting British America.

Franklin commented on the "body politic" in ways that overtly recognized such language was a metaphor for communities. In 1760, for example, he remarked in *The Interest of Great Britain Considered, With Regard to her Colonies:* "The human body and the political differ in this, that the first is limited by nature to a certain stature, which, when attain'd, it cannot, ordinarily, exceed; the other by better government and more prudent police, as well as by change of manners and other circumstances, often takes fresh starts of growth, after being long at a stand; and may add tenfold to the dimensions it had for ages been confined to." In this pamphlet, he then shifted his imagery in the next sentence by using the parent and child analogy for imperial relations to suggest that this, too, differed from human reproduction. "The mother being of full stature, is in a few years equal'd by a growing daughter: but in the case of a mother country and her colonies, it is quite different. The growth of the children tends to encrease the growth of the mother, and so the difference and superiority is longer preserv'd."[4] It was probable, therefore, that Franklin's changing choices of verbal metaphors were rhetorical adaptations to specific audiences and developing circumstances.

Throughout the decade of dissent, the various verbal images Franklin used to represent British America most frequently referred to the colonies as the "children," or "infant states," of the "mother country." On rare occasion, his prose articulated imagery of the colonies as a lower order of animal, especially in letters published over pseudonyms in London newspapers after the passage of the Townshend Duties of 1767. With some regularity, he depicted the colonies as a herd of cows, or, less often, the goose that laid golden eggs, or a cat being preyed upon by an opportunistic eagle representing Britain, or a young lion being mistreated by its foolish master. His writings animalized entire human communities in British America to dramatize and deplore their low stature within the empire, even though this imagery was, in a sense, in keeping with the colonies' subordination to Britain to the extent that humankind's domination over lower orders of animals had a basis in natural and divine law.[5] In these respects, the animal imagery reiterated associations with the colonies that he had expressed through the snake device in his earliest image of a colonial union, "JOIN, or DIE," even though he had in some measure tacitly repudiated these associations in "MAGNA *Britannia*." This pattern indicates that his vision of American community did not develop in a linear progression; rather, it had multiple elements at specific moments.

Beyond this, Franklin assumed various personae during the public debates over imperial policy by writing letters in newspapers over numerous pseudonyms throughout the decade. In these letters, published initially in the major newspapers of London and, on occasion, reprinted in the colonies, he posed, at times, as an Englishman, who was writing ineffectually to rationalize the Parliament's misguided policies. As was more typically the case than the persona of an inept English writer, he assumed the identity of a British American arguing from a concern about the colonists' "rights" in contrast with Parliament's exercise of sheer "power." His writings about "rights" during the decade of dissent, when this feature of his sensibility was pronounced, were not the productions of a mere pragmatist. They manifested the outrage of a man whose dignity and worth as an American were at stake. In some letters, he evoked the names of John Locke and Algernon Sidney, the radical republican who had been executed for his views on government.[6] These published letters, attributed to Franklin with varying degrees of certainty, employed the family imagery of the British Empire for a range of rhetorical ends articulated in often highly satirical and ironic forms. Among the most important of these letters was a series, "The Colonist's Advocate," published in the *Public Advertiser* as eleven letters over two months in 1770. But as the conflict within the British Empire deepened, his pseudonymous letters took on a sharper and darker satiric edge, as in his "Rules by Which a Great Empire May be Reduced to a Small One," which the *Public Advertiser* printed in 1773.

It is useful to distinguish among these types of writing, because they reflected variations and ambivalence in the intensity and frankness of Franklin's views. By attending to these types of prose and the major shifts chronologically in Franklin's verbal imagery representing the British Empire, this chapter follows Franklin through the process of repudiating the colonies' infantilization and subordination by Britain as well as the colonists' complicity with those representations in the interest of "protection," which he recognized as a euphemism for Britain's domination and control over the colonies. Ultimately, he repudiated the mother image of Britain altogether and, with it, the constitutional monarchy as he moved toward images suitable for a new republic.

Franklin's Verbal Imagery before "JOIN, or DIE," 1754

Before Franklin's production of "JOIN, or DIE" in preparation for the Albany Congress in 1754, he had made several references to Britain as the mother country of the colonies, a factor unifying them if only through their mutual ancestry and their subordination to the British Crown. On October 9, 1729, for example, the *Pennsylvania Gazette* affirmed with reference to the colonists of Pennsylvania: "Their happy Mother Country will perhaps observe with Pleasure, that tho' her gallant Cocks and matchless Dogs abate their native Fire and Intrepidity when transported to a Foreign Clime (as the common Notion is) yet her SONS in the remotest Part of the Earth, and even to the third and fourth Descent, still retain that ardent Spirit of Liberty, and that undaunted Courage in the Defence of it, which has in every Age so gloriously distinguished BRITONS and ENGLISHMEN from all the Rest of Mankind."[7] Remarks such as these reflected the pervasive pride that British Americans took in their heritage and status as English subjects in America. Yet the image of the British colonies as a child—an image embedded in the very word "colony"—implied the colonies' subordinated status within the British Empire, regardless of whether the idea of childhood was informed by a patriarchal or a consensual conception of the family.

In Franklin's prose, the image of Britain as the mother country justified an expectation of protection from her in return for the material benefits that her children dutifully supplied to her. On February 16, 1741, for example, Franklin wrote "An Account of the Export of Provisions from Philadelphia," which was published in the *General Magazine, and Historical Chronicle, for all the British Plantations in America* for January 1741. After listing the "Export of Provisions," he editorialized, "The above Account is a Proof of the Fertility of this Province, and of the great Plenty wherewith GOD has bless'd the Industry of the Inhabitants; who in a few Years have made a Garden of a Wilderness, and, besides living well themselves, have so much Food to spare to other Countries." He concluded, "By means of this and the neighbouring *Provision Colonies*, the British Fleet and Forces in the West-Indies are at this Time supplied with Provisions at a moderate Price, while the Enemy is starving in Want; which shows that these Colonies give Great Britain a considerable Advantage over its Enemies in an American War, and will no doubt be an additional Inducement to our Mother Country to continue us its Protection."[8]

In his subsequent prose, however, he stressed that vast distances made the colonies vulnerable to enemies' attacks and that the colonists ought not to depend upon the mother country's protection. During the 1740s, as the colonies were drawn into what they called "King George's War," Franklin felt a need to prepare their military defense. On November 24, 1747, he printed five hundred copies of a broadside titled "Form of Association," in which he wrote "that Great Britain, to which we are subject, is now engag'd in a War with two powerful Nations: That it is become too well known to our Enemies, that this Colony is in a naked, defenceless State, without Fortifications or Militia of any Sort, and is therefore exposed daily to Destruction from the Attacks of a very small Force." He emphasized, "That we are at a great Distance from our Mother Country, and cannot, on any Emergency, receive Assistance from thence."[9] Subsequently, he reprinted these comments concerning the "naked, defenceless" colony in the *Pennsylvania Gazette* for December 3, 1747.

Earlier, during mid-November 1747, Franklin had written and published his pamphlet *Plain Truth: Or, Serious Considerations on the Present State of the City of Philadelphia, and Province of Pennsylvania*, as part of his effort to promote a voluntary military association to defend the infant colony.[10] *Plain*

Truth resonated with a readership throughout Philadelphia, to judge from Franklin's having printed two thousand copies for the first edition, plus a second edition, and a German translation. Not only were excerpts of *Plain Truth* reprinted in New York, but published responses appeared from Samuel Smith on behalf of the Quakers and from Christopher Saur on behalf of the German pacifists.[11] *Plain Truth* urged the citizens of Pennsylvania to unite as one body for their defense against the increasing activities of French and Spanish privateers.[12]

In *Plain Truth*, Franklin encouraged anti-Catholic sentiments within Pennsylvania to amplify an external threat to the "Mother-Country." After observing "That our Enemies may have Spies abroad, and some even in these Colonies," Franklin affirmed, "'Tis well known, that we have Numbers of the same Religion with those who of late encouraged the French to invade our Mother-Country. *And they came,* Verse 7, *to Laish, and saw the People that were therein, how they dwelt* CARELESS, . . . QUIET *and* SECURE." Franklin added, "They *thought* themselves secure, no doubt; and as they *never had been* disturbed, vainly imagined they *never should*."[13] In these remarks, the imagery of security and tranquility, implicit perhaps in the family analogy for the mother country's protection of her colonies, was examined and rejected in ways that nonetheless drew upon a fusion of nationalism and religiosity rooted in British Americans' opposition to both France and the pervasive Catholicism in that country.[14]

Franklin recognized that the "mother country's" use of "protection" resulted from Britain's economic interests in possessing the American colonies. This idea was sufficiently important to him that he wanted it to be emphasized in his *Proposals Relating to the Education of Youth in Pensilvania* [*Pennsylvania*], which he published in Philadelphia in 1749. Among these recommendations, Franklin affirmed, "If the new *Universal History* were also read, it would give a *connected* Idea of human Affairs, so far as it goes, which should be follow'd by the best modern Histories, particularly of our Mother Country; then of these Colonies; which should be accompanied with Observations on their Rise, Encrease, Use to Great-Britain, Encouragements, Discouragements, &c. the Means to make them flourish, secure their Liberties, &c."[15] Viewing the American colonies with regard to their "Use to Great-Britain" was a commonplace in the mercantile practices for trade and commerce of the time.

Although the family imagery representing the British Empire emphasized the mother country's "protection" of the colonies, Franklin recognized that, on occasion, "protection" was a euphemism for inappropriate forms of domination. This was exemplified for him by the eighteenth-century practice of "transporting" convicted criminals away from Britain by placing them in colonies, at times, formed for that purpose. On April 11, 1751, for example, his *Pennsylvania Gazette*, which was by then under the editorship of Franklin's partner, David Hall, drew upon the family imagery of the empire to underscore this inappropriate use of power. After presenting a catalogue of murders, acts of arson, robberies, piracy, and manslaughter, the article in the *Gazette* concluded, "These are some of thy Favours, BRITAIN! Thou art called our MOTHER COUNTRY; but what good *Mother* ever sent *Thieves* and *Villains* to accompany her *Children;* to corrupt some with their infectious Vices, and murder the rest? What *Father* ever endeavour'd to spread the *Plague* in his Family! —We do not ask Fish, but thou givest us *Serpents*, and worse than Serpents!" Having evoked the family metaphor to castigate the British government's misuse of power over the colonies, the *Gazette* concluded the argument, "In what can Britain show a more Sovereign Contempt for us, than by emptying their *Jails* into our Settlements?"[16]

Subsequently, a month later, Franklin satirized the implications of the family imagery for empire in the *Pennsylvania Gazette* on May 9, 1751, in a letter over a pseudonym, "Americanus." He noted, "By a Passage in one of your late Papers, I understand that the Government at home will not suffer our mistaken Assemblies to make any Law for preventing or discouraging the Importation of Convicts from Great Britain, for this kind Reason, '*That such Laws are against the Publick Utility, as they tend to prevent the* IMPROVEMENT *and* WELL PEOPLING *of the Colonies.'*" He commented with sharp irony, "Such a tender *parental* Concern in our *Mother Country* for the *Welfare* of her Children, calls aloud for the highest *Returns* of Gratitude and Duty." Sarcastically, he added, "Our *Mother* knows what is best for us. What is a little *Housebreaking, Shoplifting,* or *Highway Robbing;* what is a *Son* now and then *corrupted* and *hang'd*, a Daughter *debauch'd* and *pox'd*, a Wife *stabb'd*, a Husband's *Throat cut*, or a Child's *Brains beat out* with an Axe, compar'd with this 'IMPROVEMENT and WELL PEOPLING of the Colonies!'"[17]

Franklin's letter drew upon his recognition of legal and commercial exploitation of colonies concealed beneath the family images depicting the British Empire. As a mark of the colonists "grateful Disposition" toward the "*Mother Country*," he mentioned, "In some of the uninhabited Parts of these Provinces, there are Numbers of these venomous Reptiles we call RATTLE-SNAKES; Felons-convict from the Beginning of the World: These, whenever we meet with them, we put to Death, by Virtue of an old Law, *Thou shalt bruise his Head.* But as this is a sanguinary Law, and may seem too cruel; and as however mischievous those Creatures are with us, they may possibly change their Natures, if they were to change the Climate; I would humbly propose, that this general Sentence of *Death* be changed for *Transportation.*" He concluded, "I would only add, That this Exporting of Felons to the Colonies, may be consider'd as a *Trade,* as well as in the Light of a *Favour.* Now all Commerce implies *Returns:* Justice requires them: There can be no Trade without them. And *Rattle-Snakes* seem the most *suitable Returns* for the *Human Serpents* sent us by our *Mother* Country." Alluding to mercantile practices, he continued, "In this, however, as in every other Branch of Trade, she will have the Advantage of us. She will reap *equal* Benefits without equal Risque of the Inconveniencies and Dangers. For the *Rattle-Snake* gives Warning before he attempts his Mischief; which the Convict does not."[18] Beneath his anger directed at the "Mother Country's" misuse of power, the passage recognized that the colonies' commerce was restricted by mercantile laws that benefitted Britain.

In 1751, Franklin wrote passages indicating his awareness that Britain, the parent state, might be threatened by the colonies' growth, as exemplified in his *Observations concerning the Increase of Mankind, Peopling of Countries, &c.* In these observations, which were later appended to William Clarke's *Observations On the late and present Conduct of the French, with Regard to their Encroachments upon the British Colonies in North America* and republished in Boston in 1755, he sought to assuage British anxieties about the colonies' burgeoning growth. For example, after commenting that "Labour will never be cheap here," he noted, "The Danger therefore of these Colonies interfering with their Mother Country in Trades that depend on Labour, Manufactures, &c. is too remote to require the Attention of Great-Britain." Instead, he noted the benefits of growth, "In Proportion to the Increase of the Colonies, a vast Demand is growing for British Manufactures, a glorious Market wholly in the Power of Britain." Franklin concluded, "Therefore Britain should not too much restrain Manufactures in her Colonies. A wise and good Mother will not do it. To distress, is to weaken, and weakening the Children, weakens the whole Family."[19]

Franklin's Verbal Imagery between "JOIN, or DIE," 1754, and "MAGNA *Britannia,*" 1765–66

Conceived of as children, the British colonies in America looked to the mother country for a model of appropriate behavior as manifested in her laws, customs, language, fashions, and conduct—taken together what eighteenth-century writers referred to as the "manners" of a nation. The idea that British Americans should endeavor to comport with the model established by the mother country was pervasive in political writings before the American Revolution. One central supposition of this thinking was articulated by Richard Jackson in a letter to Franklin on June 17, 1755. Jackson observed that "in every country in the universe, happiness is sought upon a different plan; and, even in the same country, we see it placed by different ages, professions, and ranks of men, in the attainment of enjoyments utterly unlike." After next identifying and distinguishing between what Jackson referred to as "moral habits" and "mechanical habits," he generalized, "The *cumulus* of the moral habits of each individual, is the manners of that individual; the *cumulus* of the manners of individuals makes up the manners of a nation."[20]

After surveying factors that affected the manners of nations, Jackson concluded his letter to Franklin with remarks on colonization, the mother country's process of producing children. Jackson asserted, "When we would form a people, soil and climate may be found, at least sufficiently good: Inhabitants may be encouraged to settle, and even supported for a while; a good government and laws may be framed, and even arts may be established, or their produce imported." "But," he added, "many necessary moral habits are hardly ever found among those who voluntarily offer themselves in times of quiet at home, to people new colonies; besides that the moral, as well as mechanical habits, adapted to a mother country, are frequently not so to the new settled one, and to external events, many of which are always unforeseen. Hence it is we have seen such fruitless attempts to settle colonies, at an immense public and private expence, by several of the powers of Europe: . . . none of the English colonies became any way considerable, till the necessary manners were born and grew up in the county [country]."[21] Among the implications of such thinking was the importance of attending to the people's manners.

Insofar as possible, the British Americans sought to emulate the model of appropriate manners enacted by the mother country, for example, by patterning their legislative and judicial practices after those in Britain. While Franklin was an elected representative in the Pennsylvania Assembly between 1751 and 1764, allusions to precedents and practices in the "mother country" regularly constituted a basis for the Assembly's argumentation. Other remarks in the Assembly's formal proceedings faulted the proprietors of Pennsylvania for violating the customary manners of children toward their parent.[22] Sometimes these uses of the "mother country" were combined in a single line of argument condemning the proprietors.[23] An appeal to conformity with the mother country's manners provided a powerful basis for the Assembly, not only to object to the proprietor's representatives' practices, but also to advance legislation proposed by the Assembly.[24] More common, however, were allusions to the mother country's manners to condemn the proprietor.[25] For example, on February 22, 1757, the Assembly denounced the proprietors for "the many Infractions of the Constitution, in manifest Violation of the Royal Grant, the Proprietary Charters, the Laws of this Province, and of the Laws, Usages and Customs of our Mother Country."[26] As a participating member of the Assembly between 1751 until 1757 and again from 1759 until 1764, Franklin would have helped to prepare the Assembly's positions and, in some later instances in 1764, sign the Assembly's rhetoric in his role as Speaker.[27]

Although Franklin was elected to the Assembly during the period between 1757 and 1759, he was located in London, where he served as the Assembly's agent to plead the colony's case against the proprietors. During that period, he was the colony's agent in London while the French and Indian War was concluding. At that time, the newspapers in London devoted increased attention to the American colonists' "manners," because their "manners" were a basis for gauging the prospect of the colonies' abiding unity with the British Empire. Franklin was sufficiently concerned about the depictions of the colonists' "manners" that, in his capacity as agent, he wrote a letter under a pseudonym, "A NEW ENGLAND MAN," which was published in the May 10–12, 1759, *London Chronicle*. Referring to an earlier letter in the *Chronicle*, he commented, "As there are several strokes in it tending to render the colonies despicable, and even odious to the mother country, which may have ill consequences; and no notice having been taken of the injuries contained in that letter, other letters of the same nature have since been published, permit me to make a few observations on it."[28]

Franklin devoted considerable space to refuting earlier writer's concerns that the American colonists possessed "*a levelling spirit.*" In Britain, levellers were members of a group organized during the Civil War in the previous century and composed primarily of former parliamentarians advocating universal suffrage, a written constitution, and religious toleration. The earlier writer, whom Franklin quoted, had amplified, "*This equality produces also a rusticity of manners; for in their language, dress, and in all their behaviour, they are more boorish than any thing you ever saw in a certain Northern lattitude,*"[29] an allusion to Scotland. At stake in this criticism was the extent to which the manners of the British Americans had remained sufficiently English to warrant the Americans having the same status as the English. To the extent that the colonies failed to emulate the mother country's manners, they were in danger of being considered aliens.

In reply to the earlier writer, Franklin commented at length on the colonies' "manners," detailing objections to each element of the critic's charges that they were beneath the English. For instance, he commented, "But as to their language, I must beg this gentleman's pardon if I differ from him. His ear, accustomed perhaps to the dialect practised in the *certain northern latitude* he mentions, may not be qualified to judge so nicely in what relates to *pure* English. And I appeal to all Englishmen here, who have been acquainted with the Colonists, whether it is not a common remark, that they speak the language with such an exactness both of expression and accent, that though you may know the natives of several of the counties of England, by peculiarities in their dialect, you cannot by that means distinguish a North American." In this same letter, Franklin echoed his earlier objections to the British practice of transporting criminals to the American colonies to suggest that the mother country's practices had contributed to whatever differences in "manners" existed in British America.[30] Perhaps the letter's frequent references to the "mother country" were designed both to assuage concerns about alleged differences in the manners of the colonists and the British and to evoke a basis for condemning the parent state for its behavior, which corrupted the children's manners.

During the mid-1750s, Franklin's rhetoric had noted anxieties in Britain that the children might surpass their parent, exemplified in his correspondence with William Shipley, who was an originator and initial secretary of the Society of Arts (which later became the Royal Society of Arts).[31] However, concerns about the colonies' stature compared to the mother country were transformed by the conclusion of the Seven Years War. The victory over France at Quebec during September 1759 resulted in the loss of Canada to Britain, a result that was not without disadvantages for British control over its own colonies, since the French presence had justified the mother country's "protection" of British America. This was a significant development for imperial politics that resulted in public exchanges revealing that the mother country's "protection" of her children was a euphemism for control and domination over them as resources.

In response to public suggestions that Canada be restored to the French as a means of retaining the mother country's control over the British colonies, Franklin replied with a letter over the pseudonym, "A. Z.," in the December 25–27, 1759, *London Chronicle*. His contribution to the debate, "Humourous Reasons for Restoring Canada," listed satiric reasons to give Canada back to France. Among these was his comment, "We should restore it, that the French may, by means of their Indians, carry on . . . a constant scalping war against our colonies, and thereby stint their growth; for, otherwise, the children might in time be as tall as their mother." He identified yet an additional, satiric reason, by commenting, "Our colonies, 'tis true, have exerted themselves beyond their strength, on the expectations we gave them of driving the French from Canada; but tho' we ought to keep faith with our Allies, it is not necessary with our children. That might teach them (against Scripture) to *put their trust in Princes:* Let 'em learn to trust in God."[32] He realized that allusions to the "mother Country" justified "protection" in a sense that could only be understood as domination in the British interests of economic exploitation and military control. Like his earlier letter refuting the image of the British Americans as "levellers" whose manners were no longer English, this satire demonstrated his awareness of pervasive beliefs in Britain that, as suggested by stereotypes in the popular discourse, the British Americans held a lower status than the English.

Subsequently, Franklin engaged the controversy over Canada in *The Interest of Great Britain Considered, With Regard to her Colonies,* published at London in 1760 and his most important contribution to the public debate. He framed his pamphlet as an intervention in an ongoing public exchange of views to object to comments in *Remarks on the Letters Address'd to Two Great Men,* which had been published in the *London Chronicle* on January 19–22, 1760. Many of his earlier allusions to the empire as a family recurred in this pamphlet, although they were modified in that they were situated among larger and deeper issues in imperial politics. Implicit in the family analogy for the empire was the idea that children should be grateful to their parents for protection and support. To undercut such a posture in British rhetoric, Franklin observed:

> Our North American colonies are to be considered as the frontier of the British empire on that side. The frontier of any dominion being attack'd, it becomes not merely "*the cause*" of the people immediately affected, (the inhabitants of that frontier) but properly "*the cause*" of the whole body. Where the frontier people owe and pay obedience, there they have a right to look for protection. No political proposition is better established than this. It is therefore invidious to represent the "blood and treasure" spent in this war, as spent in "the cause of the colonies" only, and that they are "absurd and ungrateful" if they think we have done nothing unless we "make conquests for them," and reduce Canada to gratify their "vain ambition," &c. It will not be a conquest for them, nor gratify any vain ambition of theirs. It will be a conquest for the whole, and all our people will, in the increase of trade and the ease of taxes, find the advantage of it.[33]

The allegation concerning the colonies' ingratitude was based upon the notion that children had a duty to be grateful to parents in exchange for support and protection. The war's outcome significantly changed the fundamental circumstances for imperial politics, because, after the French ceded Canada to Britain, the British lost their justification for "protecting" the American colonies.

Next, Franklin summarized his adversary's position in *Remarks* with regard to the colonies and then articulated the hidden relationships of power and economics concealed beneath the language depicting the children's "gratitude" for the parent's "protection." He sketched an improbable address from the colonists. Should the colonies "now humbly address the mother country in the terms and the sentiments of the *remarker,* return her their grateful acknowledgments for the blood and treasure she had spent in '*their cause,*' confess that enough had been done '*for them,*'" Franklin hypothesized, then, he imagined, might this address "not with more justice be answered" along these lines:

> We understand you, gentlemen, perfectly well: you have only your own interest in view: you want to have the people confined within your present limits, that in a few years the lands you are possessed of may increase tenfold in value! you want to reduce the price of labour by increasing numbers on the same territory, that you may be able to set up manufactures and vie with your mother country! you would have your people kept in a body, that you may be more able to dispute the commands of the crown, and obtain an independency. You would have the French left in Canada, to exercise your military virtue, and make you a warlike people, that you may have more confidence to embark in schemes of disobedience, and greater ability to support them![34]

Franklin's response developed ironies in his adversary's position, especially the alleged concern about the colonies's divisiveness, by stressing that divisiveness was necessarily entailed in the opponent's position. In addition, Franklin commented, frankly, that the writer's position would cause the colonies' need for "protection," a position amplified later in the pamphlet.

Referring to the other writer's position that Canada "would not only be of no use to us, but 'the possession of it (in his opinion) may in its consequence be dangerous,'" Franklin asked, "As how? Why, plainly, (at length it comes out) if the French are not left there to check the growth of our colonies, 'they will extend themselves almost without bounds into the in-land parts, and increase infinitely from all causes; becoming a numerous, hardy, *independent* people, possessed of a strong country, communicating little or not at all with England, living wholly on their own labour, and in process of time knowing little and enquiring little about the mother country.'" Franklin's reply underscored the implications of his opponent's position in terms of violence: "'Tis a modest word, this, *check*, for massacring men, women and children." He added, "If Canada is restored on this principle, will not Britain be guilty of all the blood to be shed, all the murders to be committed in order to check this dreaded growth of our own people? Will not this be telling the French in plain terms, that the horrid barbarities they perpetrate with their Indians on our colonists, are agreeable to us?"[35] Thus, Franklin evoked the family image of the British Empire to condemn the mother country for professing "protection" while condoning violence in British America to assure dependency on Britain.

Franklin developed his refutation of the other writer's position by endeavoring to assuage British concerns about the possibility of the colonies becoming "*dangerous*" to Britain or gaining independence. "Of this I own," he asserted, "I have not the least conception, when I consider that we have already fourteen separate governments on the maritime coast of the continent, and if we extend our settlements shall probably have as many more behind them on the inland side. Those we now have, are not only under different governors, but have different forms of government, different laws, different interests, and some of them different religious persuasions and different manners." He emphasized, "Their jealousy of each other is so great that however necessary an union of the colonies has long been, for their common defence and security against their enemies, and how sensible soever each colony has been of that necessity, yet they have never been able to effect such an union among themselves, nor even to agree in requesting the mother country to establish it for them." He asked, "If they could not agree to unite for their defence against the French and Indians, who were perpetually harassing their settlements, burning their villages, and murdering their people; can it reasonably be supposed there is any danger of their uniting against their own nation, which protects and encourages them, with which they have so many connections and ties of blood, interest and affection, and which 'tis well known they all love much more than they love one another?"[36] Thus, Franklin invoked elements of the family metaphor depicting the empire to minimize the danger the colonies posed to Britain.

Franklin concluded, "If the union of the whole is impossible, the attempt of a part must be madness: as those colonies that did not join the rebellion, would join the mother country in suppressing it." He then examined analogies with the United Provinces and the Roman Republic, mentioning in the process his awareness that one tool of imperial domination was the mother country's conscious effort to keep the colonies divided from each other. He remarked, "The Romans well understood that policy which teaches the security arising to the chief government from separate states among the governed." Even so, his assurances that the colonies were not "dangerous" probably heightened British concerns about maintaining control over commerce. Franklin's stand in this pamphlet depicted him as an advocate of the increasing economic trade between America and Britain, which would strengthen the connection between them.[37]

During the years before the 1765–66 Stamp Act controversy, Franklin's rhetoric had fully traversed the dangers to colonial America entailed in depicting the British Empire as a family. This was also the case in his views on the image's ramifications concerning taxation. As early as 1754, Franklin articulated his concerns about taxation of British America by the British Parliament in ways that evoked the family imagery of the empire. In a letter to William Shirley on December 4, 1754, for example, Franklin specified numerous specific ways in which Britain taxed the American colonies through indirect means, which he referred to as "Secondary Taxes." He prefaced these remarks with a general concern about financing the French and Indian War: "That besides the Taxes necessary for the Defence of the Frontiers, the Colonies pay yearly great Sums to the Mother Country unnotic'd."[38] Franklin enumerated varieties of indirect taxation. The expectation that the colonies supply the "Mother Country" with such economic resources was commonplace in mercantile practices during the eighteenth century. Under a patriarchal conception of the British Empire as a family, this expectation corresponded to a belief that children had a duty to provide the product of their labor to their parents.

Although these were conventional means for Britain to secure economic resources from British America, and, as such, were a source of concern, Franklin worried especially about the implications of direct taxation of the colonies by Parliament. He concluded his reasoning with a focus on the prospect of Parliament imposing taxes on British America along lines that resembled pervasive arguments a decade later during the Stamp Act controversy. In the letter of 1754, Franklin summarized, "These Kind of Secondary Taxes, however, we do not complain of, tho' we have no Share in the Laying or Disposing of them; but to pay immediate heavy Taxes, in the Laying Appropriation or Disposition of which, we have no Part, and which perhaps we may know to be as unnecessary as grievous, must seem hard Measure to Englishmen, who cannot conceive, that by hazarding their Lives and Fortunes in subduing and settling new Countries, extending the Dominion and encreasing the Commerce of their Mother Nation, they have forfeited the native Rights of Britons, which they think ought rather to have been given them, as due to such Merit, if they had been before in a State of Slavery."[39] In matters of taxation and representation, the family metaphor for the empire circumscribed Britain's treatment of the American colonies as offspring rather than slaves, even as it nonetheless still legitimated taking some of the colonies' material resources.

A decade later, Franklin continued using the family metaphor as he engaged in protesting the Stamp Act and justifying the British Americans' objections through several letters, written over pseudonyms and published in British newspapers. In addition, he sometimes published the letters of other Americans over still other pseudonyms. In his role as colony agent, Franklin may have been responsible for the printing of a letter from "a Merchant in Philadelphia," probably Charles Thompson, in the August 17–20, 1765, *London Chronicle*. In this letter "a Merchant" observed, "Heretofore we have been used to speak of England as our mother country, children have been taught by their parents to revere and love its constitution, and to risque every thing in defence and support of it; the restrictions from time to time imposed, were submitted to and born, while we solaced ourselves with the thoughts of enjoying the most substantial rights of English freemen." However, "a Merchant" added, "when those impositions are urged as arguments for laying on us still greater, when burdens are multiplied, and decrees passed, which hardly leave us the colour of freedom, we cannot be silent." The letter writer amplified the significance of the colonies' protests by remarking, "That the Colonies have borne a great deal before they complained, must be allowed, when we consider the several restrictions laid upon them."[40] He then enumerated several specific grievances concerning commerce.

On September 5, 1765, Franklin himself wrote a pseudonymously authored letter that was published in *Lloyd's Evening Post* on September 9–11, 1765. Written by "A Virginian" as a reply to "William Pym," Franklin's letter commented on the colonists' alleged ingratitude toward the mother country: "If the Americans think themselves deprived of one of their most essential rights, are they ungrateful when they resent it, only because their grievance proceeds from their benefactors?" He then justified the Americans' response, "I think they have rather shewn a great effort of virtue, in not suffering their respect for the mother country, nor gratitude for her favours, to overballance the duty they owed to their constituents." He observed, "It is much to be wished that some arguments were used that might set the right of the Parliament in clear view; for as the Americans are a reasonable people, they would acknowledge their error when convinced of it."[41] In the absence of such reasons, the Parliament's acts were a misuse of sheer political power. Franklin's other pseudonymous letters, such as those penned by "F. B." to the *Gazetteer and New Daily Advertiser* on December 19, 1765, and by "N. N." to the same paper on December 28, 1765,[42] also demonstrated that Franklin was thoroughly engaged in seeking the Stamp Act's repeal and that he drew upon the family image to condemn the mother country.

Subsequently, Franklin probably commented as "Pacificus" in a letter dated January 23, 1766, and published in the *Public Advertiser* on January 26, 1766: "THE very important Controversy being next Tuesday to be finally determined between the Mother Country and their rebellious American Children, I shall think myself happy if I can furnish any Hints that may be of public Utility." He then commented on a distinction between power and right by employing irony to discredit the proceedings of the "Mother Country": "There are some Persons besides the Americans so amazingly stupid, as to distinguish in this Dispute between *Power* and *Right*, as tho' the former did not always imply the latter. The Right of Conquest invests the Conqueror with Authority to establish what Laws he pleases, however contrary to the Laws of Nature, and the common Rights of Mankind."[43] The satire complicated the debate, by reminding readers that the colonies were not conquered territories, and by characterizing those who supported the Stamp Act as endorsing sheer power to impose legislation, regardless of the implications for milestones in British history such as the Magna Charta. The letter also complicated the debate in that Franklin posed as "Pacificus," thereby appropriating the pseudonym of an anti-American writer to satirize his stance.

During the same month, in January 1766, Franklin sketched plans for a pamphlet on the Stamp Act. Although the pamphlet was never completed for publication—parts consisted of only a sketchy outline, but, on some matters, it was written in a preliminary draft—the notes illuminated his uses of verbal imagery to depict the American colonies' relationship to Britain. Referring to the Albany Plan, he wrote, "This PLAN OF UNION, was sent to Government here, that if approv'd it might be carried into Execution. It was *not approv'd;* whether from a Jealousy that such an Union might make the Colonies in some degree formidable to the Mother Country as well as to the Enemy, or from what other good Reasons, I will not pretend to conjecture." Such remarks dispensed with illusions that the mother country would protect the colonies. He added, "It was however thought better to send Troops from hence, and they were sent accordingly, at first a few only, but many more afterwards than were either originally intended here or desired there, at an immense Expence to this Nation, which in my Opinion, and that of many Americans, might well have been spared." Because the British assumed the expense without consulting the colonists, the British should bear the debt. "And yet, however great this Expence," he noted, "the War ended in the Reduction of Canada, and Cession to Britain of all the vast Country northward, southward, and westward to the Missisipi, wherein she may from time to time plant more Colonies out of the vast Increase of the present, thereby extending her Empire."[44]

Subsequently in his plan for the pamphlet on the Stamp Act, he mentioned that British Americans, in response to Parliament's violation of their rights, had begun to reconsider their relationship to Britain. He stated, "It was now that they recollected all the former Hardships imposed on them, which their Respect for the Mother Country had induc'd them to bear in Silence. The numerous and perplex'd Restraints on their Trade, many of them requiring *Labour in vain*, and *Expence to no purpose*. The Restraints on their Manufactures, those very few that their Situation and particular Circumstances gave them some Opportunity of carrying on to Advantage: The Emptying by Law all the Gaols [jails] of this Country into their Settlements; an Instance of sovereign cruel Insolence unexampled, with which no Nation before had ever treated even a Country they had conquer'd."[45] Not only had the Stamp Act been poorly conceived legislation in that it failed to raise a revenue, it had also harmed imperial relations by causing the colonists to reconsider their role within the mercantile system. Turning to the ramifications of the British Americans' boycott, Franklin noted, "They can subsist without this Country or any Trade and being too weak to express their Resentments in any other Way it will be more strongly express'd in this." That these words were written with deep alienation may be reinforced by Franklin's note in the margin: "Germany the Mother Country of this Nation."[46]

Franklin's remarks in his planned pamphlet went unpublished, but he made a similar public statement as "A Lover of Britain" in the February 6–8, 1766, *London Chronicle*. Referring to the Albany Plan, he affirmed, "This plan was sent to the government here for approbation: had it been approved and established by authority from hence, English America thought itself sufficiently able to cope with the French, without other assistance; several of the colonies having alone in former wars withstood the whole power of the enemy, unassisted not only by the mother country, but by any of the neighbouring provinces." Although he omitted his speculation about the mother country's self-centered and mean-spirited motives, he added, "The plan however was not approved here: but a new one was formed instead of it, by which it was proposed, that 'the Governors of all the colonies, attended by one or two members of their respective councils, should assemble, concert measures for the defence of the whole, erect forts where they judged proper, and raise what troops they thought necessary, with power to draw on the treasury here for the sums that should be wanted; and the treasury to be reimbursed by a tax laid on the colonies by act of parliament.'"[47] These remarks were widely reprinted at the time, appearing in the *Gazetteer* for February 10, 1776, as well as in the February issues of the *London Magazine* and the *Gentleman's Magazine.*[48]

During the same week as Franklin's examination before the House of Commons, he may possibly have had published a letter over the pseudonym "Pacificus" in the February 11–13, 1766, *London Chronicle*. In this letter, "On Chastising the Colonies," he drew an analogy of a husband beating his wife with the permission of British law to emphasize an analogous misuse of power of Britain over America. To frame his commentary, he alluded to a recent legal case: "A Certain Judge, at an Assize, declared it from the Bench, as his Opinion, that every man had a *legal* right to chastise his wife, if she was stubborn and obstinate; but then he observed, that his right ought to be exercised with great lenity and moderation." Then he drew upon this patriarchal conception of "justice," which authorized the husband's brutal domination over this wife, to develop an analogy of the imperial relations within the British Empire: "It seems our Lawyers are of opinion, that England has an indisputable right to correct her refractory children of North America. But then, as the Judge observed, it ought to be done with temper and moderation; lest, like an unskilful Surgeon, we should *exasperate* and *inflame* the wound we ought to *mollify*. It is an old maxim, but not the less true, that it is much easier to *lead* than to *drive*."[49] Such familial imagery suggested powerfully the extent to which imperial relations between Britain and the American colonies had disintegrated into an exercise of brutal force.

Franklin's Verbal Imagery between "MAGNA *Britannia*," 1765–66, and "WE ARE ONE," 1776

In the jubilant celebrations after the Stamp Act's repeal in 1766, Franklin was, like most colonial leaders, an advocate of a closer union between America and Britain, possibly, as he suggested in correspondence with Lord Kames in 1767, through the inclusion of American representatives in the Parliament. Although such representation in "a consolidating Union" was improbable in Franklin's opinion, he believed that it would reduce the further likelihood of such controversies as those resulting from the Stamp Act.[50] In the absence of representation, he recognized other connections within the British Empire as it existed in 1766. Immediately after the Stamp Act's repeal in 1766, his constituents, political allies, and friends in Pennsylvania wrote letters that evoked the commonplace imagery of the British Empire as one family. Most of these allusions sought to renew the colonies' bonds of "affection," "gratitude," and "obedience" within the British Empire in the interest of receiving "assistance," "support," and "protection" from the "mother country." Thematic in Franklin's correspondence from his constituents and political allies in Pennsylvania were rhetorical uses of the family imagery to renew the bonds within the empire. Constituents and allies employed the image on a range of interrelated issues: land speculation, commercial trade, Indian treaties, and even the colony's form of government.[51]

In Franklin's post-repeal correspondence, he, too, employed imagery of the British Empire as one family to amplify the bonds between British America and Britain. One example of this was his reply to a series of letters that he had received from Joseph Galloway during the depths of the Stamp Act controversy. Sometime between October 8 and 14, 1765, Galloway had written to Franklin to outline ideas for unifying the American colonies within the British Empire, by enclosing Galloway's published letter over the pseudonym "Americanus."[52] In a letter on September 27, 1766, responding to Galloway's enclosure, Franklin remarked, "I purpose by the Meeting of Parliament to publish, (with a few Additions and Alterations which you have given me Leave to make) your excellent Piece on the Necessity of an Union between the Mother Country and her Colonies."[53] Although he never carried out this plan, the reply reflected his willingness in 1766 to employ the family image of the British Empire to strengthen the bonds between the colonies and Britain.

Subsequently, Franklin's views on such an imperial union changed dramatically. A decade later, he wrote to Galloway on February 25, 1775, that "when I consider the extream Corruption prevalent among all Orders of Men in this old rotten State, and the glorious publick Virtue so predominant in our rising Country, I cannot but apprehend more Mischief than Benefit from a closer Union" with Britain. He observed, "Here Numberless and needless Places, enormous Salaries, Pensions, Perquisites, Bribes, groundless Quarrels, foolish Expeditions, false Accompts or no Accompts, Contracts and Jobbs devour all Revenue, and produce continual Necessity in the Midst of natural Plenty." Franklin concluded, "I apprehend therefore that To unite us intimately, will only be to corrupt and poison us also. It seems like Mezentius's coupling and binding together the dead and the living." He amplified in Latin with an excerpt from Vergil's *Aeneid:* "Truly torture: as they floated in the poisonous, putrid blood in vile embrace, he slew them with a lingering death."[54] This transformation in his outlook resulted from a series of disturbances within the British Empire during the decade.

After the British Parliament's passage of the Townshend Duties in 1767, Franklin employed images of various animals from specific fables to represent the British colonies in America. The most common of these images referred to British America as a herd of cows. On occasion, he also depicted them as a cat, a young lion, and the goose that laid golden eggs. Because of the apparent simplicity in the form and content of these short fables, they conveyed powerful, clear messages in developing an insight about imperial relations between Britain and the American colonies. At the same time, such animalizations of entire human communities in British America were risky rhetorically insofar as they suggested that the American colonies were a lower order of animal. Both natural and divine law during the eighteenth century would have warranted humankind's domination over animals. So Franklin's rhetoric was double-edged in conceding implicitly that British domination over America was in some measure legitimate, condemning instead only specific varieties of it.

In 1768, for example, Franklin referred to British America as a "goose which lays the golden eggs" to evoke concisely a fable about the destructiveness of excessive greed. He articulated his brief allusion to this fable in an article titled "Queries," written over a pseudonym, "N. M. C. N. P. C. H.," and published in the August 16–18, 1768, *London Chronicle*. Franklin framed a series of questions as *"recommended to the Consideration of those Gentlemen who are for* vigorous Measures *with the* AMERICANS." Among these questions, he pointed out, "If that be true, which is commonly said, viz. That the Mother Country gains *two millions* a year by the Colonies, would it not have been wiser to have gone on quietly in the *happy way* we were in, till our gains by those rising and flourishing countries should amount to *three, four,* or *five* millions a year, than by these new-fashioned vigorous measures to kill the goose which lays the golden eggs?" He amplified, "Would it not have been better policy, instead of *taxing* our Colonists, to have done whatever we could to *enrich* them, and encourage them to take off our articles of *luxury,* on which we may put our own price, and thus draw them into paying us a *voluntary* tax; than deluge them in blood, thin their countries, empoverish and distress them, interrupt their commerce, force them on bankruptcy, by which our merchants must be ruined, or tempt them to emigrations, or alliances with our enemies?"[55] To Franklin, the fable was applicable in that, by seeking inappropriately to tax the colonies, the British government had not only failed to secure the taxes, but lost the wealth to be gained through commerce. Subsequently, the fable was reprinted throughout British America in the *Pennsylvania Chronicle* on October 12, in the *Newport Mercury* on December 5, and yet again in the *New-York Gazette* on December 19, 1768. Engraved prints in Britain and France reiterated the analogy.[56]

More common in Franklin's prose than the "goose which lays the golden eggs" were depictions of British America as a herd of cows being treated foolishly by their owner. Such imagery recurred in his various writings between 1768 and 1770, one of which, "On the Candidacy of Barlow Trecothick," was local in its immediate political import. Franklin may have submitted the article for publication in the *London Gazetteer*, but, in fact, it appears to have been first published in the December 5–12, 1768, issue of the *Pennsylvania Chronicle*, with a heading falsely suggesting that it was reprinted from the *Gazetteer*. He observed, "The situation of the colonies seems similar to that of the cows in the fable; forbidden to suckle their own calves, and daily drawn dry, yet they parted with their milk willingly; but when moreover a tax came to be demanded of them, and that too to be paid *in grass* of which they had already too short a provision; it was no wonder they thought their masters unreasonable, and resolved for the future to suck one another."[57] The story was reprinted in British American papers that circulated in New York, Massachusetts, and Rhode Island, including the *New-York Gazette* on December 19, 1768, the *New-York Journal* on December 22, and both the *Boston Gazette* and the *Newport Mercury* on January 2, 1769.[58]

Franklin considered his allusion to this fable to be an especially apt summary of imperial relations, because he repeated it in later letters published in London newspapers. On January 2, 1770, for example, the *Public Advertiser* carried Franklin's anonymously submitted "NEW FABLES, *humbly inscribed to the S-----y [Secretary] of St--e [State] for the* American Department." The three fables were reprinted subsequently in the *St. James's Chronicle* on January 4, 1770, and in the *Repository: or Treasury of Politics and Literature* in 1771.[59] The first of them related that "A HERD of Cows had long afforded Plenty of Milk, Butter, and Cheese to an avaritious Farmer, who grudged them the Grass they subsisted on, and at length mowed it to make Money of the Hay, leaving them to *shift for Food* as they could, and yet still expected to *milk them* as before; but the Cows, offended with his Unreasonableness, resolved for the future *to suckle one another*."[60] The story's moral was that the British government's greed, like that of the farmer, could result in lost financial benefits from the colonies. Franklin cautioned the British not to abuse its property, because the colonies could respond by becoming self-sufficient and by cutting off supplies they sent to Britain.

Subsequently, on January 29, 1770, Franklin revised the story somewhat when he wrote as "The Colonist's Advocate: VI" in the *Public Advertiser*. He prefaced the analogy between the American colonies and a herd of cows by contending, "I have shewn, that our Gains by our Colonies have been immensely great [and], but for the Grenvillian Taxation Scheme, would have soon come to be equal alone to the Whole of our necessary annual Expences of Government in Times of Peace. If so, how absurd are the Cavils of some among us, who argue, That we have been at great Expences for the Advantage of our Colonists; and that, consequently, it is very ungrateful in them to refuse to contribute to the general Exigencies of the State." Franklin then amplified this claim with his figurative analogy,

> It is an Insult on common Sense to affect an Appearance of Generosity in a Matter of obvious Interest. Is it Generosity that Prompts the Rustick to feed his Cow, which yields him Milk? Could we have been enriched by our Colonies, if we had not defended them from the common Enemy? Did we not know, that if we had left them a Prey to France, the very Accession of such a Dominion, with the additional Naval Force necessarily consequent, must have over-turned the British Empire, and unbalanced Europe? How absurd is it, then, to make a Merit of fighting our own Battles, and driving the Enemy from our Doors! Was it not the obvious Interest of both Mother-Country and Colonies to oppose the Attacks of France against whatever part of the Empire they were directed?[61]

Although this imagery for the empire mixed metaphors—the colonies were both cattle and children—Franklin claimed that Britain's "protection" of the colonies was not altruistic, but self-serving. Because the British government's mercantile policies toward America always had been based primarily upon self-interest, Franklin ridiculed the claim that the colonies should have been grateful for Britain's self-sacrifice.[62] Viewed as livestock, the British colonies were little more than commodities to be exploited or devoured.

Even though Franklin most often used cattle to represent British Americans as being a lower order of animal, he articulated other animalizations of British Americans in the "NEW FABLES" in the *Public Advertiser* on January 2, 1770. The second of these fables, which will be discussed in the final chapter, depicted British America as a cat engaged in a deadly struggle with a predatory eagle representing Britain.[63] Such animalizations of both America and Britain provided a means of depicting Britain's acts of predation in terms that the more circumscribed language of the family had tended to obfuscate in depictions of imperial relations.

The third of these "NEW FABLES" also depicted the British colonies in America by representing them in the form of an animal—a young lion. Franklin's tale began, "A Lion's Whelp was put on board a Guinea Ship bound to America as a Present to a Friend in that Country: It was tame and harmless as a Kitten, and therefore not confined, but suffered to walk about the Ship at Pleasure." The story continued, "A stately, full-grown English Mastiff, belonging to the Captain, despising the Weakness of the young Lion, frequently took it's *Food* by Force, and often turned it out of it's Lodging Box, when he had a Mind to repose therein himself. The young Lion nevertheless grew daily in Size and Strength, and the Voyage being long, he became at last a more equal Match for the Mastiff; who continuing his Insults, received a stunning Blow from the Lion's Paw that fetched his Skin over his Ears, and deterred him from any future Contest with such growing Strength; regretting that he had not rather secured it's Friendship than provoked it's Enmity."[64] Such political communication accepted a premise that sheer power was a basis for the exercise of legislative authority within the British Empire, but underscored some long-term implications of this rhetoric: increases of population and geographical size would ultimately reverse the underlying balance of power within the empire. Along similar lines, Franklin wrote another letter as "The Colonist's Advocate," published two days later on January 4, in the *Public Advertiser*, to emphasize the prospects of a fundamental reversal in relationships of power.[65] His rhetorical appeals may have sought to promote identification of the English with the British Americans by suggesting that the English consider how they would respond to similar treatment by outsiders.

Most often, however, the imagery of the British Empire as one family continued to be the single most pervasive depiction of it in Franklin's prose. These representations of the British Empire as a family changed chronologically in terms of the major political developments within the British Empire, because his rhetorical imagery shifted with major changes in the culture. Such imagery recurred in his prose immediately after the repeal of the Stamp Act in 1766, when it served, above all, to renew the bonds within the British Empire. Similarly, after Parliament's passage of the Townshend Duties in 1767 the family imagery functioned in several of his letters over pseudonyms to define, redefine, and, in noteworthy respects, reverse the implications of key terms for imperial relations.[66] After the imposition of a standing army was followed by the Boston Massacre in 1770, the imagery appeared yet again in the exchanges between the colonial agent and those colonies that he represented in London, especially Massachusetts Bay.[67]

The family image of the British Empire recurred during the controversy over Franklin's decision to transmit certain political letters to British America, where they were published at Boston to the detriment of leaders in Massachusetts Bay, primarily Thomas Hutchinson and his brother-in-law Andrew Oliver, the governor and the lieutenant-governor, respectively. As discussed previously, Franklin had imagined that, if Americans were informed that certain key American leaders had misled the British government into its harmful course of action, then the growing chasm between America and Britain could be bridged in some measure.[68] He was wrong. He paid for his error with his reputation in Britain, where the London papers assailed him as "this old snake," a "traitor," "the old veteran of mischief," a "grand incendiary," the "living emblem of iniquity in grey hairs," and "old Doubleface."[69] During the public hearing over Franklin's conduct, his political adversaries used the imagery of the mother country to magnify claims about his alleged betrayal and deceits.[70]

Throughout the decade of dissent, Franklin employed verbal images to depict the British Empire in various types of prose: political and personal correspondence with American and British leaders, pseudonymously published articles and letters in British and American newspapers, drafts and fragments for unpublished pamphlets as well as his brief, printed tracts, and, perhaps most revealing and suggestive, his handwritten marginalia in other writers' political pamphlets. Allusions to imperial politics appeared frequently in his political correspondence with allies, associates, and constituents, plus the various colonial Assemblies that had chosen him for their agent—initially, Pennsylvania, and, later, New Jersey, Georgia, and Massachusetts Bay. His marginalia on numerous pamphlets occasionally concurred with one or another of the writers' claims, but, more often than not, engaged in sharply worded disputes with them. These handwritten comments articulated Franklin's sharpening of the distinctions between the Crown and the Parliament in their distinct relationships to British America. The marginalia also articulated his recurring endeavor to prove that the colonists could not possibly be considered as subjects of the latter, because then they would be, as Franklin put it, "the Subjects of Subjects."[71]

During the decade of dissent, several of Franklin's uses of the family analogy for the British Empire reversed the analogy's usual symbolic implications. As early as the Stamp Act controversy of 1765 and 1766, for example, he and other colonial agents concentrated on the customary expectation that the colonists should follow the model set by the mother country. But they invoked the idea to undermine the usual British expectations of American compliance and obedience in that the agents emphasized some of the possible consequences of the parent state's deplorable conduct toward the British Americans: "Parental example may produce filial obedience." Such public rhetoric reversed the usual implications of the use of family imagery to describe the relationship between Britain and the colonies, suggesting that if the parent expected the child to behave appropriately, then the parent must practice appropriate behavior in imperial affairs. The agents further asserted, "They dread no enemy but the mother country, and wish to preserve America as an asylum for the wrecks of liberty."[72]

In another reversal of the usual uses of the family imagery, Franklin replied on June 2, 1765, to Lord Kames's request for what Franklin referred to as "my History from the time I set Sail for America." He mentioned, "I left England about the End of August 1762, in Company with Ten Sail of Merchant Ships under Convoy of a Man of War." Then, in subverting the typical uses of "protection" in the family imagery, he added, "We had a pleasant Passage to Madeira, an Island and Colony belonging to Portugal, where we were kindly receiv'd and entertain'd, our Nation being then in high Honour with them, on Account of the Protection it was at that time affording their Mother Country from the united Invasions of France and Spain."[73] As it turned out, Franklin's letter suggested, the children were protecting the mother country, not the other way around, as British polemicists had used the family imagery erroneously to suggest.

Subsequently, Franklin reversed yet another aspect of the family imagery in his article "Answers to the Late Queries on the Colonies," pseudonymously written by "An American" and published in the September 22–24, 1768, *London Chronicle*. Among the questions posed for his readers' consideration, Franklin asked, "Q[uestion]. 5. Whether the Mother Country . . . is not rather dependant on the Colonists, than the Colonists on the Mother Country?"[74] In 1781 he went so far in his rhetorical efforts to ridicule Britain's claims, as a parent, to rightful dominance over British America that he suggested Germany was mother country of both Britain and British America, considering the population of Germans in each place.[75]

Sometime probably between 1765 and 1772 Franklin recorded the words to "The Mother Country: A Song," which summarized abiding aspects of his use of the parent imagery for the empire during the decade of dissent. Whether Franklin wrote the song himself or merely copied it in his own handwriting is unclear, as is the identity of the person the verse alludes to as "her Man": it may be George Grenville of the Stamp Act; Charles Townshend, who proposed the duties in 1767; or even Wills Hill, earl of Hillsborough, secretary of state for the colonies and president of the Board of Trade from 1768 until 1772. But the song's words concisely conveyed Franklin's sentiments during the decade:

The *Mother Country.* A SONG.

We have an old Mother that peevish is grown,
She snubs us like Children that scarce walk alone;
She forgets we're grown up and have Sense of our own;
　　Which nobody can deny, deny,
　　Which no body can deny.
If we don't obey Orders, whatever the Case;
She frowns, and she chides, and she loses all Patience,
and sometimes she hits us a Slap in the Face,
　　Which nobody can deny, &c.
Her Orders so odd are, we often suspect
That Age has impaired her sound Intellect:
But still an old Mother should have due Respect,
　　Which nobody can deny, &c.
Let's bear with her Humours as well as we can:
But why should we bear the Abuse of her Man?
When Servants make Mischief, they earn the Rattan,
　　Which nobody should deny, &c.
Know too, ye bad Neighbours, who aim to divide
The Sons from the Mother, that still she's our Pride;
And if ye attack her we're all of her side,
　　Which nobody can deny, &c.
We'll join in her Lawsuits, to baffle all those,
Who, to get what she has, will be often her Foes:
For we know it must all be our own, when she goes,
　　Which nobody can deny, deny,
　　Which nobody can deny.[76]

Franklin's Verbal Imagery between "WE ARE ONE," 1776, and *Libertas Americana,* 1782–83

After the Declaration of Independence, Franklin almost never employed family images to depict the relationship between Britain and the United States, except for the occasional brief reference to Britain as stepmother. Perhaps the most famous of his verbal images of the British Empire during wartime was his reference to it as a shattered vase. Writing to Lord Richard Howe on July 20, 1776, only a couple of months before Franklin's departure from Philadelphia to France, he commented, "Long did I endeavour with unfeigned and unwearied Zeal, to preserve from breaking, that fine and noble China Vase the

British Empire: for I knew that being once broken, the separate Parts could not retain even their Share of the Strength or Value that existed in the Whole, and that a perfect Re-Union of those Parts could scarce even be hoped for." He added, "Your Lordship may possibly remember the Tears of Joy that wet my Cheek, when, at your good Sister's in London, you once gave me Expectations that a Reconciliation might soon take place." Alluding presumably to his being denounced by the British administration, he remarked, "I had the Misfortune to find those Expectations disappointed, and to be treated as the Cause of the Mischief I was labouring to prevent. My Consolation under that groundless and malevolent Treatment was, that I retained the Friendship of many Wise and Good Men in that Country, and among the rest some Share in the Regard of Lord Howe." Condemning the mother country for "Her Fondness for Conquest as a Warlike Nation, her Lust of Domination as an Ambitious one, and her Thirst for a gainful Monopoly as a Commercial one," he denounced Britain as having pursued a course of conduct "destructive both of Lives and Treasure."[77] Franklin's image of the empire as a shattered vase, like the pictorial images of "JOIN, or DIE," "MAGNA *Britannia*," and "WE ARE ONE," depicted the colonies as parts of a larger whole, though, unlike the earliest image, there was almost no meaningful prospect of union.

Another noteworthy image from this period depicted the United States as a "virgin," whose character was to be preserved in international diplomacy. Writing from Passy on March 21, 1777, Franklin commented to Arthur Lee, "While we are asking aids it is necessary to gratify the desires, and in some Sort comply with the Humours of those we apply to. Our Business now is to carry our point. But I have never yet changed the Opinion I gave in Congress, that a Virgin State should preserve the Virgin Character, and not go about suitering for Alliances, but wait with decent Dignity for the applications of others." Franklin added, "I was over-ruld; perhaps for the best."[78] Conceived of as a "Virgin State," the new nation was a young and innocent woman in the worldly affairs of nations, seeking a honorable marriage, as his later letter to David Hartley suggested on February 12, 1778.[79] This imagery differed from the later representation of the United States as an infant Hercules, which reflected the stature accorded to men in patriarchal American, British, and European cultures.

Although Franklin had repudiated the image of the empire as a family, having depicted Britain as an evil "Mother-in-Law" as early as 1778, his correspondents still occasionally evoked the imagery of the mother country and the colonies—the most frequent of these being his old friend Jan Ingenhousz.[80] Another example of such a correspondent was David Hartley, who wrote a letter to Franklin on July 5, 1779: "I hoped that our negotiation had done some good upon at least the minds of Men." He added, "Perhaps you may incline to the same opinion when you see the last paragraph of the King's Speech viz that those *unhappy* provinces will not persist in preferring foreign alliances &c. to *Peace & Reunion* with the Mother Country. Terms & phrases begin to soften." He hoped that the ministers "wd [would] have the experiment towards reconciliation upon a ten years peace for a good beginning."[81] Franklin's correspondent evoked the mother country's image to magnify the harms and to request reconciliation after the United States had allied with France.

Certainly, Hartley was aware of the rhetorical implications of the maternal metaphors in his letter, because he had written to Franklin years earlier on July 22, 1775, objecting to the mother image for Britain. In that earlier letter, Hartley commented, "As to my own sentiments, I have long seen the terms of parent state, over children, & c., as very misleading in themselves; if we must have allegorical terms, let us change them for Bretheren and friends. The duties annexed to the terms of Bretheren and friends in private life, woud naturally had [lead?] us to the contemplation of these duties between Great Brittain and America; which woud make a firm and everlasting bond of affection and mutual interest; but the superictious [supercilious?] usurpation of authoratative parental rights, over those whom God has made our equals, cannot fail to pervert reason at the outset." He explained, "It presupposes a parental affection which cannot exist, having no foundation in nature beyond natural parents. It presupposes a dispensation of our own private interests, in competition with that of our provincial children; the very contrary of which, constitutes in our estimation their only value to us; and under this false colouring, even respect and gratitude from our Colonies, is received as the payment of a debt, and not set to the Account of affection or merit." Hartley continued with a plea for renewed relations of a different sort, "Let us be bretheren and friends, and the mutuality of good offices required in the very terms, will impress upon the mind all those dispositions of humanity and mutual Assistance, which fellow Creatures and fellow Subjects shoud sustain towards each other." Other correspondents of Franklin also employed family imagery for the empire, writing to him on major military developments, such as Benedict Arnold's treason, and the prospect of peace negotiations.[82]

Years later, on February 12, 1778, writing to Hartley from Passy, Franklin employed some verbal metaphors himself to depict the alliance between the United States and France: "America has been *forc'd* and *driven* into the Arms of France. She was a dutiful and virtuous Daughter. A cruel Mother-in-Law turn'd her out of Doors, defamed her, and sought her Life. All the world knows her Innocence and takes her Part. And her Friends hope soon to see her honourably married."[83] As in the case of his correspondence with Hartley years earlier, though less eloquently, his 1781 suggestion that Germany was the female parent repudiated the image of Britain as the mother country. The trajectory of this process reached its logical fulfillment in his design for *Libertas Americana*, a design in which the transformations in his verbal images intersected with changes in his pictorial representations depicting the United States. His movement to the image of Britain as a mother-in-law was a shift in his vision of the United States, a shift that he magnified on the *Libertas Americana* medal's imagery of Britain as the evil stepmother, Juno, who had sent the snakes to kill Hercules.

Conclusion

In summary, certain elements of Franklin's views concerning a colonial union abided in his verbal and pictorial depictions of British America as one body politic. He suggested in every pictorial representation that unity as one symbolic body was necessary for self-preservation of the body politic, essential for the purposes of military or political defense, and important for enabling each part of the community to become stronger through its association with the others. These abiding elements recurred as well in his verbal depictions of British America. What changed in both the pictorial and verbal representations was whether the body politic designated the entire British Empire, only British America, or the lone colony of Pennsylvania. In 1747, for example, he depicted the colony of Pennsylvania as one body politic in *Plain Truth*.[84] Although Franklin's concern at the time was limited to unifying various groups within Pennsylvania and to organizing militia men to defend the colony from the French and Spanish, the pamphlet illustrated in miniature abiding factors in Franklin's later representations of the united British colonies in America as a single body politic.[85]

In *Plain Truth*, Franklin evoked an image of the colony as one body politic to urge cooperation among the diverse people in Pennsylvania. He sought to unify diverse social groups by articulating mutual interests that transcended the divisions between those in the city and the country: "Is not the whole Province one Body, united by living under the same Laws, and enjoying the same Priviledges? Are not the People of City and Country connected as Relations both by Blood and Marriage, and in Friendships equally dear? Are they not likewise united in Interest, and mutually useful and necessary to each other? When the Feet are wounded, shall the Head say, *It is not me; I will not trouble myself to contrive Relief!* Or if the Head is in Danger, shall the Hands say, *We are not affected, and therefore will lend no Assistance!* No. For so would the Body be easily destroyed: But when all Parts join their Endeavours for its Security, it is often preserved."[86] Even as Franklin promoted unity within Pennsylvania, he recognized religious, economic, and ethnic diversity within the colony. For example, he situated the Quaker's doctrine of peace in a way that affirmed respect for the dictates of the group's conscience, while emphatically encouraging others in Pennsylvania likewise to follow their convictions supporting military defense. Here as always in Franklin's rhetoric, union could make each part of the body politic stronger through its association with other parts of the community.

In later years, he depicted the entire British Empire as one body politic with the American colonies as the extremities. This was the case in his political card, "MAGNA *Britannia*." Such imagery also appeared in his political prose during the decade of dissent.[87] Assumptions derived from such imagery recurred, for example, in his commentary in "The Colonist's Advocate: III," which was published in the *Public Advertiser* on January 11, 1770. Referring to the Americans, he remarked, "They have, in their implicit Confidence . . . that no Regulation was likely ever to be made by [Parliament], which should materially injure them; as the known Consequence of injuring or impoverishing the Colonies, must be heavy Damage to the Mother Country."[88] Here, too, as always in Franklin's rhetoric, division within the body politic ineluctably harmed the entire community, though the harms varied with the members' locations.

In other respects, however, Franklin's imagery representing British America underwent some noteworthy transformations during the decades preceding national independence of the United States. With the exception of "WE ARE ONE," most of his pictorial images depicted the body politic as an organic entity consisting of either colonial America by itself, as in "JOIN, or DIE" and in *Libertas Americana*, or consisting of the entire British Empire, as in "MAGNA *Britannia*." Franklin's earliest verbal images of the empire had included both conceptions of this organic unity. In his letter to Peter Collinson on May 9, 1754, Franklin began his remarks with the image of Britain as the "mother country," with the American colonies as her offspring. But later in the same passage, he shifted to the idea of the entire British Empire as one body politic. Franklin entreated, "O let not Britain seek to oppress us, but like an affectionate parent endeavour to secure freedom to her children; they may be able one day to assist her in defending her own—Whereas a Mortification begun in the Foot may spread upwards to the destruction of the nobler parts of the Body."[89] Disease in the foot of a single body politic representing the entire empire posed dangers to all portions of the entity. But such logic would not always necessarily have followed in the case of a parent and child, because a diseased child could die while the parent survived. This juxtaposition of the images in Franklin's rhetoric indicated that the images were so closely entwined in his vision of American community at the time that it was possible to use them together without discerning noteworthy differences between them. By the late 1770s, Franklin ultimately discarded both of these images depicting colonial America, even though the American Loyalists continued to use the images interchangeably throughout the war years.[90]

The most fundamental—and elaborate—changes in Franklin's images for British America were made manifest in his rhetorical uses of the family image, which he had employed for roughly half a century and, like most contemporaneous American colonial writers and speakers, continued to use until the late 1770s. Even though the Stamp Act controversy resulted in Franklin's explicit and careful reconsideration of the parent and child image, he subsequently used it in his political prose to develop claims about imperial union. On July 7, 1773, for example, he invoked the image in a letter written in his capacity as colony agent to the Massachusetts House of Representatives. He asserted with a noteworthy conditional clause that "No one doubts the Advantage of a strict Union between the Mother Country and the Colonies, if it may be obtain'd and preserv'd on equitable Terms." He amplified, "In every fair Connection each Party should find its own Interest."[91] He went on to summarize his thoughts on imperial relations with an emphasis on the colonies' and Britain's reciprocal advantages and duties.[92]

Moreover, Franklin regularly evoked the parent and child imagery of the British Empire to amplify the bonds of affection, interest, and language uniting the American colonies with Britain. For instance, he employed such imagery when he wrote "The Colonist's Advocate: VIII," a letter published in the *Public Advertiser* on February 5, 1770. In general, he claimed with reference to British Americans, "For, what their Disposition, with Respect to the Mother-Country, was, before the Year 1763, is well known to the Public, and justly described, in the following Words, by a Gentleman, who has done great Honour, and important Service to his Country by his manly Defence of her Liberties" He then quoted Edmund Burke's famous remark that the British colonies in America "were governed by this Country at the Expence of a little Pen, Ink, and Paper. They were led by a Thread. They had not only a Respect, but an Affection, for Great Britain; for it's Laws, it's Customs, and Manners, and even a Fondness for it's Fashions, which very much increased the Trade

with them. Natives of the Mother-Country were always treated with particular Regard." In the same letter, Franklin amplified, "Their sending constantly
their Children home (for that was the affectionate Term they always used
when speaking of England) for Education, was both a very convincing Proof
of their Respect for the Principles and Manners of the Mother-Country, and
was likewise a powerful Means of attaching them to us from Generation to
Generation."[93] Yet, concurrently, Franklin's verbal depictions examined, reversed,
and ultimately discarded elements of the family imagery for the empire until
he had disposed of the family depictions altogether. By 1778, he had repudiated the family image of the empire altogether by depicting Britain as an evil
"Mother-in-Law," an image that recurred as a malevolent stepmother in 1782
and 1783 in *Libertas Americana*.

Franklin's imagery depicting British America also fundamentally shifted
from depicting the American colonies as severed, dismembered, or distinct
segments to depicting them instead as one organically unified whole. During the decades before the conclusion of the war, Franklin's verbal imagery
representing British America regularly depicted the colonies as segments or
portions of a larger whole. For example, in Franklin's satire titled "Rules by
Which a Great Empire May be Reduced to a Small One," which was published over a pseudonym in the *Public Advertiser* on September 11, 1773, he
commented on the "separation" of the colonies from the "mother country."
He wrote sarcastically, "That the Possibility of this Separation may always
exist, take special Care the Provinces are never incorporated with the Mother
Country, that they do not enjoy the same common Rights, the same Privileges in Commerce, and that they are governed by *severer* Laws, all of *your
enacting*, without allowing them any Share in the Choice of the Legislators."
He turned in his letter to a figurative analogy to amplify his point concerning
divided segments: "By carefully making and preserving such Distinctions, you
will (to keep to my Simile of the Cake) act like a wise Gingerbread Baker,
who, to facilitate a Division, cuts his Dough half through in those Places, where,
when bak'd, he would have it *broken to Pieces.*"[94] Such imagery of separate
pieces recurred in Franklin's pictorial representations of the segmented snake
of "JOIN, or DIE," the dismembered woman's body of "MAGNA *Britannia*,"
and the thirteen rings on "WE ARE ONE," as well as in his famous 1776 allusion to the British Empire as a shattered porcelain vase. But Franklin's depictions of British America as fragmented came to an end with the image of the
infant Hercules on *Libertas Americana*.

Another fundamental shift in Franklin's imagery involved the rising stature
of British America, which he initially depicted pictorially as a lower order of

animal, then as a young woman, and, finally, a mythical male god. The earliest of Franklin's pictorial image representing British America suggested that the colonies embodied a lower order of animal, specifically a segmented snake in "JOIN, or DIE." His movement away from depicting British America as a lower order of animal was not linear; rather, it varied with the political circumstances of the moment. He employed a range of such animal imagery to represent the colonies during the decade of dissent from 1765 to 1776, especially in the wake of the Townshend Duties. During the ensuing controversy, he depicted British America as the goose which lays the golden eggs, a herd of cows, a cat engaged in a struggle with the British lion, and a young but maturing lion.

Even though these animalizations of the colonies were powerful images for dramatizing Britain's deplorable treatment of British America, these metaphors were double-edged rhetorically in that humankind's dominion over lower orders of animals had a commonplace basis in both natural and divine law. Later, Franklin commented in a letter to Thomas Cushing on January 5, 1773, "For there is much Truth in the Italian Saying, *Make yourselves Sheep and the Wolves will eat you.*"[95] Eventually, Franklin cast aside such animal imagery for portraying British America, replacing the image of the segmented snake in "JOIN, or DIE" with depictions of the colonies as a young woman in "MAGNA *Britannia*" and an infant Hercules on *Libertas Americana*. After radicals in America circulated "JOIN, or DIE" on the *Constitutional Courant* in 1765 to oppose British tax laws imposed in the colonies, Franklin not only later discarded the snake's image, but also sought to enhance imperial unity by depicting the entire empire as a dismembered women in "MAGNA *Britannia*."

Even after Franklin has repudiated the image of Britain as a mother of British America by representing her as a stepmother, he continued to depict British America as a "dutiful daughter," "a wife," and, on occasion, a young "virgin" seeking alliances. Whenever Franklin depicted British America as a human during the decades before the successful conclusion of the war, he usually depicted the colonies as a young woman. Writing to David Hartley from Passy on February 12, 1778, for example, Franklin asserted with reference to the United States, "In her future Prosperity, if she forgets and forgives, 'tis all that can reasonably be expected of her. I believe she will make as good and useful a Wife as she did a Daughter, that her husband will love and honour her, and that the Family from which she was so wickedly expelled will long regret the Loss of her."[96] Within patriarchal British and American cultures, the image of the colonies as a young woman was also double-edged rhetorically. For while the image of British America as a young woman suggested her vulnerability and dependence upon the decency of men representing other nations, and while the image often depicted overt acts of misogyny to condemn British leaders' conduct, the image of British America as a young woman also implicitly conceded her subordination as consistent with the patriarchal political, legal, and economic systems throughout Britain and Europe.[97]

Ultimately, Franklin changed such implications based upon the sex of the image by depicting British America as the infant Hercules on the *Libertas Americana* medal. As such, he affirmed that British America had the stature of a youthful male in the world of nations. Other classical allusions appeared as well in Franklin's public rhetoric depicting the British Empire.[98] For example, Franklin used a classical allusion for an altogether different rhetorical objective when he commented pseudonymously as "The Colonist's Advocate" in a letter published in the *Public Advertiser* on January 4, 1770. At that time, while he was still devoted to maintaining imperial union, Franklin wrote, "Indeed, an Empire, composed of half Freemen, half Slaves (in a very few Years the British Subjects in America will equal the Number of those in the Mother Country) would resemble the Roman Empire in it's ruinous State, as it is described in the wonderful Prediction of the Prophet Daniel, by the Representation of the Legs and Feet of an Image partly of Iron, and partly of Clay, partly strong, and partly broken." He exclaimed, "God forbid that ever this Description should be applicable to the British Empire!"[99] Franklin's allusion to the Roman Republic suggested that the British Empire could likewise go into a decline, depending upon the condition and the long-term treatment of the extremities.

EIGHT

National Character and the Great Seal of the United States

For my own part I wish the Bald Eagle had not been chosen as the Representative of our Country. He is a Bird of bad moral Character.

Benjamin Franklin, letter to his daughter,
Sarah Bache, January 26, 1784

Character was a preoccupation of men in Britain and colonial America throughout the eighteenth century—not only the character of the individual men in prominent roles within the community, but also the character of entire nations in evidence in their manners. "Eighteenth-century gentlemen so jealously guarded their reputations," Gordon S. Wood observed, because a public figure's reputation was the basis for "both their social authority and the legitimacy of their arguments."[1] Reputation was a vital factor determining one's place in British colonial hierarchy, the society in which Franklin was raised and entered public life long before the American Revolution. Finding himself vilified during the mid-1760s, for example, he assured himself and his allies that "Dirt thrown on a Mud-Wall may stick and incorporate; but it will not long adhere to polish'd Marble."[2]

Yet Franklin, who worked for a living as the printer of the *Pennsylvania Gazette*, was not a "gentleman" in the eighteenth-century sense of a man who did not need to work for a living, a man of leisure. It was this shortcoming that his adversaries had sometimes targeted. Even after he had retired from publishing the *Pennsylvania Gazette*, his opponents criticized his class origins and resources. "A strong tincture of aristocratic contempt for Franklin," wrote J. Philip Gleason, "is one of the most striking things revealed by studies of his reputation."[3] On October 26, 1764, for example, opponents to Franklin's appointment as the colony agent at London had averred that "the Remonstrants cannot expect that a Gentleman of his moderate Fortune will sacrifice his Interest for the Sake of the Province, which he must necessarily do, if he but seems to oppose the Measures of the Ministry."[4] Later, at times, Franklin sought to cultivate an image of his own character as a gentleman worthy of leadership in British America. So important was it to him to be recognized as a gentleman that, on the occasion of his retirement from his business as publisher of the *Gazette* in 1748, when he formed the partnership with David Hall, Franklin commissioned Robert Feke to paint what Gordon Wood has described as "a mannered and foppish portrait to honor the occasion." Although the portrait is actually rather plain and understated by the conventions of the period, it nonetheless portrayed Franklin as a gentleman. The portrait, ordinarily forgotten in biographies of Franklin, contrasted sharply with the "wigless republican hero" he became later in life.[5]

Franklin was likewise preoccupied with the national character of the United States in evidence in its manners. In his various pictorial representations of British America, one constant was his emphasis on the character of the American community, which he hoped would be imparted to viewers. His concern with national character shaped his emphatic rejection of the bald eagle as the new nation's symbol on the Great Seal of the United States. "Predatory," "lazy," and "abusive"—these words described the eagle's character as Franklin depicted it in a letter to his daughter, Sarah Bache, during January 1784. Toward the conclusion of the American Revolution, the Continental Congress had selected the eagle's image to become the national emblem, because, to the delegates, the eagle emphasized an American commitment to classical republicanism in keeping with certain iconographic traditions. However, as Franklin pointed out, the eagle in nature was a scavenger that lived "by Sharping & Robbing." When he learned about the Congress's choice of the eagle for the national emblem, he lamented that the eagle would rather steal fish caught by a fishing hawk—better known today as an osprey—than endeavor to catch the fish itself. Despite his expression of dissatisfaction, the eagle is the most enduring of the eighteenth-century images designating the United States.

This chapter argues that Franklin meant the substance of his objections to the Great Seal to be taken as serious, not merely as humor calculated to amuse his daughter, however playful the style of the criticism. Various factors underscored his genuine dissatisfaction with the eagle's image on the Great Seal: first, his earlier political writings and pictorial symbolism represented Britain as a predatory eagle; second, his earlier proposals for specific images to represent the British American colonies involved specific criteria that he later evoked to disavow the eagle's image on the Great Seal; and, finally, his queries about publishing his criticism of the Great Seal's design in a political pamphlet at the time suggested the depth of his concern. Attention to this last factor entails examining Franklin's reliance on ridicule during an international controversy over the recent formation of the Cincinnati, a society whose use of the eagle's image had prompted Franklin's letter. Accordingly, after briefly describing the political process for approving the design for the Great Seal, the sequence of considerations in this final chapter begins with Franklin's earlier associations with the eagle's image, then turns to the enduring criteria underlying his assessment of the eagle's image, and, last, his reasons for suppressing publication of his criticism of the emblem during his lifetime. Franklin's rejection of the eagle's image on the Great Seal provides a basis for reviewing his abiding commitments and changing perceptions, particularly as they influenced his designs for emblems of American community prior to national independence.

Franklin's Disavowal of the Eagle's Image

On July 4, 1776, the Continental Congress approved a resolution appointing Franklin, John Adams, and Thomas Jefferson to serve on the first committee to "bring in a device for a seal for the United States of America."[6] Each of these men proposed a different image to represent America, none of which involved the eagle's image. Franklin, who chaired the committee, proposed an image that portrayed the destruction of the Pharaoh's army in the Red Sea. According to John Adams, Franklin proposed "Moses lifting up his Wand, and dividing the Red Sea, and Pharaoh, in his Chariot overwhelmed with the Waters.—This Motto. Rebellion to Tyrants is Obedience to God." Among Thomas Jefferson's papers, an undated note in Franklin's handwriting confirmed this description of his proposal. He referred to "Moses standing on the Shore, and extending his Hand over the Sea, thereby causing the same to overwhelm Pharaoh who is sitting in an open Chariot, a Crown on his Head & a Sword in his hand." He added, "Rays from a Pillar of Fire in the Clouds reaching to Moses, to express that he acts by Command of the Deity."[7] The other committee members also proposed images with human forms, even though a "device" traditionally did not depict human forms.[8] Ultimately, the committee submitted a proposal to the Congress on August 20, 1776, recommending a design by Pierre Eugène Du Simitière with elements from the committee members' initial suggestions (such as Franklin's proposal for a motto: "Rebellion to Tyrants is Obedience to God"). This proposal was tabled, an action that essentially killed it.

The proposal by a second committee, composed on March 25, 1780, of James Lovell, John Morin Scott, and William Churchill Houston, met essentially the same fate on May 17, 1780. Again, the Congress would not approve the imagery for the Great Seal, but rather ordered the project "recommitted." Finally, on May 2, 1782, a third committee, composed of John Rutledge, David Ramsay, and Arthur Middleton, prepared a report that for the first time alluded to the eagle's image, although as only a relatively minor element in the design. This proposal met with sufficient approval for Charles Thompson, the secretary of the Congress, to be entrusted with synthesizing the best features of the imagery proposed by the various committees; thus, the eagle's image finally came to represent the United States.

During the eighteenth century, the image of the eagle for the Great Seal received the most careful scrutiny of any image representing the United States. Congress endorsed the seal because it was based, in part, on collections of emblems and devices, on the rules governing heraldry, and, above all, on the iconographic traditions associated with flag designs during the Roman Republic. To Congress, the eagle's image emphasized an American commitment to classical republicanism, the authority and power to promote republicanism, and the predisposition of the American people toward peace through military strength.[9]

However, Franklin was not pleased with the result of the Congress's deliberations. On January 26, 1784, he articulated a now famous criticism of the Congress's decision to use the eagle for the Great Seal. In a letter to his only daughter, Sarah Bache, he commented at length on the ramifications of the eagle's image for national character. Because this image was to appear on the medallions of the Cincinnati, an honorary society composed of officers who had served under George Washington during the Revolution, he began, "The Gentleman who made the Voyage to France to provide the Ribbands & Medals has executed his Commission. To me they seem tolerably done, but all such Things are criticised. Some find fault with the Latin, as wanting classic Elegance & Correctness; and since our Nine Universities were not able to furnish better Latin, it was Pity, they say, that the Mottos had not been in English. Others object to the Title, as not properly assumable by any but Gen. Washington, who serv'd without Pay. Others object to the Bald Eagle, as looking too much like a *Dindon*, or Turkey."[10]

Franklin expressed to his daughter his dissatisfaction with Congress's choice of the bald eagle to represent the United States by concentrating on honesty, industriousness, and courage as features of national character: "For my own part I wish the Bald Eagle had not been chosen as the Representative of our Country. He is a Bird of bad moral Character. He does not get his Living honestly. You may have seen him perch'd on some dead Tree near the River, where, too lazy to fish for himself, he watches the Labour of the Fishing Hawk; and when that diligent Bird has at length taken a Fish, and is bearing it to his Nest for the Support of his Mate and young Ones, the Bald Eagle pursues him and takes it from him. With all this Injustice, he is never in good Case but like those among Men who live by Sharping & Robbing he is generally poor and often very lousy." As for the attributes of courage that Franklin had long associated with the United States, he lamented that the eagle "is a rank Coward: The little *King Bird* not bigger than a Sparrow attacks him boldly and drives him out of the District." Franklin next contrasted the eagle's character with that of the Society of the Cincinnati, complaining to Sarah that the eagle "is therefore by no means a proper Emblem for the brave and honest Cincinnati of America who have driven all the *King birds* from our Country, tho' exactly fit for that Order of Knights which the French call *Chevaliers d'Industrie*," a French expression designating crooks or swindlers.

Yet, the eagle was the choice of the men who had served General Washington, as detailed in the "Society of the Cincinnati: Circular Letter & Institution" of May 15, 1784. In the preface, this circular letter emphasized, "We have retained accordingly those Devices which recognize the manner of returning to our Citizenship; not as ostentatious marks of discrimination, but as pledges of our Friendship and emblems whose appearance will never permit us to deviate from the paths of Virtue." The letter specified that "The Society shall have an Order; which shall be a Bald Eagle of Gold, bearing on its breast the Emblems hereafter described, suspended by a deep blue ribband edged with white, descriptive of the Union of America with France." In addition, the emblem of an eagle would be a token of membership in the society.[11]

But, in light of the bald eagle's deplorable character, Franklin confided to his daughter, "I am on this account not displeas'd that the Figure is not known as a Bald Eagle, but looks more like a Turkey: For in Truth the Turkey is in Comparison a much more respectable Bird, and withal a true original Native of America. Eagles have been found in all Countries, but the Turkey was peculiar to ours, the first of the Species seen in Europe being brought to France by the Jesuits from Canada, and serv'd up at the Wedding Table of Charles the ninth. He is besides, tho' a little vain & silly, a Bird of Courage, and would not hesitate to attack a Grenadier of the British Guards who should presume to invade his Farm Yard with a red Coat on." Franklin was dissatisfied with the image of the bald eagle representing America for a number of specific reasons derived largely from his observations of the bird's behavior in the wild. His criteria were also overtly cultural in that they were derived from emblem books and heraldic traditions. The values guiding his assessment— courage, honesty, industriousness, magnanimity, and self-reliance—were as cultural as the language that he employed to express his dissatisfaction.

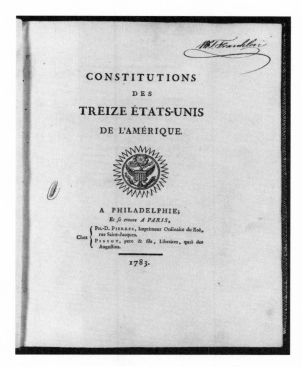

8.1. *Constitutions des Treize Etats-Unis de l'Amérique,* [translated by Louis-Alexandre, duc de la Rochefoucault], (Paris and Philadelphia: [Philippe-Denis] Pierres, 1783). Medium: engraving for the title page of a book; size: 9 ¹⁵⁄₁₆" × 7 ¾". Photograph courtesy of the American Philosophical Society.

Franklin's frank assessment has become a source of embarrassment to some, who have dismissed the remarks as merely whimsical or as a humorous commentary calculated to amuse his daughter, not a substantive criticism of the national character that the eagle's image promoted to Americans. While he employed clever puns and amusing images to make his criticism palatable, these stylistic elements may have undercut the substance of the criticism, which concentrated on the implications of the eagle's image for national character. As evidence that Franklin was just being playful, interpreters of his letter have underscored that he himself used the eagle's image on earlier occasions in the imperial dispute and, further, that he immediately used the Great Seal's image prominently on two publications concerning the recent peace agreement and the resulting nation's form of government.

Despite Franklin's displeasure with the design on the Great Seal, he later included the image in two publications: *Constitutions des Treize Etats-Unis de l'Amérique* (1783) (fig. 8.1) and *The Definitive Treaty between Great Britain,*

8.2. *The Definitive Treaty between Great Britain, and the United States of America,
Signed at Paris, the 3d day of September 1783* ([Passy: Benjamin Franklin], 1783).
Medium: engraving for the title page of a book; size: 7 7/8" × 5".
Photograph courtesy of the American Philosophical Society

and the United States of America, Signed at Paris, the 3d day of September 1783
(fig. 8.2).[12] He made a gift of these books, which prominently displayed the
emblem, to several key figures, some of whom wrote notes of thanks.[13] His use
of the seal on these publications was not dependable evidence that he was
"not writing seriously." Nor was it conclusive "evidence that his later expression of preference for the turkey as a symbol of the United States Government
is not to be taken seriously." His use of the image on these two publications
resulted from his professional responsibility to do so in his role as *ministre
plénipotentiaire.* Richard S. Patterson and Richardson Dougall observed in *The
Eagle and the Shield: A History of the Great Seal of the United States,* perhaps
the most comprehensive study of the design for the Great Seal, that "Historically, a seal established the authenticity of a document, just as a modern signature does." They added, "A great seal is the principal seal of a nation, state,

or other major political entity, used for authenticating documents of high importance or high ceremony issued in the name of the sovereign or chief executive authority."[14] Whatever private reservations Franklin had about the image, he could not have withheld the "signature" of the United States from the documents explaining the new nation's form of government or the treaty ending the war. Because the Congress had authorized the eagle's image on the Great Seal to be the legitimating signature of that august body, he was under an obligation to use the image to authenticate the later publications.

The Eagle in Franklin's Earlier Designs

Franklin himself had employed the eagle's image on two earlier occasions: first in his 1747 design for the flags for the Pennsylvania Associators, and then in his 1775 proposal to use the eagle's image on the paper currency of the Continental Congress. Although he did use the eagle to represent the Associators, he never used it to represent either the united colonies or the United States.[15] In 1747, Franklin was still loyal to the British Crown, and he would not have had grave reservations about the eagle's aristocratic associations. But he had changed markedly during the thirty-seven intervening years—the period of the French and Indian War, the decade of the dissent, the Declaration of Independence, the bloody war, and national independence. Moreover, near the end of that period, his uses of the eagle's image had consistently depicted it as an embodiment of an abusive and predatory British government. As J. A. Leo Lemay noted accurately, "The eagle was traditionally a symbol of military prowess, of aristocracy, and of feudalism. Franklin knew the traditional associations and chafed at them."[16]

Franklin employed the eagle's image on the three-dollar Continental bill in 1775, but he used it to represent Britain's abusive and predatory power, not to embody the United States. Further, at least three contemporaneous publications printed commentaries regarding the eagle's image on the paper currency in a similar light. One commentary circulated initially in the *Pennsylvania Gazette* for September 20, 1775, and, later, in the *Pennsylvania Magazine* for December 1775:

> On another [denomination of the Continental currency] is drawn an *eagle* on the wing, pouncing upon a *crane*, who turns upon his back, and receives the eagle on the point of his long bill, which pierces the eagle's breast; with this motto, EXITUS IN DUBIO EST;—*The event is uncertain.* The eagle, I suppose, represents Great-Britain, the crane America. This device offers an admonition to each of the contending parties. To the crane, not to depend too much on the success of its *endeavours to avoid* the contest

(by petition, negotiation, & c.) but prepare for using the means of defence God and nature hath given it; and to the eagle, not to presume on its superior strength, since a weaker bird may wound it mortally.[17]

Subsequently, the *Historical Magazine* reprinted this description and alluded to another copy of it in "an Almanac Published in 1777."[18] More important, this widely distributed description of the design was sometimes attributed to Franklin.[19] If the attribution was accurate, which was unlikely, then the case for the seriousness of his concerns about national character was amplified by the earlier usages of the eagle imagery, not diminished.

At least two eighteenth-century poems also alluded to the images of the eagle and the crane on the three-dollar bill. Joseph Stansbury, a Loyalist writer, commented in the following excerpts from stanzas 5 and 6 of "The History of Peru, & c.," which he wrote over the pseudonym "R. R." at Philadelphia in 1776:

> The Eagle was *Britain*—
> the Hawthorn bush *We*—
> The Mottos, explain'd
> to a Title agree!
>
> Then *We* were a Crane,
> and Great Britain a Spear
> Then *We* were the Corn
> which *She* thrash'd most severe.[20]

The Loyalist writer took poetic license with the pictorial elements by alluding to the eagle and the crane in two separate stanzas and in combination with the pictorial elements from other bills, such as the thrashing of wheat on the one-dollar bill with the Latin motto, "Depressa Resurgit," meaning "Though crushed, it rises again." Even so, Stansbury recognized the eagle as an aggressive embodiment of Britain.

An anonymous Revolutionary writer also identified the eagle as Britain and the crane as the United States in a poem titled "A Contest between the Eagle and the Crane," published in New Haven in 1778 in the Rev. Wheeler Case's collection, *Poems occasioned by several circumstances, . . . in the present grand contest of America for Liberty.* The poem's headnote affirmed that it was "Composed February 1776." The first several lines of the poetic verse recounted a witness's recollection of a predatory eagle's attack on a crane, which ended with the eagle mortally impaled through the throat by the crane's bill. Then the poem turned to the allegorical implications for the British Empire:

A lively striking emblem here you see
Of George the third and sons of Liberty
This haughty Prince, when he began to *reign*
Did great exploits, defeated *France* and *Spain*.
His heart with pride was swell'd and lifted high,
He soared aloft like the eagle in the sky.

· ·

Like the fierce Eagle darting from the skies,
Strikes down America, prostrate she lies:

· ·

With keen resentment now they raise their head,
Rush to fight and strike the Britons dead.
These with tormenting anguish feel the *Bill*,
Witness the blood that drenched all Bunkers Hill.
On this blessed land, true liberty shall reign,
While *Britain's slaves* despair and bite their chain.
The Lord's your shield *Americans* fear not,
Your *bill* has pierced the lofty Eagle's throat;
The proud imperious Prince now feels his pains,
While fainting Britain bleeds through all her veins.[21]

Presumably, the crane's "bill" was a pun for the three-dollar paper currency featuring the image of the eagle. More important, these two poems both identified the eagle as the embodiment of Britain, not the United States, despite the differences in the writers' political sympathies. Franklin's contemporaries associated the eagle with the monarchical and aristocratic power of Britain. In addition, the Revolutionary writer amplified the eagle's act of predation to denigrate the British government. Indeed, Franklin employed the eagle's image on the currency, but that usage does not discount his later letter to his daughter concerning the Great Seal. To the contrary, the currency is evidence that he was serious about the substance of his dissatisfaction with the predatory eagle as an embodiment of the United States.

Franklin employed the eagle's image to represent Britain in other noteworthy instances that, consistent with his use of the eagle's image on the currency in 1775, reflected the negative connotations he associated with the eagle. He used the image again in the article "NEW FABLES, *humbly inscribed to the S-----y [Secretary] of St--e [State] for the* American Department," published initially in the *Public Advertiser* of London on January 2, 1770, in the *St. James's Chronicle* on January 4, 1770, and yet again in the *Repository: Or Treasury of*

Politics and Literature in 1771.[22] He wrote, "AN Eagle, King of Birds, sailing on his Wings aloft over a Farmer's Yard, saw a Cat there basking in the Sun, *mistook it for a Rabbit*, stoop'd, seized it, and carried it up into the Air, *intending to prey on it*. The Cat[,] turning, set her Claws into the Eagle's Breast; who, finding his Mistake, opened his Talons, and would have let her drop; but Puss, unwilling to fall so far, held faster; and the Eagle, to get rid of the Inconvenience, found it necessary to *set her down where he took her up*."[23] Written by Franklin during the controversy after the Townshend Duties of 1767, this fable condemned the abusive power of Britain by using the eagle's image to describe predation. Years later, on November 3, 1782, John Adams inserted the fable in his diary as an apt analogy for imperial relations, despite Adams's antipathy for Franklin.[24]

In addition, Franklin's contemporaries recognized his strong convictions concerning the eagle. While he resided in France as an official representative, he was presented with various verses written in French by an anonymous author using the initials "L. A." One of these French verses was derived from Franklin's "Fable of the Eagle and the Cat," as indicated in the title, "*L'Aigle et le Chat. Fable allégorique de M. Franklin.*" In this poem, the author sustained the eagle's associations with Britain by such phrases as "*A sa Majesté l'Aigle*" ("To His Majesty the Eagle"), and the cat with the United States, "*Chat Américain*" ("American Cat").[25] Not only had Franklin continued to regard the eagle as a symbol of predatory and abusive power, his convictions about the image were well-known to his French contemporaries. If his earlier uses of the eagle's image are germane to the degree of depth of his later dissatisfaction with the Great Seal, they suggest that his concerns were genuine.

Franklin's Abiding Criteria

During the forty years prior to the Great Seal's conception, Franklin designed various images to represent British America, exemplified by "JOIN, or DIE" in 1754, "MAGNA *Britannia*" in 1766, "WE ARE ONE" in 1776, and *Libertas Americana* in 1783. Because of his long years of experience devising images of America, his criteria for a suitable image had been clearly articulated on these and other earlier occasions. The earlier commentaries suggested that the criteria he evoked were not improvised for humorous ends in his letter of January 26, 1783, which suggested that the turkey designated the United States better than the eagle. To the contrary, some of his criteria for a suitable image of British America abided over the decades, to judge from his own pictorial representations and his earlier commentaries on symbols portraying British America.

In addition, to judge from a letter published first in the *Pennsylvania Journal* on December 27, 1775, and then in the July 25–27, 1776, *London Chronicle*, Franklin supported the turkey as an emblem for the same reasons that he may have approved of the rattlesnake.[26] This letter has been plausibly, though not conclusively, attributed to Franklin. Writing pseudonymously in "An American Guesser," the author of the letter explained the choice of the rattlesnake to represent the united colonies, using criteria similar to those that Franklin offered for the turkey. For example, he stressed that the rattlesnake "never begins an attack, nor, when once engaged, ever surrenders." The turkey, as Franklin depicted it, acted strictly in defense to repel an enemy, not as an aggressive predator. To him, violence was acceptable for defending oneself, but not for seizing resources. In addition, the endorsements of both animals emphasized courage: the turkey was a "bird of courage" and the rattlesnake was "an emblem of magnanimity and true courage." Above all, the letter's author emphasized that the rattlesnake was found in "no other quarter of the world besides America, and may therefore have been chosen, on that account, to represent her." He commented likewise that the turkey was indigenous only to America, while eagles inhabited many countries. To Franklin, the turkey would therefore be an apt image to emphasize America's courage, distinctive heritage, and willingness to defend itself from aggressive enemies.

Franklin's Rhetorical Style of Ridicule

Additional factors suggest that Franklin's letter to his daughter articulated substantive objections to the eagle's image on the Great Seal, because of its implications for national character. These factors were his use of ridicule, which characterized the letter's rhetorical style as a whole; his choice of audience, his only daughter; and the broad context of the ongoing public debate over the formation of the new Society of the Cincinnati. Interpretations of his letter as private humor within the Franklin family rest on an assumption that he intended the document only for his daughter, or, possibly, for later generations of Americans. But there is evidence that he considered publishing his criticisms at the time and that certain elements from his letter found their way into the public discourse of the time. Moreover, the interpretations of the letter simply as humor assumed that ridicule was a means of amusement in the eighteenth century, not a style of substantive argumentation. However, during the eighteenth century, ridicule was a commonplace style of argument.

Finally, to understand the letter in its historical context, it is important to remember that Franklin devoted the first several paragraphs to ridiculing the entire idea of descending honors, concerned as he was that the formation of the Society of the Cincinnati could become a vehicle for the creation of a noble order in the United States. The Cincinnati had employed the image of the eagle on its symbolic artifacts because the Great Seal had used the eagle's image. So Franklin's concerns in the letter were overtly about the society's device and, only in the course of developing those concerns, about the seal that had inspired the device. This slight difference in primary focus is consequential because, situated within the international public controversy over the Cincinnati, the eagle's image would have emphatically resonated with the history of privileged classes.

During the eighteenth century, deists regarded ridicule as a powerful mode of argument for exposing the deficiency of an opposing point of view. Ridicule was not merely a style of humor calculated to amuse, but rather was regarded in some circles as a legitimate mode of argumentation. As early as 1708, Thomas Shaftesbury had suggested that truth "may bear all lights; and one of the principal lights or natural mediums, by which things are to be viewed, in order to a thorough recognition, is ridicule itself, or that manner of proof by which we discern whatever is liable to just raillery in any subject." He inquired in his *Letter Concerning Enthusiasm*, "Now what rule or measure is there in the world, except in the considering of the real temper of things, to find which are truly serious, and which ridiculous? And how can this be done, unless by applying the ridicule to see whether it will bear?" The laughter evoked by ridicule constituted proof that the described choice or belief was unacceptable to discerning people.[27] Franklin had read Shaftesbury and spoke highly of his writings.[28]

Further, at the time, Franklin considered publishing the letter in a pamphlet translated into French. But he decided not to do so, out of deference to the political judgment of his intimate friend Abbé Morellet.[29] When he returned a translated version of the letter to Franklin, Morellet, whose profession placed him in one of the privileged orders, enclosed a note that explained his reservations about publishing the letter: "If you permit me to say so, this paper, though excellent, may cause irritation to some people you do not want to antagonize; and for this reason you ought not to give it, unless you think otherwise, except to persons who have enough philosophy to know and feel all the absurdity and ridiculousness of the harmful bias you fight so well." To this advice, Franklin responded, "Your Sentiments and mine, my dear Friend, are exactly the same respecting the Imprudence of showing that Paper; it has therefore, tho' written some Months past, never been communicated to anyone but yourself, and will probably not appear till after my Decease, if it does then."[30] Political considerations of propriety convinced Franklin to suppress publication of the letter under his name during his own lifetime, because his comments concerning the Cincinnati might have offended in France, as well as in America. As the ambassador from the United States to France, he could not with propriety in public ridicule French institutions such as the nobility. In any event, French censors would not have permitted the letter's publication in France.[31]

But Franklin nonetheless indirectly engaged in the public controversy over the Cincinnati by providing materials and encouragement to other polemicists.[32] He framed the entire letter to his daughter as a response to "the Newspapers," which his daughter had sent to him "by Capt. Barney." The newspapers were filled with articles concerning the Cincinnati. Accordingly, Franklin wrote his letter in the context of the ongoing public controversy that arose in response to the society's preliminary plans: "Membership was to be hereditary in the line of the eldest son, like titles of nobility."[33] Many of those involved in the controversy associated such descending honors with the institution of the nobility. Joining their opposition, Franklin wrote to his daughter: "Honour worthily obtained (as for example that of our officers) is in its nature a personal thing and incommunicable to any but those who had some share in obtaining it." He amplified, "Descending honor, to posterity who could have no share in obtaining it, is not only groundless and absurd but often hurtful to posterity, since it is apt to make them proud, disdaining to be employed in useful arts and thence falling into poverty."

This view was a constant in Franklin's outlook, having been affirmed as early as 1751 in his *Poor Richard's Almanac*, and recurring in his later personal correspondence with other family members.[34] In the *Almanac*, he had summarized a mathematical calculation to prove "that the Pretension of such Purity of Blood in ancient Families is a mere Joke."[35] In the letter to his daughter over thirty years later, he likewise did a mathematical calculation: "A man's son, for instance, is but half of his family, the other half belonging to the family of his wife. His son, too, marrying into another family, his share in the grandson is but a fourth." After nine such generations of biological reproduction, Franklin concluded, "which would not require more than three hundred years (no very great antiquity for a family), our present Chevalier of the Order of Cincinnatus's share in the then existing knight will be but 512th part." The society's plans for hereditary membership and its use of the eagle's image would have magnified for Franklin the association of the eagle with the aristocracy and nobility.

When Aedanus Burke's *Considerations on the Society or Order of Cincinnati . . . Proving That It Creates a Race of Hereditary Patricians, or Nobility*

(Philadelphia, 1783) came to Franklin's attention, he encouraged the translation of it into French by Honoré-Gabriel de Riquette, comte de Mirabeau.[36] In 1783 alone, Burke's pamphlet went through three editions published at Charleston, Philadelphia, and Hartford—an indication that the pamphlet had struck a nerve and that it had a ready market in America.[37] Burke had criticized the Cincinnati's creation of inherited honors as the institution of a nobility that was inconsistent with the new republic's commitment to equality among men. The tenor of Burke's pamphlet, which sounded an alarm on behalf of the young republic, was suggested by the its biblical epigraph: "Blow ye the trumpet in Zion." Burke summarized his objections: "However pious or patriotic the pretence, yet any political combination of military commanders, is, in a republican government, extremely hazardous, and highly censorable. But that instituting exclusive honours and privileges of an Hereditary Order, is a daring usurpation on the sovereignty of the republic: a dangerous insult to the rights and liberties of the people, and a fatal stab to that principle of equality, which forms the basis of our government: to establish which the people fought and bled as well as the Cincinnati, though the latter are now taking every measure to rob them of the credit and the fruits of it."[38] Burke's criticisms were expanded and amplified in Mirabeau's *Considérations sur l'ordre de Cincinnatus*, which Franklin had a role in having published in London during late 1784. Franklin recorded in his journal for July 13, "Mirabeau and Champfort came and read their translation of (American) Mr. Burke's pamphlet against the Cincinnati, which they have much enlarged, intending it as a covered satire against *noblesse* in general."[39] Subsequently, on September 7, 1784, Franklin wrote a letter to Benjamin Vaughan, commending Mirabeau's "piece" written "on the subject of *Hereditary nobility*, on occasion of the order of the Cincinnati lately attempted to be established in America" and asking that Vaughan recommend the author "to an honest reasonable Bookseller, that will undertake it."[40] The publication had footnotes apparently based upon Franklin's reasoning in the letter to his daughter, because both referred to the practice of ascending honors among the Chinese and both made mathematical calculations on descending honor. Subsequently, the pamphlet was translated into English by Samuel Romilly and, likewise, published in London. Eventually, in 1786, Romilly's translation was published in Philadelphia.[41]

After commenting in his July 1784 journal entry that the translation was "well done," Franklin commented, "They say General Washington missed a *beau moment*, when he accepted to be of that society (which some affect to all an *order*). The same of the Marquis de la Fayette."[42] The two leaders had missed a "beautiful moment" in that the entire idea of Cincinnatus—the

Roman military leader who left his plow to rescue Rome only to return modestly to his fields after the danger had passed—was incompatible with the society as it was depicted in the pamphlets and newspapers. Washington's decision to accept leadership of the Cincinnati was inconsistent with the modest and unassuming character of the legendary Cincinnatus, who had declined public recognition and a prominent leadership role after the danger had passed. Then, too, there was the irony of having fought a revolution, whose Declaration of Independence asserted that all men were created equal, only to place some men and their offspring honorifically above others because of their blood lines. So the ensuing international controversy was intense and emotional, to judge from pamphlets and newspaper articles in Britain, France, and the United States. If, at the outset, the United States's most prominent military leader so flagrantly discarded the country's professed commitment to equality among men, the prospects for the republic were bleak, partisans argued.

Washington was keenly aware of at least some of the public criticisms of the Cincinnati. Not only had LaFayette written to him to secure his opinion concerning membership in the society, but Washington had exchanged letters on the subject with Thomas Jefferson, who also distrusted the very idea of forming such an organization, though his reply was tactful. In response to Washington's request on April 8, 1784, for his written opinion concerning the society,[43] Jefferson mentioned the hereditary feature among his other objections. Remarking in general to Washington that he had "wished to see you stand on ground separated from it [the Society]," Jefferson summarized additional concerns that the honorary memberships "might draw into the order all the men of talents, of office and wealth; and in this case would probably procure an ingraftment into the government." Then, too, to Jefferson there was the matter of the national meetings, which might result in further public controversy and changes in the members' understandings of the organization's reasons for existing, changes that could prove harmful over time.[44] Washington had already noted the danger, writing in his solicitation of Jefferson's opinion, "The Pamphlet ascribed to Mr. Burke, as I am told[,] had its effect. People are alarmed, especially in the Eastern States."[45]

Subsequently, Washington used his leadership role in the Cincinnati explicitly to blunt the use of the society to perpetuate descending honors and a nobility in America.[46] Ultimately, arguments such as those made by Burke and Jefferson influenced Washington to urge, as he put it in the notes he drafted on May 4, 1784, that the Cincinnati "Strike out every word, sentence, and clause which has a political tendency. Discontinue the hereditary part in all its connexions, *absolutely*, without any substitution which can be construed into concealment, or a change of ground *only;* for this would, in my opinion, encrease, rather than allay suspicions. Admit no more honorary Members into the Society." Later in those notes, he added "Abolish the General Meetings altogether."[47]

The newly born nation had a very recent history of well-established institutions and habits of thought militating against the same types of new practices it was attempting to institute; hence, the public controversy over the Cincinnati was heartfelt and serious, despite the humorous tone of much of the public discourse. In Franklin's letter to his daughter about the use of the eagle on the Great Seal's design and in the artifacts of the Cincinnati, his concerns about the eagle's aristocratic associations formed a crucial element—an element underscoring gravity beneath bemused humor. Of course, despite Franklin's concerns about inherited honor among the Cincinnati, the eagle's image was widely reproduced on an immense variety of housewares—not only on plates, pitchers, and bowls featuring Liverpool transfer designs and imported china, but also on furniture decorated with carvings—among the general public and especially among the Cincinnati, because it was the official seal of the United States. Ironically, too, despite Franklin's displeasure with the eagle's image on the Great Seal, it was sometimes combined with his design for the interlinked rings on the Continental currency in later productions of housewares.[48] (See figs. 5.10 and 5.11 on p. 137)

Conclusion

Although Franklin drew upon the European tradition of emblems and devices in his own imagery representing America, as in the case of "JOIN, or DIE," and although he was familiar with the cultural traditions that informed the Congress's decision to use the eagle's image to represent the United States, Franklin objected to the image based upon the eagle's behavior in nature and his own commitment to the values of industry, courage, and national distinction, which he thought the eagle was not well calculated to inculcate among Americans as integral to national character. In no fewer than three of his earlier depictions of the relationship between Britain and the United States, Franklin had employed the eagle's image as the embodiment of Britain's predation. To him, the eagle's image had consistently been the perfect embodiment of Britain—not the United States—precisely because the eagle was a predator whose most recent cultural associations had been with monarchy and aristocracy. Finally, he regarded the eagle as a reprehensible creature that survived by seizing the product of the fishing hawk's labor. The content of the criticism reiterated his abiding concerns about the abuse of power and the ability of individuals to profit from their own thrift and industry. Only a few year later, after Franklin had returned to the United States and had participated in the Constitutional Convention, he hinted again at the concerns that a hereditary aristocracy might pose for the new government. As Franklin was leaving the ratification of the Constitution of the United States, Mrs. Samuel Powel had called out to him, "Doctor, what have we got, a Republic or a Monarchy?" Franklin replied, "A Republic, if you can keep it."[49]

While Franklin's rejection of the eagle's image on the "Great Seal" evoked some abiding elements of his views concerning the union of British America, his various pictorial messages over the decades concisely highlight basic changes in his evolving sensibility concerning the body politic that became the United States. "JOIN, or DIE" was distinctive among Franklin's major pictorial representations of colonial America in that it depicted the unity as a lower order of animal, whose segmented body dramatized the need in 1754 for intercolonial union for defense of the British Empire's North American interests from encroachment by the French. Yet, later, from 1768 to 1770, Franklin continued to allude to British America as various types of animals in his verbal depictions of the colonies to dramatize their treatment by the British government. His movement away from such animalization of the British colonies was not linear, but rather circumstantial and shifting in that the verbal imagery resurfaced even after he had deliberately employed a human form to represent the empire in "MAGNA *Britannia*" in 1766.

After the initial distribution of "JOIN, or DIE" in 1754, Franklin's role as colonial agent in London during the conclusion of the French and Indian War impressed upon him that the British government benefited in terms of political control over America from the colonies' disunion, however much it left the colonists vulnerable to attacks by the French and Indians. Franklin's recognition of this was emphatic. Yet, despite misgivings, he remained a loyal American Whig and imperialist in support of Britain's constitutional monarchy, believing as he did that it was the finest form of government known to humankind. The abiding union of British America and Britain conferred upon both political strength among the community of nations and would lead to prosperity. The message's meanings, neither overtly radical nor revolutionary in its original context, subsequently changed dramatically during later decades in America, Britain, and France. There is, then, an historical irony in that "JOIN, or DIE" remains the most commonplace image for depicting Franklin's emerging nationalism, even though at the time there was nothing overtly radical or revolutionary about its initial circulation. Furthermore, in

1766 he not only indirectly repudiated its radical meanings through the production of "MAGNA *Britannia*," but also, after the war, actively sought in 1782 and 1783 to promote an entirely different image of the United States as a youthful god, the infant Hercules.

"MAGNA *Britannia*" represented a significant shift in Franklin's pictorial representations during 1766, not only by depicting the vital interconnections among the parts of the British Empire in North America and Britain, but also by repudiating implicitly any desire on the part of the Americans to separate from the British constitutional monarchy. Franklin used the image portraying the entire British Empire as a dismembered woman to urge Parliament's repeal of the Stamp Act legislation in Britain and to demonstrate to Americans his own moderate course of political action as their agent in London. Tacitly, he repudiated radical American protesters' appropriations of his earlier image, "JOIN, or DIE," which had come to the British government's attention prominently among the mass of documents that became known as the "American Papers"; the papers documented widespread disobedience in the colonies, which sometimes included the destruction of property. The image of Britannia with its long, deeply entrenched history and symbolism in British society dramatized Franklin's political movement toward closer connections with the constitutional monarchy. Yet, the depiction of the woman's dismembered body stressed that she was a victim of unspecified adversaries. Although the body politic was depicted as a human, and therefore in possession of greater stature than the depiction of colonial America as a snake, the image of Britannia was nonetheless that of a woman, whose subordination within patriarchal British and American cultures was certain. As such, she could plead with the men in government to change their behavior, but her future depended upon their dispensations and pleasure. Like the colonists in America, she was a subordinated being whose future depended upon actions taken by dominant men in British government, however much those men professed to idealize her virtues. Above all, the image represented Franklin's movement toward closer connection with the constitutional monarchy, a political commitment that, in his view, was sufficiently deep for him to prefer a royal colonial government to the proprietary system in Pennsylvania at least until 1765; even after the Stamp Act's repeal in 1766, he could propose means for closer union between America and Britain.

"WE ARE ONE," in turn, repudiated the constitutional monarchy altogether during 1776, representing Franklin's complete and utter rejection of the British government as a consequence of a series of unsettling, imperial controversies during the decade of dissent from 1765 until 1775: the Stamp

Act, the Townshend Duties, the Boston Massacre, and the Boston Port Act, perhaps the best known of the Intolerable Acts or the Coercive Acts—not to mention his own experience of being publicly denounced and disgraced in the Cockpit at the hands of prominent British leaders who, in his view, willfully distorted his public service. Along with Franklin's rejection of the constitutional monarchy, he distanced the American community, which he had served for roughly a decade as colonial agent in London, from an aging British government's corruption, avarice, and arrogance. Depicting the colonies pictorially as a chain, Franklin represented them as a federation. These rings were a mechanical device, lacking as they did the vital tissues and living connections among states, which, though separate, were interconnected for the purposes of military defense. The visual organization of "WE ARE ONE" amplified equality among the distinct colonial governments in the Continental Congress, because each colony had equal size and stature as a link within the circle, despite Franklin's view that each state's political representation in Congress should be proportionate to its population and financial contributions, a view that he had held consistently since at least the Albany Congress of 1754.[50] The currency design, a pictorial appeal, was a rhetorical attempt to unite its American audience, however artificial and contrived the mechanics at the outset, when the delegates to the Continental Congress could not even agree on whether the ongoing war's primary objective was for strengthening the Americans' negotiating position or for independence. Despite Franklin's familiarity with such deep divides evident in the new government, his pictorial composition portrayed unity among the thirteen American governments represented in Congress. The pictorial image coincided with the Congress's institution of the Articles of Confederation, its unanimous decision to issue paper money despite British law forbidding it, and its similarly unanimous decision to place George Washington at the head of the military.

Finally, in 1782 and 1783, *Libertas Americana* represented the birth of a new nation that was depicted, above all, as a unified whole, integrating the parts into an organic, living entity. Produced while Franklin was the United States's plenipotentiary ambassador in Paris—after the military success at Yorktown and several months before signing the formal peace treaty on September 3, 1783—the pictorial composition on the commemorative medal celebrated the founding of a new nation. Portrayed as infant Hercules, the United States's stature as a youthful, male god exceeded that of any of the earlier organic representations of colonial America as either a woman or lower order of animal in the patriarchal culture of the time. His youth, suggesting the promising future of a new nation, implicitly contrasted with the dissipation, corruption, and greed of older nations, so evident to Franklin during his years in Britain. The classical heritage associated with the imagery of Hercules made an emphatic allusion to a republican system of government. It was not the only such classical allusion in Franklin's vision of an American community. He had written to Jonathan Shipley on September 13, 1775, to claim, "Agriculture is the great Source of Wealth and Plenty. By cutting off our Trade you have thrown us *to the Earth*, whence like *Antaeus* we shall rise yearly with fresh Strength and Vigour."[51] Like this earlier verbal representation, *Libertas Americana* suggested the youthful vitality and strength of a classical god. Where Franklin had, at the outset in 1754, depicted the British colonies in America as a snake with "JOIN, or DIE," it was now Britain's armies that were the two snakes being strangled in the infant Hercules's grip. Depicted as a pouncing leopard, it was now Britain, not America, that had the stature of a lower order of animal locked in moral combat with a heroic god embodying national independence and the republican government in the United States.

More appropriate than the eagle on the Great Seal, in Franklin's estimation, was the image of the birth of the nation as the infant Hercules, whose youth, courage, industry, promise, and strength boded well for the new nation's character. Franklin himself identified closely with most of these qualities, and he sought to inculcate them in his grandson. Years earlier, during June 1775 on the eve of the American Revolution, Franklin had described his grandchild William Bache in a letter to his sister Jane Mecom as "the strongest and stoutest Child of his Age that I have seen: He seems an Infant Hercules."[52] In 1782 and 1783, by using the image of the infant Hercules on the design for *Libertas Americana*—the medal that Franklin consciously designed to represent a new republic and the emblem that he endeavored most assiduously to distribute internationally as a symbol designating the United States—the aging grandfather may have identified his own descendants' lives, strength, and future with the birth, character, and promise of the new nation. The United States possessed the courage, resilience, and tenacity of a classical god. Less than a decade before his death, Franklin devised a symbol of his legacy to the United States in the form of *Libertas Americana*'s emblem of the infant Hercules—a powerful youth with a legendary life.

ABBREVIATIONS

AAE   Archives du Ministère des affaires étrangères (Paris)
AAS   American Antiquarian Society (Worcester, Mass.)
ALS   Autograph letter signed
AHR   *American Historical Review*
Almanach royal   *Almanach royal*, 91 vols. (Paris, 1700–1792)
AN   Archives nationales (Paris)
APS   American Philosophical Society (Philadelphia)
Arch.   Archives
Autobiog.   *The Autobiography of Benjamin Franklin*, edited by Leonard W. Labaree, Ralph L. Ketcham, Helen C. Boatfield, and Helene H. Fineman. (New Haven, 1964)
Bachaumont, *Mémoires secrets*
    [Louis Petit de Bachaumont et al.], *Mémoires secrets pour servir à l'histoire de la république des lettres en France, depuis MDCCLXII jusqu'à nos jours; ou Journal d'un observateur* (London, 1784–89), 36 vols. Bachaumont, who died in 1771, wrote the first six vols.; Mathieu-François Pridansat de Mairobert the next nine; and Moufle d'Angerville the remaining vols.
BF   Benjamin Franklin
Bigelow, *Works*   *The Works of Benjamin Franklin*, ed. John Bigelow, 10 vols (New York and London, 1887–88)
Biographie universelle
    Biographie universelle, ancienne et moderne, ou histoire par ordre alphabétique, de la vie publique et privée de tous les hommes qui se sont fait remarquer, 85 vols (Paris, 1811–62)
BL   British Library (London)
BM   British Museum (London)
BN   Bibliothèque nationale de France (Paris)
Bodinier, *Dictionnaire*
    Gilbert Bodinier, *Dictionnaire des officiers de l'armée royale qui ont combattu aux Etats-Unis pendant la guerre d'Indépendance* (Château de Vincennes, 1982)
Burnett, *Continental Congress*
    Edmund C. Burnett, *The Continental Congress* (New York, 1941)
Chron.   *Chronicle*

Cobbett, *Parliamentary Hist.*
>edited by William Cobbett and Thomas C. Hansard, *The Parliamentary History of England from the Earliest Period to 1803*, 36 vols. (London, 1806–20)

Colden Papers *The Letters and Papers of Cadwallader Colden.* New-York Historical Society *Collections* for 1917–23, 1934, 1935

Coll. *Collections*

Commons Jours. *Journals of the House of Commons*, 233 vols. to date ([London], 1803–present)

Complete Poor Richard
>*The Complete Poor Richard Almanacks Published by Benjamin Franklin, Reproduced in Facsimile*, intro. by Whitfield J. Bell Jr., 2 vols. (Barre, Mass., 1970)

Contenson, *La Société des Cincinnati*
>Baron Ludovic de Contenson, *La Société des Cincinnati de France et la Guerre d'Amérique, 1778–1783* (Paris, 1934)

Corresp. Correspondence or correspondance

Crane, Letters *Benjamin Franklin's Letters to the Press*, ed. Verner W. Crane (New York, 1950)

DAB *Dictionary of American Biography*

DBF *Dictionnaire de biographie française*, 17 vols. to date (Paris, 1933–present)

Dictionnaire historique
>*Dictionnaire historique, critique et bibliographique, contenant les vies des hommes illustres, célèbre ou fameux de tous les pays et de tous les siècles*, 30 vols. (Paris, 1821–23)

Div. Division

DNB *Dictionary of National Biography*

Dull, *Diplomatic* Jonathan R. Dull, *A Diplomatic History of the American Revolution* (New Haven, 1985)

EB Elias Boudinot

ECS *Eighteenth-Century Studies*

Etat militaire de France
>*Etat militaire de France, pour l'année . . .* , 36 vols. (Paris, 1758–93)

Evans Charles Evans, *American Bibliography*, 14 vols. (Chicago and Worcester, Mass., 1903–59)

f. folio

Fortescue, *George Third*
>*The Correspondence of King George the Third from 1760 to December 1783*, ed. Sir John William Fortescue, 6 vols. (London, 1927–28)

Gaz. *Gazette*

Gaz. de Leyde *Nouvelles extraordinaires de diverse endroits*, commonly known as *Gazette de Leyde*

Gent. Mag. *The Gentleman's Magazine, and Historical Chronicle*

Hatin   Eugène Hatin, *Bibliographie historique et critique de la presse périodique française* (Paris, 1866)

Hist.   *History, Historic, Historical,* or *Histoire*

HLRO   House of Lords Record Office, Parliament (London)

HSP   Historical Society of Pennsylvania (Philadelphia)

JCC   *Journals of the Continental Congress, 1744–1789,* edited by Worthington C. Ford et al., 34 vols. (Washington, D.C., 1904–37)

Jour.   *Journal*

Lasseray, *Les Français*

André Lasseray, *Les Français sous les treize étoiles, 1775–1783,* 2 vols. (Paris, 1935)

LC   Library of Congress. The collections of manuscripts in the Library of Congress will be abbreviated as follows: Papers of Benjamin Franklin (BF), the Robert R. Livingston Collection (RRLP), and the Elias Boudinot Collection (EB)

LC Phila.   Library Company of Philadelphia

Lescure, *Corresp. secrète*

Adolphe Mathurin de François-Adolphe Lescure (pseud. Paul Breton), *Corresp. secrète inédite sur Louis XVI, Marie Antoinette, la Cour, et la Ville, de 1777 à 1792* (Paris, 1866)

Lopez, *Mon Cher Papa*

Claude-Anne Lopez, *Mon Cher Papa: Franklin and the Ladies of Paris* (New Haven and London, [1966])

Mag.   *Magazine*

Mazas, *Ordre de Saint-Louis*

Alexandre Mazas and Théodore Anne, *Histoire de l'ordre royal et militaire de Saint-Louis depuis son institution en 1693 jusqu'en 1830,* 2nd ed., 3 vols. (Paris, 1860–61)

MHS   Massachusetts Historical Society (Boston)

MMNY   Metropolitan Museum of New York

MS, MSS   Manuscript, Manuscripts

Musée des arts   Musée des arts décoratifs (Paris)

Musée à Blérancourt

Musée nationale de la Coopération Franco-Américaine (Blérancourt)

NA   National Archives (Washington, D. C.)

Newcomb, *Franklin*

Benjamin H. Newcomb, *Franklin and Galloway: A Political Partnership* (New Haven and London, 1972)

Newman, *Paper Money*

Eric P. Newman, *The Early Paper Money of America* (Racine, Wis., 1967)

NNHS   New Hampshire Historical Society

NYHS   New-York Historical Society

NYPL New York Public Library

Olson, *Emblems* Lester C. Olson, *Emblems of American Community: A Study in Rhetorical Iconology* (Washington D.C., 1991)

Pa. Arch. *Pennsylvania Archives*, edited by Samuel Hazard et al., 9 series, each comprising multiple volumes (Philadelphia and Harrisburg, 1852–1935)

Papers *The Papers of Benjamin Franklin* (New Haven, 1959–present)

Phil. Philosophy or Philosophical

PMHB *Pennsylvania Magazine of History and Biography*

PRO Public Record Office (Kew and London)

Proc. *Proceedings*

Pubs. *Publications*

QJS *Quarterly Journal of Speech*

Rev. *Review*

Rochambeau, *Mémoires* Rochambeau, *Mémoires militaires, historique, et politique de Rochambeau* (Paris, 1809)

RRLP Robert R. Livingston Papers

Sellers, *Franklin* Charles Coleman Sellers, *Benjamin Franklin in Portraiture* (New Haven and London, 1962)

Sheffield RO Sheffield Record Office

Smith, *Letters* *Letters of Delegates to Congress*, edited by Paul H. Smith and others, 15 vols. to date (Washington D.C., 1976–present)

Smyth, *Writings* *The Writings of Benjamin Franklin*, ed. Albert Henry Smyth, 10 vols. (New York, 1905–7)

Soc. *Society*

Sparks, *Works* *The Works of Benjamin Franklin*, ed. Jared Sparks, 10 vols. (Boston, 1836–40)

Stourzh, *Franklin* Gerald Stourzh, *Benjamin Franklin and American Foreign Policy*, 2d ed. (Chicago, 1954; reprinted 1969)

t. tome

Trans. Translator or translated

Trans. *Transactions*

USL University of Sheffield Library

Van Doren, *Franklin* Carl Van Doren, *Benjamin Franklin* (New York, 1938)

Van Doren, *Franklin-Jackson* Carl Van Doren, ed., *Letters and Papers of Benjamin Franklin and Richard Jackson, 1753–1785* (Philadelphia, 1947)

Van Doren, *Franklin-Mecom* Carl Van Doren, ed., *The Letters of Benjamin Franklin & Jane Mecom* (Princeton, 1950)

VHS   Virginia Historical Society

WMQ   *William and Mary Quarterly*

Wharton, *Diplomatic Corresp.*

The Revolutionary Diplomatic Corresondence of the United States,
ed. Francis Wharton, 6 vols. (Washington D.C., 1889)

WTF   William Temple Franklin

NOTES

Preface

1. *Papers*, 3:397–421, esp. 407–8, 414, and 4:101–8, esp. 104–5, 107. BF made additional references to "rhetoric" in *Papers*, 2:16, 8:93, as well as *Autobiog.*, 64–65.

Chapter 1. Franklin's Emblems and Devices

1. Frank H. Sommer, "Emblem and Device: The Origin of the Great Seal of the United States," *Art Quarterly* 24 (spring 1961): 57–76.

2. *Pa. Gaz.*, Sept. 20, 1775, p. 1, col. 1; *Pa. Mag.* 1 (Dec. 1775): 561. The explanation was later published in an almanac for 1777, judging from a citation for it in *The Hist. Mag. and Notes and Queries* 5 (March 1861): 71–73. The explanation was also reprinted in Henry Phillips Jr., *Hist. Sketches of the Paper Currency of the American Colonies: Prior to the Adoption of the Federal Constitution*, 2 vols. (Roxbury, Mass.: W. Elliot Woodward, 1865–66), 2:251–56.

3. For the attribution to BF, Eric P. Newman, "Benjamin Franklin and the Chain Design," *Numismatist* 96 (Nov. 1983): 2272–73; J. A. Leo Lemay, *The Canon of Benjamin Franklin, 1722–1776* (Newark: U of Delaware P, 1986), 122–24. A contemporary, Joseph Stansbury, also attributed the articles to BF, *Loyalist Rhapsodes*, ser. 8D, no. 90, reel 49, Peter Force Coll., MS Div., LC.

4. For an analysis of distinctions drawn in France, Daniel S. Russell, "Differences between the Emblem and the Device," in *The Emblem and Device in France* (Lexington, Ky.: French Forum, 1985), 142–60.

5. Russell, 145; Sommer, 58. BF's article about the Associator flags in 1747, for instance, employed the term "devices," with reference to a list of ten designs, some of which portrayed animal forms, while others depicted human forms (*Papers* 5:267–69). Further, although the image on "JOIN, or DIE" depicted the British colonies in America as a snake, not a human, and although the motto was expressed in the vernacular, not Latin or a foreign language, he employed the word "emblem" to describe it in his letter to Richard Partridge (*Papers* 5:273). Three decades later, in 1776, when Franklin chaired a committee charged by Congress "to prepare Devices for a Great Seal" of the United States, he proposed an image that portrayed the destruction of the Pharaoh's army in the Red Sea. Other committee members, Thomas Jefferson and John Adams, also proposed images with human forms (*Papers* 22:563). Franklin used the term "device" in a letter to his sister Jane Mecom on May 30, 1757, when he commented upon designs to be placed on "the papers" and "the crown soap" (he objected to Peter

Mecom's use of "the Franklin arms" on the latter). Franklin seems here to have employed the term "device" as a synonym for a "mark," which would identify the maker of a product (*Papers* 7:222).

6. For an alternative account, J. A. Leo Lemay, "The American Aesthetic of Franklin's Visual Creations," *PMHB* 111 (1987): 465–99, esp. 473, 475, and 494.

7. *Papers*, 1:50.

8. A. B. [pseud.], "*On the Use and Abuse of* MOTTOS," *Supplement to the Pa. Mag. for the Year 1775* ([1775]): 587–89, quote on 588, col. 1.

9. For frontispieces, *Papers*, 3:189–90. On this letter, Alfred Owen Aldridge, "Franklin's Letter on Indians and Germans," *Proc. of the APS* 94, no. 4 (Aug. 1950): 391–95.

For flags, *Autobiog.*, 183. These flags were described in the *Pa. Gaz.* for Jan. 12, 1748, and April 16, 1748, and in *Papers*, 3:267–69. For commentaries on the flags, Lemay, "American Aesthetic," 471–75, 496–97; Sally F. Griffith, "'Order, Discipline, and a few Cannon': Benjamin Franklin, the Association, and the Rhetoric and Practice of Boosterism," *PMHB* 116 (April 1992): 131–55. Contemporaneous evidence exists for the attribution of the flag designs to BF: James Logan to Peter Collinson, Feb. 28, 1749/50, *Papers*, 3:470. For paper currency, BF's [Preliminary ink sketch of wind blowing waves design for Continental currency], 1776, APS, Franklin Papers, vol. 50 (ii) f. 45; *Papers*, 22:357–58, and facing page; Newman, *Paper Money*, 32–33; Newman, "Benjamin Franklin and the Chain Design," 2271–81; Eric P. Newman, "Continental Currency and the Fugio Cent: Sources of Emblems and Mottoes," *Numismatist* 79 (Dec. 1966): 1587–98. For medals, *Papers*, 31:489–90, 33:174. For photographic reproductions and commentary on these medals, Vladimir and Elvira Clain-Stefanelli, *Medals Commemorating Battles of the American Revolution* (Washington, D.C.: Smithsonian Institution, 1973). Elvira Clain-Stefanelli forwarded to me a photocopy of her notes regarding the production of these medals, L. W. Vosloh, letter to author, May 17, 1993. For BF's general reflections on honorary medals, BF to John Jay, May 10, 1785, (BF) MS Div. LC and Papers of the Continental Congress, NA. For sword, *Papers*, 30:260–61. For seal, Sommer, 63–64, 74. For several germane comments about BF's role in the creation of the Great Seal, see Richard S. Patterson and Richardson Dougall, *The Eagle and the Shield: A History of the Great Seal of the United States* (Washington, D.C.: GPO, 1976). For relevant primary sources, John Adams to Abigail Adams, Aug. 14, 1776, *Adams Family Corresp.*, ed. L. H. Butterfield (Cambridge, Mass.: Belknap of Harvard UP, 1963), 2:96–97. BF's handwritten description of the design was on an undated note (Aug. 1776), Thomas Jefferson Papers, MS Div., LC.

In regard to the monument, on Dec. 16, 1781, Robert R. Livingston conveyed to BF a Nov. 7, 1781, resolution, "By The United States in Congress assembled" (University of Pa. Library). *Papers*, 36:262, 644. BF to Robert R. Livingston, Aug. 12, 1782, NA, Papers of the Continental Congress. For metal money, *Papers*, 30:429–30; 31:129–30. For portraits, *Papers*, 32:421–22, 590–91. For soap, *Papers*, 7:222. For BF's interest in heraldry, *Papers*, 2:229. BF had further exposure to heraldry in 1753, when he was awarded the Copley Medal. For a reproduction, *Papers*, 5:127.

10. *Pa. Gaz.*, Feb. 7, 1740, p. 3, col. 1; May 21, 1741, p. 2, col. 1; June 4, 1741, p. 4, col. 2; Nov. 26, 1741, p. 3, col. 1; Jan. 6, 1742, p. 3, col. 1; Aug. 12, 1742, p. 3, col. 1; May 19, 1743, p. 3, col. 1; May 31, 1744, p. 3, col. 2; July 12, 1744, p. 4, col. 2. For examples of advertisements, *Papers*, 2:323, 451. Another, earlier advertisement in the *Pa. Gaz.* on Dec. 6, 1738, mentioned "The Emblem of a Friend" in the *Poor Richard's Alamanck for the Year 1739*, but this was evidently an allusion to a short verse for September (*Papers*, 2:216, 223; *Complete Poor Richard*, 1:159). With some regularity, the term "emblem" recurred in verses (e.g., *Papers*, 3:254, 343).

11. The following advertisements by David Hall in the *Pa. Gaz.* included Quarles's emblems in the same list with "Moral virtue delineated": April 5, 1748, p. 5, col. 1; April 16, 1748, p. 2, col. 3, and p. 3, col. 1; May 12, 1748, p. 3, col. 1; March 14, 1749, p. 2, col. 3, and p. 3, col. 1; June 22, 1749, p. 2, cols. 2–3; Oct. 12, 1749, p. 2, col. 3, and p. 3, col. 1; Dec. 19, 1749, p. 2, cols. 2–3; Feb. 6, 1750, p. 3, cols.1–2 ; the following included only "Quarrle's emblems": Sept. 22, 1748, p. 2, col. 3; May 30, 1751, p. 2, col. 3; June 13, 1751, p. 2, col. 3; June 20, 1751, p. 3, col. 2; and Dec. 10, 1751, p. 2, col. 2.

12. Sommer, 61.

13. *A Catalogue of Choice and Valuable Books* (Philadelphia: B. Franklin, 1744), 15.

14. *Autobiog.*, 59.

15. Ibid., 97. Douglas Anderson, *The Radical Enlightenments of Benjamin Franklin* (Baltimore: Johns Hopkins UP, 1997), 6, 221–22.

16. Edwin Wolf II, a librarian at the LC Phila., devoted many years to reconstructing Franklin's library. During the summer of 1989, Mr. Wolf generously allowed me to consult the four boxes of cards that he had compiled in his endeavor. Edwin Wolf II, "A Key to the Identification of Franklin's Books," *PMHB* 80 (1956): 407–9.

17. For a list of corresponding images, see Newman, "Continental Currency and the Fugio Cent," 1596. I consulted the volumes held at the LC Phila. and confirmed that these volumes contained designs resembling several denominations of the Continental Currency in 1775. Although Newman mentioned that only volumes 2, 3, and 4 had the shelf marks (C 22 N 24–26) written in pencil on the inside cover, I noticed that volume 1 also contained a distinctive shelf mark (C 22 N 23). Perhaps this volume surfaced during the intervening years.

18. This claim is based upon a computer search of the three CDs containing the *Pa. Gaz.*, plus the experimental CD of Franklin's papers. It is possible that a variant spelling of the author's name or title appears in these works, however.

19. *Papers*, 20:459. On identifying this ed., *Papers*, 20:460 n. 6; R. T. H. Halsey, *Benjamin Franklin and His Circle: A Catalogue of an Exhibition* (New York: Plantin Press for the Metropolitan Museum of Art, 1936), 9; Winfried Schleiner, "The Infant Hercules: Franklin's Design for a Medal Commemorating American Liberty," *ECS* 10, no. 2 (1976–77): 240 n. 12.

20. *Pa. Gaz.*, April 5, 1748, p. 5, col. 1; April 16, 1748, p. 2, col. 3; May 12, 1748, p. 3, col. 1; March 14, 1749, p. 2, col. 3, and p. 3, col. 1; June 22, 1749, p. 2, cols. 2–3; Oct. 12, 1749, p. 2, col. 3, and p. 3, col. 1, Dec. 19, 1749, p. 2, cols. 2–3; Feb. 6, 1750, p. 3, cols.1–2 .

21. Sommer, 62.

22. Clarence William Miller, *Benjamin Franklin's Philadelphia Printing, 1728–1766* (Philadelphia: APS, 1974), 279–80, quote on 280. Examples resembling the currency include the images opposite pages 1, 68, 294, 300, 638, and 672 in Arndt's book.

23. Albert Matthews, "The Snake Devices, 1754–1776, and the *Constitutional Courant* 1765," Dec. 1907, *Pubs. of the Colonial Soc. of Mass.* (Cambridge: John Willson and Son, 1908), 11: 409–53; Philip Davidson, *Propaganda and the American Revolution* (Chapel Hill: U of N.C. P, 1941), 14, 15; Frederic R. Kirkland, "An Unknown Franklin Cartoon," *PMHB* 73 (1949): 76–79; Edwin Wolf II, "Benjamin Franklin's Stamp Act Cartoon," *Proc. of the APS* 99 (1955): 388–96; David P. McBride, "Linked Rings: Early American Unity Illustrated," *Numismatist* 92 (Nov. 1979): 2374–93; Newman, "Benjamin Franklin and the Chain Design"; Newman, "Continental Currency and the Fugio Cent"; Carl Zigrosser, "The Medallic Sketches of Augustin Dupré in American Collections," *Proc. of the APS* 101 (Dec. 1957): 535–50; and Winfried Schleiner, "The Infant Hercules: Franklin's Design for a Medal Commemorating American Liberty," *ECS* 10 (1976–77): 235–44.

24. Halsey, "Benjamin Franklin: His Interest in the Arts," in *Benjamin Franklin and His Circle*, 1–16.

25. Sellers, *Franklin*. Additional studies that examine BF's image in portraiture include Wayne Craven, "The American and British Portraits of Benjamin Franklin," and Ellen G. Miles, "The French Portraits of Benjamin Franklin," in *Reappraising Benjamin Franklin: A Bicentennial Perspective*, ed. J. A. Leo Lemay (Newark: U of Delaware P, 1993), 247–71, 272–89, respectively. Bernard Bailyn, *To Begin the World Anew* (New York: Knopf, 2003), 60–99.

26. Olson, *Emblems*, 21–74.

27. Anderson, 36.

28. H. W. Brands, *The First American: The Life and Times of Benjamin Franklin* (New York: Random House, 2002), 234, 369, 373; Edmund S. Morgan, *Benjamin Franklin* (New Haven: Yale UP, 2002), 237; Esmond Wright, *Franklin of Philadelphia* (Cambridge, Mass.: Harvard UP, 1986), 89, and an illustration following 66; and Walter Isaacson, *Benjamin Franklin: An American Life* (New York: Simon & Schuster, 2003), 159, 225, 228, plate 19.

29. Van Doren, *Franklin*, 220, 491–92, 628.

30. Anderson, xv.

31. Crane, *Letters*, 42; *Papers*, 12:414.

32. Barbara B. Oberg, "'Plain, insinuating, persuasive': Benjamin Franklin's Final Speech to the Constitutional Convention of 1787," in *Reappraising Benjamin Franklin*, 175–95, quote on 176.

33. *Papers*, 14:101.

34. Ibid., 15:272–73.

35. Claude-Anne Lopez, "Was Franklin Too French?" in *Reappraising Benjamin Franklin*, 143–53.

36. Verner W. Crane, "Franklin's Marginalia and the Lost 'Treatise' on Empire," *Papers of the Michigan Academy of Science, Arts, and Letters* 42 (1957): 163–76.

37. Jack P. Greene, "The Alienation of Benjamin Franklin, British American," *Jour. of the Royal Society for the Arts* (now the *RSA Jour.*) 124 (1976): 52–73; rptd. with minor revisions in Jack P. Greene, *Understanding the American Revolution* (Charlottesville: UP of Va., 1995), 247–84.

38. An instance of the former is J. A. Leo Lemay, "The American Aesthetic of Franklin's Visual Creations," *PMHB* 111 (1987): 465–99. An example of the latter is Clinton L. Rossiter, "The Political Theory of Benjamin Franklin," *PMHB* 74 (1952): 259–93; rptd. in Esmond Wright, ed. *Benjamin Franklin: A Profile* (New York: Hill and Wang, 1970), 148–87, and Clinton L. Rossiter, *Seedtime of the Republic* (New York: Harcourt, 1953), 290, 309–10.

39. Anderson, xiv.

40. *Papers*, 5:417.

41. Gordon S. Wood, *The Radicalism of the American Revolution* (New York: Knopf, 1992).

42. *Autobiog.*, 155.

43. Ibid., 156.

44. Russell, 149–50.

Chapter 2. Franklin's Earliest Commentary Envisioning Colony Union

1. BF to James Parker, originally printed in [Archibald Kennedy], *The Importance of Gaining and Preserving the Friendship of the Indians to the British Interest, Considered* (New York: James Parker, 1751), 27–31. *Papers*, 4:117–121. Lois K. Mathews inquires into the origins of the broad outlines of BF's plan of union at Albany based upon this letter, "Benjamin Franklin's Plans for a Colonial Union, 1750–1775," *American Political Science Rev.* 8 (1914): 393–412, esp. 395–97. Stourzh, *Franklin*, 50–54, 61.

2. *Papers*, 4:118–19.

3. Ibid., 4:117. BF had written on Oct. 11, 1750, to Cadwallader Colden about securing the Iroquois Confederacy's "Attachment to the British Nation" (*Papers*, 4:68). Robert C. Newbold, *The Albany Congress and Plan of Union of 1754* (New York: Vantage, 1955), 33.

4. Kennedy, 18.

5. *Papers*, 4:117.

6. Ibid., 4:120.

7. For an alternative interpretation, Douglas Anderson, *The Radical Enlightenments of Benjamin Franklin* (Baltimore: Johns Hopkins UP, 1997), 160, 162–63.

8. *Papers*, 4:234. For research on the context of BF's concerns about the Germans, Dietmar Rothermund, "The German Problem of Colonial Pennsylvania," *PMHB* 84 (1960): 3–21. For an account of BF's specific opinions on the Germans in Pennsylvania, Francis Jennings, "Germans," in *Benjamin Franklin: Politician* (New York: Norton, 1996), 72–80.

9. *Papers*, 4:477–86; for a note on Collinson, 3:49 n. 8.

10. BF, *Remarks concerning the Savages of North America* (London, 1784), rptd. in Smyth, *Writings*, 10:97–105, quote on 97. The draft of the manuscript for this pamphlet was undated. So it is not known precisely when BF composed it. For research on

BF's attitudes toward "Indians" in the early 1750s, Jennings, "Indians," *Benjamin Franklin*, 81–93.

11. *Papers*, 35:547.

12. James E. Hutson, "The Campaign to Make Pennsylvania a Royal Province, 1764–1770, Part I," *PMHB* 94 (1970): 427–63; James E. Hutson, "The Campaign to Make Pennsylvania a Royal Province, 1764–1770, Part II," *PMHB* 95 (1971): 28–49.

13. *Papers*, 4:117–118.

14. Ibid., 4:118.

15. For an alternative view of BF's pragmatism, William S. Hanna, *Benjamin Franklin and Pennsylvania Politics* (Stanford, Calif.: Stanford UP, 1964).

16. *Papers*, 4:118.

17. Ibid., 4:119.

18. Ibid.

19. Mathews, 396. She stresses that no solid documentary establishes a causal link, however. For alternative views, Samuel B. Payne Jr., "The Iroquois League, the Articles of Confederation, and the Constitution," *WMQ*, 3rd ser., 53 (July 1996): 612; Donald A. Grinde Jr. and Bruce E. Johansen, "Sauce for the Goose: Demand and Definition for 'Proof' Regarding the Iroquois and Democracy," *WMQ*, 3rd ser., 53 (July 1996): 628.

20. *Papers*, 4:120–21.

21. Alfred Owen Aldridge, "Franklin as Demographer," *Jour. of Economic Hist.* 9 (1949): 25–44.

22. *Papers*, 4:119.

23. BF, "Convention speech proposing prayers," June 28, 1787, MS Div., (BF) LC; rptd. in Smyth, *Writings*, 9:600.

Chapter 3. "JOIN, or DIE," 1754

1. Robert C. Newbold, *The Albany Congress and Plan of Union of 1754* (New York: Vantage, 1955), 32.

2. "JOIN, or DIE" appeared in *Pa. Gaz.*, May 9, 1754, p. 2, col. 1; *New-York Gaz.*, May 13, 1754, p. 2, col. 3; *New-York Mercury*, May 13, 1754, p. 2, col. 3; *Boston Gaz.*, May 21, 1754, p. 3, col. 1; and *Boston Weekly News-Letter*, May 23, 1754, p. 1, col. 1. Allusions to "JOIN, or DIE" occurred in *Virginia Gaz.*, July 19, 1754, p. 3, col. 1, and *South Carolina Gaz.*, Aug. 22, 1754, p. 2, col. 2.

3. The most comprehensive studies of the snake device are Albert Matthews, "The Snake Devices, 1754–1776, and the *Constitutional Courant* 1765," Dec. 1907, *Pubs. of the Colonial Soc. of Mass.* (Cambridge: John Willson and Son, 1908), 11:409–53; Lester C. Olson, "Benjamin Franklin's Pictorial Representations of the British Colonies in America: A Study in Rhetorical Iconology," *QJS* 73 (1987): 18–42; Olson, *Emblems*, 21–74; and Karen Severud Cook, "Benjamin Franklin and the Snake That Would Not Die," in *Images and Icons of the New World: Essays on American Cartography*, ed. Karen Severud Cook (London: British Library, 1996), 88–111.

4. Alison Gilbert Olson, *Making the Empire Work: London and American Interest Groups, 1690–1790* (Cambridge, Mass.: Harvard UP, 1992), 122.

5. "JOIN, or DIE," as produced in 1754, is sometimes misread as a protest symbol and, as such, it is related to BF's earlier satire, "A Rattlesnake for Felons," *Papers*, 4:130–33. Such an interpretation is unwarranted. For an alternative account, J. A. Leo Lemay, "The American Aesthetic of Franklin's Visual Creations," *PMHB* 111 (1987): 479.

6. For a more detailed account of the transformations than is necessary here, Olson, *Emblems*, 21–74.

7. For BF's own words to this effect, *Papers*, 13:225.

8. Most historians have attributed "JOIN, or DIE" to BF, because he was an ed. of the *Pa. Gaz.* Matthews, "The Snake Devices," 409 n. 1, has suggested that the evidence is not conclusive, because David Hall was BF's partner in the publication of the *Pa. Gaz.* The eds. of the *Papers* commented, *Papers*, 5:272–273; however, see the letter from Hutchinson to BF, *Papers*, 12:380–81. Martha G. Falls, "Heraldic and Emblematic Engravers of Colonial Boston," *Boston Prints and Printmakers, 1670–1775*, ed. Walter Muir Whitehill, vol. 46, *Proc. of the Colonial Soc. of Mass.* (Meriden, Conn.: 1973), 218, has speculated that James Turner cut the woodcut of "JOIN, or DIE" for the *Pa. Gaz.*

9. Alison Olson, *Making the Empire Work*, 156–58.

10. Michael G. Kammen, *A Rope of Sand: The Colonial Agents, British Politics, and the American Revolution* (Ithaca, N.Y.: Cornell UP, 1968), 8.

11. The circular letter is recorded at C.O. 5:211, f. 9–10, PRO (Kew). A transcription is readily available in Charles Henry Lincoln, ed., *Corresp. of William Shirley, Gov. of Mass. and Military Commander in America, 1731–1760*, 2 vols. (New York: Macmillan, 1912), 2:13. For background on Shirley, John A. Schutz, *William Shirley: King's Governor of Massachusetts* (Chapel Hill: U of N.C. P, [1961]), esp. 180–86.

12. *Pa. Arch.*, 8th ser., 5:3639; *Papers*, 5:222.

13. For the governors' use of the instructions to justify the Albany Congress, *Papers*, 5:252 n. 3; Lincoln, *Corresp. of Shirley*, 2:46; Roger R. Trask, "Pennsylvania and the Albany Congress, 1754," *Pa. Hist.* 27 (1960): 274–75.

14. *Papers*, 5:223.

15. *Pa. Arch.* 8th ser., 5:3698.

16. *Pa. Gaz.*, May 9, 1754, p. 1, cols. 2–3, Belcher quote in col. 3; p.1, cols. 1–2, Shirley quote in col. 2.

17. Ibid., May 16, 1754, p. 1, cols. 1–3.

18. *Jour. of the Proc. of the Congress Held At Albany, in 1754, for the Purpose of Treating with the Six Nations of Indians and Concerting a Scheme of General Union of the British American Colonies*, a MS printed in the *MHS Coll.*, 3rd ser., 5 (1836): 5–74. Beverly McAnear, "Personal Accounts of the Albany Congress of 1754," *Mississippi Valley Hist. Rev.* 39 (1952–53): 727–46.

19. *Papers*, 5:394. Trask, 273, 282 n. 35.

20. *Papers*, 3:193–94, 4:67.

21. For background on the 1744 treaty at Lancaster, Francis Jennings, *The Ambiguous Empire: The Covenant Chain of Indian Tribes with English Colonies from the Beginnings to the Lancaster Treaty of 1744* (New York: Norton, 1984), 356–66; Francis

Jennings, "'Pennsylvania Indians' and the Iroquois," in *Beyond the Covenant Chain: The Iroquois and their Neighbors in Indian North America 1600–1800*, ed. Daniel K. Richter and James H. Merrell (Syracuse, N.Y.: Syracuse UP, 1987), 75–92.

22. *Indian Treaties Printed by Benjamin Franklin, 1736–1762*, with an introduction by Carl Van Doren, notes by Julian P. Boyd (Philadelphia: HSP, 1938), 78. This book is an "exact facsimile" of thirteen treaties published by BF between 1736 and 1762. This passage has been quoted in numerous articles about the Iroquois influence thesis. On one side of this controversy are Donald A. Grinde Jr. and Bruce E. Johansen; on the other, Philip A. Levy, Samuel B. Payne Jr., and Elisabeth Tooker. Donald A. Grinde Jr., *The Iroquois and the Founding of the American Nation* (San Francisco: Indian Historian, 1977), 31; Bruce E. Johansen, *Forgotten Founders: How the American Indian Helped Shape Democracy* (Boston, Mass.: Harvard Common, 1982), 61–62; Elisabeth Tooker, "The United States Constitution and the Iroquois League," *Ethnohistory* 35 (1988): 305–36, reference on 309; Donald A. Grinde Jr. and Bruce E. Johansen, *Exemplars of Liberty: Native America and the Evolution of Democracy* (Los Angeles, Calif.: U of Calif. Los Angeles, 1991), 56, 93–94, 163; Philip A. Levy, "Exemplars of Taking Liberties: The Iroquois Influence Thesis and the Problem of Evidence," *WMQ*, 3rd ser., 53 (1996): 588–603, reference on 591–92; Samuel B. Payne Jr., "The Iroquois League, the Articles of Confederation, and the Constitution," *WMQ*, 3rd ser., 53 (1996): 604–20, reference on 609; Donald A. Grinde Jr. and Bruce E. Johansen, "Sauce for the Goose: Demand and Definitions for 'Proof' Regarding the Iroquois and Democracy," *WMQ*, 3rd ser., 53 (1996): 621–36, reference on 626–28; Donald A. Grinde Jr., "The Iroquois and the Development of American Government," *Historical Reflections/Reflexions Historiques* 21 (1995): 301–18, reference on 306; and Bruce E. Johansen, "Native American Roots for Freedom of Expression as a Form of Liberty," *Jour. of Communication Inquiry* 15 (1991): 48–69, reference on 60.

23. *Indian Treaties*, 41–79, facsimile of title page on 41.

24. For a careful study of the Albany Congress with judicious attention to the differing perspectives of the Six Nations, the British government, and American colonists, including Franklin, see Timothy J. Shannon, *Indians and Colonists at the Crossroads: The Albany Congress of 1754* (Ithaca: Cornell UP, 2000).

25. *Papers*, 5:399–400.

26. Stourzh outlines BF's motives for promoting colonial union, *Franklin*, 50–54.

27. *Papers*, 5:459, 462.

28. *Benjamin Franklin's Autobiographical Writings*, ed. Carl Van Doren (New York, 1945), 87.

29. Frank H. Sommer, "Emblem and Device: The Origin of the Great Seal of the United States," *Art Quarterly* 24 (1961): 63–65.

30. Sommer, 63–65, suggested the possibility with reference to *Recueil* (1696). As reported in my doctoral diss. in 1984, I located the same image in an earlier coll., *Livre Curieux*, and a later ed. of *Recueil* (1724). To date, I have not located any ed. of Verrien's emblem books that has Franklin's distinctive shelf mark in it. Edwin Wolf's file of information on BF's library does not include any of these emblem books by Verrien. Even so, after examining countless emblem books, I have not located the design

for "Se rejoindre ou mourir" in other colls. of emblems, despite Verrien's book's use of a section title suggesting the image had ancient origins. Huston Diehl does not refer to this image under either "serpent" or "snake" in *An Index on Icons in English Emblem Books, 1500–1700* (Norman and London: U of Oklahoma P, 1986), nor does Daniel S. Russell in *The Emblem and Device in France* (Lexington, Ky.: French Forum, 1985).

31. As mentioned previously this claim is based on a computer search using CD-ROM. On French books available in Philadelphia, see Howard Mumford Jones, "The Importation of French Books in Philadelphia, 1750–1800," *Modern Philology* 32 (Nov. 1934): 157–77.

32. Subsequently, in 1755, the image from Verien's collections was reprinted in *Emblems for the Improvement and Entertainment of Youth* (London: Printed for R. Ware, 1755), 103–5.

33. *Pa. Gaz.*, May 9, 1754, p. 2, col. 1; rptd. in *Papers*, 5:272–75, quote on 274.

34. *New-York Gaz.*, May 13, 1754, p. 2, col. 2; *New-York Mercury*, May 13, 1754, p. 2, col. 2; *Boston Weekly News-Letter*, May 23, 1754, p. 1, col. 1; *Boston Gaz.*, May 20, 1754, p. 2, col. 2 through p. 3, col. l; *Boston Evening Post*, May 20, 1754, p. 4, col. 1; *South Carolina Gaz.*, May 28–June 4, 1754, p. 1, col. 2–3.

35. *South Carolina Gaz.*, June 11–20, 1754, p. 1, col. 1; *Boston Gaz.*, Aug. 13, 1754, p. 3, col. 1; *Boston Evening-Post*, Aug. 12, 1754, p. 2, col. 1. Lois K. Mathews, "Benjamin Franklin's Plans for a Colonial Union, 1750–1775," *American Political Science Rev.* 8 (1914): 393–412.

36. Isaiah Thomas, *Hist. of Printing in America*, 2 vols. (Worcester, 1810), 2: 328–329; Isaiah Thomas, *The Hist. of Printing in America with a Biography of Printers & an Account of Newspapers*, ed. Marcus A. McCorison from 2d ed. (1810; rptd., New York: Weathervane, 1970), 435.

37. Mathews, 396. On the authorship and origins of the Albany Plan, Lawrence H. Gipson, "Thomas Hutchinson and the Framing of the Albany Plan of Union, 1754," *PMHB* 74 (1950): 5–35, esp. 29–35, and a reply by Verner W. Crane, *PMHB* 75 (1951): 350–53, with Gipson's response, 353–62.

38. Thomas Hutchinson, *The Hist. of the Colony and Province of Mass.-Bay*, ed. Lawrence Shaw Mayo (Cambridge, Mass.: Harvard UP, 1936; rptd., New York: Kraus, 1970), 3:15.

39. "JOIN, or DIE" appeared in *Pa. Gaz.*, May 9, 1754, p. 2, col. 1; *New-York Gaz.*, May 13, 1754, p. 2, col. 3; *New-York Mercury*, May 13, p. 2, col. 3; *Boston Gaz.*, May 21, p. 3, col. 1; and *Boston Weekly News-Letter*, May 23, p. 1, col. 1. Allusions to "JOIN, or DIE" occurred in *Virginia Gaz.*, July 19, 1754, p. 3, col. 1, and *South Carolina Gaz.*, Aug. 22, 1754, p. 2, col. 2.

40. *Virginia Gaz.*, July 19, 1754, p. 3, col. 1. Robert Dinwiddie, *The Official Records of Robert Dinwiddie, Lieutenant-Governor of the Colony of Virginia, 1751–1758*, with an introduction and notes by R. A. Brock, in *Coll. of the VHS*, n.s., 3 vols. (Richmond, Va.: VHS, 1883), 3:146; *Boston Gaz.*, Aug. 13, 1754. p. 3, col. 1.

41. *South Carolina Gaz.*, Aug. 22, 1754, p. 2, col. 2; *Pa. Gaz.*, Aug. 1, 1754, p. 2, cols. 1–2.

42. Additional MSS, 32,735, f. 133, 134, MSS Dept., BL; *Boston Weekly News-Letter,* April 25, 1754, p. 1, col. 2, and p. 2, col. 1 (rptd. with typographical changes in *Corresp. of Shirley,* 2:43–44).

43. *Boston Weekly News-Letter,* April 25, 1754, p. 1, cols. 1–2, and p. 2, col. 1; *New-York Gaz.,* May 13, 1754, p. 1, cols. 1–3; *Boston Evening-Post,* April 29, 1754, p. 1, col. 2 (identified by Matthews, "The Snake Devices"); *Pa. Gaz.,* May 16, 1754, p. 1, cols. 1–3; *Whitehall Evening-Post,* July 16–18, 1754, p. 1, cols. 1–3.

44. Additional MSS, 32,735, f. 117, f. 134, MSS Dept., BL; *Corresp. of Shirley* 2:112.

45. C.O. 5:1328, f. 83, PRO (Kew). This was received May 15, 1754, and read on May 21, 1754.

46. "Votes and Proceedings of the General Assembly of the Colony of New York," C.O. 5:14, f. 552, PRO (Kew). A note on this document indicates that it was "in Lt. Gov. Delancey's Letter of Oct. 8, 1754," indicating he sent it after news of Virginia's July 3 defeat on the Ohio River.

47. Newbold, *Albany Congress,* 170.

48. *Papers,* 4:118

49. Ibid., 5:338.

50. Ibid., 5:400, 453–54; 6:88, 170, 231–32.

51. C.O. 5:1088, f. 50, PRO (Kew); *Corresp. of Shirley,* 2:113; Colden Papers, *NYHS Coll.* 54 (1921): 25.

52. C.O. 5:14, f. 156, and C.O. 5:14, f. 160, PRO (Kew). For a transcript, *Papers,* 5:272–75.

53. C.O. 5:1274, f. 11–12, PRO (Kew). Whether the materials pertaining to "JOIN, or DIE" were among these is conjecture, since the records do not identify the extracts. No substantial study of Richard Partridge exists, which is unfortunate, because he was Pa.'s agent since 1740, and he represented N.Y., N.J., Mass., R.I., and Conn. at various times (*Papers,* 5:11–12 n. 4).

54. Jack D. Marrietta, "Conscience, the Quaker Community, and the French and Indian War," *PMHB* 95 (1971): 8–9. For a list of other members of the Ohio Company, including Gov. Robert Dinwiddie, see Kenneth P. Bailey, *The Ohio Company of Virginia and the Westward Movement, 1748–1792* (Glendale, Calif.: Arthur H. Clark, 1939), 35–36, 41.

55. Additional MSS, 32,850, f. 229, 231, MSS Dept., BL. Another copy of the extract and the letter to John and Capel Hanbury is also in Additional MSS, 33,029, f. 130, 132–35. The *Virginia Gazette's* allusion to the emblem is in Additional MSS, 33,029, f. 134–35, 32,850, f. 234.

56. Additional MSS, 32,850, f. 234, MSS Dept., BL.

57. Ibid., 33,029, f. 130, 132–35, respectively.

58. Dinwiddie, *Official Records,* 3:208 n. 135.

59. Additional MSS, 35,593, f. 4, MSS Dept., BL. This document does not have a date of receipt written on it.

60. Ibid., 32,736, f. 436.

61. Ibid., 32,736, f. 424.

62. Ibid., 32,736, f. 432.

63. An extract of Dinwiddie's letter without reference to the *Gaz.* is in Additional MSS, 35,909, f. 186–88, MSS Dept., BL. Another, more complete copy is in Additional MSS, 32,736, f. 85–90. The ALS along with the newspaper is held at the C.O. 5:14, f. 422–23, PRO (Kew); for yet another copy, C.O. 5:14, f. 439, PRO (Kew). The last page of the newspaper has a handwritten note, "in Lt. Gov. Dinwiddie's Letter of July 24, 1754." Rptd. in Dinwiddie, *Official Records,* 3:242.

64. Dinwiddie, *Official Records,* 3:237, 245, 247, 251, 253.

65. Ibid., 3:239–43, 243–44, 249.

66. Ibid., 3:259, 275, 277. The copies in *Official Records* of Dinwiddie's letters to Gov. James Hamilton of Pa. and Gov. Horatio Sharpe of Maryland comment upon the defeat and the capitulation, but do not explicitly mention the newspaper. However, the original in Sharpe's corresp. does have an addendum, "The inclos'd News Paper contains a true acct of the action from our officers," which was possibly written on the newspaper itself and as a consequence not included in Dinwiddie's *Official Records.* (Horatio Sharpe, *Corresp. of Gov. Horatio Sharpe,* 3 vols., ed. William Hand Brown, vols. 6, 9, and 14 of *Arch. of Maryland* [Baltimore: Maryland Hist. Soc., 1888], quotation from 6:77). The volume numbers are complicated in that there are two different volume numbers corresponding to each book. Subsequent notes will use the volume number from the *Arch.*

67. Dinwiddie, *Official Records* 3:257.

68. *London Evening-Post,* Sept. 5–7, 1754, p. 1, cols. 1–2; *Whitehall Evening-Post,* Sept. 5–7, 1754, p. 1, col. 3; *Public Advertiser,* Sept. 10, 1754, p. 1, col. 3; *Gent. Mag.* 24 (Sept. 1754): 399–400, quote on 400.

69. C.O. 5:14, f. 483, PRO (Kew). The newspaper is at C.O. 5:14, f. 505–9. The image representing the snake is on f. 506, col. 2, PRO (Kew).

70. Additional MSS, 32,995, f. 309, MSS Dept., BL. Alison Gilbert Olson, "The British Government and Colonial Union, 1754" *WMQ,* 3d ser., 17 (1960): 31. To learn about Arthur Onslow's other comments at this time, I consulted without success *The MSS of the Earl of Buckinghamshire, the Earl of Lindsey, the Earl of Onslow, Lord Emly, Theodore J. Hare, Esq., and James Round, Esq.* (London: Printed for His Majesty's Stationery Office, by Eyre and S. Pottiswood, 1895). J. M. Bumsted, "'Things in the Womb of Time': Ideas of American Independence, 1633–1763," *WMQ,* 3d ser., 31 (1974): 539–540.

71. Horace Walpole, *Memoirs of the Last Ten Years of the Reign of George II* (London, 1822), 1:344. This quote is also in Horace Walpole, *Memoirs of the Last Ten Years of the Reign of George the Second,* ed. John Brooke (New Haven, Yale UP, 1985), 2:16.

72. Additional MSS, 32,736, f. 512–13, MSS Dept., BL.

73. Ibid., 32,737, f. 16–17.

74. Ibid., 32,736, f. 244, 591.

75. The existing literature on the plan of union is misleading in that it suggests that the plan was simply set aside in mid-Sept., following Newcastle's meeting with Arthur Onslow. There is evidence to the contrary (Additional MSS, 32,736, f. 253, and 32,737, f. 411, MSS Dept., BL; similarly, C.O. 5:6, f. 139, and C.O. 5:6, f. 136, PRO [Kew]).

76. *Papers,* 5:417; quote from Alison Olson, "British Gov.," 34.

77. C.O. 5:211, f. 96, PRO (Kew). Also Additional MSS, 32,851, f. 142, MSS Dept., BL.

78. Alison G. Olson discusses the two letters in "British Gov." Shirley to Morris, Oct. 21, 1754, and Shirley to Robinson, Dec. 24, 1754, *Corresp. of Shirley,* 2:96, 117. The latter document is at C.0. 5:15, f. 54, PRO (Kew).

79. H. W. Brands, *The First American: The Life and Times of Benjamin Franklin* (New York: Random House, 2002), 238–40.

80. *Coll. of the MHS,* 1st ser., (Boston: Freeman and Bolles, 1801; rptd., [Boston]: Charles C. Little and James Brown, 1846), 7–8:209, 211.

81. William Smith, *A Brief State of the Province of Pennsylvania* (London: Printed for R. Griffiths, 1755), 10. For an account of the local ramifications for this pamphlet in Pennsylvania politics, Melvin H. Buxbaum, *Benjamin Franklin and the Zealous Presbyterians* (University Park: The Pennsylvania State UP, 1975), 162–63.

82. P. D. G. Thomas, *British Politics and the Stamp Act Crisis: The First Phase of the American Revolution, 1763–1767* (London: Oxford UP, 1975), 84 (quote), 86. For an orientation in addition to P. D. G. Thomas on the Stamp Act controversy in Britain, John L. Bullion, *A Great and Necessary Measure: George Grenville and the Genesis of the Stamp Act, 1763–1765* (Columbia: U of Missouri P, 1982), 193–210; and Edmund S. Morgan and Helen M. Morgan, *The Stamp Act Crisis* (Chapel Hill: U of N.C. P, 1953).

83. *Constitutional Courant,* Sept. 21, 1765, masthead. Thomas, *Hist. of Printing in America* 2:322–323 of the 1810 ed., or 524–525 of the 1970 ed. In the 1810 ed. Isaiah Thomas erroneously referred to the newspaper as the *Constitutional Gazette* (2:322–23), but the error was corrected in later editions (*Papers,* 12:287 n. 4). Ward L. Miner, *William Goddard, Newspaperman* (Durham, N.C.: Duke UP, 1962), 50–52, has proven that Goddard published the *Courant,* though it is often attributed to Parker.

84. *Boston Evening-Post,* Oct. 7, 1765, p. 3, col. 1; *Newport Mercury,* Oct. 7, 1765, p. 2, cols. 1–3.

85. Thomas, *Hist. of Printing in America* 2:322 in 1810 ed.; 524 in 1970 ed.

86. Morgan and Morgan, 201.

87. The ALS is at C.O. 5:1097, f. 170–72, PRO (Kew). The *Courant* with the snake on the masthead is on f. 172, which has a handwritten note on it, "In Lieut. Gov. Colden's of the 12th Oct. 1765." Additional abstracts are in C.O. 5:43, f. 103, and f. 114; also C.O. 5:217, f. 24, PRO (Kew). Another copy is in the House of Lords Papers, Jan. 14, 1766, American Papers, E.f. 448, HLRO. Still another is in the Stowe MSS 264, f. 287–306, MSS Dept., BL, complete with a hand drawing of the snake device on f. 289. For background on the publication and comment on the colony's council meeting, Isaiah Thomas, *Hist. of Printing in America* 2: 322–323 of 1810 ed., 524–525 of the 1970 ed.

88. Henry Seymour Conway to Major General Thomas Gage, Dec. 15, 1765, in the coll. titled Great Britain, Privy Council Letterbook, 1765–66, MS Div., LC. Another letter in this coll. from Conway to Colden mentions his letters of Nov. 5 and the minutes of the Council of N.Y., all of which Conway "immediately laid before the King,"

but does not explicitly mention the letter of Oct. 12. Even so, the later appearance of the letter among those placed by the king before the Parliament proves that at some point it too was presented to the king.

89. Morgan and Morgan, 100, 129–30; *Papers*, 13:188.

90. The ALS of the October 12, 1765, letter is held at the C.O. 5:891, f. 300, PRO (Kew). Copies are in the House of Lords Papers, Jan. 14, 1766, American Papers, D.f.292, and American Papers, F.f.638, HLRO. Additional copies are at the Stowe MSS 265, f. 78, and 265, f. 169–70, MSS Dept., BL. The ALS of the October 17, 1765, letter is held at C.O. 5:891, f. 302, PRO (Kew). Copies are held in the House of Lords Papers, Jan. 14, 1766, American Papers, D.f.294; another copy is in F.f.640–41, HLRO. Additional copies are held in the Stowe MSS 265, f. 79–80, and f. 171–72, MSS Dept., BL. For the text of Bernard's speech, Hutchinson, *History*, 3:334–38, and for an account of the political events, 3:93–94.

91. C.O. 5:891, f. 308, PRO (Kew). House of Lords Papers, Jan. 14, 1766, American Papers, D.f.296; another copy, F.f.645, HLRO. Contemporaneous copies are also held in the Stowe MSS 265, f. 83–84, and f. 176–77, MSS Dept., BL.

92. Isaiah Thomas, *Hist. of Printing in America*, 524; Matthews, "The Snake Devices," 435.

93. C.O. 5:891, f. 307, PRO (Kew). House of Lords Papers, Jan. 14, 1766, American Papers, D.f.296; another copy, F.f.644, HLRO. Contemporaneous copies are also held in the Stowe MSS 265, f. 82, and f. 175, MSS Dept., BL.

94. State Papers, Foreign Office, France, S.P. 78/268, f. 216–17, PRO.

95. *Jour. of the Commissioners for Trade and Plantations, 1764–1767* (London: His Majesty's Stationery Office, 1936), 235 (vol. 72: f. 375). For background, P. D. G. Thomas, *British Politics*, 150.

96. House of Lords Papers, Jan. 14, 1766, American Papers, D.f. 288, HLRO.

97. Ibid., F.f. 565.

98. *Acts of the Privy Council*, Colonial Series, ed. James Munno and Almeric W. Fitzroy (London: His Majesty's Stationery Office, 1912), 6:412–16.

99. Additional MSS, 32,972, f. 190, and Additional MSS, 32,972, f. 214, MSS Dept., BL; P. D. G. Thomas, *British Politics*, 155.

100. Cobbett, *Parliamentary Hist.*, 16:83–84, 84; P. D. G. Thomas, *British Politics* 154–55.

101. C.O. 323:18, f. 171, PRO (Kew), where a notation on the document indicates, "Read December 19, 1765"; *Jour. of Commissioners, 1764–1766*, 236 (vol. 72, f. 378); House of Lords Papers, Jan. 14, 1766, A.f.85, HLRO.

102. C.O. 323:18, f. 178, PRO (Kew), where a notation indicates that it was "Read Dec. 20, 1765," and also T. 1:437, f. 354 for the similar letter to the treasury; *Jour. of Commissioners*, 238 (vol. 72, f. 384); House of Lords Papers, Jan. 14, 1766, A.f.85, HLRO.

103. These are held at the PRO (Kew). Colden's letter of Oct. 12, 1765, is at T1:447, f. 148. Bernard's letters of Oct. 12, 17, and 19, 1765, are at T1:447, f. 155. The precise date that these copies found their way to the Treasury Dept. is not clear, because a note on T1:447, f. 156, indicates when each letter was received, and all of

the above were marked Dec. 15, but another note on T1:447, f. 135, states, "17 Decr Received Representation of ye Board of Trade on Govr Bernard's Letters Concerning ye proceedings subsequent to the Riot."

104. *Acts of the Privy Council,* 6:412–16.

105. Charles Watson-Wentworth, *Memoirs of the Marquis of Rockingham and His Contemporaries,* ed. George Thomas, earl of Albemarle, 2 vols. (London: Richard Bentley, 1852), 1:258.

106. Horace Walpole, *Memoirs of the Reign of King George the Third* (London: Richard Bentley, 1845), 2:237. Walpole's language is almost identical to Rockingham's language in the previous note.

107. Fortescue, *George Third,* 1:203.

108. The quotes from Grafton and the king are taken from P. D. G. Thomas, *British Politics,* 158.

109. Conway to the King, Dec. 19, 1765, Fortescue, *George Third,* 1:205; *Memoirs of Rockingham* 1:259.

110. Additional MSS, 32,972, f. 239, MSS Dept., BL; Additional MSS, 32,972, f. 344, MSS Dept., BL.

111. Ibid., 32,972, f. 333.

112. For further background, Fortescue, *George Third,* 1:206; P. D. G. Thomas, *British Politics,* 169–70.

113. House of Lords Papers, Jan. 14, 1766, f. 658, HLRO; Cobbett, *Parliamentary Hist.,* 16:91, with minor typographical changes.

114. *Papers,* 13:39 n. 7.

115. Walpole, *Memoirs of the Reign of King George the Third,* 2:268 (on printing the American Papers, also 2:290); House of Lords Papers, Jan. 16, 1766, f. 690, HLRO. *Journals of the House of Commons* 30 (Jan. 10, 1765–Sept. 16, 1766): 448.

116. House of Lords Papers, Jan. 16, 1766, f. 690, HLRO; Fortescue, *George Third* 1:233. For further background on the motions to publish the American Papers, Fortescue, *George Third,* 1:233, 236. For a scholarly disagreement about the availability of the American Papers and for a discussion of motions as late as Jan. 29, P. D. G. Thomas, *British Politics,* 158 n. 1, 179, respectively.

117. Burke Papers, Copeland Transcript at Sheffield, O 237; rptd. in Edmund Burke, *The Corresp. of Edmund Burke,* ed. Thomas W. Copeland, 10 vols. (Chicago: U. of Chicago P., 1958), 1 (April 1744–June 1768): 232.

118. Walpole, *Memoirs of the Reign of King George the Third,* 2:268. For additional details on the printing of the American Papers, Walpole, 2:290; P. D. G. Thomas, *British Politics* 178.

119. Villiers Journal, Additional MSS, 47,584, f. 39, MSS Dept., BL. Both motions were also noted in Burke, *The Corresp. of Edmund Burke,* 1:232.

120. Burke Papers, Copeland Transcript at Sheffield, O 237; rptd. in Burke, *The Corresp. of Edmund Burke,* 1:232.

121. William Wildman Barrington and Francis Bernard, *The Barrington-Bernard Corresp. and Illustrative Matter, 1760–1774,* in *Harvard Hist. Studies,* ed. Edward Channing and Archibald Cary Coolridge (Cambridge, Mass.: Harvard UP, 1912), 27:92.

122. House of Lords Papers, Jan. 14, 1766, American Papers, D.f. 309–62, HLRO. The snake device is on f. 310; the *Courant* is on f. 310–13, and the reprint of the *Courant* in the *Newport Mercury* is on f. 316–19. Several copies of the 108-page document, printed sometime at the end of January or during February 1766, are in various MSS Coll., cited below (the BL shelf mark for the document is 9603.g.7.)

123. Villiers Journal, Additional MSS, 47,584, f. 39, MSS Dept., BL; *Memoirs of Rockingham*, 1:291; Sharpe, *Corresp.*, 14:257–58.

124. Charles Garth to the S.C. Committee of Corresp., Feb. 9, 1766, Misc. MSS, MSS Div., NYHS.

125. Grenville Papers, Additional MSS, 57,835, f. 98 and f. 100 respectively, MSS Dept., BL.

126. Additional MSS, 35,911, f. 151–56, the handwritten note is on f. 151, the masthead with the snake device is on f. 152, MSS Dept., BL; summary quote from Additional MSS, 35,911, f. 45, MSS Dept., BL.

127. Additional MSS, 32,971, f. 109, MSS Dept., BL. The date for the receipt of the letter is inconsistent with the ALS of the letter, but the broad outlines of the information conveyed in it make it clear that this is the same document.

128. Hist. MSS Commission, *Manuscripts of the Earl of Dartmouth*, 3 vols. (London: 1887–96). These contain an undated MS identified as "Minutes in Lord Dartmouth's Hand" that includes June-Nov. 1765 letters from Americans such as Francis Bernard and Cadwallader Colden about affairs relative to the Stamp Act (2:30); abstracts of "letters and enclosures received by or communicated to the Lords Commissioners for Trade and Plantations relative to the Stamp Act," including references to Francis Bernard's letters of Oct. 12, 17, 19, and 26 (2:31); and, most important, two copies of the *Constitutional Courant*, Sept. 21, 1765, described as consisting of "1 leaf each" (2:19). The two copies of the *Courant* are reproduced on reel 4 of *The American Papers of the Second Earl of Dartmouth in the Stafford Record Office*, with an introduction by Colin Bonwick (East Ardsley, England: Microform Academic Publishers, 1993), consisting of sixteen microfilm reels. *Papers*, 12:362 n. 6.

129. Rockingham Papers, R22, Sheffield Archives Wentworth Woodhouse Muniments, "Précis of letters from American Governors relating to the Stamp Act," Sheffield Central Library, Sheffield, Britain. (The Wentworth Woodhouse Muniments have been accepted in lieu of inheritance taxes by H.M. Government and allocated to Sheffield City Council. Excerpt courtesy of the Head of Leisure Services, Sheffield City Council.)

130. William Pitt, first earl of Chatham, *Corresp. Of William Pitt*, ed. William Stanhope Taylor and John Henry Pringle (London: John Murray, 1838–40), 2:374–75. B. R. Smith, "The Committee of the Whole House to Consider the American Papers (Jan. and Feb. 1766)" (master's thesis, University of Sheffield, 1956). For the use of Bernard and Colden's letters in the protest of the minority in the House of Lords, see *Papers*, 13:213, 219; also, Sharpe, *Corresp.*, 14:286, 288–89.

131. P. D. G. Thomas, *British Politics*, 191.

132. Conway quote from Fortescue, *George the Third*, 1:249. For Stamp Act debate, Alison G. Olson, *Making the Empire Work: London and American Interest Groups,*

1690–1790 (Cambridge, Mass.: Harvard UP, 1992), 155–58; and Lawrence H. Gipson, "The Great Debate in the Committee of the Whole House of Commons on the Stamp Act, 1766, as Reported by Nathaniel Ryder," *PMHB* 86 (1962): 15.

133. Nathaniel Ryder, "The Parliamentary Diaries of Nathaniel Ryder, 1764–1767," ed. Peter D. G. Thomas, in *Camden Miscellany* (London: Royal Hist. Soc., n.d.), vol. 23, Camden 4th ser., 7:263 (henceforth, "Ryder Diaries"). The first portion of this quotation is also printed in Gipson, "Great Debate," 15–16.

134. "Debates on the Declaratory Act and the Repeal of the Stamp Act, 1766," *American Hist. Rev.* 17 (April 1912): 563–86, quote on 566.

135. *Memoirs of Rockingham*, 1:289. This reference was made in association with events on the evening of Jan. 27, 1766, while the American Papers were still being read.

136. Walpole, *Memoirs of the Reign of King George the Third*, 2:270.

137. Additional MSS, 35,912, f. 86, MSS Dept., BL. Quotation from the original, but it is reprinted with minor typographical differences in "Debates" *American Hist. Rev.* 581.

138. "Debates" *American Hist. Rev.*, 582.

139. Additional MSS, 22, 358, f. 30, MSS Dept., BL.

140. Ms. Letters, vol. 53, 1766, f. 20, Bedford Office (Woburn Abbey, Bedfordshire). (Excerpt by kind permission of the Marquess of Tavistock and the Trustees of the Bedford Estates.)

141. Walpole, *Memoirs of the Reign of King George the Third*, 2:270–71. P. D. G. Thomas, *British Politics*, 189–90.

142. "Ryder Diaries," 7:275. P. D. G. Thomas, *British Politics*, 198.

143. "Ryder Diaries," 7:312–13.

144. *Annual Register for 1765*, 5th ed. (London: J. Dodsley, 1793), 50–51; rptd. with minor changes in Edward Barnard, *The New, Comprehensive and Complete Hist. of England* (London: Printed for the Author and Published by Alex. Hogg, [1782]), 666. The publication date of the first ed. of the *Annual Register for 1765* is not known with precision: *Public Ledger*, Oct. 10, 1765, p. 3, col. 4; *London Chron.*, Nov. 30–Dec. 3, 1765, p. 529, col. 1; and Jan. 18–21, 1766, p. 71, col. 3.

145. *London Evening-Post*, Nov. 2–5, 1765, p. 3, col. 1; *Gazetteer and New Daily Advertiser*, Nov. 6, 1765, p. 2, col. 3; and *Lloyd's Evening Post*, Nov. 6, 1765, p. 441, cols. 1–2.

146. "Rationalis," *Public Ledger*, Nov. 16, 1765, p. 1, col. 3; "From the Public Ledger," *Pa. Jour.*, Feb. 20, 1766, p. 1, col. 3."Rationalis" wrote in several British newspapers during 1765 and 1766, including the *Gazetteer and New Daily Advertiser* on Sept. 6, 1765, p. 2, col. 2; Sept. 7, 1765, p. 4, cols. 1–2; Oct. 23, 1765, p. 4, cols. 2–3; Nov. 1, 1765, p. 4, cols. 2–3; the *Lloyd's Evening Post* for Oct. 30–Nov. 1, 1765, p. 426–27; the *London Chron.* for Oct. 22–4, p. 395, cols. 1–2; Oct. 24–26, p. 402, cols. 2–3; Oct. 31–Nov. 2, 1765, 420, cols. 2–3; Nov. 7–9, 1765, p. 449, col. 1; Nov. 19–21, 1765, p. 489, cols. 1–2; March 6–8, 1766, p. 229, col. 1. Crane asserts that, despite John Mein's claims to the contrary, "Rationalis" was not BF, but Crane does not specify the basis for this assertion in *Letters*, xxviii. Reprinting news under the dateline Feb. 20, New

York, the *Pa. Gaz.*, Feb. 27, 1766, p. 1, col. 3, and the *Pa. Jour.* for Feb. 27, 1766, p. 3, col. 1, both used asterisks to identify "Nicholas Ray" as "A native and formerly an inhabitant of this city [New York], to whom all the English colonies are highly obliged for his unwearied assiduity in their behalf in England, and for his sensible judicious writings published weekly in the London papers, under the titles of Marcus Aurelius and Rationalis." *New-York Gaz.* (James Parker, editor), Feb. 20, 1766, p. 2 col. 2, had carried this article identifying Nicholas Ray as "Rationalis." For BF's intelligence on Ray, *Papers*, 13:498.

147. "Rationalis," *Public Ledger*, Nov. 16, 1765, p. 2, col. 1; "From the Public Ledger," *Pa. Jour.*, Feb. 20, 1766, p. 1, col. 3.

148. "Pacificus," *Gazetteer and New Daily Advertiser*, Nov. 15, 1765, p. 1, col. 3. Crane, *Letters*, indicates that BF may have used the pseudonym "Pacificus" during this period in a later letter (57), but comments that one of the anti-American writers also employed it during this period (55). *Papers*, 13:54, succinctly summarizes the evidence that "Pacificus" was BF's pseudonym for a later letter. Neither source mentions this earlier letter, which was also a defense of the colonies' interests.

149. *The Charters of the Following Provinces of North America . . . To Which is Prefixed, a Faithful Narrative of the Proceedings of the North American Colonies, In Consequence of the Late Stamp-Act* (London: Printed for W. Owens; J. Almon, F. Blyth, 1766), 7; copy in Hardwicke's MSS in the Additional MSS, 35,912, f. 11, MSS Dept., BL; Barnard, *Hist. of England*, 666.

150. I identify and discuss an immense variety of these objects in Olson, *Emblems*, 21–74.

151. Crane, *Letters*, 110–12. *Papers*, 15:36–38. The attribution of this letter to BF is probable, but not certain.

152. *Papers*, 13:240, 207.

153. Ibid., 13:212.

154. Ibid., 13:213, 214.

155. Bernard Bailyn, *The Ideological Origins of the American Revolution* (Cambridge, Mass.: Harvard UP, 1967), provides background on the concept of sovereignty, 198–229, quote on 198.

156. *Papers*, 13:219–20.

157. Ibid., 13:224.

158. Verner W. Crane, "The Stamp Act Crisis," in *Benjamin Franklin: A Profile*, ed. Esmond Wright (New York: Hill and Wang, 1970), 126.

159. *Papers*, 5:417. For a careful argument that BF's account here was not perhaps the most fundamental explanation, see Alison Olson, "British Gov.," 34, and Shannon, *Indians and Colonists at the Crossroads of Empire*.

Chapter 4. "MAGNA *Britannia: her Colonies* REDUC'd," 1765–66

1. Essays that comment at length on "MAGNA *Britannia*" are *Papers*, 13:66–72; Frederic R. Kirkland, "An Unknown Franklin Cartoon" *PMHB* 73 (Jan. 1949): 76–79; Edwin Wolf II, "Benjamin Franklin's Stamp Act Cartoon," *Proc. of the APS* 99 (Dec. 1955): 388–96; M. Dorothy George, *English Political Caricature to 1792: A Study of*

Opinion and Propaganda (Oxford: Clarendon, 1959), 136–37; Lester C. Olson, "Benjamin Franklin's Pictorial Representations of the British Colonies in America: A Study in Rhetorical Iconology" *QJS* 73 (Feb. 1987): 18–42; Olson, *Emblems*, 219–25; Karen Severud Cook, "Benjamin Franklin and the Snake That Would Not Die," in Cook, ed., *Images and Icons of the New World: Essays on American Cartography* (London: British Library, 1996), 88–111, esp. 99–101.

2. Albert Matthews, "The Snake Devices, 1754–1776, and the *Constitutional Courant* 1765," Dec. 1907, *Pubs. of the Colonial Soc. of Mass.* (Boston: Colonial Soc. of Mass., Dec. 1908), 11: 409–453.

3. *Papers*, 13:170; Wolf, 389.

4. *Papers*, 13:189; Van Doren, *Franklin-Mecom*, 92; Wolf, 390.

5. *Papers*, 13:67–68. The editors speculate on earlier sources of the image, 13:67.

6. *Papers*, 13:176; Wolf, 389.

7. *Papers*, 13:68; Wolf, 390.

8. A copy of the broadside with a handwritten, contemporaneous note is held at the APS (Wolf, 390). Wolf was correct in his claim that the exact date of publication of the Philadelphia broadside version must remain at issue, reasoning that it was probably published between 1767 and 1769. But he may have erred when he dismissed Ford's initial dating of the engraving in 1766, by claiming that "it hardly seems likely that Franklin's London original would have reached any of his American correspondents much before the news of the repeal of the act; hence its republication then would have lacked point" (390–92). By that reasoning, however, the *Examination*, which transpired on Feb. 13, 1766, only eleven days before BF sent "MAGNA *Britannia*" to David Hall, also would not have been circulated in 1766. Strahan did not send a copy of the *Examination* to Hall until May 1766, but it was printed and distributed by Sept. 1766 to vindicate BF's conduct and to influence the fall elections in Pennsylvania. "MAGNA *Britannia*" could have served similar ends. Therefore, the 1766 date for the Philadelphia version remains plausible, though even if it were later published between 1767 and 1769, it still could have been used as an apologia to vindicate BF, since the endeavor to rehabilitate his reputation persisted for years. Ward L. Miner, *William Goddard, Newspaperman* (Durham: Duke UP, 1962), 73.

9. Many years later, WTF articulated a similar account of the use of the print, *Memoirs of the Life and Writings of Benjamin Franklin*, 6 vols. (Philadelphia: William Duane, 1800–18), 1:270–71. Sparks, *Works*, 4:456.

10. Wolf, 390.

11. *Papers*, 13:124–62. The *Papers* address the extent to which the proceedings during the *Examination* were a pre-orchestrated affair at 13:128. The *Papers'* position is endorsed tacitly by G. Jack Gravlee and James R. Irvine in "Franklin Reexamined: A Rejection of Parliamentary Manipulation," *Southern Speech Communication Jour.* 48 (winter 1983): 167–81.

12. *Papers*, 13:509.

13. Thomas Hollis to John [or Jonathan] Mayhew, June 19, 1766, MHS. Rptd. in Bernhard Knollenberg, ed., "Thomas Hollis and Jonathan Mayhew: Their Corre-

spondence, 1759–1766," *Proc. of the MHS* (Portland, Maine: Anthoensen, 1956), 69:190.

14. For an analysis of the political factors entailed in the change of government, Peter D. G. Thomas, "The Change of Ministry in 1765," in *British Politics and the Stamp Act Crisis: The First Phase of the American Revolution, 1763–1767* (Oxford: Clarendon, 1975): 115–30. For George Grenville's political role, John L. Bullion, *A Great and Necessary Measure: George Grenville and the Genesis of the Stamp Act, 1763–1765* (Columbia: U of Missouri P, 1982). For the broad outlines of the controversy, Edmund S. Morgan and Helen M. Morgan, *The Stamp Act Crisis: Prologue to Revolution* (Chapel Hill, U of North Carolina P, 1953).

15. Michael G. Kammen, "The Agents and the Stamp Act Crisis, 1765–1766," in *A Rope of Sand: The Colonial Agents, British Politics, and the American Revolution* (Ithaca, N.Y.: Cornell UP, 1968), 123. P. D. G. Thomas, *British Politics*, 140.

16. I discuss this exchange later in the chapter on *Libertas Americana*, 1782–83 on pp. 183–84.

17. Wolf, 388–96; *Papers*, 13:66–72; Kirkland, 76–79.

18. *Papers*, 12:287–88.

19. The *Papers*, 12:287 n. 3, specify that the version of the *Courant* sent to BF was one with a snake device on the masthead. On the incorrect attribution to Parker, see Matthews, "The Snake Devices," 441; Isaiah Thomas, *History of Printing in America*, 2 vols. (Worcester, 1810) 2: 323; 441; Thomas, *The Hist. of Printing in America with a Biography of Printers & an Account of Newspapers*, ed. Marcus A. McCorison from 2d ed. (rptd., New York: Weathervane, 1970), 525. Miner 50–52. *Papers*, 12:287 n. 4.

20. *Papers*, 13:12. For further background, see my earlier chapter on "JOIN, or DIE," 1754 on pp. 54–57.

21. Thomas, *Hist. of Printing in America* 2: 323 in 1810 ed.; 525 in 1970 ed.

22. *Papers*, 12:287, 288 n. 5.

23. Thomas Hutchinson, *The Hist. of the Colony and Province of Mass.-Bay*, ed. Lawrence Shaw Mayo (Cambridge, Mass.: Harvard UP, 1936; rptd., New York: Kraus, 1970), 3:90–91. Bernard Bailyn, *The Ordeal of Thomas Hutchinson* (Cambridge, Mass.: Harvard UP, 1974), 35–37, 68–72. P. D. G. Thomas, *British Politics* 135. BF was aware of the destruction of Hutchinson's home (Van Doren, *Franklin-Mecom*, 86–87, 92; *Papers*, 12:417–19, 13:188).

24. *Papers*, 12:380–81.

25. Lawrence Henry Gipson, "Thomas Hutchinson and the Framing of the Albany Plan of Union, 1754," *PMHB* 74 (1950): 5–35, esp. 9, 21. Bailyn, *Ordeal* 15, 81, 143.

26. *Papers*, 12:380–81.

27. Among the other papers placed before the House of Commons, was a letter "from Lieut. Governor *Hutchinson* to Mr. Secretary *Conway*. Boston, 27th Oct. 1765. Inclosing . . . Printed Copy of the *Boston Evening Post* and *Supplement* [,] Printed Copy of the *New Port Mercury*." This letter, received by Conway's office on Dec. 13, 1765, was placed before the House of Commons on Jan. 14, 1766 (*Journals of the House of Commons* 30 [Jan. 10, 1765–Sept. 16, 1766]: 448). A note in C.O. 5:755, f. 384, PRO (Kew), indicates that this was a complete copy of the *Newport Mercury* with excerpts

from the *Constitutional Courant*, but without the snake device. C.O. 5:755, f. 361, PRO (Kew), indicates that Conway received it on December 13, 1765. I have been unable to ascertain which issue of the *Boston Evening Post* was enclosed in the letter.

28. These publications are discussed in the chapter on "JOIN, or DIE" on pp. 66–68.

29. For example, BF used the pseudonym "W. S." in the *Public Ledger*, Nov. 20, 1765, p. 4, cols. 2–3. For the attribution of this article to BF, see Crane, *Letters*, 35–38. The piece was printed initially in the *London Chron.*, Nov. 16, 1765, p. 471, cols. 1–2.

30. For a list of the publications impugning and promoting Franklin's career in 1764, see Melvin H. Buxbaum, *Benjamin Franklin, 1721–1906, A Reference Guide* (Boston: G. K. Hall, 1983), 4–9.

31. *Papers*, 11:434.

32. G. B. Warden, "The Proprietary Group in Pennsylvania, 1754–1764," *WMQ*, 3d ser., 21 (1964): 367–89, esp. 370.

33. Quotes from Warren, 369–70, 378, respectively.

34. Ibid., 369.

35. Ibid., 383–84.

36. John Penn to Thomas Penn, May 5, 1764, Penn Papers, HSP; *Papers*, 11:173 n. 7.

37. [Isaac Hunt], *A Looking-Glass for Presbyterians, Number II* (Philadelphia, 1764) [Evans 9703], 30. Newcomb, *Franklin*, 86.

38. Melvin H. Buxbaum, *Benjamin Franklin and the Zealous Presbyterians* (University Park: The Pennsylvania State UP, 1975), 5.

39. *Papers*, 4:234.

40. *Papers*, 11:329. For accounts of the 1764 campaign, Marc Egnal, "The Politics of Ambition: A New Look at Benjamin Franklin's Career," *Canadian Rev. of American Studies* 6 (1975): 151–64; David L. Jacobson, "The Fight Against Royal Government, 1764," *John Dickinson and the Revolution in Pennsylvania, 1764–1776* (Berkeley: U of Calif. P, 1965), 9–26; and Robert Middlekauff, *Benjamin Franklin and His Enemies* (Berkeley: U of Calif. P, 1996), 22–114. For the use of political cartoons in the campaign, E. P. Richardson, "The Birth of Political Caricature," in *Philadelphia Printmaking*, ed. Robert F. Looney (Westchester, Pa.: Tinicum, 1977), 72; Sellers, *Franklin* 379–82.

41. *The Counter-Medly* [Evans 9943].

42. Jacobson, 22; Samuel Purviance Jr. to James Burd, Sept. 10, 1764, Shippen Papers, Corresp., vol. 6, HSP, quoted in William Hanna, *Benjamin Franklin and Pennsylvania Politics* (Stanford, Calif.: Stanford UP, 1964), 166.

43. *The Plot. By way of burlesk, to turn F[rankli]n out of the Assembly* (Philadelphia, 1764) [Evans 9799]; J. Philip Gleason, "A Scurrilous Colonial Election and Franklin's Reputation," *WMQ*, 3d ser., 18 (1961): 79.

44. *To the Freeholders and Other Electors of Assembly-Men for Pennsylvania* (Philadelphia, 1765), in a footnote on the broadside [Evans 10184].

45. *Papers*, 11:397; William Allen to Thomas Penn, Oct. 21 1764, Penn MSS: Official Corresp., 9:282, HSP.

46. Crane, *Letters*, 24.

47. *Papers*, 11:408–12. Gleason, 68–84. For John Dickinson's role, Jacobson, 9–26.

48. *Papers,* 11:430–41. Buxbaum, *Zealous Presbyterians,* 112, 215–17.

49. Verner W. Crane, "The Stamp Act Crisis," in *Benjamin Franklin: A Profile,* ed., Esmond Wright (New York: Hill and Wang, 1970), 116. On Franklin's adversaries, Robert Middlekauf, *Benjamin Franklin and His Enemies* (Berkeley: U of Calif. P, 1996).

50. *Pa. Jour.,* Dec. 20, 1764, p. 3, col. 2, and Jan. 10, 1765, p. 2, cols. 1–3, and p. 3, col. 1.

51. *Pa. Jour.,* Oct. 3, 1765, p. 3, col. 3. On the life of William Franklin, Sheila L. Skemp, *William Franklin: Son of a Patriot, Servant of a King* (New York: Oxford UP, 1990).

52. *Papers,* 12:388.

53. Crane, "Stamp Act Crisis," 107; Newcomb, *Franklin,* 109. For background on Grenville's meeting with the colonial agents, Morgan and Morgan, 54–66.

54. *Papers,* 13:449.

55. Newcomb, *Franklin,* 111.

56. *Papers,* 13:449.

57. Joseph Galloway to William Franklin, Dec. 21, 1766, APS; Crane, "Stamp Act Crisis," 109.

58. *Papers,* 12:47–60; Newcomb, *Franklin,* 111 n. 14; Morgan and Morgan, 8.

59. *Papers,* 5:339 n. 5

60. Ibid., 12:207–8.

61. Newcomb, *Franklin,* 113–14.

62. Bullion, 197.

63. For John Hughes's experiences during the protests, Morgan and Morgan, 238–57.

64. *Pa. Jour., Supplement,* Sept. 18, 1766, p. 2, col. 2.

65. Newcomb, *Franklin,* 108, 115; Benjamin H. Newcomb, "Effects of the Stamp Act on Colonial Pennsylvania Politics," *WMQ,* 3d ser., 23 (1966): 260–61. James E. Hutson, "The Campaign to Make Pennsylvania a Royal Province, 1764–1770, Part II," *PMHB* 95 (1971): 28–39.

66. For the text of BF's *Examination* with ed. notes, *Papers,* 13:124–62; also, an annotated transcript is located in the Rockingham MSS, R27, f. 35–69, Sheffield RO. For a contemporary witness's account, Lawrence H. Gipson, "The Great Debate in the Committee of the Whole House of Commons on the Stamp Act, 1766, as Reported by Nathaniel Ryder," *PMHB* 86 (1962): 10–41, esp. 34–35; and Peter D. G. Thomas, ed., "Parliamentary Diaries of Nathaniel Ryder, 1764–7," *Camden Miscellany* (London: Royal Hist. Soc., n.d.), vol. 23, Camden 4th ser., 7:300–302. For background concerning publication of BF's *Examination,* "Corresp. Between William Strahan and David Hall, 1763–1777," *PMHB* 10 (1886): 96–97, 217, 220–21.

67. Newcomb, *Franklin,* 133, 140.

68. Crane, "Stamp Act Crisis," 113. On Strahan, see "Corresp. Between Strahan and Hall" 92.

69. Crane, *Letters,* 35–76.

70. Crane, "Stamp Act Crisis," 113; Miner 73.

71. John Fothergill to James Pemberton, February 27, 1766, held at the HSP. Betsy Copping Corner, "Dr. Fothergill's Friendship with Benjamin Franklin," *Proc. of the APS* 102, no. 5 (October 1958): 413–19, esp. 415. *Pa. Gaz.*, May 8, 1766, p. 2, col. 3; for other letters concerning BF's performance, May 1, 1766, p. 3, col. 2; May 8, 1766, p. 1, col. 2.

72. During the process of repealing the Stamp Act, several members of the House of Lords who were opposed to the repeal prepared two protests in March 1766, one following the second reading of the legislation in the House of Lords, the other following the third reading. These protests were published shortly later, possibly during the same month but certainly before mid-April 1766, in two pamphlet forms. One of these was titled *Protest against the Bill To repeal the American Stamp Act, of the Last Session,* and the other was titled *Second Protest, with a List of Voters against the Bill to Repeal the American Stamp Act.* These contain statements that provide evidence of the parliamentarians' expectations. They are discussed in the previous chapter on pp. 72–75.

73. For examples, *Papers,* 4:233–34, 9:78–79.

74. Ibid., 13:132; Stephen E. Lucas, *Portents of Rebellion: Rhetoric and Revolution in Philadelphia, 1765–1776* (Philadephia: Temple UP, 1976), 13; Merrill Jensen, "America in 1763," *The Founding of a Nation* (New York: Oxford UP, 1968), 10.

75. *Papers,* 13:150.

76. Herbert M. Atherton, "The Allegory of Patriotism," *Political Prints in the Age of Hogarth: A Study of the Ideographic Representation of Politics* (Oxford: Clarendon, 1974), 89–97.

77. For BF's private reasoning, *Papers,* 21:417.

78. For example, *Papers,* 9:90.

79. Ibid., 12:380–81.

80. John Penn's message to the Pa. Assembly, June 3, 1766, *Papers,* 13:292–93 n. 2, which cites *Pa. Arch.,* 8th ser., 7:5877–79, 5881.

81. *Papers,* 13:72.

82. Douglass Adair, "The Stamp Act in Contemporary English Cartoons," *WMQ,* 3d ser., 10 (Oct. 1953): 538–42. E. P. Richardson, "Stamp Act Cartoons in the Colonies," *PMHB* 96 (July 1972): 275–97.

83. *Annual Register for 1766,* 5th ed. (London: J. Dodsley in Pall Mall, 1793), 35. On the existing economic recession in Britain, P. D. G. Thomas, *British Politics,* 214–15, and Morgan and Morgan, 264.

84. *Papers,* 13:72.

85. Gipson, "Great Debate" 40.

86. *Papers,* 13:71–72.

87. Franklin Papers, vol. 51, f. 95, held at APS.

88. *Papers,* 13:72.

89. *Annual Register for 1766* 35. For commentary on economic considerations in repealing the Stamp Act, P. D. G. Thomas, *British Politics* 214–215; Gipson, "Great Debate" 40.

90. *Papers,* 13:220. Crane, "Stamp Act Crisis," 125.

91. This concern is discussed in the chapter on "JOIN, or DIE, 1754" on pp. 72–75.

92. There is disagreement about whether BF's letter to Lord Kames was sent on April 11, 1767, or on Feb. 25, 1767. The *Papers* comment on the issue, 14: 62–64, 116. Quote from 14:65.

93. For example, Crane, *Letters*, 42; *Papers*, 12:414.

94. *Papers*, 14:65. Also on this point, *Papers*, 13:426.

95. Ibid., 13:84, 83. Crane, *Letters*, 72, 71.

96. Ibid., 17:320–21, 321.

97. Ibid., 13:396–97.

98. Ibid., 13:479, 488. Quote from 13:488; similarly, from *Poor Richard's Almanac* in 1757; rptd., *Papers*, 7:85.

99. *Papers*, 13:144–45, 153, 156.

100. On BF's pragmatism, Clinton Rossiter, "The Political Theory of Benjamin Franklin," in *Benjamin Franklin*, ed. Esmond Wright, 151, and Crane, *Letters*, 129 n. 3.

101. Crane, "Stamp Act Crisis," 129; also, *Papers*, 14:69.

102. *Papers*, 13:225.

103. Ibid., 17:379–80.

104. *Papers*, 12:376. On BF's relationship to Galloway, see Newcomb, *Franklin*.

105. *Papers*, 13:37.

106. John E. Ferling, *The Loyalist Mind: Joseph Galloway and the American Revolution* (University Park: Pennsylvania State UP, 1977). Mary Beth Norton, "The Loyalist Critique of the Revolution," in *The Development of a Revolutionary Mentality*, with an introduction by Richard B. Morris (Washington D.C.: Library of Congress, 1972), 127–48, esp. 133–34.

107. *Papers*, 29:614. For an analysis of the republican political economy BF envisioned for the colonies, Drew R. McCoy, "Benjamin Franklin's Vision of a Republican Political Economy for America," *WMQ*, 3rd ser., 35 (1978): 605–28.

108. *Papers*, 21:417. Similarly, *Papers*, 13:84; Crane, *Letters*, 73.

Chapter 5. "WE ARE ONE," 1776

1. Although sometimes attributed to Franklin, the epigraph was actually by an Italian historian, Charles (Carlo G.) Botta, in an English translation of his history of the United States. Richard T. Hoober attributed the remark to Franklin twice—once in Hoober's essay "Franklin's Influence on Colonial and Continental Paper Money," *Numismatist* 69 (Dec. 1956): 1362 and again in Hoober's essay "Franklin, The Money Printer," *Numismatic Scrapbook Mag* 32 (Feb. 1966): 268. Neither paragraph had any citations for original sources. A similar passage can be found in Henry Phillips, Jr., *Hist. Sketches of the Paper Currency of the American Colonies: Prior to the Adoption of the Federal Constitution*, 2 vols. (Roxbury, Mass.: W. Elliot Woodward, 1865–66): 2:31. But the attribution in Phillips's book was ambiguous because of a passive-voice construction, making it seem like the comment might have been by Franklin. However, Phillips cited "Botta," referring only to a chapter title, "The American War," from Botta's history. Translated from Italian into English by George Alexander Otis, Charles (Carlo Giuseppe) Botta's *Hist. of the War of the Independence of the United*

States of America went through several editions. Botta's remark can be found, for example, in the seventh edition (New Haven: Nathan Whiting, 1837) 1: 271.

2. The most comprehensive studies of the design include Newman, *Paper Money*, 20, 32–33, 46; David P. McBride "Linked Rings: Early American Unity Illustrated," *Numismatist* 92 (Nov. 1979): 2374–93; Eric P. Newman, "Benjamin Franklin and the Chain Design," *Numismatist* 96 (Nov. 1983): 2271–84; and Eric P. Newman, "Continental Currency and the Fugio Cent: Sources of Emblems and Mottoes," *Numismatist* 79 (Dec. 1966): 1587–98. There is a brief discussion of the image in Olson, *Emblems*, 214–16. The 1956 issue of *Numismatist* had several articles on BF's contributions to numismatics.

3. Maurice Charland, "Constitutive Rhetoric: The Case of the *Peuple Québécois*," *QJS*, 73 (1987): 133–50.

4. *Papers*, 22:572–74.

5. John Adams, *Diary and Autobiography of John Adams*, ed. L. H. Butterfield (Cambridge, Mass.: Belknap Press of Harvard UP, 1961), 2:245. H. W. Brands, *The First American: The Life and Times of Benjamin Franklin* (New York: Random House, 2002), 513; Edmund S. Morgan, *Benjamin Franklin* (New Haven: Yale UP, 2002), 238–39.

6. William H. Nelson, *The American Tory* (Oxford: Clarendon, 1961), 64; Janice Potter, *The Liberty We Seek* (Cambridge, Mass.: Harvard UP, 1983), 5. On using the terms "Tory" and "Loyalist," see Mary Beth Norton, "The Loyalist Critique of the Revolution," in *The Development of a Revolutionary Mentality*, with an introduction by Richard B. Morris (Washington D.C.: Library of Congress, 1972), 126–48.

7. For examples of such verses concerning the currency, see Winthrop Sargent, *The Loyalist Poetry of the Revolution* (Philadelphia: [Collins], 1857), 2, 28, 32, 37, 71; Phillips 2:245–51. For the Loyalists' poetry in general, also Winthrop Sargent, *The Loyal Verses of Joseph Stansbury and Doctor Jonathan Odell Relating to the American Revolution* (Albany: J. Munsell, 1860).

8. William B. Willcox, "Franklin's Last Years in England: The Making of a Rebel," in *Critical Essays on Benjamin Franklin*, ed. Melvin H. Buxbaum (Boston: G. K. Hall, 1987), 96–110.

9. Smith, *Letters*, 2:166.

10. Ibid., 3:271, 294. *JCC*, 2:103, 105–6, 3:390, 398, 4:157, 164–65. *Papers*, 22:358 n. 2.

11. Newman, *Paper Money* 18, 20.

12. Franklin Papers, vol. 58, f. 151, APS. Newman, *Paper Money*, 32–33. *Papers*, 22:358 n. 3.

13. For other evidence supporting the attribution to BF, see *Papers*, 22:358. McBride points out that "Others thought to have been possible designers of the notes are Francis Hopkinson and David Rittenhouse" (2375), but Newman explains why these sources are much less likely than BF ("Benjamin Franklin and the Chain Design," 2272). Germane to the attribution of currency designs in 1775 to BF is William Browne to Samuel Curwen, Jan. 8, 1776, in *Jour. and Letters of the Late Samuel Curwen, 1775–1784*, ed. George Atkinson Ward (London: Wiley and Putnam, 1842), 46.

14. Hoober, "Franklin's Influence," 1357–62. Hoober, "Franklin, the Money Printer," 258–69.

15. *Papers*, 1:139–57.

16. BF's [Preliminary ink sketch of wind blowing waves design for Continental currency], 1776, Franklin Papers, vol. 50 (ii) f. 45, APS.

17. *Papers*, 9:90–91. For the attribution to BF, *Papers*, 9:53–54.

18. Ibid., 15:3.

19. McBride, 2375.

20. An unpublished MS by Samuel Breck, "Hist. Sketch of the Continental Bills of Credit, from the Year 1775 to 1781," facing p. 18, APS.

21. Eric P. Newman, "Poor Richard's Mottoes for Coins," *Numismatist* 69 (Dec. 1956): 1363. Francis Hopkinson, who is sometimes suggested as a possible designer, sought compensation for seven designs on the 1778–79 currency, but not for any issued in 1776. On this matter, George E. Hastings, *Life and Works of Francis Hopkinson* (Chicago: U of Chicago P, 1926), 240–57; also, Newman, "Continental Currency and the Fugio Cent," 1594–1596.

22. Olson, *Emblems*, 214–15.

23. Phillips, 2:204.

24. Smith, *Letters*, 1:492. For examples, see 1:502, 503, 508, 518. For additional letters from the delegates of Congress about the paper currency, 1:496, 498, 507, 515, 524–26, 528, 543, 561. For documents about how the currency was to be backed by each colony, see 1:482, 687, 689.

25. Smith, *Letters*, 1:503.

26. *Papers*, 22:125, 121–22.

27. Smith, *Letters*, 3:83 n. 2.

28. Ibid., 2:524, 3:83.

29. Bigelow, *Works*, 8:352, quote from photocopy of original MS. For an interpretation of BF's economic views, Tracy Mott and George W. Zinke, "Benjamin Franklin's Economic Thought: A Twentieth Century Appraisal," in *Critical Essays*, 111–28.

30. Olson, *Emblems*, 209–18.

31. McBride, 2374, comments on the similarities with Greek symbolism.

32. For example, *Papers*, 5:93.

33. Donald A. Grinde Jr. and Bruce E. Johansen, *Exemplars of Liberty: Native America and the Evolution of Democracy* (Los Angeles, Calif.: U of Calif. Los Angeles, 1991), 143, 149, 278 n. 27.

34. Several books and articles address the Iroquois influence thesis. The case supporting "the Iroquois influence thesis" may be exemplified by Donald A. Grinde Jr., *The Iroquois and the Founding of the American Nation* (San Francisco: Indian Historian, 1977); Bruce E. Johansen, *Forgotten Founders: How the American Indian Helped Shape Democracy* (Harvard and Boston, Mass.: Harvard Common, 1982); and Grinde and Johansen, *Exemplars of Liberty*, The case opposing the Iroquois influence thesis may be exemplified by Elisabeth Tooker's stinging critique in 1988 in "The United States Constitution and the Iroquois League," *Ethnohistory* 35 (fall 1988): 305–36, as well as a series of articles in a forum in *WMQ*, 3d ser., 53 (July 1996): Philip A. Levy, "Exemplars of Taking Liberties: The Iroquois Influence Thesis and the Problem of Evidence," 588–603; and Samuel B. Payne Jr., "The Iroquois League, the Articles of Confederation, and the Constitution," 604–20.

For replies to these objections by Tooker, Levy, and Payne, see Donald A. Grinde Jr. and Bruce E. Johansen, "Sauce for the Goose: Demand and Definitions for 'Proof' Regarding the Iroquois and Democracy," *WMQ*, 3rd ser., 53 (1996): 621–36. In addition, Donald A. Grinde Jr., "The Iroquois and the Development of American Government," *Hist. Reflections/Reflexions Historiques* 21 (1995): 301–18; and Bruce E. Johansen, "Native American Roots for Freedom of Expression as a Form of Liberty," *Jour. of Communication Inquiry* 15 (summer 1991): 48–69.

35. For the thirteen treaties, see *Indian Treaties Printed by Benjamin Franklin, 1736–1762*, with an introduction by Carl Van Doren and notes by Julian P. Boyd (Philadelphia: HSP, 1938), 54. This book is an "exact facsimile" of thirteen treaties published by BF between 1736 and 1762.

36. *Pa. Gaz.*, Aug. 28–Sept. 7, 1732, p. 4, col. 1; *Papers*, 1:277; *Pa. Gaz.*, Sept. 30–Oct. 7, 1736, p. 3, col. 2. For a history of the "covenant chain," see Francis Jennings, "The Constitutional Evolution of the Covenant Chain," *Proc. of the APS* 115 (April 1971): 88–96; Gunther Michelson, "The Covenant Chain in Colonial History," *Man in the Northeast* 21 (1981): 115–26.

37. Brands, 222–27.

38. "Jour. of the Proceedings of the Congress Held at Albany, in 1754," *MHS Coll.*, 3d ser., 5 (1836): 9, 10, 14, 15.

39. Ibid., 21, 35, 37, 40, 41, 44, 45.

40. George Hamell, Senior Museum Exhibits Planner in Anthropology, New York State Museum, letter to author, Feb. 16, 1995.

41. Perry Miller, "From the Covenant to the Revival," in *The Shaping of American Religion*, ed. James Ward Smith and A. Leland Jamison (Princeton, N.J.: Princeton UP, 1961), 325.

42. *Papers*, 36:171; John Adams to Charles Dumas, Sept. 10, 1783, C. W. F. Dumas *Papers*, vol. 1, MS Div., LC.

43. Richard S. Patterson and Richardson Dougall, *The Eagle and the Shield: A Hist. of the Great Seal of the United States* (Washington D.C.: GPO, 1976), 16–25. Richardson, *Standards*, 10–11.

44. *Papers*, 22:218.

45. Quotation from *Papers*, 22:344. For examples of letters abroad, *Papers*, 22:34, 86, 93–94, 217–18, 288–89.

46. Smith, *Letters*, 1:496.

47. Ibid., 1:528.

48. Ibid., 1:496, 567; *Papers*, 22:525.

49. John Adams to Hezekiah Niles, Feb. 13, 1818, in *Works of John Adams*, ed. Charles Francis Adams, 10 vols. (Boston: Little, Brown, and Co., 1850–56), 10:283.

50. Sargent, *Loyalist Poetry*, 32, 28, 2, respectively. Another example is "A Fragment," *Loyalist Rhapsodes*, ser. 8D, no. 90, reel 49, Peter Force Coll., MS Div., LC.

51. "Mud Island," *Loyalist Rhapsodes*.

52. R. R. [Joseph Stansbury], "The History of Peru & c.," in *Loyalist Rhapsodes*. The verses quoted in the next several paragraphs are from this source. The poem is reprinted in Eric P. Newman, *Numismatist* 96 (1983): 2282–84, with slight typographical differences from the MS at the LC.

53. Newman, "Poor Richard's Mottoes," 1363. The mistaken attribution is discussed above in n. 21.

54. On ridicule as argument, James A. Herrick, "Miracles and Method," *QJS* 75 (1989): 323.

55. Max Farrand, ed., *The Records of the Federal Convention of 1787*, rev. ed., 4 vols. (New Haven: Yale UP, 1937), 2:648. Van Doren, *Franklin*, 754–55. William G. Carr, *The Oldest Delegate: Franklin in the Constitutional Convention* (Newark: U of Delaware P, 1990), 122.

56. Herrick, 321–34.

57. *London Chron.*, June 4–6, 1776, p. 542, col. 2; Nov. 5–7, 1776, p. 446, cols. 2; Dec. 28–31, 1776, p. 630, col. 1.

58. Quotes from ibid., March 5–7, 1776, p. 229, col. 1. On Continental Congress's resolution, p. 232, col. 2.

59. Rutledge quote from Smith, *Letters*, 5:295; Hooper quotes, 5:439–40; Morris quote, 5:623; Rush quotes, 5:639.

60. For examples, Smith, *Letters*, 4:148, 295, 424, 5:295, 424, 440, 623, 647.

61. Ibid., 5:639.

62. Olson, *Emblems*, 215.

63. Eric P. Newman, "The Continental Dollar of 1776 Meets Its Maker," *Numismatist* 72 (Aug. 1959): 914–26; Eric Newman, "The 1776 Continental Currency Coinage," *Coin Collector's Jour.* 19 (July-Aug. 1952): 1–9. Newman, *Paper Money*, 17; McBride, 2376.

64. *London Chron.*, Dec. 21–24, 1776, p. 606, col. 3.

65. McBride, 2376.

66. For a contemporaneous description of the design on the Vermont currency, William Bentley, *Diary of William Bentley*, 4 vols. (Salem, Mass.: 1905–14), 1:99, entry for April 27, 1788. Newman, *Paper Money*, 105–6, 324.

67. McBride, 2378.

68. Ibid., 2378, 2379.

69. Newman, *Paper Money*, 324.

70. Bentley, 1:99. Olson, *Emblems*, 215–16.

71. *Papers*, 30:37. Morgan, 253–54.

72. Richardson, *Standards* 101, 209, plate 31; McBride, 2377. The flag is held at NHHS. It is possible that the "Colors of a Newburyport Company" featured an elaborate design influenced by the interlinked rings (Richardson, *Standards*, 96–97, 204, plate 26).

73. For additional examples, Richardson, *Standards*, 5–7, 47–50.

74. Isaiah Thomas, *Hist. of Printing in America*, 2 vols. (Worcester, 1810), 2: 266; Isaiah Thomas, *The Hist. of Printing in America with a Biography of Printers & an Account of Newspapers*, ed. Marcus A. McCorison from 2nd ed. (New York: Weathervane, 1970), 278.

75. Charles Wyllys Betts, *American Colonial Hist. Illustrated by Contemporary Medals* (New York: Scott Stamp and Coin, 1894), no. 614. McBride, 2380. Olson, *Emblems*, 215; #015857, Dept. of Coins and Medals, BM.

76. McBride, 2379–80.

77. Ibid., 2380–81.

78. Eric P. Newman, "Varieties of the Fugio Cent," *Coin Collector's Jour.* 19 (July–Aug. 1952): 10–20. McBride, 2382–83. Olson, *Emblems*, 215, 289 n. 14. For examples of both versions of the Fugio coin, MHS.

79. McBride, 2382–84.

80. *Papers*, 22:358.

81. *The Argus* (Boston), March 26, 1793, p. 2, col. 4. McBride, 2389, quotes *The Mail or Claypoole's Daily Advertiser* for March 18, 1793.

82. Jean McClure Mudge, *Chinese Export Porcelain for the American Trade, 1785–1835* (New York: U of Delaware P, 1962), 152–53, 171–72, 174. Examples of the Martha Washington China are reproduced in Elinor Gordon, *Chinese Export Porcelain: An Hist. Survey* (New York: Main Street/Universe, [circa 1975]), 71, 116. McBride, 2390; held at MHS and at "Mount Vernon Ladies Association."

83. McBride, 2390; held at HSP.

84. Robert H. McCauley, *Liverpool Transfer Designs on Anglo-American Pottery* (Portland, Maine: Southworth-Anthoensen, 1942), has several examples of housewares with this motif, e.g. plates 23, 28, 29, 31. McBride, 2391; held at the Henry Francis du Pont Winterthur Museum.

85. McBride, 2391.

86. This pitcher is held at the National Museum of American History, Smithsonian Institution, and is reproduced in Nobel E. Cunningham Jr., *Popular Images of the Presidency from Washington to Lincoln* (Columbia: U of Missouri P, 1991), 3.

87. McBride, 2284. Alphaeus H. Albert, *Political Campaign and Commemorative Buttons* (Hightstown, N.J.: Boyertown, 1966), 9–10. Alphaeus H. Albert, *Washington Hist. Buttons* (Hightstown, N.J.: Princeton UP, 1949), 21–23, 42, 53.

88. McBride, 2384–85. For another example, Wendy C. Wick, *George Washington: An American Icon* (Washington, D.C.: Smithsonian Institution, 1982), 34, 99–101; Cunningham, 113; Richardson, *Standards*, 8.

89. McBride, 2381–82; an example of this medal is held by the American Numismatic Society, New York, N.Y.

90. McBride, 2286–87.

91. Cunningham, 86, held by AAS; for similar engravings, 92–93, 96–100.

92. For photographs and descriptions of these artifacts, see McBride, 2381–82, 2384–87, and 2390–91, held at MHS.

93. Olson, *Emblems*, 34–35.

94. *New-York Gazetteer*, Aug. 25, 1774, p. 3, col. 2. Olson, *Emblems*, 35–36.

95. *Papers*, 22:117.

Chapter 6. *Libertas Americana*, 1782–83

1. The most helpful essays on *Libertas Americana* are Carl Zigrosser, "The Medallic Sketches of Augustin Dupré in American Collections," *Proc. of the APS* 101 (1957): 535–50; Winfried Schleiner, "The Infant Hercules: Franklin's Design for a Medal Commemorating American Liberty," *ECS* 10 (1976–77): 235–44; and Lester C. Olson, "Benjamin Franklin's Commemorative Medal, *Libertas Americana:* A Study in

Rhetorical Iconology," *QJS* 76 (1990): 23–45. Charles Saunier alluded to *Libertas Americana* in "Les Médailles Françaises de l'indépendance américaine," *Les Arts* 172 (1918): 2–6. Brief commentary about the medal can be found in two articles by William S. Appleton, "Augustin Dupré, and his Work for America," *Proc. of the MHS,* 2d ser., 5 (1890): 348–52, and "Medals and Coins Relating to America," *Proc. of the MHS* 11 (1869–70): 293–305. Another brief commentary is R. T. H. Halsey, "Benjamin Franklin's Peace Medal," *Légion d'Honneur* 8 (April 1938): 248–50. A brief, inaccurate description is in James Mease, "Description of Some of the Medals Struck in Relation to Important Events in North America," *NYHS Coll.* 3 (1821): 8. For another brief account, W. C. Moore, "The *Libertas Americana* Medal," *Numismatist* 25 (Dec. 1912): 466–68.

2. BF to Robert R. Livingston, April 15, 1783, (BF), MS Div., LC.

3. The most useful references for medals during the Revolutionary era are Charles Wyllys Betts, *American Colonial History Illustrated by Contemporary Medals* (New York: Scott Stamp and Coin, 1894), and Laurence Brown, *A Catalogue of British Hist. Medals, 1760–1960,* vol. 1 of *The Accession of George III to the Death of William IV* (London: Seaby, 1980). For medals produced during the period in France, Saunier, "Les Médailles Françaises de l'indépendance américaine."

4. BF drew up a list of the medals, recorded on Feb. 17, 1780, *Papers,* 31:489–90. The medals are discussed in Vladimir and Elvira Clain-Stefanelli, *Medals Commemorating Battles of the American Revolution* (Washington, D.C.: Smithsonian Institution, 1973). I was unaware of this vol. when I published my essay on *Libertas Americana* in *QJS* during 1990. I want to thank the authors for forwarding their worksheets on *Libertas Americana* during May 1993. BF identified Stewart and Lee as "Lieutenant Colonels," but Vladimir and Elvira Clain-Stefanelli identify both men as majors.

5. Stourzh, *Franklin,* 164–79, specified BF's motives for a diplomacy of gratitude to France. On gratitude in America during the war, Sarah J. Purcell, *Sealed with Blood: War, Sacrifice and Memory in Revolutionary American* (Philadelphia: U of PA P, 2002), 49–91.

6. For an alternative assessment, Esmond Wright, *Franklin of Philadelphia* (Cambridge, Mass.: Harvard UP, 1986), 299.

7. On BF's diplomacy in France, Stourzh, *Franklin;* Dull, *Diplomatic;* Jonathan R. Dull, "Benjamin Franklin and the Nature of American Diplomacy," *International Hist. Rev.* 3 (Aug. 1983): 346–63. Esmond Wright, *Franklin of Philadelphia* (Cambridge, Mass.: Harvard UP, 1986), 297.

8. *Papers,* 36:115, 454. There is an earlier reference to the United States as the infant Hercules in his cradle, expressed in a letter from Arthur Lee to Schulenberg on June 10, 1777: "We are left, like Hercules in his cradle, to strangle the serpent that annoys all Europe." The letter is printed in Wharton, *Diplomatic Corresp.,* 2:334.

9. *Papers,* 36:180; John Adams to Major Jackson, Dec. 1, 1781, Adams Family Papers, MHS, Boston, rptd. in John Adams, *Adams Family Corresp.,* ed. L. H. Butterfield and Mark Friedlaender (Cambridge, Mass.: Harvard UP, 1973), 4:248. Adams also repeated the observations about the rarity of the events in a letter to Abigail Adams, *The Book of Abigail and John: Selected Letters of the Adams Family, 1762–1784,* ed.

L. H. Butterfield, Marc Friedlaender, and Mary Jo-Kine (Cambridge, Mass.: Harvard UP, 1975), 305. Jay to BF from *Papers*, 36:559. For commentary about the condensation of time in pictorial narrative, Rudolf Arnheim, *New Essays on the Psychology of Art* (Berkeley: U of California P, 1986), 5.

10. *Papers*, 25:651.

11. *Papers*, 36:644.

12. BF to George Washington, April 2, 1782, (BF), MS Div., LC.

13. Robert R. Livingston to BF, May 30, 1782, [letterbook copy], NA. This and all subsequent letters from the NA were in the Papers of the Continental Congress, 1774–1789. Robert R. Livingston's draft copy with abbreviated language was in the Robert R. Livingston Papers (henceforth, RRLP), NYHS.

14. BF to Robert R. Livingston, Aug. 12, 1782, NA; BF to Robert R. Livingston, April 15, 1783, (BF), MS Div., LC, also at NA.

15. An exhibit about Brongniart featured his career as an architect, *Alexandre-Théodore Brongniart, 1739–1813: architecture et décor, [exposition] Musée Carnavalet 22 avril-13 juillet 1986* (Paris: Musées de la ville de Paris, 1986), 310, mentions the role at the Military School. For Ségur's 1782 letter nominating Brongniart for this role, shelf code MM, 676:45, AN.

16. *Almanach royal* (1783), 523; *Almanach royal* (1784), 524; Bachaumont, *Mémoires secrets*, 21:202. "Liste des membres de l'académie d'architecture, depuis sa fondation, le 31 décembre 1671, jusqu'au 8 août, jour de la suppression," *Archives de l'art français: recueil de documents inédit relatifs à l'histoire des arts en France* (Paris: F. de Nobele, 1851), t. 1:419–24, for Brongniart, 423.

17. Alexandre-Théodore Brongniart to BF, Sept. 22, 1782, APS. Jacques S. Silvestre de Sacy, *Alexandre-Théodore Brongniart, 1739–1813, sa vie, son oeuvre* (Paris, 1940). Louis-Alphonse de Launay, *Une Grande famille de savants: Les Brongniart* (Paris, 1940), 22–23.

18. J. B. Dacier, *Hist. de l'Académie royale des Inscriptions et Belles-Lettres* (Paris: Imprimerie royale, 1736–1809), 45:69–70, 47:303–6. In addition, I examined the materials in numerous, unpublished files at the Académie française (Paris). There is no mention of *Libertas Americana* in *Les Registres de l'Académie française: 1672–1793* (Paris, 1895).

19. There was also no mention of *Libertas Americana* in Académie royale d'architecture (W. Viennot), *Procès-verbaux de l'Académie royale d'architecture, 1671–1793, publié pour la Société de l'histoire de l'art français, sous les auspices de l'Académie des beaux-arts, par H. Henry Le Monnier* (Paris, 1929).

20. Louis Auvray and Emile Bellier, *Dictionnaire général des artistes de l'école française* (Paris, 1880), 1:644. For later notices about Gibelin's work as a fresco painter, Bachaumont, *Mémoires secrets*, 30:36, which describes his subsequent frescoes at the Royal Military School and elsewhere. Jules Belleudy, *J.-S. Duplessis, peintre du Roi* (Chartre, 1913), 211 n. 1.

21. Esprit-Antoine Gibelin to BF, fév. 7, 1785, APS. It would have been two years, not one, as the letter affirms. Subsequently, Gibelin authored *De l'origine et de la forme du bonnet de la Liberté* (Paris, 1794).

22. Sketches at the Musée à Blérancourt and at the APS were discussed by Zigrosser, 537, and Schleiner, 237. Clain-Stefanelli mentions two sketches at Bléran-court and the Musée des arts (37).

23. *Almanach royal*, 1783, p. 494; *Biographie universelle*, 6:321–22; *Procès-verbaux . . . architecture*, 9:92. Cadet de Vaux described himself in a letter dated avril 8, 1783, AAE, Corresp. Politique., Etats-Unis, t. 23, f. 386.

24. [Antoine-Alexis-François] Cadet de Vaux to BF, jan. 13, 1783, APS.

25. [Alexandre-Théodore] Brongniart to BF, jan. 23, 1783, APS.

26. Print Dept., Boston Public Library. Zigrosser, 538.

27. [Alexandre-Théodore] Brongniart to BF, jan. 31, 1783, APS. The medal was not the only project that he undertook for BF, to judge from a letter on aug. 13, 1783.

28. R. T. H. Halsey discusses BF's pragmatic view of the arts in "Benjamin Franklin: His Interest in the Arts," in *Benjamin Franklin and His Circle: A Catalogue of an Exhibition* (New York: Plantin Press for the Metropolitan Museum, 1936), 9.

29. Zigrosser, 540; Charles Saunier, *Augustin Dupré: orfèvre, médailleur et graveur général des monnaies* (Paris: Société de Propogation des Livres d'Art, 1894), 19–20. Charles Blanc, *Notice sur la vie et les ouvrages d'Augustin Dupré, graveur général des monnaies de la République* (Paris, 1870).

30. *Papers*, 36:646.

31. This contrast was noted explicitly by at least one of BF's contemporaries, Peter P. Burdett to BF, Jan. 17, 1786, APS, whose response is discussed later in the chapter on pp. 181–82.

32. This translation from Latin to English is by Schleiner, 236.

33. *Papers*, 18:201 n. 2.

34. BF to W. Jones, March 17, 1783, Beinecke Rare Book and MS Library, Yale Univ. Library. My thanks to George Miles for forwarding a photocopy of the letter.

35. Garland Cannon, *The Life and Mind of Oriental Jones: Sir William Jones, the Father of Modern Linguistics* (Cambridge: Cambridge UP, 1990), for a passing reference to the medal, 192; for Jones's visit to Passy and the contemporaneous speculation, 174–15. I consulted the two vols. of *The Letters of Sir William Jones*, ed. Garland Cannon (Oxford: Clarendon, 1970), seeking a response from Jones to BF, but without success.

36. On Jules-François de Cotte, *Almanach des monnoies (1784–1789), année 1784* (Paris, [1784]), 15. *Almanach royal*, 1783, p. 338. Fernand Mazerolle, *l'Hôtel des Monnaies. Les bâtiments–le musée–les ateliers* (Paris, 1907), 174. Robert Laulan, "La construction de l'école militaire (1765–1788)," *Bulletin de la Société d'histoire et d'archéologie des 7e et 15e arrondissements de Paris* (1937–1938): 145, 147. F. Bluche, *Les magistrats de la Cour des Monnaies de Paris au XVIIIe siècle, 1715–1790* (Paris, 1966). At the AN (Paris), I examined germane colls. for materials on *Libertas Americana*, including "Cours de la Monnaie, Registres, 1780–1789," "Cours de la Monnaie (1782–1784)," "Bibliothèque du roi, Dept. des Médailles," and "Cours de la Monnaie Procès-verbaux, 1779–1790." None of these yielded specific information about the production of BF's medal.

37. *Almanach des monnoies*, 1784, p. 3, 16. For a general history of the institution, Roger Debray, *La chambre des monnaies et l'administration des monnaies sous l'ancien*

régime (Paris, 1919). For an orientation to archival material pertaining to the institution, Suzanne Clémencet,"Cours des monnaies," in *Guide des recherches dans les fonds judiciaires de l'ancien régime*, ed. Michel Antoine and others (Paris, 1958), 237–46.

38. [Robert] de Cotte to BF, mars 26, 1783, APS.

39. WTF to Caleb Whitefoord, July 27, 1785, in William Albert Hewins, *The Whitefoord Papers: Being the Correspondence and Other Manuscripts of Colonel Charles Whitefoord and Caleb Whitefoord, from 1739 to 1810* (Oxford: Clarendon, 1898), 198. Earlier, Caleb Whitefoord had written to WTF to place "an order" for silver and copper medals from "the Mint," April 26, 1783, APS. George Fox to WTF, May 15, 1783, APS; Elias Boudinot to Robert R. Livingston, Sept. 16, 1783, NYHS (RRLP). For another version of the letter, MS Div., LC. BF to Elias Boudinot, Sept. 13, 1783, NA.

40. Zigrosser, 538–40, quote on 538. For background on Morellet, *Biographie universelle*, 29:282–86; *Almanach royal*, 1789, p. 504.

41. *Papers*, 19:177 n. 5.

42. This letter is held in the Franklin Papers, B: F85, vol. 44, f. 126, film 54–34, APS. On April 6, 1990, Dorothy Medlin sent me the proof sheets for the then-forthcoming vol. that she, Jean-Claude David, and Paul Le Clerc were preparing for *Lettres d'André Morellet* (Oxford: Voltaire Foundation, 1991).

43. Copies of this pamphlet are held by the BN, the HSP, the Univ. of Pa. Library, and the APS.

44. BF to Thomas Brand Hollis, Oct. 5, 1783, LC. Another reference to Liberty's head appears in [Alexandre-Théodore] Brongniart to BF, jan. 31, 1783, APS.

45. Cotton Mather, *Magnalia Christi Americana* (London, 1702), bk. 7, p. 42 (ch. 6, p. 1); Schleiner, 237, 244. BF's copy is held at the APS (shelf mark 277.4.M42).

46. Cobbett, *Parliamentary Hist.*, 18:347.

47. On typology in eighteenth-century public address, Ronald F. Reid, "Apocalypticism and Typology: Rhetorical Dimensions of a Symbolic Reality," *QJS* 69 (Aug. 1983): 229–48.

48. *Gaz. de Leide* or *Nouvelles extraordinaires de divers endroits*, avril 18, 1783, no. 31, p. 3, col. 1. Similar information in the *Gaz. des Deux-Ponts*, avril 19, 1783, no. 31, p. 245, col. 1; and the *Courrier de l'Europe*, avril 22, 1783, vol. 13, no. 32, p. 1, col. 1.

49. *Gaz. des Deux-Ponts*, mars 4, 1783, no. 18, p. 139, col. 1; mars 11, 1783, no. 20, p. 158, col. 2; avril 19, 1783, no. 31, p. 245, col. 1.

50. *Gaz. de Leide*, "Supplement aux nouvelles extraordinaries de divers endroits du numero XX," mars 11, 1783, p. 2. *Jour. politique de Bruxelles*, mars 15, 1783, no. 11, pp. 120–21. *Courrier de l'Europe*, mars 18, 1783, vol. 13, no. 22, p. 2, col. 2, and p. 3, col. 1.

51. *Gaz. des Deux-Ponts*, mars 11, 1783, no. 20, p. 158, col. 2; *Courrier d'Avignon*, mars 14, 1783, no. 21, p. 83, col. 2.

52. *Jour. Politique de Bruxelles*, mars 15, 1783, no. 11, pp. 120–21. Hatin, 26, 73.

53. *Jour. Politique, ou gaz. des gaz.*, avril 1–15, 1783, p. 45; *Affiches Américaines*, mai 21, 1783, p. 1, col. 2, p. 2, col. 1. Hatin, 63.

54. *Jour. historique et politique de Genève*, mars 15, 1783, no. 11, p. 505; *Courrier de l'Europe*, mars 18, 1783, vol. 13, no. 22, p. 2, col. 2, p. 3, col. 1. Hatin, 74.

55. *London Chron.*, March 13–15, 1783, p. 252, col. 1; *Morning Chron.*, March 15, 1783, p. 2, col. 3; *Morning Herald & Daily Advertiser,* March 15, 1783, p. 2, col. 2; *Gent. Mag.* 53 (March 1783): 269.

56. *Maryland Jour.*, May 23, 1783, p. 1, col. 3; *Virginia Gaz.*, May 31, 1783, p. 2, col. 1.

57. Charles W. Dumas to BF, mars 14, 1783, (BF), MS Div., LC; Charles Dumas to John Adams, mars 18, 1783, MHS, reproduced on microfilm of the Adams Family Corresp., reel 360.

58. [Luigi] de Pio to BF, mars 20, 1783, APS; [Luigi] de Pio to BF avril 20, 1783, APS. An earlier letter from de Pio to BF, nov. 16, 1782, identified him as the "Chargé des affaires de la Cour de Naples," APS. Antonio Pace, *BF and Italy* (Philadelphia: APS, 1958), 149–52. Otto Friedrich Winter, *Repertorium der diplomatischen Vertreter aller Länder. III. Band. 1764–1815* (Graz-Köln: Verlag Hermann Böhlaus Nachf, 1965), 423.

59. *Gaz. de Leide,* avril 18, 1783, no. 31, p. 3, col. 1; *Gaz. des Deux-Ponts,* avril 19, 1783, no. 31, p. 245, col. 1; *Courrier d'Avignon,* avril 22, 1783, no. 32, p. 126, col. 2; *Suite des nouvelles d'Amsterdam,* avril 18, 1783, no. 31, p. 1, col. 1; *Courrier de l'Europe,* avril 22, 1783, vol. 13, no. 32, p. 1, col. 1; *London Chron.*, April 22–24, 1783, p. 392, col. 2; *Pa. Jour.* June 18, 1783, p. 2, col. 2; *New-Jersey Gaz.*, June 25, 1783, p. 392, col. 2.

60. [Philippe-Henri, marquis] de Ségur to BF, avril 11, 1783, APS. On Ségur, *Almanach royal,* 1783, pp. 190, 191, 195, 209, 210, 212, 217.

61. [Jean-François] Joly de Fleury to BF, avril 11, 1783, and [Antoine-Jean] Amelot de Chaillou to BF, avril 12, 1783, both at the APS. On Joly de Fleury, *Almanach royal,* 1783, pp. 209, 210, 215. He had resigned his post shortly before the gift of the medal, to judge from articles in the *Gaz. de France,* avril 1, 1783, p. 123, col. 1, and *Le Courrier d'Avignon,* avril 11, 1783, p. 113, col. 2. On Amelot, *Almanach royal,* 1783, esp. pp. 504, 507, also pp. 210, 211, 216, 245. On Amelot's resignation, *Gaz. de France,* nov. 21, 1783, no. 93, p. 4, col. 1.

62. For a list of the secretaries of state, *Almanach royal,* 1783, pp. 215–17; for a list of members in the four Councils of the King, 209–11. Emmanuel, maréchal duc de Croÿ, *Jour. inédit du duc de Croÿ, 1718–1784,* ed. Emmanuel-Henri de Grouchy and Paul Cottin (Paris 1906–7), 4:278.

63. On Castries, *Almanach royal,* 1783, pp. 209, 210, 211; Contenson, *La Société des Cincinnati,* 151. In the Reserve at the AN (Paris), I consulted the unpublished *Jour. de Castries* (MS 306 AP 17), as well as the germane papers listed in Archives nationales (Yves Chassin du Guerny), *Le Chartrier de Castries: (306 AP) Inventaire* (Paris, 1975).

64. On Vergenne, *Almanach royal,* 1783, pp. 209, 210, 211, 216, 243, 528. On Vergenne's appointment, *Jour. de Castries,* fév. 20 [1783], p. 158.

65. Contenson, *La Société des Cincinnati,* 186; Rochambeau, *Mémoires* 1:319–20; Claude Blanchard, *Jour. de campagne de Claude Blanchard . . . 1780–83* (Paris, 1881), 93; *Etat militaire de France,* 1783, p. 111.

66. [François-Joseph-Paul,] comte de Grasse to BF, avril 13, 1783, APS.

67. Rochambeau, *Mémoires* 1:296.

68. [Yves-Marie Desmaretz, comte de] Maillebois to BF, mai 15, [1783], APS. On Maillebois, *Almanach royal*, 1783, esp. p. 507, also p. 194; *Etat militaire de France*, 1783, p. 104. Brief mentions of comte de Maillebois are in Bachaumont, *Mémoires secrets*, 5:247, and Lescure, *Corresp. secrète*, 2:732.

69. [Palteau de] Veimerange to BF, avril 13, 1783, APS. John Laurens to BF, May 22, 1781, APS, mentions Veimerange's role under the marquis de Ségur. *Etat militaire de France*, 1783, p. 9. *Almanach royal*, 1783, p. 179. BF to Veimerange, July 10, 1781, specifies Veimerange's role, too. There are passing references to Veimerange in Lescure, *Corresp. secrète*, 1:529, 596, 2:120.

70. For examples, BF to de Veimerange, Feb. 17, 1782, LC; BF to de Veimerange, March 4, 1782, LC; Palteau de Veimerange to BF, mars 11, 1782, APS; Palteau de Veimerange to BF, sept. 6, 1782, APS.

71. Vicomte de la Houssaye to BF, mai 1, 1783, APS.

72. [Marianne Camasse], comtesse de Forbach, duchesse douairière du duc de Deux-Ponts to BF, avril 13, 1783, APS. Lopez, *Mon Cher Papa*, 190–91.

73. "Supplement à la Gaz.," *Gaz. de France*, nov. 20, 1781, p. 442. Rochambeau, *Mémoires*, 1:294.

74. Mazas, *Ordre de Saint-Louis*, 2:298; also, there is mention of the Deux-Ponts on 2:296, and in Rochambeau, *Mémoires*, 1:293, 301; Blanchard, *Jour.*, 101–2, 104; *Etat militaire de France*, 1783, s.v. "DRAGONS."

75. Lopez, *Mon Cher Papa*, 192–93, quote on 192.

76. *Almanach royal*, 1783, pp. 191, 506. *Papers*, 25:413 n. 5. On the resignation, Ségur to Timbrune, mai 20, 1783, AN, under MM676:92.

77. [Agathon] chevalier de Kéralio to BF, avril 18, 1783, APS.

78. [Agathon] chevalier de Kéralio to WTF, mai 21, 1783, requesting the medals, and mai 22, 1783, acknowledging receiving them. Both letters are held by the APS.

79. *Almanach royal*, 1783, 191, 208; *Etat militaire de France,*1783, 460; Chesnaye-DuBois, *Dictionnaire de la noblesse*, 2nd ed., 12:655–656. Jean-Baptiste-César, marquis de Timbrune later wrote the *Instructions pour les enfants qui ont été agréés pour les écoles royales militaires* (Paris, 1784).

80. Mazas, *Ordre de Saint-Louis* 2:311; *Etat militaire de France*, 1783, 460; *Almanach royal*, 1783, 191.

81. Mazas, *Ordre de Saint-Louis*, 2:300; Contenson, *La Société des Cincinnati*, 234; Bodinier, *Dictionnaire*, 356.

82. Contenson, *La Société des Cincinnati*, 275–76; Bodinier, *Dictionnaire*, 310. *Biographie universelle*, 43:9. It is possible, though less likely, that the medal was given to Louis Gabriel, marquis de Vauban, who, according to the *Gaz. de France*, preceded comte de Rochambeau and his officers to the court during mid-February 1783, having been charged to do so by Rochambeau's dispatches. For the marquis de Vauban's role, *Gaz. de France*, mars 7, 1783, no. 19, p. 92, col. 1. [Agathon] chevalier de Kéralio to BF, juillet 20, 1783, APS.

83. [Claude-Gabriel, marquis] de Choisy and [Pierre-François, chevalier] de Béville to BF, avril 28, 1783, APS.

84. For Claude-Gabriel, marquis de Choisy, Bodinier, *Dictionnaire*, 100; Contenson, *La Société des Cincinnati*, 157–59. *Etat militaire de France*, 1783, 83.

85. "Supplement à la Gaz.," *Gaz. de France*, nov. 20, 1781, p. 448, col. 2, p. 441, cols. 1–2, respectively. Rochambeau, *Mémoires*, 1:291; Blanchard, *Jour.*, 99, 101.

86. Rochambeau, *Mémoires*, 1:320. Contenson, *La Société des Cincinnati*, 139; Bodinier, *Dictionnaire*, 49. *Etat militaire de France*, 1783, 83.

87. [Barnabé-Eugène, comte de] Messey to BF, [1783], APS. *Etat militaire de France*, 1783, 83; Mazas, *Ordre de Saint-Louis*, 1:596.

88. *Papers*, 23:231; *Papers*, 14:205 n. 6.

89. [Guy-Claude, comte de] Sarsfield to BF, mai 4, 1783, APS. *Papers*, 14:205 n. 6.

90. *Almanach royal*, 1783, p. 206. Contenson, *La Société des Cincinnati*, 228. *Etat militaire de France*, 1783, 111. On the service under comte de Grasse, *Gaz. de France*, nov. 20, 1781, p. 446, col 2. Mazas, *Ordre de Saint-Louis*, 2:438.

91. [François-Aymar,] chevalier de Monteil to BF, mai 23, 1783, APS. *Jour. Politique de Bruxelles*, mars 15, 1783, p. 119; *Gaz. de France*, mars 17, 1783; *Le Courrier d'Avignon*, mars 18, 1783, no. 22, p. 87, col. 1. Georges Lacour-Gayet, *La Marine militaire de France sous le règne de Louis XV* (Paris, 1910), 534.

92. [Jacques-Dominique] de Cassini fils to BF, jan. 2, 1784, APS. *Almanach royal*, 1783, 513.

93. On vicomte de Mory, Contenson, *La Société des Cincinnati*, 203; Bodinier, *Dictionnaire*, 283. There is a slight variation of the spelling of his name ("de La Mire" becomes "Lamire") in Mazas, *Ordre de Saint-Louis*, 3:11; François Saint Christo, *Les ordres du Roi* (Paris, 1925), 438.

94. Contenson, *La Société des Cincinnati*, 139, 151, 157–59, 186–87, 203, 228–29, 234, 275–76.

95. [Jacques-Hippolyte, comte de] Sarsfield to BF, mai 4, 1783, APS.

96. *Almanach royal*, 1783, pp. 502, 504, 514–15. René Poupardin, *Catalogue des manuscrits des collections Duchesne et Bréquigny* (Paris, 1905), xxi. According to Poupardin, Bréquigny was also a collaborator for the *Mémoires de l'Académie des Inscriptions, ou Jour. des savants* (xxv).

97. [Bon-Joseph, baron] Dacier *et al.* to BF, juin 6, 1783, APS. On Dacier, *Almanach royal*, 1783, p. 505. For his role as perpetual secretary of the academy, *Nouvelles de la République des Lettres et des Arts*, jan. 1, 1783, no. 1, p. 6, col. 2, and mai 7, 1783, no. 19, p. 152, col. 2; Bachaumont, *Mémoires secrets*, avril 29, 1783, 22:235.

98. *Assemblées et délibérations de l'Académie Royale, 1783–84*, 79, held at the Academy of Inscriptions and Belles-Lettres in the Académie français (Paris).

99. Académie des sciences (Paul Dorveaux), *Les membres et les correspondants de l'Académie royale des sciences (1666–1793)* (Paris, 1931), 6, 49, 133, 143, 145, 154. On de Chaillou, *Papers*, 29:285 n. 5.

100. On Jean-Baptiste Le Roy, *Almanach royal*, 1783, pp. 505, 509, 521; *Almanach royal*, 1784, p. 522; Académie des sciences (Dorveaux), *Les membres*, 143. *Papers*, 10:61 n. 2. Lopez, *Mon Cher Papa*, 355. Hippolyte Buffenoir, *La comtesse d'Houdetôt, sa famille, ses amies* (Paris, 1905), 67.

101. [Jean-Baptiste] Le Roy to BF, circa avril 1783, APS.

102. Académie des sciences (Dorveaux), *Les membres*, 193.

103. *Almanach royal* (1783), 505, 521.

104. [Louis-Alexandre], duc de la Rochefoucauld to BF, avril 12, [1783], APS. *Almanach royal*, 1783, p. 507.

105. Joseph Bartoli to BF, avril 11, 1783, APS. On Bartoli, *Almanach royal*, 1783, 506. Pace, 239.

106. Elie de Beaumont to BF, avril 14, 1783, APS. On Elie de Beaumont, *Almanach royal*, 1783, 368; Bachaumont, *Mémoires secrets* 20:150–51. Lescure, *Corresp. secrète*, 2:2. *Papers*, 16:205 n. 4.

107. [Jean-André] Mongez to BF, avril 1, [1783], APS. Bachaumont, *Mémoires secrets*, mentions Antoine Mongez as a member of the "Académie des Inscriptions et Belles-Lettres" and describes his activities in entries for nov. 15 and 23, 1783, vol. 23:320, 342, and avril 5, 1785, 28:234. *Gaz. de France*, nov. 21, 1783, no. 93, p. 4, col. 2.

108. Frère Félix Nogaret to BF, avril 1, 1783, APS. There are brief passages about Nogaret's relationship to BF in Sellers, *Franklin*, esp. 176–77, also, 215–16.

109. *Almanach royal*, 1783, p. 280. On Nogaret's writing, Belleudy, *J.-S. Duplessis*, 258; Bachaumont, *Mémoires secrets*, 2:108–9, 140, 158.

110. [Jean-Baptiste] Artaud to BF, mai 10, 1783, APS. On Artaud, *Biographie universelle*, 2:299–300.

111. [Michel-Guillaume] St. Jean de Crèvecoeur to BF, [May 1783?], APS. Robert de Crèvecoeur, *Saint-John de Crèvecoeur, sa vie et ses ouvrages* (Paris, 1883).

112. [Michel-Guillaume] St. Jean de Crèvecoeur to BF, Jan. 3, 1783, APS.

113. Lopez, *Mon Cher Papa*, 158–67. Gilbert Chinard, *Les Amitiés Américaines de Madame d'Houdetôt, d'après sa corresp. inédite avec Benjamin Franklin et Thomas Jefferson* (Paris, 1924), 13, 17–18.

114. George Fox to WTF, May 15, 1783, APS.

115. Additional examples of this include Kéralio's letters of mai 21 and 22, 1783 (APS); Caleb Whitefoord's letter of July 27, 1785; and Henry Grand's request to WTF for a copper medal ([Henry] Grand to WTF, juin 1783, APS).

116. On Pierres's role in publishing the translation of the constitutions, AAE, Corresp. politique, Etats-unis, t. 23, f. 372; t. 24, f. 4, 31.

117. Philippe-Denis Pierres to BF, mai 5, 1783, APS.

118. Mazas, *Ordre de Saint-Louis* 2:326.

119. Le comte de Beaujeu to BF, avril 18, 1783, APS.

120. Bachaumont, *Mémoires secrets*, 22:154–55.

121. Dull, *Diplomatic*, 159; also Jonathan R. Dull, "Vergennes, Rayneval, and the Diplomacy of Trust," *Peace and the Peacemakers: The Treaty of 1783* (Charlottesville: U of Virginia P, 1986), 101–31.

122. Friedrich Melchior Grimm and Denis Diderot, *Corresp. littéraire, philosophique et critique de Grimm et de Diderot depuis 1753 jusqu'en 1790* (Paris: Chez Furne, Libraire, 1829–31), 11:360–61.

123. Joseph Bartoli, "Description de la Médaille sur l'Indépendance de l'Amérique à l'occasion de la Paix," APS. Although undated, this verse was almost certainly

enclosed in Joseph Bartoli to BF, avril 11, 1783, APS. Thanks to Daniel S. Russell for suggesting improvements in my translations of the poems by Bartoli and Coquillot.

124. Coquillot, prior of Epinay, verses written to BF, aug. 1, 1783, APS.

125. "Explication de la Médaille Frappée Par Les Américains en 1782," APS and BN.

126. Zigrosser, 538.

127. *Affiches, Annonces, et Avis Divers*, avril 15, 1784, no. 46, p. 225, col. 2.

128. R. T. H. Halsey, "Benjamin Franklin's Peace Medal," *Légion d'Honneur* 8 (April 1938): 250. R. T. H. Halsey, "The Rooms of the Early Republic in the New American Wing," *Bulletin of the Metropolitan Museum of Art* (Sept. 1924): 214–19. C. Gabillot, *Les Hüet, Jean-Baptiste et ses trois fils* (Paris: Libraire de l'Art, 1892), 86. Henri Clouzot, *Hist. de la manufacture de Jouy et de la toile imprimée au XVIIIe siècle* (Paris, 1926), 3:15–16; also in the 1928 edition, t. 1:16, t. 2: plate 8. "List chronologique des membres de l'académie de peinture et de sculpture, depuis son origine, le 1re février 1648, jusqu'au 8 août 1793, jour de la suppression," *Archives de l'art français* (1re série), t. 1:392.

129. Corresp. on this authorization in F 12:1405A, AN. For further background on terms imprinted on the edging, F 12:1403.

130. For a series of articles on these fabrics, A. Juvet-Michel, "Textile Printing in Eighteenth Century France," *Ciba Review* (March 1940): 1090–1128, esp. 1122. For background on the process of production, F 12:1404B, AN.

131. Juvet-Michel, 1092–95; Henri-René d'Allemagne, *La Toile imprimée et les Indiennes de Traite* (Paris, 1942), 1:51–76, 93–95.

132. On the commercial interest in the U.S. market for textiles, Penide to BF, jan. 16, 1783; Jean-Bernard Linckh to BF, fév. 12, 1783; François de Launey to BF, mars 9, 1783; de Pinelli to BF, mars 12, 1783. All of these letters are held by the APS.

133. de Coch to BF, mars 17, 1783, APS.

134. A. Storelli, *Jean-Baptiste Nini, sa vie–son oeuvre, 1717–1786* (Tours, 1896), 23–24, 113–22. A. Villers, *Jean-Baptiste Nini, ses terres cuites* (Blois, 1862), 18–19, 56–57. Halsey, "Rooms of the Early Republic," 215. For Nini's other terra cotta medallions depicting BF, Lopez, *Mon Cher Papa*, 125, 127. Pace, 286. H. W. Brands, *The First American: The Life and Times of Benjamin Franklin* (New York: Random House, 2002), 551.

135. Sellers, *Franklin*, 344–48; Lopez, *Mon Cher Papa*, 127.

136. Hatin, 74–75. Lescure, *Corresp. secrète*, 1:546.

137. Linguet, *Annales politiques, civiles, et littéraires*, 10:342.

138. Ibid., 10:370.

139. BF to Robert R. Livingston, April 15, 1783, NA; also at (BF), MS Div., LC. BF reiterated the information about the distribution of medals in France in his corresp., BF to James Logan, Sept. 16, 1789, LC.

140. BF's corresp. with Thomas Digges indicates that BF was aware of the convention that gold medals were reserved only for the king (*Papers*, 32:27).

141. Stourzh, *Franklin*, 165.

142. Elias Boudinot to BF, June 18, 1783, (BF), MS Div., LC.

143. BF to Elias Boudinot, Sept. 13, 1783, NA.

144. Elias Boudinot to Robert R. Livingston, Sept. 16, 1783, (EB), MS Div., LC; rptd. in Burnett, *Continental Congress*, 7:298.

145. Elias Boudinot to Robert R. Livingston, Sept. 16, 1783, (RRLP), NYHS. One of the two earlier letters was dated Aug. 29,1783: "The Medal I wrote you about, is at Philadelphia otherwise I should have sent it long since" ([RRLP], NYHS).

146. Elias Boudinot to Robert R. Livingston, Sept. 27, 1783, (EB), MS Div., LC; rptd. in Burnett, *Continental Congress* 7:314.

147. Elias Boudinot to BF, Nov. 1, 1783, APS; also on microfilm at (EB), MS Div., LC. For a list of the ninety-six Congressmen in 1783, *Biographical Directory of the American Congress, 1774–1971* (Washington, D.C.: GPO, 1971), 40–43. For a list of the fourteen govs., Roy R. Glashan, comp., *American Govs. and Gubernatorial Elections, 1774–1978* (Westport, Conn.: Meckler, 1979).

148. Robert R. Livingston to Elias Boudinot, Sept. 29, 1783, (RRLP), NYHS.

149. Elias Boudinot to Robert R. Livingston, Oct. 23, 1783, (RRLP), NYHS.

150. BF to Robert R. Livingston, July 22, 1783, NA.

151. Claude-Anne Lopez, "Was Franklin Too French?" in *Reappraising*, 143–53.

152. William Dunlap, *Diary of William Dunlap*, vol. 1, in *NYHS Coll.* 62 (1929): 176. William B. Evans, "John Adams' Opinion of Benjamin Franklin" *PMHB* 92 (1968): 220–38.

153. *Papers*, 33:162.

154. Ibid., 33:163, 163 n. 7.

155. Ibid., 33:315 n. 9.

156. BF to [James Logan,] Sept. 16, 1789, (BF), MS Div., LC.

157. *London Chron.*, March 13–15, 1783, p. 252, col. 1, and April 22–24, 1783, p. 392, col. 2; *Maryland Jour.*, May 23, 1783, p. 1, col. 3; *Virginia Gaz.*, May 31, 1783, p. 2, col. 1; *Pa. Jour.* June 18, 1783, p. 2, col. 2; *New-Jersey Gaz.*, June 25, 1783, p. 392, col. 2.

158. BF to Emmanuel de Rohan, April 6, 1783, [copy forwarded by BF to the Congress], NA.

159. Emmanuel de Rohan to BF, juin 21, 1783, APS; also in copy forwarded by BF to the Congress, NA. In the copy that he forwarded to Congress, BF omitted the clause concerning his role.

160. [Gerard Van de] Brantsen to BF, April 29, 1783, APS. *Almanach royal*, 1784, p. 151. Winter, *Repertorium*, 263. There was also mention of Brantsen's role in *Suite des Nouvelles d'Amsterdam*, jan. 21, 1783, no. 6, p. 4. col. 1; Charles Dumas to BF, sept. 4, 1782, APS.

161. [Baron Otto] de Blôme to BF, avril 30, 1783, APS. *Almanach royal*, 1783, p. 149. There is also mention of de Blôme's official role in *Jour. Politique de Bruxelles*, jan. 11, 1783, p. 69.

162. For Luigi de Pio's political role, de Pio to BF, nov. 16, 1782, APS. Pace, 149–152.

163. P[eter] P. Burdett to BF, Jan. 17, 1786, APS. He mentioned the gift again in a later letter (P[eter] P. Burdett to BF, Aug. 19, 1787, APS).

164. William Carmichael to WTF, Nov. 26, 1783, APS; William Carmichael to BF, Jan. 15, 1784, (BF) LC.

165. Esmond Wright, "The Peace Treaties of 1782 and 1783," in *Reappraising,* 164–165.

166. Caleb Whitefoord to WTF, April 26, 1783, APS; Caleb Whitefoord to WTF, May 9, 1783, APS. Subsequent correspondence, WTF to Caleb Whitefoord, July 27, 1785, alluding to the medal in Hewins, *The Whitefoord Papers,* 198.

167. BF to Robert R. Livingston, July 22, 1783, NA.

168. BF to Elias Boudinot, Sept. 13, 1783, NA. Boudinot to BF, Nov. 1, 1783, APS; also in (EB), MS Div., LC.

169. For the provocative passage about BF's character, [Francis Blackburne, ed.], *Memoirs of Thomas Hollis, Esq.* (London, 1780), 1:335–36. I discuss the passage at greater length in the chapter on "MAGNA *Britannia,*" pp. 85–86. BF to Thomas Brand Hollis, Oct. 5, 1783, (BF), MS Div., LC.

170. T[homas] Brand Hollis to BF, June 21, 1784, APS (Bache Coll.).

171. Jan Ingenhousz to BF, April 29, 1783, APS. BF to Jan Ingenhousz, May 16, 1783, LC. *Papers,* 14:4 n. 1. Jan Ingenhousz to BF, Aug. 15, 1783, APS.

172. BF to George Whatley, May 23, 1785, LC; George Whatley to BF, July 7, 1785, APS. Another reference to a medal is in George Whatley to BF, Sept. 14, 1787, APS. For background on BF's relationship to Whatley, *Papers,* 21:169–71. On Whatley's pamphlet, *Papers,* 21:169–77.

173. BF to Mather Byles, June 1, 1788, LC. For background on Byles, see introduction in Mather Byles, *Works,* comp. and with an introduction by Benjamin Franklin V (Delmar, N.Y.: Scholars Facsimiles, 1978), v–xix.

174. BF Bache to BF, March 30, 1783, APS. On the grandson's life, James Tagg, *Benjamin Franklin Bache and the Philadelphia Aurora* (Philadelphia: U of Pa. P, 1991). On de Marignac, *Papers,* 29:342 n. 1, 344–45. On Johonnot, *Papers,* 33:121 n. 7. BF to BF Bache, May 2, 1783, APS; BF Bache to BF, May 30, 1783, APS.

175. Van Doren, *Franklin-Mecom,* 281.

176. Ibid., 280.

177. Jane Mecom to BF, Sept. 13, 1786, APS. Van Doren, *Franklin-Mecom,* 281.

178. Jane Mecom to BF, May 22, 1787, APS. Van Doren, *Franklin-Mecom,* 292.

179. Matthias Christian Sprengel, *Allgemeines historisches Taschenbuch; oder Abriss der merkwürdigsten neuen Welt-begebenheiten enthaltend für 1784 die Geschichte der Revolution von Nord-America* (Berlin: Haude und Spener, 1784), 182 ff. On Sprengel, *Biographie universelle,* 40:87–88.

180. A lengthy review of Hilliard d'Auberteiul's book was printed in *Nouvelles de la république des lettres et des arts,* juillet 23, 1783, no. 29, pp. 260–62. On the list of French officers, Lasseray, 73.

181. Hilliard d'Auberteuil to BF, avril 12, 1783, APS.

182. Charles Spener to BF, mai 26, 1783, APS. This letter may have been conveyed as an attachment to Bauer and Treuttel to BF, juin 1, 1783, APS.

183. Fisher Ames to William Tudor, April 25, 1789, in "Memoir of Tudor," *MHS Colls.,* 2d ser., 8 (1819): 317; Jonathan Boucher, *A View of the Causes and Consequences of the American Revolution* (London, 1797), lxv. Philip Evanson, "Jonathan Boucher: The Mind of an American Loyalist," *Maryland Hist. Mag.* 58 (June 1963): 123–36.

184. Bibliothèque nationale (Paris), *Benjamin Franklin et la France* (Paris, 1956).

185. For Duplessis's portrait, Sellers, *Franklin*, 114–15, 124–29, 249–53; Lopez, *Mon Cher Papa*, 127; Léon Honoré Labande, "Notes sur le peintre Joseph-Siffrein Duplessis et sur les portraits de Franklin exécuté par lui," *Mémoires de l'Académie de Vaucluse* 17 (1898): 393–402; Jules Belleudy, *J.-S. Duplessis, peintre du roi* (Chartre, 1913). For textile design, Henri-René d'Allemagne, *La Toile Imprimée*, t. 2: plate 131. For "L'Amérique Indépendante," Sellers, *Franklin*, 120–21, 195–97, plate 32. For "Au Génie de Franklin," Sellers, *Franklin*, 120–22, 284–86, plate 33; Mary D. Sheriff, "'Au Génie de Franklin': An Allegory by J.-H. Fragonard," *Proc. of the APS* 127, no. 3 (June 1983): 180–93. For "Benjamin Franklin," Sellers, *Franklin*, 283–84.

186. Sellers, *Franklin*, 275–77. Zigrosser, 542–43.

187. *Papers*, 29:612.

188. James A. Leith, "Le culte de Franklin en France avant et pendant la Revolution Française," *Annales historiques de la Révolution Française* 48, no. 225 (1976): 543–71.

Chapter 7. Interludes and Transformations

1. Edwin G. Burrows and Michael Wallace, "The American Revolution: The Ideology and Psychology of National Liberation," *Perspectives in American History* 6 (1972): 168. This article has been criticized and supplemented by Jay Fliegelman, *Prodigals and Pilgrims: The American Revolution against Patriarchal Authority, 1750–1800* (Cambridge, England: Cambridge UP, 1982), esp. 38–40. Melvin Yazawa, *From Colonies to Commonwealth: Familial Ideology and the Beginnings of the American Republic* (Baltimore: Johns Hopkins UP, 1985). J. Vernon Jensen, "British Voices on the Eve of the American Revolution: Trapped by the Family Metaphor," *QJS* 63 (February 1977): 43–50. Olson, *Emblems*, 125–99.

2. *Papers*, 4:233–34. BF commented on the "Polypus" in his 1751 almanac, *Complete Poor Richard*, 2:129, 131. Douglas Anderson, *The Radical Enlightenments of Benjamin Franklin* (Baltimore: Johns Hopkins UP, 1997), 161–62, comments on the analogy, as does Stourzh, *Franklin*, 59.

3. Paul W. Conner, "The Continentalist," in *Benjamin Franklin: A Profile*, ed. Esmond Wright (New York: Hill & Wang, 1970), 80.

4. *Papers*, 9:78–79, 79.

5. On animalizations representing British America, Olson, *Emblems*, 238–51.

6. Crane, *Letters*, 41, 169, 189; *Papers*, 12:413, 17:6, 47–48.

7. *Pa. Gaz.*, Oct. 9, 1729; rptd. in *Papers*, 1:161.

8. *General Magazine, and Historical Chronicle, for all the British Plantations in America* 1 (Jan. 1741): 75; rptd. in *Papers*, 2:303–4. The attributed date of BF's prose is a month after the publication date, but the eds. gave no explanation. Perhaps the magazine was published after the imprinted publication date.

9. *Papers*, 3:205.

10. Ibid., 3:189.

11. Ibid., 3:184. For further background on BF's role, Sally F. Griffith, "'Order, Discipline, and a few Cannon': Benjamin Franklin, the Association, and the Rhetoric and Practice of Boosterism," *PMHB* 116 (April 1992): 131–55.

12. *Papers*, 3:180.

13. Ibid., 3:192.

14. H. W. Brands, *The First American: The Life and Times of Benjamin Franklin* (New York: Random House, 2002), 181–86.

15. *Papers*, 3:415.

16. *Pa. Gaz.*, April 11, 1751; rptd in *Papers*, 4:131 n. 5.

17. *Pa. Gaz.*, May 9, 1751; rptd. in *Papers*, 4:131, 131–32, 133.

18. *Papers*, 4:132, 133.

19. Ibid., 4:229. Stourzh, *Franklin*, 87.

20. *Papers*, 6:76. Van Doren, *Franklin-Jackson*, 59–60.

21. *Papers*, 6:82. Van Doren, *Franklin-Jackson*, 67–68.

22. For additional examples, *Papers*, 6:264; 7:108, 125, 127.

23. For example, ibid., 6:159.

24. For example, ibid., 7:108.

25. For example, ibid., 7:125.

26. Ibid., 7:137.

27. Ibid., 11:349–50.

28. Ibid., 8:340–41.

29. Ibid., 8:341.

30. Ibid., 8:342, 351.

31. Ibid., 6:276, 500.

32. *Papers*, 8:450, 451. Crane, *Letters*, 14.

33. Ibid., 9:74–75.

34. Ibid., 9:75–76.

35. Ibid., 9:77, 93–94.

36. Ibid., 9:90.

37. Ibid., 9:90, 92, 59.

38. Ibid., 5:446.

39. Ibid., 5:446–47.

40. Ibid., 12:184, 185.

41. Ibid., 12:253–54.

42. For "F. B.," *Papers*, 12:407; Crane, *Letters*, 39. For "N. N.," *Papers*, 12:415. Crane, *Letters*, 43.

43. *Papers*, 13:55. Crane, *Letters*, 55.

44. *Papers*, 13:76–77. Crane, *Letters*, 65–66.

45. *Papers*, 13:78–79. Crane, *Letters*, 67–68. "Gaols" is spelled as such in Crane's quotation, but *Papers* prints it as "Goals."

46. *Papers*, 13:82–83, 83. Crane, *Letters*, 70.

47. *Papers*, 13:120. Crane, *Letters*, 62.

48. Crane, *Letters*, 60.

49. *Papers*, 13:163. Crane, *Letters*, 294.

50. *Papers*, 14:65.

51. For examples, *Papers*, 13:278–79, 396, 15:71, 89–90, 231, 278.

52. Ibid., 12:304–6.

53. Ibid., 13:426.

54. Ibid., 21:509, 509 n. 9.

55. Ibid., 15:187, 188.

56. Crane, *Letters*, 122, and Olson, *Emblems*, 243, 240–44, comment on pamphlets and prints invoking the fable.

57. *Papers*, 15:66–67. Crane, *Letters*, 115.

58. Crane, *Letters*, 112.

59. Verner W. Crane, "Three Fables by Benjamin Franklin," *New England Quarterly* 9, no. 3 (Sept. 1936): 499–503. Crane, *Letters*, 166.

60. *Papers*, 17:3. Crane, *Letters*, 166.

61. *Papers*, 17:45. Crane, *Letters*, 183–84.

62. Olson, *Emblems*, 239–40.

63. *Papers*, 17:3. Crane, *Letters*, 166. This fable is discussed in "National Character and the Great Seal of the United States" on p. 242.

64. *Papers*, 17:3–4. Crane, *Letters*, 167.

65. *Papers*, 17:5–8. Crane, *Letters*, 167–70.

66. *Papers*, 15:208.

67. Ibid., 17:188–89, 282–83, 301.

68. Ibid., 19:411–12, 20:515–16, 21:416–18, 428.

69. For a poignant, dramatic account of these events, see H. W. Brands, *The First American: The Life and Times of Benjamin Franklin* (New York: Random House, 2002), 1–8, 452–54, 464–90, quotes on 481. BF's rationale is discussed in "'WE ARE ONE,' 1776" on p. 115.

70. *Papers*, 21:58–59, 60, 63–64.

71. Ibid., 15:36–38.

72. Ibid., 12:120.

73. Ibid., 12:158–59.

74. Ibid., 15:208.

75. For examples, *Papers*, 20:118; also, 35:547.

76. *Papers*, 12:431–32.

77. *Papers*, 22:520–21. Stourzh, *Franklin*, 111–12. Esmond Wright, "'The fine and noble vase, the British empire': Benjamin Franklin's 'Love-Hate' View of England," *PMHB* 111 (1987): 435–64. Brands, 514–16.

78. Ibid., 12:431.

79. *Papers*, 23:511. Stourzh, *Franklin*, 123–24.

80. Quote from *Papers*, 25:651. For examples of Ingenhousz's correspondence, *Papers*, 23:12, 42, 115, 24:241, 25:288, 382, 26:634–35.

81. Ibid., 30:39.

82. Ibid., 22:129, 34:124, 35:100.

83. Ibid., 25:651.

84. Ibid., 3:180–204.

85. Stourzh, *Franklin*, 44–47, 61.

86. *Papers*, 3:195.

87. For example, *Papers*, 17:7–8.

88. Ibid., 17:21.

89. Ibid., 4:486.

90. I discussed these mixed metaphors in Loyalists' rhetoric in "An Ideological Rupture: Metaphorical Divergence in Loyalist Rhetoric During the American Revolution" *Rhetorica: An International Jour. of the Hist. of Rhetoric* 10 (1992): 405–22.

91. *Papers*, 20:282.

92. Stourzh, *Franklin*, 88.

93. *Papers*, 17:59, 59–60.

94. Ibid., 20:391.

95. Ibid., 20:10.

96. Ibid., 25:651. Stourzh, *Franklin*, 148.

97. Linda K. Kerber, *Women of the Republic: Intellect & Ideology in Revolutionary America* (New York: Norton, 1980). Mary Beth Norton, *Liberty's Daughters: The Revolutionary Experience of American Women, 1750–1800* (Boston: Little, Brown, and Co., 1980).

98. *Papers*, 22:199.

99. Ibid., 17:7–8.

Chapter 8. National Character and the Great Seal of the United States

1. Gordon S. Wood, *The Radicalism of the American Revolution* (New York: Knopf, 1992), 39.

2. *Papers*, 13:488. Similarly, *Poor Richard's Almanac* in 1757, rptd. in *Papers*, 7:85.

3. J. Philip Gleason, "A Scurrilous Colonial Election and Franklin's Reputation," *WMQ*, 3d ser., 18 (1961): 68–84, quote on 68.

4. Crane, *Letters*, 24.

5. Wood, 86. I concur here with Wayne Craven, "The American and British Portraits of Benjamin Franklin," in *Reappraising Benjamin Franklin: A Bicentennial Perspective*, ed. J. A. Leo Lemay (Newark: U of Delaware P, 1993), 249–51, with a reproduction of the portrait.

6. *JCC*, 5:517–18.

7. Richard S. Patterson and Richardson Dougall, *The Eagle and the Shield: A History of the Great Seal of the United States* (Washington, D.C.: GPO, 1976), 6. Frank H. Sommer, "Emblem and Device: The Origin of the Great Seal of the United States," *Art Quarterly* 24 (spring 1961): 58, 63–64. John Adams to Abigail Adams, Aug. 14, 1776, *Adams Family Corresp.*, ed. L. H. Butterfield (Cambridge, Mass.: Belknap of Harvard UP, 1963), 2:96. BF's handwritten description of the design was on an undated note (Aug. 1776), Thomas Jefferson Papers, MS Div., LC; rptd. in *Papers*, 22:563.

8. Sommer, 64.

9. Patterson and Dougall, 30.

10. BF to Sarah Bache, Jan. 26, 1784, LC; French translation of a revised version in *Journal de la Société de 1789, July 24, 1790*; Durard Echeverria, *Bulletin de l'Institut Français de Washington*, n.s., no. 3 (Dec. 1953): 119–26.

11. "Society of the Cincinnati: Circular Letter & Institution," May 15, 1784, APS.

12. *Constitutions des Treize Etats-Unis de l'Amérique*, [translated by Louis-Alexandre, duc de la Rochefoucault] (Paris and Philadelphia: [Philippe-Denis] Pierres,

1783). *The Definitive Treaty between Great Britain, and the United States of America, Signed at Paris, the 3d day of September 1783* ([Passy: B. Franklin,] 1783).

13. For example, P. P. Burdett to BF, Jan. 17, 1786, APS.

14. Patterson and Dougall, 31, 384, 2, respectively.

15. These flags were described in the *Pa. Gaz.* of Jan. 12, 1748, and April 16, 1748, rptd. in *Papers*, 3:267–69. There are additional references to the flags in *Autobiog.*, 183. *Papers*, 3:268. Other contemporaneous evidence also attributes the designs to BF: James Logan to Peter Collinson, Feb. 28, 1750, rptd. in *Papers*, 3:469–70. For commentaries on the flags, J. A. Leo Lemay, "The American Aesthetic of Franklin's Visual Creations," *PMHB* 91 (Oct. 1987): 471–75, 496–97; Sally F. Griffith, "'Order, Discipline, and a few Cannon': Benjamin Franklin, the Association, and the Rhetoric and Practice of Boosterism," *PMHB* 116 (April 1992): 131–55.

16. Lemay, "The American Aesthetic," 497, quote on 499.

17. *Pa. Gaz.*, Sept. 20, 1775, p. 1, col. 2.; *Pa. Mag.* 1 (Dec. 1775): 562.

18. *Hist. Mag., and Notes and Queries* 5 (March 1861): 71–73.

19. Eric P. Newman, "Benjamin Franklin and the Chain Design: New Evidence Provides the Missing Link," *Numismatist* 96 (Nov. 1983): 2272–73; J. A. Leo Lemay, *The Canon of Benjamin Franklin, 1722–1776* (Newark: U of Delaware P, 1986). 122–24. Joseph Stansbury, *Loyalist Rhapsodes*, ser. 8D, no. 90, reel 49, Peter Force Coll., MS Div., LC. I discuss my misgivings about the attribution in chapter 1 on p. 4.

20. R. R. [Joseph Stansbury], "The History of Peru & c." in *Loyalist Rhapsodes*, ser. 8D, no. 90, reel 49, Peter Force Coll, MS Div., LC. The poem is reprinted in Eric P. Newman, "The Hist. of Peru, Etc. by Joseph Stansbury," notes and introduction by Newman, *Numismatist* 96 (1983): 2282–84, with slight typographical differences from the MS at the LC.

21. The poem was reprinted in Henry Phillips Jr., *Hist. Sketches of the Paper Currency of the American Colonies: Prior to the Adoption of the Federal Constitution*, 2 vols. (Roxbury, Mass.: W. Elliot Woodward, 1865–66), 2: 256–58.

22. Verner W. Crane, "Three Fables by Benjamin Franklin," *New England Quarterly* 9, no. 3 (Sept. 1936): 499–504. Crane, *Letters*, 166–67. *Papers*, 17:3–4.

23. *Public Advertiser*, Jan. 2, 1770, p. 1, col. 4 and p. 2, col. 1.

24. Crane, "Three Fables," 500.

25. "*L'Aigle et le Chat. Fable allégorique de M. Franklin*," circa 1778, APS.

26. *Pa. Jour.*, Dec. 27, 1775, p. 1, col. 1; *London Chron.*, July 25–27, 1776, p. 1, col. 3, p. 2, col. 1. This article was attributed to BF in Lemay, *Canon*, 124–26. The arguments for the attribution, though plausible, are not conclusive.

27. James A. Herrick, "Miracles and Method," *QJS* 75 (1989): 323. On ridicule, see James A. Herrick, *The Radical Rhetoric of the English Deist* (Columbia: U of S.C. P, 1997).

28. Douglas Anderson, *The Radical Enlightenments of Benjamin Franklin* (Baltimore: Johns Hopkins UP, 1997), 9, 11–12, 24–25, 58, 102–5, 122.

29. Van Doren, *Franklin*, 709–10. Lopez, *Mon Cher Papa*, 288–90.

30. Both men are quoted in Lopez, *Mon Cher Papa*, 289.

31. Van Doren, *Franklin*, 709.

32. For a concise overview of the controversy, Contenson, *La Société des Cincinnati* esp. 39–50.

33. Van Doren, *Franklin*, 707.

34. BF to Richard Bache, Nov. 11, 1784, rptd. in Smyth, *Writings*, 9:279.

35. *Papers*, 4:98. *Complete Poor Richard*, 2:137.

36. For the evidence on this point, Bernard Faÿ, "Franklin et Mirabeau collaborateurs," *Revue de littérature comparée* 8 (1928): 5–28.

37. Aedanus Burke's *Considerations on the Society or Order of Cincinnati . . . Proving That It Creates a Race of Hereditary Patricians, or Nobility*, was published at Charleston by A. Timothy, at Philadelphia by Robert Bell, and at Hartford by David Webster [Evans 17862–64].

38. Burke, 14 (Philadelphia edition).

39. Smyth, *Writings*, 10:354.

40. Faÿ, "Franklin et Mirabeau," 15.

41. Honoré-Gabriel de Riquette, comte de Mirabeau, *Considerations on the Order of Cincinnatus*, [trans. Samuel Romilly] (Philadelphia: T. Seddon, 1786). The note on Chinese customs appears on p. 34. The mathematical calculation is on p. 36. Evans 19803. Van Doren, *Franklin*, 710.

42. Smyth, *Writings*, 10:354. Van Doren, *Franklin*, 710.

43. George Washington, *The Writings of George Washington*, ed. John C. Fitzpatrick (Washington, D.C.: 1931–44), 27:388.

44. Thomas Jefferson, *The Papers of Thomas Jefferson*, ed. Julian P. Boyd and others (Princeton, N.J.: Princeton UP, 1953), 7:105–10.

45. Washington, *Writings*, 27:388.

46. Garry Wills, *Cincinnatus: George Washington and the Enlightenment* (New York: Doubleday, 1984), 13, 20, 23, 103, 112, 140–42.

47. Washington, *Writings*, 27: 393–94, 395.

48. Robert H. McCauley, *Liverpool Transfer Designs on Anglo-American Pottery* (Portland, Maine: Southworth-Anthoensen, 1942), has several examples of housewares with this motif, e.g., plates 23, 28, and 31. Elinor Gordon, *Chinese Export Porcelain: An Hist. Survey* (New York: Main Street/Universe, [1975]). In this book, see two especially helpful essays by Homer Eaton Keyes: "Lowestoft: Exclusively American," 115–23, and "The Cincinnati and Their Porcelain," 133–38. Alphaeus H. Albert, *Washington Hist. Buttons* (Hightstown, N.J.: Princeton UP, 1949), 25–33, 39, 45–48.

49. Max Farrand, ed., *The Records of the Federal Convention of 1787*, rev. ed., 4 vols. (New Haven: Yale UP, 1937), 3:85. William G. Carr, *The Oldest Delegate: Franklin in the Constitutional Convention* (Newark: U of Delaware P, 1990), 122.

50. *Papers*, 22:572–74.

51. Ibid., 22:199.

52. Ibid., 22:67.

GENERAL INDEX

(Please find specific works grouped by media in the Media Index.)

MEDIA INDEX